Emotional Development and Families

Julie Hakim-Larson

# Emotional Development and Families

## Socialization across the Lifespan

This edition published 2018 by
RED GLOBE PRESS

Red Globe Press in the UK is an imprint of Springer Nature Limited, registered in England, company number 785998, of 4 Crinan Street, London N1 9XW.

Red Globe Press® is a registered trademark in the United States, the United Kingdom, Europe and other countries.

ISBN 978–1–137–35632–1 paperback

This book is printed on paper suitable for recycling and made from fully managed and sustained forest sources. Logging, pulping and manufacturing processes are expected to conform to the environmental regulations of the country of origin.

A catalogue record for this book is available from the British Library.

A catalog record for this book is available from the Library of Congress.

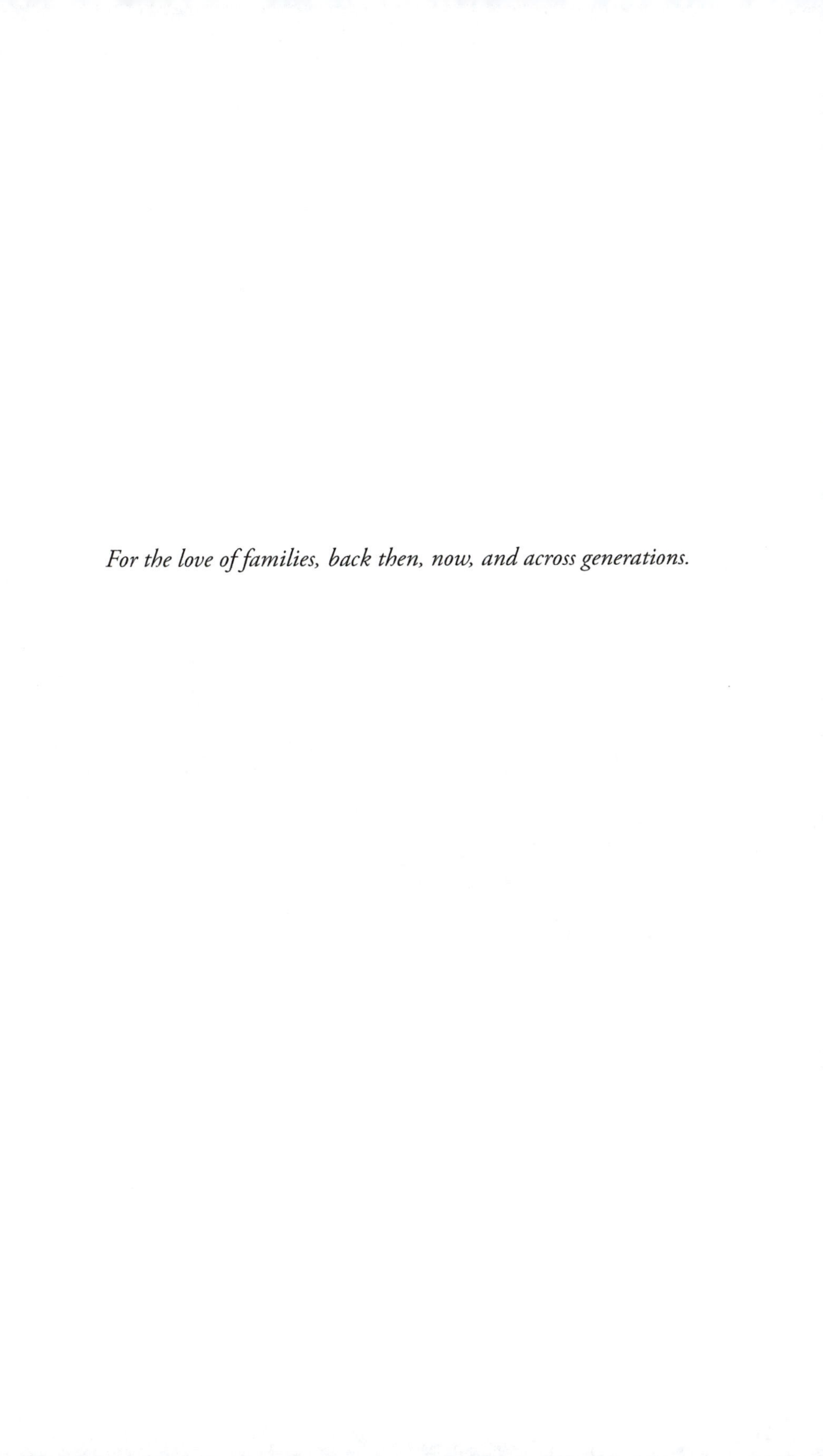

*For the love of families, back then, now, and across generations.*

# Contents

# List of Tables

# List of Figures

# List of History Feature Boxes

# Acknowledgements

Writing this book has been a career-long dream for over 30 years. During this time, I enjoyed reviewing many great works on emotion science and development. I would like to thank those scholars before me who have championed the importance of understanding emotions, many of whom I have at least tried to mention somewhere in the book. Undoubtedly, I have inadvertently missed many important contributors. I am nonetheless grateful to them for helping to shape my thinking in numerous ways. Many thanks also go to the knowledgeable reviewers who provided scholarly constructive feedback to me at various points during my work on the book. I appreciate your willingness to take the time to engage in the review process. This book has benefited greatly from your insights and suggestions!

My heartfelt thanks go posthumously to my dear parents, Yvonne M. (Barrack) and Simon D. Hakim, for teaching me the most important life lesson – how to love with empathy for others. I will be forever grateful to them, my husband Curtis C. Larson, my siblings and sister-in-law and their spouses and children, and our large extended multi-generational family for the warmth, tolerance, and moral sense of justice that seems to be the default for our emotional interactions with each other through both good and bad times. I have learned about emotional development from you, as well as from my students and colleagues at the University of Windsor whom I have had the pleasure of getting to know throughout my years of teaching. I wish I could name all of you here! My heartfelt thanks to each of you for your inspiration and support!

Since my first encounter with Palgrave at a conference where I was looking for a textbook for my courses on emotional development, I have had the good fortune of working with a wonderful team of open-minded and conscientious editors and staff members who have believed in this project from the beginning. Thanks to all of you for your patience and steady guidance throughout the process. In addition to Nicola Jones, who was the first to give my project a chance, I want to thank those who helped me during the various stages of the process (e.g., Isabel Berwick, Aléta Bezuidenhout, Alice Clarke, Jenny Hindley, Ann Martin, Cecily Wilson, Amy Wheeler). Cathy Scott, Gogulanathan Bactavatchalane and Cathy Tingle provided invaluable and much-appreciated help during the last stages of manuscript preparation and editing. Finally, I am forever grateful to Paul Stevens for his encouraging words, motivating ideas throughout the writing and editorial process, and reassuring leadership. Thank you so much! What a great team of staff and editors at Palgrave!

The author and publisher would like to thank the following for their permission to reproduce copyrighted material:

Gerald and Deborah Newmark and NMI Publishers for permission to use the excerpt from Newmark (2008, p. 9) in Chapter 1.

Oxford University Press for Table 1.1, which was taken from Lazarus (1991, p. 122).

W.W. Norton & Company for permission to use the excerpt in Chapter 1 from Gottman (2011, p. 191).

Elsevier for Figure 3.1 taken from Somerville and Casey (2010, pp. 236–241, Figure 1).

The Guilford Press for permission to use the case summary from Leung and Boehnien (1996, p. 299) in Chapter 5, and the case summary from Saarni (1999, p. 7) in Chapter 8.

Taylor and Francis for permission to use the case summary and excerpts from McGillicuddy-DeLisi (1992, pp. 115–116) in Chapter 6, and for Table 11.3 taken from Waters and Waters (2006, p. 190, Table II).

John Wiley & Sons for Table 6.1 taken from Grusec and Davidov (2010, p. 694, Table 1), and for the case summary from Nassar-McMillan and Hakim-Larson (2014, pp. 67–70) in Chapter 11.

Pearson Education, Inc. for permission to use the excerpt from Garrod, Smulyan, Powers, and Kilkenny (2012, pp. 213–214) in Chapter 9.

Todd Hochberg for permission to use the case summary from *Other Rituals: Parents Stories of Meaning Making* (© Copyright Todd Hochberg, 2010) in Chapter 12.

# Preface

## The Structure of the Book

The structure of this book on emotional development comes from the fields of life-span developmental psychology, child clinical psychology and developmental psychopathology, all of which highlight how families socialize emotion within the constraints of interacting biological and sociocultural processes over time. Where possible, research that includes various cultural perspectives and ethnic diversity is considered. Although the contemporary trend is for the internationalization of psychology with research perspectives becoming more global, the fact is that many publications tend to favour a Western (i.e., European and North American) point of view, and this Western view has inevitably influenced some implications that I draw in this book.

For each of the 12 chapters, there is a story or case study depicting one or more characters who display some of the important constructs featured in the chapter. Important terms are italicized in the text, and those that are included in the glossary at the end of the book are put in bold italicized text. Chapter 1 provides an overview of emotional development and socialization with specific attention given to the various roles played by family members. Chapter 2 summarizes the major methodological issues and approaches used by emotion researchers. Chapter 3 introduces the neurobiological foundations of emotional development with an emphasis on the plasticity of the brain based on genetics and experiences, and the emergence of consciousness as a function of these processes. Further expanding on the biological foundation of emotion, Chapter 4 includes an examination of temperament variation in family members, and the implications of temperament for life course trajectories. Chapter 5 on culture and emotion addresses the sociocultural foundations of emotional development, while Chapter 6 focuses on the emotion-related beliefs, goals and values of parents. Chapter 7 incorporates a review of the literature on non-verbal emotional expressions in families beginning with the early preverbal learning during infancy in which a budding sense of feelings about the self in relation to others emerges. Chapter 8 addresses the self-conscious emotions which emerge in infancy and that help to form the basis for identity and self-esteem in later years. Chapter 9 focuses on emotion language and the verbal communication of emotion in families, while Chapter 10 includes a review of the burgeoning literature on emotion regulation and coping in families. Finally, the book concludes with a discussion of developmental psychopathology and emotions in families in Chapter 11, and with an emphasis on how family members can promote emotional resilience in each other in Chapter 12.

## Back Then and Now: History Feature Boxes

There is ample evidence that emotions and the passions have been of interest to artists, writers, philosophers and scientific scholars since the earliest historical recordings. While a comprehensive review of the history of emotions is well beyond the limits of this book, each chapter provides a glimpse into the history of past ideas and research relevant to the chapter topic. The History Feature Boxes in each chapter introduce the reader to historical issues primarily from a Western viewpoint.

## About the Author: How I Came to Write this Book

I grew up in an actively changing multi-ethnic working class neighbourhood on the lower east side of Detroit, Michigan, USA from the 1950s to the 1970s. Unwittingly, I became a first-hand witness to the cultural upheaval and dramatic changes that occurred in American families as they adapted to the civil strife and unrest of the 1960s, the Vietnam War, the influx of illegal drugs into the everyday life of high school students, and general urban decay. In spite of the insulated safe haven of my large Catholic multi-generational Lebanese-American extended family, these and other social events affected me deeply. By the time I left for college, I knew of distal neighbours who engaged in all sorts of illegal acts including child abuse and neglect, drug abuse and prostitution. I had seen the authorities remove the remains of an entire family in body bags from a home after a father murdered his wife and then committed suicide, leaving the young children to starve to death. I saw many transient and immigrant families from the Southern United States, from French-speaking Canada, from Europe, and from the Middle East move in and try to adapt to the American way of life, and saw many families including my own struggle to leave the city in search of a more routine and less chaotic existence. It increasingly became clear that there was no returning to the now seemingly idyllic 1950s when the streets of Detroit were lined with majestic arches of elm trees, and childhood life was easy, simply fun, and teenagers cruised along Jefferson and Woodward Avenues in their now classic cars. The 1960s brought death to the trees with Dutch elm disease, death to American national heroes such as the Kennedys and Martin Luther King, and a feeling of uneasiness as the culture changed, heading towards unknown territory through uncharted waters. As if that was not enough at that time, wives and husbands were also wrestling with how to put their changing gender roles into practice, and issues involving race/ethnicity and sexual orientation were beginning to become open topics for public discussion and debate.

As a third-generation Arab American growing up in the Motor City of Detroit, I knew first-hand and observed many instances of labour disputes, prejudice and discrimination. Much good came out of those times with positive changes in attitudes and greater equity for women and minorities. The social changes that occurred back then continue to affect all of us in some way developmentally. In many ways, it is not surprising that my professional life led me to study the emotional lives of families in my academic work, and to work with individuals and family members of various ethnic backgrounds clinically and in my research.

College life at Michigan State University (MSU) with its traditional sprawling Midwestern campus helped to form my budding professional identity. There, as an undergraduate psychology major, I worked with a paediatric psychologist in local hospitals and discovered then that I was just as interested in parents' feelings of guilt, love and hope for their children as I was in the adjustment of their hospitalized children. I also met the love of my life, my husband, Curtis Larson, at MSU. Eventually, my academic pursuits led to doctoral work in life-span developmental psychology and postdoctoral work in child clinical psychology.

In the early 1980s, there were big debates about the relative importance of cognition and emotion. My dissertation, which I completed in 1984 at Wayne State University in Detroit, reflected my interest in both. My research involved observing the communication between mothers and their teenage daughters. I found that mothers asked more questions than daughters to regulate the conversations, although older adolescent girls asked more questions than younger ones. Emotionally, the conversations were more negative in tone between younger adolescent girls and their mothers in comparison to older adolescent girls and their mothers. My study illustrated that there is often a delicate balance between parental regulation and guidance, and adolescents' striving for autonomy that gets acted out in conversational structure and emotional tones (Hakim-Larson & Hobart, 1987).

Postdoctorally, in the mid to late 1980s, I worked with my dissertation supervisor, Dr. Gisela Labouvie-Vief, at Wayne State University on examining emotional development from middle childhood through the older adult years using both interviews and questionnaires; the findings from these studies are described later in this book. In the late 1980s, I felt that my research on emotion could only benefit from hands-on clinical practice, so I then undertook postdoctoral studies and training in child clinical psychology. I maintained a life-span focus and interest in family members across generations. Since 1991, I have been a full-time faculty member in Child Clinical Psychology at the University of Windsor in Ontario, Canada – right across the Detroit River and my home in Michigan. Among my research interests are emotions in the family, and culture and emotion. Much has happened in the field of emotion science since the 1980s and I feel that it is important for students in mental health disciplines to have a firm up-to-date developmental foundation that considers adaptive and maladaptive emotional functioning in families based on the latest theories and research findings.

The purpose of this book is to review current theories and research findings and to introduce concepts and ideas on how we can best foster healthy emotional functioning within families in both our work and in our everyday lives. Throughout the book, I have tried to take various levels of analysis into account and thus molecular and genetic microsystems as well as broad cultural macrosystems are discussed in the context of the emotional lives of families. Though I have placed emphasis on what is known about typical or more normative developmental patterns, life trajectories that are unique, atypical and psychopathological are also highlighted. The emotional life experiences reviewed in the book are ones that each of us may potentially encounter either directly ourselves or vicariously through our observations of others.

# 1

# Introduction: Emotional Development and Socialization in Families

*One day, while working for a research corporation, my work wasn't going well. Discouraged, I left work early. When I arrived home and walked into the kitchen, my son was already home from school. He was having some corn flakes and milk, and I noticed the refrigerator door had been left slightly open. I started scolding him for being thoughtless, and how all of the food in the refrigerator would spoil, and how we couldn't afford that kind of waste. Suddenly, David started to cry.*

*"What are you crying about?" I shouted.*

*"I didn't do it on purpose; you act like I'm some sort of criminal," he replied.*

*"What a big baby!" I exclaimed, and left the house.* (Newmark, 2008, p. 9)



## Overview of Emotion Socialization in Families

As family members have conversations and arguments with each other, such as the one in the example given by Newmark (2008), they are also teaching or socializing each other about emotions. This process goes in multiple directions from parent to child, and from child to parent, as well as between and among grandparents, spouses, brothers, sisters, cousins, aunts, uncles, and other extended family members. Later in the day, this father, educator and author reflected upon what happened and realized that he had displaced his feelings about himself and work onto his son. Thus, he became consciously aware that he had treated his son quite disrespectfully during this emotional interchange. Indeed, Newmark (2008), who cites this personal example in his book on emotions, was concerned about what he was teaching his son in this encounter. Towards his own efforts at self-improvement during such emotional family encounters, Newmark identified five ways that parents can foster their children's emotional health. One of these is by treating children with the same high levels of *respect* and consideration that they would afford to adults or even strangers. In addition to feeling *respected*, children need to feel *important, accepted, included* and *secure* (Newmark, 2008). Although we often treat emotions, such as the anger and sadness experienced by the father and son in this example, as taking place within individuals, emotions clearly have something to do with how we relate interpersonally with each other or with objects, events or situations in the environment. So just what, then, are emotions per se, and how does the definition of "emotion" differ from that of related terms such as "feelings", "affect", emotional "states" and "traits"?

Lewis (2014) provides a concise definition of emotions as "thoughts about our evolutionary-derived action patterns that occur within and are molded by our social niche" (p.1). Because the terms "emotion", "feelings" and "affect" are used very often in the literature on emotional development, it is important to consider how they are defined. Although sometimes used interchangeably throughout history, they do have distinct meanings; therefore, care should be taken in how each term is used (Lazarus, 1991). The broadest category in use is that of *emotion*, which Lazarus (1991) has described as a complex configuration involving two primary components, one that includes observable behaviours that have resulted from our evolutionary heritage and the other that includes our personal experiences, human capacity for self-reflection, and the conscious appraisal of events. Thus, the first component involves ***phylogenetic*** development (changes in species over time) and has an evolutionary basis stemming from the work of Charles Darwin (1872/2008) on emotional expressions in both animals and humans. This includes observable and measurable behavioural reactions to the environment, such as physiological and muscular bodily reactions (e.g., hormonal secretions, facial expressions), and action-tendency responses (e.g., to approach or avoid) that have developed over the course of many generations. With ***ontogenetic*** development (changes within individuals over their lifespans), we experience emotional changes based on our maturation and evolutionary heritage. The result is that our emotions place us in a ***state of action readiness*** to either approach or withdraw from others and the situation (e.g., Frijda, 2008).

The second component involves *affect* or inner subjective experiences, such as thoughts in the form of cognitive appraisals and judgements, and the awareness of bodily sensations in the form of *feelings* (e.g., bodily feelings of inner turmoil and conflict). It is not until typically developing children are about 15 to 24 months old that they have the brain maturation needed for such conscious self-awareness (Lewis, 2014). Thus, under the broad category of "emotion", there is the subcategory of "affect", and underneath the subcategory of affect is "feelings". As noted by Lazarus (1991) in his cognitive-motivational-relational theory, it is our ***cognitive appraisal*** and the meaning that we ascribe to our emotional experiences that is most important in determining whether we energetically approach another person out of anger or out of passionate love. Lazarus (1991) defines ***core relational themes*** as "the central (hence core) relational harm or benefit in adaptational encounters that underlies each specific kind of emotion" (p. 121). See Table 1.1 for Lazarus's core relational themes. As we will discuss later in the text, it is also possible to experience ambivalence about which way to act (Lewis, 2008a, 2008b).

There are temporal qualities to emotion depending on the stability and duration of the experience. Sometimes we have emotion episodes that are limited in time and scope (Oatley & Jenkins, 1996). When an emotional encounter with the environment is transient, fleeting and depends on the

**Table 1.1** Core Relational Themes for Each Emotion (Lazarus, 1991)

| | |
|---|---|
| Anger | A demeaning offense against me and mine. |
| Anxiety | Facing uncertain, existential threat. |
| Fright | Facing an immediate, concrete and overwhelming physical danger. |
| Guilt | Having transgressed a moral imperative. |
| Shame | Having failed to live up to an ego-ideal. |
| Sadness | Having experienced an irrevocable loss. |
| Envy | Wanting what someone else has. |
| Jealousy | Resenting a third party for loss or threat to another's affection. |
| Disgust | Taking in or being too close to an indigestible object or idea (metaphorically speaking). |
| Happiness | Making reasonable progress toward the realization of a goal. |
| Pride | Enhancement of one's ego-identity by taking credit for a valued object of achievement, either our own or that of someone or group with whom we identify. |
| Relief | A distressing goal-incongruent condition that has changed for the better or gone away. |
| Hope | Fearing the worst but yearning for better. |
| Love | Desiring or participating in affection, usually but not necessarily reciprocated. |
| Compassion | Being moved by another's suffering and wanting to help. |

Source: Emotion and Adaptation by Lazarus (1991) Tab 3.4. p.122 ©1991 by Oxford University Press, Inc. By permission of Oxford University Press, USA.

situation, it is termed an *emotional state*, and when it is a more stable personality characteristic of a person that is less bound to the constraints of the environment, it is an *emotional trait* (Lazarus, 1991). In between the temporary emotional states and more stable personality patterns of emotion, are emotional *moods*, which can last from hours to weeks, and may become symptomatic of an *emotional disorder* (Oatley & Jenkins, 1996). One basic idea presented in this textbook is that this complex configuration known as emotions changes developmentally over time as the individual changes and ages, not merely due to biological foundations including genetic history, temperament or maturation, but also due to emotion socialization within family relationships and because of the social and cultural contexts.

## Emotional Development and Socialization

As noted by Fabes, Valiente and Leonard (2003):

> [E]motions are involved in almost every aspect of family development: from the beginnings of family formation (e.g., dating, courting, attraction, and marriage), to the transition to parenthood (e.g., pregnancy, birth, bonding, and attachment), parenting (e.g., socialization and discipline), as well as the dissolution of family relationships (e.g., divorce and death). (pp. 3–4)

As family members work on such developmental tasks, many emotions are felt and released in ways that vary along the adaptive to maladaptive spectrum. That is, some family members have been found to be more competent than others in their emotion understanding and knowledge and in their ability to appropriately control and express emotions in a manner that is consistent with their own values and the norms of their culture (Saarni, 1999). One way that such ***emotional competence*** seems to be acquired is through direct observation of competent family members who serve as role models. In other words, family members learn vicariously about emotions by watching and listening to each other during everyday life.

Though the process of emotion socialization involves the learning of emotional behaviours that vary along the dimension of emotional competence, the focus of this book is on how to foster the development of the more competent end of the spectrum. Thus, research on pathological and deviant emotional functioning in families will be integrated throughout the book with the goal of fostering the prevention of psychopathology and the improvement of our understanding of how best to socialize family emotional and social competence.

Emotional and social competence within families has been called ***affective social competence***, and has been defined by Halberstadt, Denham and Dunsmore (2001) as the "efficacious communication of one's own affect, one's successful interpretation and response to others' affective communications, and the awareness, acceptance, and management of one's own affect" (p. 80). Children and adults learn from each other how to communicate emotions, interpret them, and respond to each other's feelings. They also learn how to be more aware of emotions and how to regulate or cope with them. They learn how to identify and label emotions, express them in vocal intonations and intensity, in words, facial expressions and gestures, and change them to achieve a whole range of minor and major goals that are consistent with what they value as important and meaningful in living a good life.

Eisenberg, Cumberland and Spinrad (1998a) have developed a model of how parents socialize emotions in their children using a variety of ***emotion-related socialization behaviours (ERSBs)***. They define emotional competence as including:

> an understanding of one's own and others' emotions, the tendency to display emotion in a situationally and culturally appropriate manner, and the ability to inhibit or modulate experienced and expressed emotion and emotionally derived behavior as needed to achieve goals in a socially acceptable manner. (p. 242)

In this model, parenting practices are influenced by child characteristics such as the child's age and sex, temperament and personality, and parent characteristics such as parenting style and beliefs, as well as cultural factors and the more immediate local context. Parenting practices or ERSBs include how parents react to children's emotions by what they say verbally in discussing emotions and what they do in their own emotional expressions. The family's immediate local environment (e.g., the neighbourhood, schools, religious and government agencies) and the broader cultural values, beliefs and traditions influence the socialization of emotion within families (e.g., Kitayama & Markus, 1994).

In this textbook, I provide an overview of the various domains of study that researchers such as Denham (e.g., 1998; Denham, Bassatt & Wyatt, 2007), Eisenberg et al. (1998a, 1998b), Fabes (2002), Halberstadt et al. (2001), Lewis (2008a, 2008b, 2014) and Saarni (1999, 2000), among many others, have identified as important for socializing emotion in children. Keeping in mind that cultural context plays a role, it is also important to understand the developmental foundation of neurobiology, physiological arousal and emotional states, as well as the influence of each family member's unique inborn predisposition or temperament on family communication. Non-verbal emotional expressions such as facial expressions and gestures are a *precursor* to the more developmentally advanced inner subjective conscious experience of emotion (e.g., as reflected in the self-concept and feelings of self-esteem) and its verbal expression. Finally, the ability to self-regulate emotions and to facilitate the emotional regulation of others develops across the course of the lifespan. The process of socialization in the family affects both self- and other-regulation, both of which are topics covered in more detail in later chapters.

In considering how parents socialize emotions in their children, it is important to take a *life-span developmental perspective* in which developmental changes occur at each stage of life from infancy to older adulthood based on: age-graded influences, history-graded influences or non-normative life event influences (Baltes, Reese & Lipsitt, 1980). *Normative age-graded* influences are those that occur in a common way to most people of a similar background and age (see Table 1.2). Infants in the second half of the first year of life,

**Table 1.2** Normative Age-Graded Developmental Tasks Influenced by Emotion Socialization

***I. Infancy***
- learn to interact socially, and have some self-control
- attachment: build relationship with primary caregivers
- develop consciousness and emerging feelings of self-worth
- utilize social/affective referencing
- develop self-control (interacts with temperament)

***II. Early To Later Childhood***
- adopt group norms, rules and values
- expand emotion word vocabulary
- learn non-verbal cultural display rules and feeling rules
- internalize rules of culturally sanctioned behaviours
- foster relationships with sibling, peers and extended family
- develop areas of competence in social, physical (sensory and/or kinaesthetic), academic and behavioural domains

***III. Adolescents/Emerging Adults***
- evaluate group norms, rules and values
- implement behaviours based on beliefs and internalized values
- manage hormonal and physiological influences and bodily changes
- manage intrapsychic conflicts and dualistic/egocentric thinking and feeling
- participate in intimate relationships
- manage feelings about self linked to competence and self-worth

***IV. Adults***
- balance emotional control and expression according to the situation
- continue to manage feelings about self as linked to competence and self-worth
- learn emotional attunement skills in intimate relationships
- learn to accept and cope adaptively with inevitable losses

for example, develop a fear of novelty and strangers (Kagan, 1994), which is around the same time that they develop an attachment to their primary caregiver (see History Feature Box 1).

**History Feature Box 1**

**Back Then and Now: The Study of Parent–Child Attachment – John Bowlby and Mary Ainsworth**

Taking an ethological perspective, Bowlby's (1969) attachment theory incorporated the notion that human infants have an extended period of dependency on their caregivers to allow their brains and bodies to mature more fully outside of the womb. To promote survival during this period of dependency, the need for emotional security as well as proximity promoting (e.g., crying to attract the caregiver to come close) and proximity seeking (e.g., actively crawling or moving towards the caregiver) behaviours evolved, with both infants and their mothers having a biologically based predisposition to become emotionally attached to each other (Bowlby, 1969). For Bowlby and Ainsworth, basic emotions involving love, interest, anger, fear and sadness were intimately involved in the ongoing process that extended across the lifespan (e.g., pleasure/enjoyment in the shared affection during caregiver and others' availability; exploratory interest and curiosity in the environment under conditions of feeling secure; separation anxiety, despair and/or angry protests during and after separations from loved ones; feelings of sadness/loss when the caregiver or other attachment figures are unavailable; and fear of unfamiliar strangers and situations). Ainsworth's findings, coupled with her own naturalistic observations of mother–child interactions in Kampala, Uganda, Africa, and Baltimore, Maryland, USA, and those of John Bowlby and his colleagues, James and Joyce Robertson, in the United Kingdom, led to the conclusion that healthy emotional development *around the world* required the consistent accessibility of an emotionally sensitive primary caregiver (Bowlby, 1969; Fitton, 2012). Usually, the caregiver was the mother or a mother figure, who was attuned to the child and responsive to the child's needs (Bowlby, 1969; Fitton, 2012).

Using her findings from Uganda to guide her, Ainsworth operationalized the concept of emotional security through her creation of the Strange Situation laboratory task. Secure attachment style and two anxious insecure attachment styles (avoidant or ambivalent-resistant) could be identified on the basis of how infants responded to the following eight episode standardized sequence of situations in an unfamiliar lab room with toys: (1) infant and caregiver enter the lab room, (2) infant is allowed to play while caregiver is seated, (3) a stranger enters and talks with the caregiver before playing with the infant, (4) the caregiver leaves and the stranger attempts to console infant, (5) the caregiver returns (first reunion) and the stranger leaves, (6) the caregiver leaves the infant alone, (7) the stranger enters and tries to console the infant if necessary, and (8) caregiver returns and reunites with the infant (second reunion). This sequence is moderately stressful for infants in Western cultures and allows then for comparisons among typical and atypical responses to the stress (Ainsworth, Bell & Stayton, 1973; Ainsworth & Wittig, 1969; Sroufe, 1996). Infants classified as secure cried for their primary caregivers when separated, but contacted them once they were reunited; they were easily consoled and returned to play using their caregivers as safe, secure bases from which to explore toys in the room (Bretherton, 2003). Infants classified insecure/*avoidant* were also distressed upon separation, sometimes only if left alone, but looked or turned away from the caregiver when reunited, and seemed detached and uninterested in the caregiver upon reunion. Insecure/*ambivalent-resistant* infants strongly protested separation from their caregivers, but were resistant and angry upon being reunited, and showed ambivalence with some desire for contact (Bretherton, 2003).

By the mid-1980s, researchers had noted that not all infants could be easily classified as secure, avoidant or ambivalent-resistant; thus, some were left unclassified. However, Mary Main, one of Ainsworth's students, and Judith Solomon examined the videotaped data from these unclassified cases that was made available to them from other researchers; they identified a fourth pattern that they called *disorganized/disoriented* (Main & Solomon, 1986; Hesse & Main, 2000). Some of the insecure disorganized infants appeared to be avoidant during the first reunion with their mothers in the Strange Situation procedure and then appeared to be ambivalent-resistant during the second reunion, or vice versa in a mixed manner, thus making them difficult to classify as either avoidant or ambivalent; however, it was clear that they fitted best in the insecure general category. In studies on the disorganized category in the 1980s and 1990s, children classified as disorganized showed the following behaviours: stilling or freezing for a period of time as if they were in a daze or state of dissociation; contradictory or misdirected actions such as trying to establish contact with the stranger rather than the caregiver; stereotypical behaviours (e.g., hair pulling, rocking) under stress; and apprehensive wariness/fear in reaction to the caregiver (e.g., Hesse & Main, 2000; van IJzendoorn, Schuengel & Bakermans-Kranenburg, 1999). In their meta-analyses of these studies, van IJzendoorn et al. (1999) were able to demonstrate a clear link between risk of later psychopathology and the lack of an organized pattern of reacting to a caregiver. They indicated that many of those children classified as disorganized also had experienced maltreatment and their reactions seemed to be the result of having a history of experiencing fright without solution as to how to be comforted as conflicting biological systems were activated (i.e., both approach and avoid). Judith Solomon and Carol George (1999, 2011) further emphasized the fact that caregivers of children classified as disorganized were themselves disorganized in their approach to the Strange Situation task. They sometimes frightened their children with sudden, abrupt behaviours without providing anticipatory signals of what was to come; they also tended to behave in a helpless manner with respect to interacting with their children and in knowing how to handle and regulate their own emotions. Not surprisingly, then, infants classified as disorganized were sometimes found in later childhood to engage in controlling, role-reversal types of behaviours with their caregivers, such as ordering their parents about (e.g., Hesse & Main, 2000). In addition, although research findings do not suggest that temperament alone is responsible for whether a child is classified as secure, avoidant, ambivalent or disorganized, temperament does play a role in the way a child demonstrates a secure or insecure pattern. In addition, temperament may interact with caregiver responsivity and sensitivity, thus affecting the likelihood of a secure or insecure outcome (Steele & Steele, 2014).

As Sroufe (1996) describes, this is also the time when the infant starts to assign meanings to his or her emotional experiences based on the social context and the infant's own personal background. *History-graded* influences are those that are common to a generation or birth cohort of people who experience similar historical events at about the same time, such as occurs during wars, famines or the introduction of new technologies such as smartphones and tablets. For example, today's children do not remember a world without instant access to information via computers and other electronic devices, while many of their grandparents do. The specific socio-economic conditions under which people live affects their emotional development, whether the conditions are peace and prosperity or economic depression and daily hardships (e.g., Elder, Modell & Parke, 1993). *Non-normative* influences are those that do not occur in a normative manner and are unique to the individual regardless of age or generation. For example, falling in love for the first time may occur at many different ages and the death of a beloved family member may result in feelings of grief no matter what the person's age or historical circumstances. In taking a life-span perspective to the study of emotion socialization in families, it becomes apparent that the social and cultural contexts of family members of different ages and generations interact with each other and affect each family member in unique ways. So not only are parents important to consider in understanding the developing individual but also siblings, grandparents, extended family members, peers, and the broader social and cultural context in which families are embedded.

Assisting effectively in others' emotional understanding and regulation is one of the hallmarks of healthy family life as a parent, son, daughter, sister, brother, grandparent, aunt, uncle, or cousin. This chapter includes a discussion of how family members teach both adaptive and maladaptive emotion-relevant skills to each other during everyday life. By learning and practising effective emotion skills themselves, family members are better poised to help socialize adaptive emotional functioning in each other. Interestingly, there is increasing scientific evidence that early socialization experiences may have an impact on both the physiological foundation and the social behaviours of family members during interactions. This is not to say that the adaptive emotion action patterns (e.g., angry expression and activity to remove a blocked goal) that are present early in life become completely superseded by socialization, a point clearly made by Lewis (2014). Although many studies have examined parents and children as individuals who act as individuals who affect each other, another approach stems from the family systems theoretical approach. In *family systems theory*, the relationships among family members are viewed as the most important unit of analysis (Parke, 2004). Therefore, it becomes essential to consider how parents interact with each other and each of their children and how children interact with each other and each parent, as well as how extended family (aunts, uncles, grandparents) interact with each parent and child. This is a higher *level of analysis* and one that is significantly more complicated than merely looking at parents and their children as individuals.

As summarized next, several major family subsystems are addressed in this book using a developmental psychopathology approach. These are the parent–child, sibling, marital partner subsystems (Parke, 2004), the grandparent–adult child–grandchild subsystem and subsystems involving other extended family members, as well as the systems inherent in the broader social and cultural environment. The field of ***developmental psychopathology*** addresses continuities and discontinuities over time of both *adaptive* and *maladaptive* development within these family subsystems across the lifespan (Rutter & Sroufe, 2000). In contrast to related fields of study, such as clinical psychology or social work, less emphasis is placed on diagnosis and treatment when taking a developmental psychopathology approach (Ross & Jennings, 1995).

Parents are often the primary emotion socializers in the family, and thus there is a large research base of findings addressing their roles and the outcomes of their influences as introduced next.

## The Parent–Child Relationship

Historically, studies of the adaptive parent–child relationship have examined feelings of love, displays of affection, and attachment in relation to the gender of both parent and child. Of these, the most observed and studied relationship around the world is that of the mother and child extending as far back as we can go into ancient historical records and artefacts, sculptures and paintings. The developing infant becomes mobile, crawling and then walking in the first and second year of life, and attempts to maintain proximity to the mother figure. Gradually, the infant begins in a very rudimentary way to comprehend that the mother figure has feelings and motivations towards goals that may or may not be different from those of the infant (Bowlby, 1969). Eventually, an attachment and partnership develop as the mother and child interact in what appears to outsiders to be a finely tuned and well-orchestrated dance of emotional give and take, called ***interactional synchrony***, in which the rhythm and pattern of infant movements correspond to those of speech vocalizations in the social environment (Condon & Sander, 1974).

Researchers today know that dyadic synchrony between typical mothers and their infants is hardly a perfect Fred Astaire and Ginger Rogers type of dance in which one partner bubbles with love and happy excitement, smiles a big smile, and the other reciprocates with a lovely big smile in return and lots of hugs and kisses (Tronick, 2007; Tronick & Beeghly, 2011). Rather, Tronick and his colleagues note that the typical interaction is more of a messy yet normal dance with lots of false starts, uncoordinated missteps, mismatched behaviours, and unreciprocated bids for love, affection and attention. In other words, there are many random "errors". Thus, parental expectations and the infants' basic needs are not met in a perfect idealized way, and this is reflected in how they interact with each other on a moment-to-moment everyday basis. Nonetheless, functional and adaptive interactions can and do include strategies for repairing the interactive errors that occur in such messy everyday interactions. A mother who gets interrupted by an important phone call in the middle of playing a fun game of peek-a-boo with her infant may later come back to her disappointed infant, apologise remorsefully, and re-enact where they left off to try and reconstruct the earlier pleasurable experience. Such reparative behaviours are also part and parcel of the imperfect but normal dances of mothers with their infants (Tronick & Beeghly, 2011). In interacting with her infant in this way, the mother is communicating the unspoken parental expectation to her infant that their interactions with each other will not always be perfect and that everything will still be okay; that is, they will be able to pick up wherever they left off. Furthermore, the infant is socialized to learn that forgiveness in such situations is not only permissible, but highly desirable as part and parcel of everyday interactions.

Parental expectations for emotion-related behaviours in their children fall along a spectrum from functional to dysfunctional. Functional parental expectations for children are adaptive and consistent with the developing child's abilities and include the expectation that the child will learn prosocial emotions such as empathy for others and the ability to forgive. Dysfunctional parental expectations for children are maladaptive and may include such expectations as the child using emotions in self-serving ways; thus, dysfunctional parental expectations are not in the best interest of fostering the healthy development of children. Functional and adaptive parental expectations are consistent with the developmental tasks of children at each stage of their lives. For example, some evidence reviewed by Stipek (1992) suggests that parents who expect their school-age children to have age-appropriate school achievement successes do have children who are more likely to try and strive for achievement in their schoolwork because they anticipate self-esteem enhancing feelings of pride (when they succeed) and shame in disappointing parents (when they fail). On the other hand, dysfunctional and maladaptive parental expectations for children may involve age-inappropriate demands on a child and/or the encouragement of the violation of social or moral norms. For example, it may be reasonable for a parent to expect an average 10 year old to sit quietly without overt complaints, fidgeting and emotional distress while paying attention for an hour to a religious service meant for adults. However, the same parental expectation would not be age appropriate for an average 3 year old, and thus might lead to the child's overt expressions of distress and boredom, which in turn may result in parent–child conflict. Another extreme dysfunctional example here would be parents with a criminal history who expect their children to find pleasure in successfully assisting them in illegal activities, such as selling drugs or shoplifting. Thus, various parent characteristics, such as the parent's knowledge of typical child development or lack thereof and the parent's mental status, directly affect the emotional socialization of the child.

In addition to parental expectations, other personality and demographic background characteristics of mothers and fathers affect the emotion socialization of the child. However, there are *bidirectional influences* because the temperamental and background characteristics of the child, such as whether the child is a boy or girl, temperamentally difficult or easy-going, also result in child behaviours that influence how parents respond to their children. For example, some research suggests that mothers and fathers socialize emotions differently in their sons and daughters based on gender roles, although the exact findings for various emotions across studies are equivocal and in need of further clarification. When researchers have found gender differences, they note that mothers tend to talk more with their children about emotions than fathers do, and this is especially the case for mothers talking with daughters. There is some evidence that both mothers and fathers talk differently with daughters than with sons, emphasizing issues of interpersonal relationships, sadness and anxiety more with daughters and disharmonious relationship issues more with sons such as occurs during angry interactions (e.g., Chaplin, Cole & Zahn-Waxler, 2005; Fivush et al., 2000).

In addition to directly socializing emotion based on parent and child gender, the family's routines and rituals around the house may vary depending on whether it is a mother or a father interacting with a son or a daughter. For example, gender-based activities could include such chores as daughters helping mothers make dinner and sons helping fathers with the yard work such as lawn-mowing (Grusec & Davidov, 2007). Children may be reluctant or willing partners in chores and they may experience such tasks as repetitive and boring, emotionally reassuring, or occasionally fun; such activities potentially provide a sense of family stability for both parents and children.

## The Role of Siblings

*Family constellation* refers to the underlying characteristics of a family based on the ages, gender and birth order of the children. The birth of a child into a family not only changes the family constellation but also changes the underlying emotional tone of the couple for the first child and for the entire family with subsequent births. Initially, there may be excitement over anticipating a new family member; however, for many first-born or earlier-born children, the introduction of a new sibling presents emotional challenges. What if a 4 year old really wants a little brother and instead gets a little sister? What will happen if the new sibling is born with a disability? In many cases, the new sibling commands a large portion of parental time, attention and emotional resources, and this has an impact on the earlier-born siblings. Researchers have begun to consider the bidirectional influence of siblings in the emotional life of families (Kramer, 2014), a topic introduced here but discussed further throughout the textbook.

Studies of siblings have examined the consequences of having a warm and loving relationship, sibling rivalry and sibling involvement in arguments or conflicts including violence. Along with peers and friends outside of the family, siblings play an important role in socialization experiences because of the unique features of the sibling relationship (Dunn, 2007). Consider that sibling relationships are among the most emotionally intense and enduring of relationships that may last over the course of one's entire life or nearly so. In comparison to peers and friends, there is less threat of relationships being entirely cut off, especially during childhood. Thus, children are relatively freer than they are with peers and friends to test out and engage in more emotionally overt and intense expressions, risky interpersonal manipulations involving teasing, and poorly self-regulated behaviours, sometimes just to see what will happen next (e.g., Kramer, 2014).

Thus, sibling relationships are rich in opportunities to learn the dos and don'ts of interactions with others involving how one's own behaviour and feelings affect the emotional life and behaviours of another person. Adaptive sibling relationships may involve siblings who display warm, affectionate interactions with each other as well as non-violent conflicts with effective resolutions; such interactions, however, are influenced in several ways by what happens in the family between parents as well as between each parent and each child (Dunn, 2007). Furthermore, there is evidence that parents' relationships with their children have an impact on siblings. For example, some studies indicate that siblings who do not have emotionally supportive parents may form their own positive alliance with each other; in contrast, if parents differentially favour one or some children over others, this may exacerbate jealousy and fuel negative interactions and longstanding feuds between siblings (Dunn, 2007). Dunn (2007) reviews evidence that attachment security with a caregiver and positive marital/spousal/parental interactions form a foundation for more positive sibling relationships. Thus, the relationship between the adult partners in a family is an important facet of the emotional life of siblings as discussed further next.

## The Role of Partners/Couples

The emotional tone set by the adults within a family pervades the other interactions within the family, and stresses such as unemployment, financial burdens and illness affecting adults within the family will have an influence on more than just one individual. Researchers have begun to examine a variety of types of couples, such as heterosexual, lesbian/gay couples, divorced adults who co-parent, couples with stepfamilies, and cohabiting as well as married couples; for all types of couples, stressful life experiences are a common underlying theme. Bodenmann (2005) uses the term "dyadic stress" to refer to "a specific stressful encounter that affects both partners within a defined time frame and a defined geographic location" (p. 33). Also, partners within the family often must engage in what Bodenmann calls ***dyadic coping*** in addition to their individual coping efforts because of their interdependence, common concerns and joint goals. Sometimes the resulting synergy is an emotionally positive one and involves reality-based effective problem solving as well as tangible and emotional social supports; in other cases, the result is one in which the partners attempt to cope using maladaptive strategies such as substance abuse and hostile, ineffective forms of communicating. A large part of emotion socialization in families involves how family members appraise and cope with stressful interactions within their social and physical environments.

John Gottman and his colleagues have made the study of emotions within the family a lifelong career, and I will refer to his many contributions throughout this textbook. Recently, Gottman (2011) has emphasized the critical role that feelings of *trust* play in adult partners who form a couple; in trusting relationships, each partner can count on the other to have due consideration for their wants, needs and desires instead of merely acting based on self-interest. There is an implicit understanding that acting only with self-interest or being disloyal to your partner would lead to feelings of betrayal that would be difficult if not impossible to repair. This "science" of trust is based on decades of laboratory research on couples and families carried out by Gottman and his colleagues (2011). Based on the couples research of Yoshimoto (2005) and Gottman (2011), questions arise as to whether partners show an ***emotional attunement*** to each other in their everyday interactions and to the dynamics of the broader family. That is, do partners in the couple seem to "be there" for each other? Are they emotionally connected and aware of their partners' feelings within the broader family context? Do they make good eye contact, turn towards their partners, and actively pay attention during interactions? Do they do their best to maintain a positive problem-solving stance as they attempt to resolve disputes? If they hurt the feelings of the other person, is there some attempt to make amends and repair what has gone wrong?

To describe the concept of emotional attunement, Gottman (2011) uses ATTUNE as an acronym that stands for:

> Awareness of the emotion
> Turning toward the emotions
> Tolerance of the emotional experience
> Understanding the emotion
> Nondefensive listening to the emotion
> Empathy toward the emotion
>
> (p. 191, *The Science of Trust*, Copyright ©2011 by John M. Gottman. Reprinted with permission from W.W. Norton & Company)

The bottom line of Gottman's research findings is that couples in well-functioning long-term relationships show a wide range of emotional interactions including some that are quite negative in emotional tone, such as bitter complaining or feeling let down by the partner. Conflicts may or may not be effectively resolved, although there may be attempts to repair the hurt; some conflicts may even be longstanding 'issues' that are never resolved even in these well-functioning couples. However – and this is critical – the balance of positive moment-to-moment everyday interactions, such as showing affection, complimenting, or agreeing with the partner far outweigh the negative conflictual moments by a ratio of about 5:1 (Gottman, 2011).

Also, Gottman's scientific findings (2011) regarding the communication pattern known as the ***four horsemen of the apocalypse*** is well known for demonstrating the ability to accurately predict partners on a pathway to breaking up or divorcing (also see Gottman & Levenson, 2002). The four horsemen of the apocalypse are: *defensiveness, criticism, stonewalling and contempt.* Of these, the feeling of contempt towards a partner is the most toxic, and conveys both a feeling of disgust and hostile anger at the partner. Defensiveness involves not acknowledging the other's point of view, but rather engaging in self-protecting strategies to show how "I am right" and "You are wrong." Criticism should be clearly differentiated from complaining, in that being critical attacks the core of a person's sense of self and identity, whereas a complaint is an expressed wish for a person to alter behaviour. Refusing to interact by withdrawing and not responding are the defining features of stonewalling. Repairing breaches that signal any of the four horsemen of the apocalypse are critical to preserving a couple's relationship. Cowan, Cowan and Barry (2011) found that it is indeed possible to intervene with a couple parenting children in order to have a lasting impact on their children. They achieved a positive influence on school-age children that lasted even 10 years later by enhancing the parents' relationship with each other or by training parents to work on their parenting skills as a common goal. In addition to the role of siblings and marital partners/couples in affecting emotion socialization, other family members such as grandparents and extended family members can also play a role, as described next.

## The Role of Grandparents and Extended Family Members

Like parents, grandparents, aunts, uncles and cousins are sometimes present in the life a child from the time of the child's birth, and a variety of emotional ties may be forged. For the adult looking forward to the new role as a grandparent, aunt or uncle, or the child looking forward to a new cousin, there may be feelings of joy and excitement over the prospect of a budding relationship that promises to be emotionally close, warm, affectionate or fun. Grandparents looking forward to this new role may overtly express their love for their grandchildren, show that they are concerned and interested in the daily life and activities of the child, and celebrate, along with the child's family, special events such as birthdays and holidays (Mansson, 2013). Developing such emotional closeness across generations from child through parents to grandparents and other extended family members assists in teaching children how to maintain and value stability, trust and long-term emotional commitment within their family relationships.

Positive *intragenerational* emotional bonds may form between siblings or between cousins within the same generation; similarly, *intergenerational* emotional bonds beyond the typical nuclear family parent–child bond may also form between grandparent and grandchild, or between aunts and uncles and their nieces and nephews (Milardo, 2005, 2009; Ponzetti, 2011). "*Aunting*" and "*uncling*", as described by Milardo, have not been widely researched thus far, although many people have rich memories of their aunts and uncles and can readily describe their influential impact as surrogate parents and mentors who provide advice, criticism, support and meaning to their lives. For example, in African American black families, maternal aunts sometimes play an important role by taking over the mothering of their sisters' children (e.g., Davis-Sowers, 2012), and uncles may provide social support and advice regarding the upbringing of their nephews in father-absent homes (Richardson, 2009). The important role played by grandparents in raising and socializing grandchildren has been increasingly noted in North America in a wide diversity of families (e.g., and in other regions around the world, including but not limited to China, Spain and Italy). Grandparents may act as a surrogate when there is the loss of one or both parents, as a caregiver while parents work, or just as an extended family member who checks in on the family and child occasionally during holidays and special events (e.g., Hakoyama & Malonebeach, 2013; Mansson, 2013).

The extended family has effects on the emotion socialization of children in both direct and indirect ways. In addition to direct live family interactions and phone conversations, recent technological advances via the internet and social media enable real-time as well as delayed audiovisual contacts that directly and/or indirectly influence emotion socialization. Indirectly, family members affect the emotion socialization of each other through observing emotional expressions and regulation efforts, conflicts and conflict resolutions. Another mechanism for the indirect transmission of emotion-related socialization behaviours occurs when one family member interacts with another with an indirect influence on the emotional life of a third person. For example, as a mother and father grieve over the death of one of their children, the family context is imbued with a focus on transitions and changes that may involve people within and outside of a family, such as the child's school, neighbourhood peers and friends, and the family's religious institution. A surviving child in the family may be emotionally neglected and feel the fear of uncertainty regarding what the future will bring. The importance of the overall sociocultural context in which emotional development occurs is addressed next.

## Contextual Influences: Neighbourhoods, Communities and Culture

As noted above, individuals within immediate families are not the only ones who provide emotion-socializing experiences; other relatives who may or may not reside in the same household provide a social and emotional context and are thus additional agents of socialization. Similarly, the broader social and cultural network of the family provides opportunities for a variety of emotional encounters from venues for local entertainment (e.g., a neighbourhood comedy theatre) and recreation (e.g., a park with a beautiful lake for swimming and boating) to local religious institutions, shopping centres and community centres.

As *bio-ecological models* of development demonstrate (Bronfenbrenner, 1994; Swick & Williams, 2006), individuals and their family members are embedded within layers of nesting contextual influences. Bronfenbrenner's (1994) model is particularly noteworthy and relevant to understanding some of the complexities of emotion socialization in families. Immediate and extended family members, teachers, peers and co-workers directly influence the everyday emotional life of each other and are part of the inner circle of the target individual's life, called the *microsystem* in Bronfenbrenner's model. The *mesosystem* is the next highest level in which various microsystems interact with each other and have an emotional impact on each involved family member. These microsystems each directly involve the targeted individual. For example, father–child conflict over the target child's participation in extracurricular soccer training at school interacts at the mesosystem level with the alliance between the mother and child, and the nature of the relationship between the child and soccer coach at the school. The complexity of the microsystems and mesosystems as they interact are embedded within the *exosystem*. Exosystems involve the interaction of multiple systems, at least one of which *indirectly* involves the target individual. An example here would be a mother who is emotionally distressed about having to work unexpectedly on frequent occasions on an overtime basis. The influence of the mother's employment setting on a target child is indirect, and interacts with the emotional quality of the mother–child interaction at home. *Macrosystems* incorporate microsystems, mesosystems and exosystems with the underlying organization involving social norms and roles (such as those within neighbourhoods and surrounding communities) and the broader society's cultural belief systems. Finally, the *chronosystem* in this model refers to the relative stability and changes in the various systems and the environments in which they function over time. Bronfenbrenner's model is one in which both genetics and environment are influential; it is commonly pictured as nesting circles of influence with the individual at the centre embedded within the layers of microsystems, mesosystems, exosystems and macrosystems, all of which are affected by the chronosystem.

Using Bronfenbrenner's model, Eamon (2001) provides an analysis of how family poverty relates to children's socio-emotional development, noting that family poverty has broader effects than just that of adding to a family's coping difficulty with everyday stresses at a microsystem level. Eamon (2001) reviews research on the outcomes of the many microsystem influences. Children affected by poverty are more likely to attend schools with fewer resources, and to have peer conflicts and rejection. They are more likely to have emotional/behavioural disorders, low sociability, and to display disruptions at school. Furthermore, poor children have fewer opportunities to engage in peer group activities due to event or travelling costs; they may feel different and be perceived as being different by peers because it may be more difficult for them to obtain and wear clothing, for example, that conforms to the group norms locally or at the broader cultural levels (Eamon, 2001). Studies of the mesosystem and exosystem are rarer. At the mesosystem level, Eamon (2001) summarizes evidence that mothers affected by poverty are less likely to be actively involved at the schools their children attend, and this shows a relation with their children's social adjustment at school, and their interactions with schoolmates and teachers. At the exosystem level, an example of an indirect effect on the socio-emotional development of a child would be poverty-affected parents having difficulty with their own social support or community networks, and this lack of support indirectly influencing the parent–child relationship (Eamon, 2001). Culture, which resides within the macrosystem, is the broadest emotion socialization agent addressed in this textbook. Culture consists of symbolic meanings ascribed to tangible things – music, art, language, situations and events – as well as less tangible ideas that are common to a group of people often residing within a community (e.g., Shweder et al., 2008). For parents and children affected by poverty, there are often race/ethnicity disparities in material resources, educational and employment opportunities, housing and neighbourhood quality, as well as nutrition and health at the macrosystem level (Eamon, 2001). Finally, the chronosystem includes a consideration of how income loss affects individuals based on the person's age or developmental level, or based on the historical time period in which the person has lived, such as the Great Depression (Eamon, 2001).

While cultural differences allow emotion socialization practices in families to differ widely from one place to another over the course of time, culture and the environment do not directly influence some features of the emotional life of individuals, at least at certain critical points. Lewis (2014), for example, contends that culture does not influence those aspects of early emotional development that are part of our innate biological heritage, such as the ability to engage in self-reflection or the acquisition of *consciousness* in the second year of life, a topic that is introduced in Chapter 3. The various methods used by researchers to contribute to our knowledge base of the microsystems, mesosystems, exosystems, macrosystems and chronosystems is the topic of the next chapter.

## Summary of Chapter Key Points

It is important to distinguish the various defining features of emotion, affect and feelings in coming to an understanding of emotional development and competence in families. This chapter provided introductions to three approaches to understanding the socialization of emotion within families: family systems, developmental psychopathology, and bio-ecological. The *family systems* approach accounts for various subsystems within the larger extended family. Included here are the parent–child, sibling and partner/couple subsystems, as well as those subsystems involving extended family such as grandparents, aunts, uncles and cousins. Researchers have begun to identify specific forms of emotion socialization that take place within each family subsystem. The *developmental psychopathology* approach considers both adaptive and maladaptive developmental pathways and the emotional ramifications that affect family members. In Bronfenbrenner's (1994) *bioecological* approach, embedded systems situate individuals and their families within increasingly broader spheres of influence including that of culture situated in place and time. Although cultural influences on emotions in families are pervasive and provide meaningful experiences over the lifespan, biological and evolutionary influences such as the emergence of consciousness and the ability to self-reflect are also important. Researchers have used a variety of methods to contribute to our understanding of these important influences.

## Further Reading

Gottman, J. M. (2011). *The science of trust: Emotional attunement for couples.* New York: Norton.

This book provides useful tips on communication within family relationships based on recent research findings. Much to his chagrin, the media has often treated John Gottman as the relationship or 'love guru' because of his studies that predict relationship successes and failures such as divorce. In this book, Gottman acknowledges that communication processes need to be better understood especially with respect to how trust is built and maintained over time.

Lazarus, R. S. (1991). *Emotion and adaptation.* New York: Oxford University Press.

In this classic volume, Richard Lazarus presents an in-depth look at his cognitive-motivational-relational theory as it relates to how people cope with stressful life experiences, manage their emotions, and adapt to their social and physical environments. Sections of his book summarize and critique the functions of various emotions and how they motivate us towards actions. Lazarus also highlights the significance of his theoretical approach for life-span emotional development, relationships, and physical and mental health.

Newmark, G. (2008). *How to Raise Emotionally Healthy Children: Meeting the Five Critical Needs of Children ... and Parents Too!* Tarzana, CA: NMI Publishers.

Gerald and Deborah Newmark founded the *The Children's Project* (www.emotionallyhealthychildren.com) to help foster family emotional health through the education of parents, teachers, childcare workers and policy makers. In this short, readable and practical guide, Newmark's important message is one that is easily understood and accessible to a wide variety of audiences. The book describes the five critical emotional needs of children and adults with many practical tips and exercises for how to promote fulfilment of these needs.

# 2

# Methodological Issues in the Study of Emotional Development in Families

The following is an excerpt from an emotionally focused family therapy (EFFT) session in the United States reported by Stavrianopoulos, Faller and Furrow (2014). The session consisted of the therapist, the father and mother (who were in their 40s), and their four sons: Stephen (17 yrs), Tony (14 yrs), Michael (12 yrs) and Ben (10 yrs). The identified patient was Tony who had a history of attention deficit disorder and disruptive, oppositional behaviours. The family was seeking help because they wanted to alleviate family conflicts.

> *THERAPIST: Last time we talked about the different ways people learn to protect themselves when they feel threatened. Some of us try to go away to avoid further threat while others actively force the issue. I realize we all do some of both but I'm trying to get a feel for the predominant way each one of you protects yourself during a fight or when you are stressed. (Therapist assessing family members' awareness of their predictable secondary, emotional responses.)*
>
> *MICHAEL: Well, Stephen, Ben, and Dad all go to their rooms when they are mad. Mom and Tony usually start yelling at everyone, and I try to keep the peace by talking it out.*
>
> *TONY: Yeah, right! You cause just as much trouble as me. You cause most of our fights by stealing my stuff; it's just that everyone blames me.*
>
> *MOM: Hey, quit it you two. We are not here to fight.*

*One minute into the session and the therapist can already see the negative cycle taking off; Mom, Tony, and Michael jump into the conversation while Dad, Stephen, and Ben stay out.* (Case study from Stavrianopoulos, Faller & Furrow, 2014, pp. 31–32)

## Watching and Listening to Families

Observation is perhaps the most direct and widely used informal method of assessing the emotional life of a family. It is personally relevant for laypersons and professionals alike, such as the family therapist in the opening vignette. It forms the basis for the daily stories we hear and watch in the media or those that we read in books and magazines. It is possible to identify and relate to such family members based on our own inner emotional experiences by actively feeling empathy and emotional connectedness with them. They remind us of feelings we have had in the past and of events that we have processed emotionally at least to some degree. In some cases, though unaware of the source of our feelings, we may have an uncomfortable, unsettled feeling about what we observe in a family as it stirs up some unfinished emotional business or highlights complex interpersonal events that are beyond our own current level of comprehension.

Thus, given that observing and reacting to people in families is so pervasive, each of us already has some experience in judging the quality of the emotional life of families. As observers of family members interacting with each other, we may conclude that there is primarily harmony or conflict that binds the observed family together. We deem that a given family *seems to be* a "happy" functional family or one that is "troubled" and dysfunctional. Although there is no absolute, ultimate test or gold standard for which is which, researchers have made great strides in clarifying emotional functioning in families and in understanding emotional change processes during psychotherapy with individuals and families. Researchers have begun to identify emotion components that are measurable in the effort to understand emotion communication.

Klaus Scherer (2005) has suggested that there are five measurable emotion components: appraisal; physiological symptoms; motor expressions in face and body; action tendencies or behaviours including verbalizations; and subjective feelings of arousal, intensity, duration, valence and tension. Similarly, Robert Solomon (2002) and others have endorsed these aspects of emotion as being important to assess along with the interactive social context in a manner that is holistic, multi-method and non-reductionistic (e.g., Zeman et al., 2007). In addition to formal methods of measuring these aspects of emotions, our own informal observations and assessments take place in everyday settings.

As described throughout this book, methodological considerations are important in contemporary studies of emotional development in individuals and families. These are: (1) developing sound theoretical concepts with the potential for practical applications, (2) reliably and validly assessing emotional development, (3) proactively enhancing adaptive emotion regulation strategies and preventing maladaptive ones, (4) identifying and diagnosing emotional dysfunction, and (5) evaluating the evidence for the effectiveness of interventions (such as EFFT in the opening vignette) that attempt to promote adaptive changes in emotion over time. In addition, research design issues that consider cohort effects, within and across family differences, and the pros and cons of cross-sectional and longitudinal studies of family emotion are important. See History Feature Box 2. This chapter provides an overview of some methodological issues encountered in interpreting emotion within families.

**History Feature Box 2**

**Back Then and Now: Family Emotion – Methods and Research Designs**

In conducting research on emotion in families, *quantitative methods* involve gathering numerical data through questionnaires, experiments and coded data, while *qualitative methods* involve gathering reports of subjective experiences through interviews, focus groups, diaries, field observations and case studies (Greenstein, 2006). Researchers sometimes pragmatically make use of both by using a ***mixed methods*** approach (Greenstein, 2006). Research designs with families can focus on what is happening between parents and children in a *within-family design*; for example, Shewark and Blandon (2015) studied maternal and paternal emotion socialization and regulation in families with two children between 2 and 5 years of age. This design allowed researchers to compare parents' reactions to emotions in the older and younger siblings, and to identify patterns of socialization that differed for mothers and fathers. In contrast, *between-family designs* address family differences according to categorical classifications such as race, ethnicity, or culture. For example, Wörmann, Holodynski, Kärtner and Keller (2012) compared the socialization of smiling in mother–infant interactions cross-culturally in families from Germany (Europe) and Cameroon (Africa). Hypotheses took into consideration the independent worldview of German mothers and the interdependent worldview of Cameroonian mothers. Consistent with expectations, Wörmann et al. found that there were no differences in the groups when the infants were 6 weeks old. However, by 12 weeks of age, German mothers and infants showed more smiling and imitation than the Cameroonian mothers and infants, thus illustrating the likely influence of culture on emotion socialization.

Developmental researchers have identified some methodological issues in conducting studies across the lifespan. In making age comparisons, emotion researchers must make sure that what they are comparing at different points in the lifespan is the same underlying construct. In other words, what they are measuring must have ***measurement equivalence*** (e.g., Miller, 2013). For example, a verbal measure of emotion understanding suitable for a 7 year old might be too demanding for the cognitive abilities of a 4 year old. When there is measurement equivalence, age comparisons are important in showing *continuity* or *discontinuity* over time. To make such comparisons, researchers use cross-sectional, longitudinal, time-lag and sequential research designs (Lerner, 2002). *Cross-sectional designs* involve comparing different age groups consisting of separate individuals at about the same point in time, while *longitudinal designs* consist of a relatively homogeneous group of individuals from the same birth cohort who are followed up over time to assess how they have remained the same (continuity) or how they have changed (discontinuity). One disadvantage to cross-sectional studies is that age and birth cohort are confounded resulting in potential ***cohort effects***, where the differences are due to the biology and/or experiences of a specific generation rather than due to their age (e.g., Lerner, 2002; Miller, 2013). Time-lag studies examine one age group, but at different points in time consisting of different groups of people; for example, a researcher might ask: "How can I describe the emotional experiences of 13 year olds independent of their birth cohort?" The researcher might then design a study to compare 13 year olds in 2018, 2021 and 2024, in order to understand better the similarities and differences by cohort. However, the influence of *time of testing* (historical events occurring that year) is confounded with the birth cohort, so it is difficult to know which is responsible for the observed differences. Longitudinal studies allow for repeated testing of the same individuals over time and thus control for possible cohort effects, but the person's age is confounded with the time of testing. To address the limitations of each of these approaches, ***sequential designs*** combine cross-sectional, longitudinal and time-lag designs (e.g., Lerner, 2002); the researcher can then sort through the results to make inferences about the relative influence of age, cohort and time of testing.

Historically, there have been many longitudinal studies conducted that involve emotion, personality and adaptation. Glen Elder and colleagues conducted interviews and observations, or gathered retrospective reports at various points in the lives of individuals who were children or adolescents during the Great Depression in the United States; the main question that they addressed was why this disadvantaged World War II cohort nonetheless overcame the adversities of their youth (Elder & Hareven, 1993). The New York Longitudinal Study (NYLS), described in Chapter 4, was a catalyst for much of the research on temperament that has followed since then (Chess & Thomas, 1977; Thomas et al., 1963). Lewis Terman's longitudinal study of gifted individuals began in the 1920s and has resulted in numerous studies since then regarding what it means to develop with the advantage of gifted intelligence. For example, Holahan, Holahan, Velasquez and North (2008) analysed data on happiness in old age in the Terman sample and found that positive expectations for old age in the 60s age range was related to greater self-reported happiness later. Although these gifted participants reported moderately high levels of happiness in old age, there were small declines in happiness from age 66 to 86, consistent with findings from studies on the general population. In the Block and Block Longitudinal Study that took place from 1969 to 1999 in the United States, Jack and Jeanne Block (2006, 2010) studied socio-emotional development and personality in individuals from 3 to 32 years old. The Blocks described the importance of *ego-control* (how the person usually responds to impulses) and *ego-resiliency* (how adaptive and flexible the person is to changing life circumstances). The Blocks' research has inspired other longitudinal studies. For example, a longitudinal study by Causadias, Salvatore and Sroufe (2012) showed how ego-resiliency, but not ego-control, in high-risk children predicted their adaptive functioning in early adulthood.

Some personality researchers have reviewed longitudinal studies and conducted quantitative ***meta-analyses***, which involves averaging the effect sizes found across many studies; *effect sizes* are the strength or magnitude of the relation among the main study variables (e.g. Miller, 2013). Roberts and DelVecchio (2000) conducted a meta-analysis of 152 longitudinal studies on personality traits reported from the 1930s to the 1990s, and found that there was an increase in rank order consistency from childhood to the middle adult years, with evidence for some personality change occurring even into older adulthood. Karney and Bradbury (1995) studied marital quality and stability in 115 longitudinal studies from the 1930s to the 1990s and examined vulnerability, stress and adaptive processes. They concluded that future studies need to: (1) use multiple approaches, (2) contain homogenous samples to control for family distress, and (3) include couples even before marriage using cross-sectional designs and retrospective reports in combination with longitudinal data gathering.

Currently, the US National Longitudinal Study of Adolescent and Adult Health (ADD Longitudinal Project) exemplifies a multiple method approach to data gathering (Resnick et al., 1997). In a first wave report of cross-sectional findings on the influence of family and school risk and protective factors on adolescent behaviours, Resnick et al. (1997) found that connectedness to parents, family and school served a protective function against many problematic health outcomes (e.g. emotional distress, substance abuse). In another ADD Longitudinal Project study, researchers followed up and assessed 13 year olds later at age 14 and again between 18 and 20 years of age for family and school risk and protective factors and violent behaviours (Bernat et al., 2012). In a recent study from the ADD Longitudinal Project, Gambrel, Faas, Kaestle and Savla (2016) use the compelling theory of Daniel Siegel (2001, 2006) on interpersonal neurobiology to interpret the results; the contention of this theory is that interpersonal experiences, such as those that occur during the attachment process, have direct implications for brain functioning and mental processes. Gambrel et al. found that emotional support from mothers and fathers was linked to self-acceptance in adolescence, which was linked to emotional stability in adulthood; it was emotional stability in turn that was associated with adult relationship quality. This latest longitudinal study demonstrates how attachment theory continues to have relevance for contemporary research interpretations.

## Observing Families: Theory, Research and Practical Applications

Theories of family functioning are often born of observations of families and the theorist's own experiences (e.g., Nichols & Schwartz, 1995). Good theories of emotion are, of course, necessary because they can lead to reliable, valid assessments and measurement, and sound research; and well-designed and executed research in turn can lead to useful, practical applications clinically, at home, and in other relevant everyday settings such as at school or work (e.g., Plutchik, 2000). John Bowlby's *attachment theory*, discussed in Chapter 1, is a quintessential example. I was fortunate enough to hear Bowlby discuss his theory and answer questions about surrogate parenting in a talk that he gave to community mental health workers in Michigan in the 1980s. Bowlby proposed that mothers and their newborn babies are biologically predisposed to developing a meaningful and lasting emotional bond. In his theory, evolutionary processes and the need for infant survival in the human species have resulted in babies developing a strong need for love, nurturance and physical proximity to a consistent caregiver.

Around the time that I heard Bowlby speak in the 1980s, I was looking for a film on attachment to show to one of my child development classes. At that time, I discovered the film *John, Aged Seventeen Months, For Nine Days in a Residential Nursery* from a classic British film series by James and Joyce Robertson on the separation of young children from their mothers (also see Robertson & Robertson, 1989). Like Bowlby, these colleagues of his were interested in the effects of separation from the mother figure on personality development. Like many others who saw the film, I watched with great interest and compassion as John tried to cope with being left in a residential nursery while his mother went to the hospital to have her second child, and his father went to work during the day and left him to stay overnight. At first, John seemed to adapt well and to form an attachment to a substitute caregiver, but once the caregivers rotated in their duties and became inconsistent, and once he realized that his father's visits were only temporary, he became increasingly withdrawn and he refused to play or eat. By the time John reunited with his mother, he seemed ambivalent and angry with his mother and father as evidenced in his non-verbal behaviour towards them once they were reunited. The Robertsons and Bowlby observed similar results in other case studies.

In the preface to his seminal book *Attachment*, Bowlby (1969) suggests that it was observations such as the one that I just described that helped to confirm his contention that early separation or loss of the mother figure (in combination with other yet unidentified variables) is related to later personality problems and psychopathology. Based on such observations and the relevant literature available then, Bowlby (1969) developed his comprehensive theory of attachment. Bowlby's contention was that if the attachment process was disrupted or deviant, the consequences would be severe and far-reaching, resulting in negative patterns of relating to others out of fear, anger and mistrust. Other observations of children separated from their caregivers, such as the classic films of Rene Spitz that depicted institutionalized children of incarcerated mothers, helped to consolidate the view that nurturing, consistent caregivers are vital to the mental health and well-being of children (NOVA/WGBH, 1986).

Since the early observations of Spitz, the Robertsons and Bowlby, researchers such as Mary Ainsworth have developed reliable and valid ways to assess attachment behaviour in young children and to measure the perceived attachment relationship in adults (Cassidy & Shaver, 2008; also, see Chapters 1 and 5). For example, Ainsworth developed the Strange Situation approach to the observational assessment of attachment quality. In this approach, an infant and caregiver are videotaped in a variety of interpersonal situations that all occur within a short period. To recap, these include the child and caregiver alone, the child and caregiver together with a stranger present, the child and stranger without the caregiver, the child alone, and the child reunited with the caregiver. During these episodes, the child experiences increasing levels of stress within a strange setting as he or she is introduced to the stranger. These experiences include various separations with the caregiver (Lamb, Ketterlinus & Fracasso, 1992). The caregiver and child's behaviours and reactions are assessed and a determination is made about whether the child is securely or insecurely attached to the caregiver. Currently, there are thousands of research studies relating the quality of attachment (as being either secure or insecure) to various aspects of mental health such as positive peer relations or psychopathology. Such research has led to the identification of attachment trauma as a serious causal factor in understanding problematic family relationships (e.g., Coleman, 2003). Both laypeople and professionals speak meaningfully of the parent–child bond as being either secure or insecure in their informal discussions. Because of attachment theory and research, paediatricians, hospital staff, day care providers, clinicians, teachers and many well-informed parents understand the importance of warm, nurturing, consistent caregivers in children's lives; consequently, they have applied this knowledge to the benefit of children and their families (e.g., James, 1994). A variety of attachment interventions have been put into practice (e.g., Levy, 2000). The field of attachment studies addresses emotions such as love, anger, jealousy and betrayal, separation anxiety and fear of strangers all within the family context. Perhaps in no other area of the psychology of families do we so clearly see the links between observation, theory, research and application than in the field of attachment studies.

In the opening chapter excerpt from an ***emotionally focused family therapy (EFFT)*** session, Stavrianopoulos et al. (2014) provide an illustration of an intervention approach that uses constructs and ideas that have emerged from attachment theory. The techniques of EFFT are an extension of ***emotion-focused therapy (EFT)*** for couples. In EFT, emotional reactions can be primary or secondary, and adaptive or maladaptive. ***Primary emotions*** include biologically based adaptive emotions such as sadness in reaction to a loss or maladaptive learned emotions such as fear or shame in reaction to trauma or abuse (Greenberg, 1993). However, primary emotions may be thwarted or blocked, and instead defensive, reactive ***secondary emotions*** may be enacted (such as crying out of frustration, when the underlying primary emotion is anger) (Greenberg, 1993). Both the therapeutic relationship and the processing of activated primary emotions are important in EFT; during therapy, processing occurs in awareness and arousal, emotion regulation, reflection and the transformation of emotional meanings (e.g., Greenberg, 1993; Greenberg & Pascual-Leone, 2006; Paivio, 2013). In EFFT, an early goal in treatment is to help each family member to understand how maladaptive attachment-related emotions and patterns of relating to each other can be transformed into adaptive emotional expressions and attachment patterns reflecting the love and genuine concern family members have for each other (e.g., Johnson, 2008). Therapeutic changes occur in three stages. First, the therapist facilitates a *de-escalation* of negative cycles after it is initially activated in a session (as in this chapter's opening excerpt); then, the therapist assists the family in *restructuring* their attachment-relevant ways of relating to each other, and, finally, helps them in a *consolidation* of the attachment pattern changes (Johnson, 2008). Emotionally focused family therapy research is *process-oriented* and has increasing empirical support for its effectiveness in work with couples, parents, children and adolescents (e.g., Johnson, 2008). Similarly, researchers have found successful emotion processing in attachment-based family therapy in which the unresolved anger of young adults towards their parents is addressed (Diamond et al., 2016).

The success of the study of attachment and its implications for treating families sets a high standard for what researchers need to study emotion and families on a broader scale. Studies of attachment-related disorders and psychopathology have incorporated attachment theory across the lifespan, often with cross-cultural relevance and implications (Cassidy & Shaver, 2008). As observers of the emotional lives within families, we need viable, testable theories, reliable and valid measures, and useful guidelines on how to translate research findings into practice. Thus far, there are numerous measurement approaches in use that are relevant for the study of emotional development in families, with a review of some of these provided below. Table 2.1 also provides a list of some methods used by researchers in studying emotion in families.

**Table 2.1** Examples of Measurement Methods for Assessing Emotions in Family Members

| Measurement Method | Some Examples |
|---|---|
| **Naturalistic observation** | • Audio- or videotaped recordings and coding (Mesman & Emmen, 2013) |
| **Self-report and other-report measures** | • Paper-and-pencil questionnaires (Shields & Cicchetti, 1998)<br>• Electronic diaries (Suveg et al., 2010)<br>• Experience sampling (e.g., Carstensen et al., 2011) |
| **Projective tests** | • Sentence completion (e.g., Hy & Loevinger, 1996; Drewes & Westenberg, 2001)<br>• Drawings (Bonoti & Misalidi, 2015)<br>• Projective pictures (Zurbriggen & Sturman, 2002) |
| **Interviews** | • Meta-emotion parent interview (Gottman, Katz & Hooven, 1997)<br>• Use of props, stories, pictures, or puppets during child interviews (Adrian, Zeman & Veits, 2011) |
| **Physiological and genetic measures** | • Skin conductance (Kochanska et al., 2015)<br>• Electroencephalogram (Strang, Hanson & Pollak, 2012)<br>• Electrocardiogram/vagal tone (Gottman, Katz & Hooven, 1996)<br>• Neuroendocrine assessments (e.g., cortisol, oxytocin) (e.g., Fox & Calkins, 2000; van IJzendoorn & Bakermans-Kranenburg, 2012)<br>• Genetic markers (e.g., Pappa et al., 2015) |
| **Facial expressions, vocal expressions, gestures and body posture** | • Coding systems of discrete emotions based on muscle movements (e.g., Izard's MAX and Ekman's FACS) (Camras & Fatani, 2008)<br>• Emotion encoding and decoding accuracy (Halberstadt et al., 2011) |
| **Narratives and stories (oral, written, audio-visual)** | • Autobiographical memory tasks (Fivush & Nelson, 2004; Fitzgerald, 2010)<br>• Writing about traumatic events (Pennebaker & Seagal, 1999)<br>• Story stem completion (Shields, Ryan & Cicchetti, 2001)<br>• Reminiscing tasks (Fivush & Nelson, 2006)<br>• Life story narratives (McAdams, 2001; McAdams et al., 2006) |
| **Problem solving and prosocial tasks** | • Delay-of-gratification tasks (Vaughn, Kopp & Krakow, 1984)<br>• Frustration in solving problem tasks (Dennis et al., 2009)<br>• Prosocial behaviour tasks (Dunsmore, 2015) |

*Continued*

Table 2.1 *(Continued)*

| Measurement Method | Some Examples |
| --- | --- |
| **Family interaction and family therapy** | • Couple conflicts and resolution (Carstensen, Gottman & Levenson, 1995)<br>• Dyadic and triadic family interactions (Kerig & Lindahl, 2001; Volling, McElwain & Miller, 2002)<br>• Parent–adolescent conflicts and resolution (Robin & Foster, 1989)<br>• Family interaction with therapist (Stavrianopoulos et al., 2014; Diamond et al., 2016) |

Note: Additional sources are Adrian, Zeman & Veits (2011), Malatesta (1981) and Zeman et al. (2007).

## Assessing Emotions in Families: Stories, Narratives, Drawings and Interviews

The general population appears to be very motivated to understand their own emotions and those of others as attested to by the popularity of self-help books, specialized popular magazines and children's picture books on feelings. Such books often contain information for parents on how to listen to their children to validate their feelings, and how to teach children to cope with common stresses such as separation, death, moving, starting school, peer conflict, and parental divorce and remarriage. Clinicians sometimes make use of "bibliotherapy" for their clients in which they prescribe books to read or films to watch outside of their therapy sessions. Clients then discuss emotional reactions to the book or film in the session and the therapist may use this information informally to assess the client's emotional status.

Part of the delight in hearing or reading a good story is that it stirs up our feelings. Emotional provocation in the receiver is considered the essential feature of a good novel or film (e.g., Nafisi, 2003; Tan, 1996), and the field of narrative studies is replete with examples of how oral, written and filmed stories (i.e., narratives) can be used to informally assess and alter emotions in others (also see Chapter 9). While the negative impact of videogames is often noted, even the positive emotional potential of videogames has been tapped for its therapeutic uses in working with children (e.g., Griffiths, 2003). The therapeutic uses of games, stories and movies in working with children allow parents, teachers and therapists to make use of written and visual media in their informal assessment and interventions into the emotional lives of children.

Everyday stories of fact and fantasy told by children are often rich in emotional meaning, and conscientious, attentive parents who converse and interact with children can utilize this information to transform and extend children's emotion understanding (e.g., Engel, 1995; Gardner, 1992; Mills & Crowley, 1986). Gardner (1992) was one of the earliest therapists to use stories as a means of treating children. In Gardner's mutual storytelling technique, the therapist supports the child in telling a make-believe story about anything he or she desires. The therapist listens for the emotional significance behind the metaphors in the child's story and constructs a similar but modified new story with a moral that results in a more positive and mentally healthy framework. The therapist then tells the child this new story as part of the therapeutic process. Similarly, Mills and Crowley (1986) devised a variety of techniques for parents and therapists to help children express their feelings. For example, as part of the assessment process, the adult ask a child or adolescent to draw three pictures. For Picture 1, the instructions are to draw what their problem feels like, or to draw their "problem". Picture 2 is a picture of what the problem feels like once it is "all better", or the problem is resolved. Finally, for Picture 3, the child is asked to draw who or what will help in going from the first to the second picture (i.e., the child is asked to reflect on and draw perceived resources).

Such drawings serve two purposes. First, a child may have a different perception of the problem than the caregivers who are the main informants. Thus, the child's perspective is gained by examining Picture 1 and discussing it with the child. For instance, caregivers may identify the problem as oppositionality, disobedience and poor school performance, while the child identifies it as feeling lonely and bullied, and being emotionally provoked by schoolmates. A child may not verbalize these problems and feelings during an interview, and the caregivers may be unaware of the problem or minimize it. Yet, the child may feel otherwise and may best be able to convey in a picture what he or she cannot convey well in words. Thus, those problems provided by the child supplement the problems identified by the caregivers. Tapping into ***inter-informant agreement*** is an important methodological consideration in assessing emotion in families. Second, in Pictures 2 and 3, it is possible to understand whether the child has some idea of goals (i.e., what he or she thinks things should be like) and what will help to achieve those goals (i.e., resources). This helps in assessing how aware the child is of emotions and how to regulate them. It is then possible to help the child clarify goals and resources by using the child's own ideas as a point of departure. Individuals, including children, have their own life stories, and the idea behind a narrative approach to assessment is that emotional themes pervade the stories we have about others we know as well as ourselves. The use of stories in the formal assessment of emotions is not new, as some readers may already know.

Historically, projective techniques often involved the idea that if individuals are asked to tell stories about story characters with whom they identify rather than autobiographical stories with direct questions about themselves, they are less likely to be defensive and distort their feelings. That is, they will project their own feelings onto the story characters (also see History Feature Box 9).

Some studies have made use of real stories told by adults, rather than stories told that are stimulated from pictures. For instance, Daniel McAdams and his colleagues have conducted research with college students and midlife adults in which they are encouraged to tell their own personal life stories (e.g., Bauer & McAdams, 2004; McAdams et al., 2001). Such oral and written narratives provide a rich database of information about the themes of identity (i.e., knowing who you are and what you believe in) and generativity (i.e., concern for the next generation). The researcher presents autobiographical questions in either an oral or written format. The researcher then analyses responses according to themes of *redemption* in which a bad sequence of life events turn good (e.g., being saved or redeeming yourself after experiencing the hardships of life), and themes of *contamination* in which positive life events and sequences turn bad (e.g., failing to survive life's hardships). McAdams and his colleagues have studied these responses for their emotional content and implications for personality. They have found clear evidence for redemption and contamination in the narratives of midlife adults (McAdams et al., 2001). However, they reported finding fewer contamination sequences in young adult undergraduate students. Measures of self-reported well-being and generativity correlated positively with redemption and negatively with contamination.

Another similar line of research has been conducted by Fiese and her colleagues from the Family Narrative Consortium (e.g., Fiese et al., 1999, 2001; Fiese & Wamboldt, 2003). They have developed a family narrative coding system to assess which experiences are meaningful to a family and how the family perceives their relationships and interactions. For instance, Fiese and Wamboldt (2003) have examined the narratives of the primary caretakers of school-age children with asthma. Researchers asked parents to tell the story of their children's asthma and how the family copes with it. Coding of interview data occurred along three dimensions. First, *narrative coherence* involves the degree to which the story is organized, concise and well-constructed. Second, *relationship beliefs* include whether the family member expects family interactions and relationships to be more rewarding, positive, trustworthy and safe, or in contrast, more disappointing, negative, hostile and unreliable. Third, the researcher assesses *interviewer intimacy*, which refers to interactions with the interviewer as either more guarded, private and withholding, or as more open, detailed and connected. Fiese and Wamboldt (2003) found that family members who reported better problem solving, communication and affective responsiveness on self-report measures were more likely to score high in narrative coherence and interviewer intimacy. In addition, the child's asthma had less effect on the family and their coping with the illness if relationship beliefs included expectations that were generally rewarding, positive, and involved feelings of trustworthiness. In the work of McAdams, Fiese and their colleagues, we see that having a relatively high ratio of positive or supportive emotional expressions as compared to unsupportive, negative ones during family interactions has a beneficial influence. This finding, which is one that we might expect based on everyday observations, is also reflected in the research studies of John Gottman and his colleagues that involve meta-emotion interviews and observed family interactions that are discussed in a later section of this chapter and Chapter 6. However, one limitation to the study of narratives, interviews and family interactions is that data coding is time intensive. Thus, many researchers have developed easy-to-administer and score self-report tests and ability measures to assess emotion, and it is to this topic that we turn next.

## Self-Report and Other-Report Questionnaire Measures of Emotional Skills

To be practical, psychological measurement tools need to be easy to take, administer, and learn to score. This, of course, is why self-report questionnaires continue to proliferate. This book addresses such self-report and other-report measures throughout and includes such emotion-relevant issues as the assessment of temperament, self-esteem, emotional expressiveness and emotion regulation. In addition to traditional paper-and-pencil versions, it is now possible to participate in research studies online over the internet. If you are curious enough about this and haven't already participated in an online study, you may want to consider visiting the website www.outofservice.com and try out a few of the tests there which are free and anonymous. Your responses are used as part of a research study, and you receive immediate feedback about what your responses mean. This website was created by a team of psychologists to gather data for their research on adult personality (e.g., Gosling et al., 2004; Srivastava et al., 2003). The American Psychological Association has guidelines for conducting online research (Kraut et al., 2003, 2004), and it is now possible for family members to be recruited for studies on emotion through a variety of online advertisements.

Although online studies are increasing in popularity, face-to-face interviews or video interviews, observations, and the paper-and-pencil versions of tests continue in use. There are many paper-and-pencil type tests to measure emotional intelligence or competence. Schutte and Malouff (1999) summarized many of the early tests and published a book on the psychometric properties of measures of emotional intelligence, understanding, expression, regulation, impulse control, and other emotional aspects of relationships and individual personality. Where they could get permission from the author of the test, they also reproduced the test in its entirety in their book, including their own test, the Emotional Intelligence Scale (EIS). The EIS is based on the theory of emotional intelligence originally proposed by Salovey and Mayer in 1990, and the authors and their colleagues, as well as other researchers, report evidence for the measure's reliability and validity (e.g., Austin et al., 2004; Schutte et al., 1998). The EIS is a self-report measure of adults' or adolescents' own awareness and understanding of emotions and how to regulate or control them (e.g., Chan, 2003; Ciarrochi, Chan & Bajgar, 2001). For each measure that Schutte and Malouff reproduced, they described the research leading to the measure's reliability and validity.

Several tests of emotional intelligence (EI) are currently available from test publishers. Many scholars distinguish *ability EI* from *trait EI*. Among the most well-known of the comprehensive ability EI measures is the Mayer-Salovey-Caruso Emotional Intelligence Test (MSCEIT). Evidence suggests that the MSCEIT is a reliable and valid means of assessing adults' *emotional problem-solving ability* (e.g., Brackett & Mayer, 2003; Brackett, Mayer & Warner, 2004; Mayer et al., 2003). The youth research version is for children and adolescents from 10 to 18 years of age (MSCEIT-YRV; Mayer, Salovey & Caruso, 2005; Rivers et al., 2012; Wols, Scholte & Qualter, 2015). Using specific structured tasks as part of the assessment process, emotional problem-solving ability includes adaptively using emotions to solve everyday problems or solving everyday problems that involve an emotional component. Because the MSCEIT involves problem-solving skills, some view it as primarily assessing *cognitive abilities* that are related to emotion (Barchard & Hakstian, 2004). In contrast, some assessment tests are related more to *personality traits* than to cognitive abilities; included among these are some *self-report tests of emotional intelligence* (Barchard & Hakstian, 2004). For example, the Trait Emotional Intelligence Questionnaire (TEIQue; Petrides & Furnham, 2003) has increasing evidence for its reliability and validity (e.g., Petrides, Fredrickson & Furnham, 2004; Petrides, Pita & Kokkinaki, 2007; Siegling et al., 2015). Some studies show that the TEIQue general score of trait emotional intelligence is positively related to various indices of mental health and negatively related to indices of psychopathology (e.g., Petrides et al., 2004; Petrides et al., 2006).

Another self-report measure for those 16 years of age and older with an emphasis on personality traits related to emotion is the BarOn Emotional Quotient-Inventory (BarOn EQ-i; Bar-On, 1997). The youth version (EQ-i:YV) is for children and adolescents between 7 and 18 years of age. It has positive and negative impression validity scales and assesses the following 15 areas of emotional life: emotional self-awareness; assertiveness; self-regard; self-actualization; independence; empathy; interpersonal relationships; social responsibility; problem solving; flexibility; reality testing; stress tolerance; impulse control; optimism; and happiness. The scales of the EQ-i correlate with some personality factors (e.g., see Schutte & Malouff, 1999). Thus, one current research issue in the study of emotional intelligence measures is the extent to which the constructs measured are distinct and the extent to which they overlap with other well-known and widely used measures of cognitive abilities and personality (e.g., Barchard & Hakstian, 2004). Another issue concerns the impact of the person's developmental level. Developmental considerations are especially important for assessing infants and children, but remain important over the course of the lifespan.

## Developmental Considerations in Measuring Emotional Skills and Abilities

Developmental tasks vary by age groups and the person's level of emotional maturity. For children and adolescents, who spend most of their time in school, the popularity of the emotional intelligence construct has led to emotion assessments by multiple informants including teachers and peers (e.g., Rivers et al., 2012). Likewise, in workplace settings for adults, emotion assessments include the perspectives of others (boss, peers, workplace subordinates, friends, family members and clients) (e.g. Boyatzis & Sala, 2004). In addition to using multiple informants to establish reliability in school and the workplace, the use of multiple informants and determining inter-informant agreement are important in measuring family emotion between spouses, siblings, and between parents and their children (e.g., Culbertson, 1999). While family members may agree about some aspects of emotional functioning in each other, they are also likely to differ depending on the emotional maturity of those being assessed.

As discussed in Chapter 10, emotional maturity in adults entails critical self-reflection and an awareness of emotions in self and others. However, it also includes active use of healthy coping strategies and self-control in everyday situations at home or work that are part of the adult's overall life plan and consistent with his or her moral standards or life philosophy (e.g., Labouvie-Vief et al., 1987; Labouvie-Vief et al., 1989; Lazarus, 1991; Malatesta & Izard, 1984). Inherent in measures of adult emotional intelligence (e.g., MSCEIT as described above) and competence in adults are specifications of which emotional skills and abilities best reflect emotional maturity and adaptive emotional functioning. Researchers continue to identify features of adult emotional competence in their studies measuring personality (e.g., John & Srivastava, 1999), subjective well-being and happiness (e.g., Fredrickson & Cohn, 2008; Lucas & Diener, 2008), emotion regulation (e.g., John & Eng, 2014) and emotional development (Magai, 2008).

However, because healthy well-adapted infants, children and adolescents have not yet achieved the same level of emotional maturity as well-adapted adults who can report on their self-reflections, assessments of youth emotional functioning must consider what is normal or expected by age, gender and background experiences. Consistent with developmental considerations, researchers have conducted most studies on emotion regulation involving longitudinal or observational studies with infants or preschool children, and most self-report studies of emotion regulation with individuals in middle childhood or adolescence (Adrian, Zeman & Veits, 2011).

In infants and young children, assessments often include the child's temperament, physiology, non-verbal behaviours or facial expressions, or family interactions. After Mary Ainsworth's studies on attachment theory (e.g., Ainsworth et al., 1973; Sroufe, 1996), many observational measures and coding systems were developed by other researchers to identify parental responsivity or sensitivity; in their literature review, Mesman and Emmen (2013) conclude that no new measures are needed to assess parental sensitivity. Instead, researchers need to focus on refining behavioural indicators used to operationalize the sensitivity construct.

Because of young children's limited thought and language skills, the assessment of emotions in infants and preschoolers often involves the use of measures of their physiology such as their heart rate, their brain wave activity and the hormones that they produce during emotion-provoking situations (see Fox & Calkins, 2000). Fox and Calkins (2000) review studies that they and others have conducted that examines the links between emotion, physiology and social behaviour in babies. Researchers have found that various measures of cardiovascular activity such as heart rate acceleration and deceleration, and breathing patterns in infants relate to their emotional reactivity. Some studies show that brain wave patterns measured by the electroencephalograph

(EEG) suggest temperamental differences in babies from birth, with some babies showing more activation in their right frontal lobes as compared to the left. This baseline pattern includes a lower threshold for expressions of negative emotion. Such babies are more likely to cry when they separate from their mothers for example. On the other hand, more left frontal lobe activation occurs during happy expressions in babies in contrast to sad ones. Fox and Calkins (2000) also discuss research on adrenocortical activity. The adrenal glands are located on top of the kidneys. The adrenal glands result in the production of the hormone cortisol, which can be measured through saliva samples. In reaction to distress, such as separations from caregivers, researchers have found that cortisol levels in young children go up. In adults, secure and insecure attachment patterns also have been linked to emotion regulation as assessed by physiological reactivity, cortisol level and brain imaging studies (Shaver & Mikulincer, 2014).

Throughout the lifespan, researchers have assessed emotions by analysing the movement of facial muscles into patterns or facial expressions. These expressions are found either universally across cultures (e.g., smiles and frowns) or uniquely within a given culture, as described in the discrete emotions approach of Izard (e.g., Izard, 1993; Izard & Abe, 2004; Izard & Ackerman, 2000) and Ekman (Ekman & Friesen, 1975; Keltner & Ekman, 2000) (see Chapter 7). In this evolutionary approach that follows upon the studies of Charles Darwin, specific discrete emotions such as anger, sadness, fear and happiness are thought to be biologically based and universal in human experience. However, once infants and children are exposed to their culture's rules about emotions, they learn to regulate their emotions and constrain their expressions to some extent depending on the social situation. Interestingly, Izard and Abe (2004) found developmental differences in the facial expressions of 13- and 18-month-old infants during some of the more stressful episodes of the Strange Situation attachment assessment. Full facial expressions involve both upper and lower parts of the face (e.g., a full smile includes crinkles around the eyes and the corners of the lips turned upwards). Component expressions involve only one component of the face – the upper or lower component, for example. The older infants in the study by Izard and Abe were more likely than the younger ones to display component expressions. The authors interpret this finding as suggesting that older infants were better able to regulate their expressions or alternatively, they were less reactive and aroused in the Strange Situation. The coding of facial expressions in this study and many others makes use of the Max-Affect Coding system in which researchers translate specific facial movements into one or more discrete emotion verbal labels such as angry, sad, fearful or happy.

## Family Interaction Assessments

Emotion often occurs in the context of interactions and communication with others and the family setting is rich with examples of emotional situations. Observing and measuring emotion in the family is a challenge, because the reactions and coping depend on which family members or outsiders are present at the time of the assessment (Kerig, 2001). A parent may have a different emotional reaction to a child's misbehaviour if the spouse or family friend or neighbour is present, for example, than if he or she would have if alone with the child.

Because of this complexity, researchers have taken a variety of approaches to the study of family interactions. They must decide which family members should be present during the assessment, what tasks they will ask the family members to complete, how long they will observe them, where they will complete the tasks (e.g., at home or in a laboratory setting), and how they will record and code the observations (Lindahl, 2001). Lindahl (2001) notes that it is best if the task is something family members might do in their normal day-to-day life because this increases the chances that the findings are valid and that the results will likely apply and generalize to other families. Researchers have used a vast array of family interaction tasks to study emotions and problem-solving behaviours in families. As examples, three approaches to the study of family interactions are presented below to illustrate how researchers have used family interaction tasks with toddlers, school-age children, and with adolescents.

As a first example, 2 year olds are learning how to have self-control and regulate their emotions. Initiating play with toddlers and ending it with clean-up of toys is one everyday typical interaction between parents and children. Using family systems and attachment theory as their framework, Paley, Cox and Kanoy (2001) have developed the Young Family Interaction Coding System (YFICS) in which they assess the emotional quality and parenting strategies of parents with their 24-month-old child. The researchers observe parents playing with their toddlers and then ask them to gain their toddlers' compliance in helping them to clean up and put the toys away after the playtime. The researchers rate the family as well as the child's emotional responses. For instance, some of the family ratings assess how child-centred the parents are and how "in-sync" they are with the child, how much positive emotion is shared such as warmth and affection, and how much negative emotion is displayed such as hostility, criticism and disagreement. The researchers rate the child's responses as well and include ratings of the child's enthusiasm, eagerness to play and confidence, the child's displays of anger, and how compliant the child is to parental requests and suggestions.

As a second example, researchers have studied *emotional reciprocity* in school-age children to find out how family members reciprocate positive and negative emotions. For example, Lindsey, MacKinnon-Lewis, Campbell, Frabutt and Lamb (2002) studied emotional reciprocity between mothers and their 7- to 9-year-old sons. In this approach, the researchers were interested in how often a mother's or son's facial display of positive emotion (smiling, giggling) or negative emotion (disgust, frowning) was likewise returned by the other person during an interaction, and how often it was not. Briefly, they found that marital conflict leads to negative interactions between mothers and sons, and that this then relates to negative interactions with peers, thus affecting the boys' friendships and social behaviours.

As a third and final example, we turn to the study of parent–adolescent conflict resolution, which is often one major spark that ignites intense family emotions. One method of assessing families with teenagers and training them to communicate better in family therapy is through a problem-solving interaction task developed by Robin and Foster (1989). First, parents and their adolescent identify and define an issue that is a problem for them by using non-accusatory "I" statements such as "I get worried when you come home late and don't call me" or "I get mad when you treat me like a child and insist that I repeatedly call you to tell you what I'm doing". After each person verifies that they understand the positions and feelings of others, the family members each take turns stating proposed solutions to the problem. They are encouraged to be creative and list as many ideas as they can without judging or evaluating them. After a sufficiently long list is generated, the family is asked to take turns evaluating each idea as a "plus" if it is feasible and will address the problem effectively or a "minus" if it will not. Surprisingly, a consensus occurs about 80 per cent of the time (Robin, 1998). If a family cannot reach a consensus, the therapist works with them on developing some negotiation skills and coming up with compromise alternatives that everyone might agree to. Finally, once the family agrees to a solution, they decide how to implement it and what the consequences will be for following through or not following through. They then report what happened in their next therapy session.

## Culturally Sensitive Assessment of Emotion in Families

Psychologists and other social scientists who study emotions in different cultures, such as anthropologists and sociologists, are often interested in whether their findings apply across many different cultural settings or whether they are unique and specific to the culture they are studying (Saarni, 1998). One qualitative method that is important for understanding the deeper meaning of emotional events is called the ***ethnographic approach***, in which the researcher spends time observing, interviewing, and recording data within a culture among the people; such fieldwork takes time to organize and interpret but provides a rich source of information (e.g., Marinosson, 1998; Sue, Kuraski & Srinivasan, 1999). Although their methods and interpretations differ, social scientists from different fields of study appear to agree that we need to understand cultural values and beliefs about emotions and how they affect the adaptation and adjustment of individuals and their families. We need to know, for example, which specific emotional events are focused upon in a specific culture (e.g., individual pride related to achievement; or, shame and dishonour to one's family), and which coping strategies are widely used within a given culture (e.g., Frijda & Mesquita, 1994). For instance, cultures vary in the extent to which they emphasize individualistic values (goals of autonomy and personal achievement) and collectivistic values (goals that involve group cohesion and belongingness) (e.g., Triandis, 1994). In addition to providing values and norms to guide emotion regulation, cultures provide routine social practices and socially sanctioned ways of interacting (Mesquita, Leersnyder & Albert, 2014). Researchers need to be cognizant that valued emotions in one culture (e.g., happiness in Western cultures) may be perceived as being less than optimal in a culture that values self-restraint and upholding one's social duties and obligations (Mesquita et al., 2014).

As discussed in Chapter 5, each of us has a cultural and ethnic background that comes to us from the broader culture and from our caregivers, and the result constitutes our unique ethnic identity that may include Native/Aboriginal, Hispanic, Asian, European, African, Middle Eastern or other diverse ethnic roots (e.g. Markus & Kitayama, 1991; McGoldrick, Giordano & Pearce, 1996). Our emotional lives are intimately bound up with who we are and our sense of self that is tied in with our ethnic backgrounds. To assess the impact of cultural background on emotion in individuals and within families, many social scientists have relied on anthropological comparisons using an ethnographic approach. In this approach, they interview members of various cultures and attempt to interpret the meaning and functions of emotion within and across cultures (e.g., White, 1993). Saarni (1998) notes that psychologists have come up with ways to compare aspects of emotions that they feel may be universal (e.g., a smile denotes positive feelings) and aspects of emotions that may have unique cultural interpretations (e.g., the exact meaning of a smile may depend on the cultural context). She highlights the need to explore the variability of human emotions within and across cultures to look for patterns and to develop theories of culture and emotion. There remains a great need for more research on the culturally sensitive assessment of emotion in families both within and across cultures.

## Summary of Chapter Key Points

Interesting contemporary trends have emerged in the study of emotion within families. As shown in Table 2.1, psychologists now have a variety of measurement tools available to assess and research emotion in families. Informal and naturalistic observations of families help to provide initial impressions of the emotional climate within a family, and may lead to the identification of important variables for further study and clarification. Oral, written and visual narratives or stories provided by family members about emotions within their family are perhaps the most engaging and comprehensive of the methods of assessment since they have the opportunity for the most creativity and afford a richness of detail that often cannot be matched by other methods. Closely related, the information provided by interviews can also be rich in detail, but much depends here on how structured the interview is, and how comfortable the family member is with the person conducting the interview. Self- and other-report questionnaires give us concise, objective information, but are similarly limited in the information that they can provide and must meet professional standards of reliability and validity to be worthwhile. For instance, to be valid, such measures need to be appropriate for the ethnic groups and age groups to which they are applied and proper norms of comparison need to be established. Physiological measures of emotion and facial expression research studies have yielded interesting results thus far, and hold promise as methods that researchers can use across different cultural settings and with different age groups. Research on emotional problem-solving tasks in individuals and conversation during family interactions have the potential to help us to better understand family emotions in the everyday, real world. In addition, the processing of emotions in psychotherapy sessions offers promise as a method of showing how meaningful changes can occur in our emotional lives through our interactions with others. Finally, researchers have used ethnographic approaches to compare emotions in families around the world, and are continuing to develop methods to compare and contrast emotion in families across cultures.

## Further Reading

Cassidy, J. & Shaver, P. R. (Eds.) (2008). *Handbook of attachment: Theory, research, and clinical applications* (2nd ed.). New York: Guilford.

Leading attachment researchers have contributed chapters to this comprehensive and informative volume on the theoretical foundations of research into relationships across the lifespan. Measurement issues specific to each phase of the lifespan and across various methods are covered (e.g., observational, interview, questionnaires, story completion). Psychotherapy and family-based interventions and applications are also addressed. This volume is an excellent resource for understanding how emotion-relevant theory, research and application can be successfully integrated to promote progress in emotion science.

Kerig, P. K. & Lindahl, K. M. (Eds.) (2001). *Family observational coding systems: Resources for systemic research.* Mahwah, NJ: Erlbaum.

This edited book provides a sampling of family research methods and issues involved in coding observational family data. The emotions observed and how each family member regulates emotion is likely related to who is present during the interaction (dyad, triad, whole family) and whether there is conflict in one or more subsystems. Constructs and their measurement, levels of analysis in coding, ecological validity, generalizability of findings and ethnic diversity are among the many topics covered.

## Relevant Film

Davidson Films Inc., Films for the Humanities & Sciences & Films Media Group. (2007). *John Bowlby: Attachment theory across generations* (Giants of Psychology). New York: Films Media Group.

This engaging and highly informative 40-minute film is available through Films on Demand in university libraries. The film begins with an overview of John Bowlby's personal history and life, the development of his theory, and his early observations. Mary Ainsworth's Strange Situation paradigm is demonstrated with a boy who is assessed again in childhood and later in adulthood. The importance of attachment across the lifespan and across generations is emphasized. The film ends by demonstrating how attachment theory can be applied to psychotherapy and clinical interventions.

# 3

# The Developmental Neurobiology of Emotion and Consciousness

*Heather, a 19-year-old university student, acquired a traumatic brain injury after an automobile accident left her with impaired vision and brain damage to the frontal lobe region. Multiple surgeries and corrective lenses helped to improve her vision so that she could resume many of her former activities, including her studies in the field of communications. After the accident, her parents and brother noticed that Heather's personality changed; she was more subdued and less flexible than she was before the accident. Fortunately, Heather's university health centre offered an acceptance-based form of psychotherapy. Heather's family and school counsellor encouraged her participation in the psychotherapy programme, and Heather agreed. The psychotherapy proved to be beneficial in helping Heather regain self-awareness, acceptance of the changes in her functioning, and commitment to her values and career goals. Heather started actively monitoring her memory by making and checking lists as needed at school and at home. Her family noticed that she appeared to be more animated and emotionally motivated to try and cope better with the challenges she faced.*

## Developmental Neurobiology and the Orthogenetic Principle

Successful rehabilitation after a traumatic brain injury (TBI), such as that experienced by Heather, involves acceptance of limitations, an awareness of one's own values, and committed proactive attempts to compensate for emotional difficulties and memory problems that could affect the survivor's relationships with family, friends and co-workers (Schutz, 2007; Whiting et al., 2017). Heather sustained damage to the frontal lobe region of her brain, which is the region just above the eyes (LeDoux, 1996). The frontal lobe is highly interconnected with other regions of the brain including those that influence emotions, and is known to play an important role in working memory and conscious attention (Siegel, 1999). Like Heather, individuals who sustain brain damage may have some personality changes; their family members may experience *ambiguous loss*, defined by Pauline Boss as the feeling that your loved one is physically present but psychologically absent (as might occur with mental impairment), or physically absent but psychologically still present (as when someone in the military is missing in action) (Boss, 2016; Kreutzer, Mills & Marwitz, 2016). Individuals with TBI and their family members may feel that the injured person has lost an identity, and may grieve the fact that the lost identity may never be fully recovered (Kreutzer et al., 2016). Thus, family members need to be aware of how their relative's brain injury may affect their own emotions. Also, they need to be aware of the emotional and financial supports that are needed to promote the adaptation of their injured loved one (Schutz, 2007). As a treatment option, *acceptance and commitment therapy (ACT)* encourages the acceptance of the new reality along with a commitment to cherished values and goals, some of which may be from the former identity and some of which may be part of the newly forming identity (Whiting et al., 2017).

Recently, there has been much media attention given to sports-related brain concussions or functional brain impairments in athletes (Talavage et al., 2014); additional reasons for injuries include motor vehicle and bicycle accidents, accidental injuries at home or work, physical abuse and assaults (Schutz, 2007). In each case, in addition to emotionally reacting to the traumatic event itself, some aspect of the person's consciousness, personality, sense of self or ability to manage thoughts and emotions during interactions with others is often affected. Although it is unfortunate that non-normative traumatic brain injuries such as the one sustained by Heather ever occur, there is hope for recovery because the human brain is more adaptable than previously recognized, and successful therapeutic rehabilitation is sometimes possible with the attempt to get the person back onto a more typical developmental path (Schutz, 2007).

Research in the field of developmental neurobiology addresses the potential changes in structure, function and processes that may occur *normatively* in the human brain from infancy and childhood, through adolescence, and into the adulthood and ageing years. Issues related to how the materialistic brain is related to psychological processes and consciousness have been of great interest historically to scholars as discussed further in History Feature Box 3.

Throughout this chapter, understanding normative developmental changes provides a foundation for interpreting deviations in emotional development in families precipitated by non-normative and/or traumatic life events that affect brain development.

**History Feature Box 3**

**Back Then and Now: Mind–Body Dualisms and Dualistic Thinking**

Dualistic thinking has been present since the earliest philosophical writings and attempts to understand human functioning (e.g., Shobris, 1994). Many philosophers have focused on the importance of the mind and reason in controlling bodily passions and emotions since the writings of the ancient Greek philosopher Aristotle (384–322 BC) who emphasized the superiority of mind, reason, rationality, masters, men and humans over the body, passion, emotions, slaves, women and animals (e.g., Seldes, 1985; Solomon, 1993). Many dualisms have been identified and studied in psychology (see Table 3.1); the dualism between mind and matter (including the body) is among the foremost, as articulated by the French philosopher and father of modern philosophy, Rene Descartes (1596–1650) (Rockwood, 2007). Mind–body *dualism* is the belief that the mind is separate from the functioning of the body. Descartes upheld a dualistic position but also maintained a mind–body *interactionism* in which mind and body interacted at the base of the brain in the pineal gland (a structure that is now thought to be responsible for producing sleep-enhancing melatonin) (Goodwin, 2010; Shobris, 1994). Mind–body dualism can be contrasted with *monism*, the belief that mind and body are merely dual aspects of the same being or existence (Solomon, 1993). Baruch (Benedict) Spinoza (1632–1677), the Dutch philosopher and theologian, was a proponent of monism and rejected Descartes' dualism in favour of viewing mind and matter/body as two attributes linked with a pantheistic God and the ultimate substance of the world that is absolute and infinite (Rockwood, 2007). As summarized by Solomon (1993), Spinoza's view showed that he was ahead of his time; he anticipated the ideas behind much contemporary research on emotions, cognitions and the functioning of the brain from a monistic viewpoint. The role of learning, nurturing (including that from parents and teachers) and experience in the functioning of the human mind was brought to the foreground by the English empiricist and philosopher John Locke (1632–1704). Locke maintained that our thoughts and ideas were not inborn, but only come to us through our experiences and reflections on what we perceive (e.g., Benjafield, 2010; Munger, 2003; Shobris, 1994). In contrast to many other philosophers, the Scottish philosopher David Hume (1711–1776) relegated an important role to emotions and passions in human functioning: "What motivates us to right and (wrong) behavior, Hume insisted, are our passions, and rather than being relegated to the margins of ethics and philosophy, the passions deserve central respect and consideration." (Solomon, 1993, p. 7) Throughout the 18th, 19th and 20th centuries, philosophers and early psychologists sought to understand emotions in relation to both the body and the mind.

The American psychologist William James (1842–1910) wrote extensively about the mental, feeling aspects of emotions and the human stream of thought or consciousness, as well as the bodily manifestations of emotions (James, 1890/2013). James proposed that we experience bodily reactions (e.g., pounding heart) and show physiological reactions and expressions to emotional events before we become aware of having an emotional experience (Goodwin, 2010). For James, having bodily sensations or reactions was essential to having an emotional experience (Benjafield, 2012). Because this theory was proposed at about the same time in history by the Dutch physiologist Carl Lange, it is known as the *James–Lange* theory (Goodwin, 2010). Walter B. Cannon (1871–1945) challenged and critiqued James's theory by demonstrating that internal visceral changes in the body were not necessary for an emotion to occur; this criticism, however, did not address the fact that James's theory incorporated many other bodily reactions, including muscular ones, and were not restricted to the viscera (Benjafield, 2010).

The theoretical views of William James on emotion were consistent with those of later cognitive appraisal theorists. Magda Arnold (1960) was the first to emphasize the role of cognition and cognitive appraisal in emotional actions (Cornelius, 2006). The mind–body dualism took on a contemporary spin with some psychologists, such as Richard Lazarus (1991) continuing to emphasize the necessity of considering cognition in emotional processing, while others, such as Robert Zajonc (1984), emphasized the view that emotions are primary and functionally independent from cognitive processing. Other cognitive appraisal researchers have tried to reconcile how the mind and cognitive processing operates together with physiology. Examples here are the classic studies by Stanley Schachter and Jerome Singer (1962), in which they contend that physiological arousal is unfocused and requires hints from the social environment about the possible emotions that are experienced by the individual (Lazarus, 1991). Antonio Damasio (2010) has attempted to move beyond the mind–body problem and to reconcile consciousness with physiology; Damasio claims that the human body maps onto the human brain and thus the body is represented in the mind of the individual, which assists in moment-to-moment *consciously minded regulation*.

A developmental approach to dualistic thinking comes from the seminal work on forms of intellectual and ethical development during the college years as studied by William G. Perry (1970). Perry (1970) found that as students enter university, many tend to construe the world in terms of *absolute dualisms* (unqualified rights and wrong), but they are soon confronted with many opposing viewpoints that lead them to a *generalized relativism*, and an eventual *commitment within relativism* outlook. Based on Perry's work, this progression from dualistic thinking to thinking more relativistically and eventually committing to a point of view after considering and integrating multiple perspectives is a marker of adult emotional maturity in models of adult development and ageing (Labouvie-Vief & Hakim-Larson, 1989).

In normative development, the young child first must be able to engage in conscious self-reflection to have emotional experiences with others, an ability that Lewis (2014) describes as being the result of brain maturation. As discussed further in this chapter and throughout this book, among the regions of the brain thought to be central to the functional networks and systems involved in the development of consciousness and the processing of emotions are the *prefrontal cortex*, the *amygdala*, and the *hippocampus* (e.g., LeDoux & Phelps, 2008). The cerebral cortex of the brain consists of a wrinkled outer layer and includes regions for specific sensory and motor functions (LeDoux, 2002). The prefrontal cortex is the portion of this outer layer that is in the very front of the frontal lobes on both sides of the brain and does not include

**Table 3.1** Dualisms in the History of Psychology and Philosophy

| | |
|---|---|
| Mind | Body |
| Free will | Determinism |
| Reason | Passion |
| Logic/cognition | Emotion |
| Left brain | Right brain |
| Master | Slave |
| Human | Animal |
| Learned | Inborn/innate |
| Empiricism | Nativism |
| Nurture | Nature |

specific sensory or motor functions; rather, it serves a higher order integrative function as do other similar association regions of the cortex (Damasio, 2010). Together, the amygdala, hippocampus and *hypothalamus* are sometimes called the limbic system; the limbic system is a brain region often noted as being important in the study of emotions given that the hypothalamus regulates sex hormones (oestrogen, progesterone, and androgens such as testosterone) (Arain et al., 2013). Because cognitive self-control (i.e., using thoughts and self-talk) is important in managing emotions, especially in emotionally charged situations, another subcortical (below the outer layer of the cortex) region called the *striatum* has been studied (Somerville & Casey, 2010). These various brain regions are subject to many changes in structure and processing over time. As shown in Figure 3.1, the ***functional neurocircuitry*** of the brain

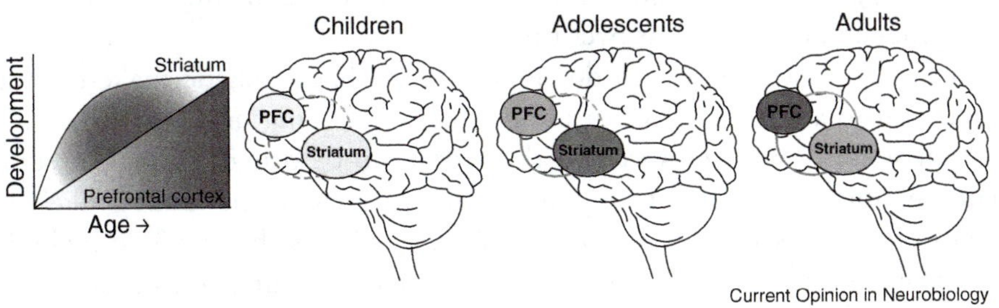


Cartoon model of striatal and prefrontal interactions across development. Deeper color indicates greater regional signaling. Line represents functional connectivity, with solid line indicating mature connection and dotted line indicating immaturity.

**Figure 3.1** Functional Neurocircuitry in Children, Adolescents and Adults (Somerville & Casey, 2010)

Source: Reprinted from *Current Opinion in Neurobiology, Vol. 20/No. 2*, Leah H. Somerville and B. J. Casey, *Developmental neurobiology of cognitive control and motivational systems*, pp. 236–241, Copyright © (2010), with permission from Elsevier.

is different in children, adolescents, and adults; children have weak connections (dashed lines), and even though these start to strengthen during adolescence, connections between brain regions that are important for processing emotions are still weaker in adolescents than they are in adults. Thus, the emotional ups and downs and risky behaviours often observed in adolescents may at least partially be due to the immaturity of connections between areas of their brains (Somerville & Casey, 2010).

Like other systems that grow, change and develop, the neurobiological system develops in accordance with the ***orthogenetic principle***; that is, the form and structure of the brain becomes increasingly differentiated, organized and hierarchically arranged and integrated with maturation (Brent, 1984; Valsiner, 2005; Werner, 1957). As embryonic brain cells (i.e., neurons) multiply, they emerge as primitive, undifferentiated cell types (Stiles & Jernigan, 2010). However, the cells eventually transform and serve more specific and varied purposes over time depending on the cell type, as well as on nutritive (or toxic) and interactive environmental stimulation. Although there is a genetic blueprint or map for how this early neural development is to take place, there is also plenty of room for modification in adaptive or maladaptive directions. These modifications depend on the soft boundaries or limits set by the underlying *genotype* (i.e., genetic make-up of the individual), and how the cells are prompted to function based on the quality of the mother's nutrition prenatally or that of the developing individual postnatally. This modifiability or malleability of the brain is known as neural or ***brain plasticity*** and it is thought to be responsible for the flexible adaptive or maladaptive changes that occur in human development over time extending throughout the entire lifespan (Lerner, 1984). The resulting *phenotype* (i.e., overt expression of the underlying genetic make-up) is thus the result of the dynamic interaction of both genes and environment over time.

For example, assume that a developing foetus has a genetic make-up that would lead to a normal range of intellectual functioning under healthy environmental conditions. However, if the mother-to-be drinks alcohol in sufficient amounts at certain critical points in her pregnancy, the result is likely to be a disorder known as *foetal alcohol syndrome*, which is characterized by brain abnormalities and anomalies in overt physical facial features (Grossman et al., 2003). The plasticity of the brain of the developing foetus means that a variety of developmental outcomes are thus possible depending on the environment provided within the mother's body at specific points in time. Similar plasticity of changes in the brain occur throughout the human lifespan. Thus, the brain of the pregnant mother who abuses alcohol is also subject to impairment depending on how long the abuse takes place and whether she abuses other drugs.

The term *plasticity* in the field of psychology dates to the 19th century and William James (1890/2013), who used the term to refer to both the behavioural and neural openness to change after an organism interacts with outside influences. Although there are other important neuroglial cell types in the human brain, which serve crucial supportive and ancillary roles, the *neuron* is typically the focus of research on brain plasticity. The neuron is a brain cell that is composed of a cell body, dendrites, which accept neurotransmitter chemical input, and axons that transmit neurochemical output after an electrochemical discharge. *Myelination* of axons increases throughout child, adolescent and emerging adult development up to about the age of 25 years; this process involves the addition of insulating myelin sheath fibres around the axons, which speed up the efficient transmission of neural impulses (Arain et al., 2013). *Synapses* are the small gaps between the neurons in which this electrochemical communication between neurons takes place after an electrical impulse is triggered in a neuron by internal or external stimulation (LeDoux, 2002). A complex interconnected active circuitry of the human brain is the result, which is characterized by an open system of ongoing *synaptic remodelling* or reorganization (e.g., Stiles & Jernigan, 2010; Tau & Peterson, 2010).

Prenatally and in early child development, there is an initial overproduction of neurons and an overly dense network of connectivity. As child development proceeds, there is selective cell death based on experiences, the 'pruning' of synaptic connections, structural changes in neurons, all of which accompany increased myelination of the surviving active neurons, thus making neural transmission more efficient. In addition, cell death and new synaptic connections are possible throughout life in response to brain insults/traumas and injuries (e.g., hitting your head after falling off your bike) or other adaptive or maladaptive experiences including physical abuse (Grossman et al., 2003). For example, Foley et al. (2013) describe evidence showing that many young infants worldwide are victims of what is sometimes called "shaken baby syndrome" in which caregivers or others have difficulty tolerating the infant's crying and, consequently, shake the baby vigorously (often out of anger) to get the baby to stop crying. The result is often severe brain injury or death (e.g., Foley et al., 2013). In the US, abusive head trauma (AHT) is a leading cause of severe injury in maltreated children (Niederkrotenthaler et al., 2013). Studies have shown that AHT during infancy is more severe and lethal than accidental head injuries. Follow-up studies of such children into school age show that they are more likely than normally developing children and those with accidental head injuries to have long-term physical, emotional and behavioural difficulties (e.g., Lind et al., 2016). Fortunately, many countries are implementing educational prevention programmes to reduce the incidence of AHT (e.g., Foley et al., 2013).

Two major types of neural plasticity are *experience-expectant plasticity* and *experience-dependent plasticity* (Grossman et al., 2003). Experience-expectant plasticity involves the notion that there is a genetically pre-preprogrammed expectation within *already existing neural cells* that certain environmental experiences will be forthcoming, even if the exact qualitative nature or content of the input is unknown. Examples here would include input such as the primary language spoken by a child's mother, or the types of visual input a child is exposed to (dimly lit indoor or bright outdoor lighting) which vary considerably from person to person. As humans, we expect genetically that members of our species will get exposure to some form of language and some form of lighting, but that form depends on the environmental context and personal experiences. With plasticity, the language or visual skills of the child are fine-tuned by selective pruning of some neural connections and the strengthening of others. Experience-dependent plasticity, in contrast, includes novel and unexpected experiences that result in the actual production of new cells and new dense connections based on unusual or non-normative life experiences, which can be either adaptive or maladaptive. For instance, some family members are exposed right from birth to an enriched array of unusual emotional experiences involving physical activity, the arts, literature or music. Likewise, an unpleasant, unexpected array of abusive or neglectful maladaptive emotional experiences can result in changes in the brain due to plasticity (e.g., maltreatment, foetal alcohol syndrome). Families are, of course, critical in providing the social context in which changes in the brain due to plasticity takes place.

While the plasticity of the human brain allows for variability and changes in functioning over time, there also are limits or constraints placed on the possible changes that can occur due to genetics and existing environmental opportunities (Lerner, 2002). Two controversial concepts of historical importance to the study of the developmental neurobiology of emotional development are relevant here: reaction range and canalization.

***Reaction range*** can be defined as the genotype of a person setting an upper and lower limit on the range of possible phenotypes, with some people having a broader range of possible reactions to different environments and others a narrower one (Griffiths & Tabery, 2008). In the literature, historically, the controversial concept of reaction range has sometimes been used synonymously with the terms *norm of reaction* or *reaction norm*; at other times, the terms have been differentiated and distinguished from each other with no clear consensus on their use (for more information on this topic, see Griffiths & Tabery, 2008). Griffiths and Tabery attribute the concept of reaction range to the Russian-American geneticist Theodosius Dobzhansky in the 1950s, when it was used synonymously with the terms "norm of reaction" and "reaction norm"; these terms were later differentiated by Irving Gottesman, who popularized the term "reaction range" in psychology in the 1960s and later. However, for contemporary psychologists such as Gilbert Gottlieb, the concept of reaction range is too simple, deterministic, and not useful as a guide for research. For Gottlieb, the concept of reaction range should be abandoned, because it does not address gene modifiability, nor does it account for how genes at molecular and cellular levels interact with each other and with other higher-level systems of the body and the environment (Gottlieb & Lickliter, 2007). In the past, genes were thought of as the fixed starting point for development to occur within different environments, but genes are not fixed and are very much open to change with various environmental inputs. Importantly, Gottlieb goes beyond the nature-nurture controversy and proposes instead a *relational causality* to development, where it is the relation between and within developmental components at various levels of analysis (genetic, neural, behavioural, environmental) that propel development (Gottlieb & Lickliter, 2007; Lerner, 2002). For Gottlieb, both genes (i.e., nature) and the environment (i.e., nurture) are modifiable and equally unpredictable. Thus, the bidirectional coaction of genes with information at the genetic level and at the other three levels of analysis leads to probabilistic (not deterministic) outcomes.

Gottlieb's (Gottlieb & Lickliter, 2007) theory of ***probabilistic epigenesis*** can be understood as a developmental systems approach to the emergence of *qualitatively new* forms within an individual over time. Probabilistic epigenesis, as defined by Gottlieb, involves a new higher level of complexity or a new non-linear change that takes place over time and development that cannot be completely predicted by any known earlier precursors; thus, such changes are probabilistic and uncertain rather than deterministic and certain in nature (Lerner, 2002).

Another idea challenged by Gottlieb (Gottlieb & Lickliter, 2007) in his theory of probabilistic epigenesis is the notion of canalization. ***Canalization,*** as originally introduced by Waddington (1957), refers to the idea that there is a bumpy rolling epigenetic landscape along which development proceeds within canals based on a person's genetic make-up. Initially, there are many possible pathways of phenotypic expression, but once development proceeds along a given trajectory, there may be perturbations or environmental assaults that may temporarily derail or hinder the developmental course (Brent, 1984); however, there is also a tendency due to the genetically based *canalization* for development to return to its original developmental course. Brent (1984) cites examples of such canalization in poorly nourished children with stunted growth at one point early in their lives; later on once these children were adequately fed, they were able to get back on their normal developmental growth track and many were thus able to reach their growth potential based on their underlying genetics. For Gottlieb (1991), however, the concept of canalization as originally proposed by Waddington is flawed because it conveys the notion that genes act as strong buffers against environmental experiences; thus, in this early view, genetics are given a strong, deterministic causal role in development. Gottlieb (1991), in contrast, prefers to emphasize the important role of what he has called *experiential canalization*. Thus, according to Gottlieb, the environment and experiences can actually trigger specific genetic activity within a biological system and these actions may result in either *plasticity* of the neural system, in which case there are new connections or reorganizations, or *experiential canalization*, in which case responsivity narrows and changes are constrained (Lerner, 2002). Thus, it may be more fruitful given Gottlieb's analysis to think of the psychobiology of emotional development as a complex pattern of genes being turned on and/or off with the opposing functions of plasticity and experiential canalization at play (Lerner, 2002). Experiential and environmental factors include micro-levels of analysis at the molecular and cellular levels, topics which are beyond the scope of this chapter but are addressed again briefly in Chapter 12.

In addition, macro-levels of analysis are involved, such as those involving face-to-face social interactions, a topic to which we now turn. As primary environmental and experiential factors, social interactions have reciprocal influences on the emotional brains of those communicating with each other. One way that this may occur is through *body maps,* which is the mapping of bodily experiences of self and others within our brains (Damasio, 2010).

## Mirror Neurons and Consciousness

Our changing brains must continuously and repeatedly create body maps in anticipation of experiencing an emotion to physiologically prepare us to act. At any given time, we need to have some mental representation of our bodies in space and to have some awareness of our senses and body positioning so that we will have options for acting. Damasio (2010) proposes that humans can *simulate* body states through this body mapping and new body maps may emerge *as if* the experience of an emotion and a bodily reaction had already taken place. Damasio has suggested that being able to map the body within the brain is crucial to the development of a sense of self. He further claims that ***mirror neurons*** are the ultimate "as if body device" (Damasio, 2010, p. 110). Mirror neurons are neurons that fire and activate in one of two primary ways: either directly through personal experience that does not involve mimicking another person, or indirectly by visually observing and imitating the actions of another person (Rizzolatti & Craighero, 2004). What this means is that when an adult makes an emotional facial expression (e.g., sticking his or her tongue out in disgust), an infant observing that adult will motorically represent this action in his or her own brain and thus may mimic or imitate the expression (Walker-Andrews, 2008; Wicker et al., 2003). As theorized by Damasio (2010), observing another person's emotional actions are amplified and represented within mirror neurons. Even if individuals have not directly experienced an emotional event, they feel "as if" they did and they are then prepared to act as if they did. Thus, a person may encode an event represented in mirror neurons but suppress the corresponding action depending on his or her ability to self-regulate voluntarily.

Interestingly, Hoffman (2008), who has studied empathy, suggests that such underlying neural mapping and mirror neurons may also be involved in the development and formation of empathic responses to other people. Thus, when infants, children, adolescents, parents and other family members observe each other's emotional states and bodily reactions, features of the event may be represented at a neural level and modelled either immediately or after a delay under the right circumstances. The well-known neuroscientist V. S. Ramachandran has described the discovery of mirror neurons in psychology as being like the discovery of DNA in biology. To some scientists, this discovery is *that* important because it potentially explains (at least theoretically) how and why humans can learn so quickly from each other within families and within and across cultures during relatively short time periods. The discovery of mirror neurons by Giacomo Rizzolatti and his colleagues has already started to generate much research (see Kilner & Lemon, 2013), as well as much controversy, leading to mirror neurons being called "the most hyped concept in neuroscience" (Jarrett, 2012, 2013). Nonetheless, as of December 2013, there were already over 800 published scholarly topics on mirror neurons, with the clearest and most conclusive findings coming from non-human primates (Kilner & Lemon, 2013). Kilner and Lemon review evidence showing that mirror neurons in the motor system of the brain are modulated (either excited or suppressed) both by executing and observing actions, while other neurons have a more limited range of functioning.

Interestingly, the study of mirror neuron systems has had a significant impact on the study of social cognition, the sense of self and consciousness at the neural level. This has led researchers such as V. S. Ramachandran and his colleagues to suggest that difficulties in the mirror neuron system may underlie some of the emotional and behavioural deficits observed in the autism spectrum disorders (e.g., Oberman & Ramachandran, 2008). Indeed, Lewis (2014) describes studies of children with autism. He highlights that various indicators of self-representation and conscious intentional behaviours and experiences involving self and others seem to be either delayed or absent altogether in children with autism.

## Qualia, Intentionality and Decisions

While mirror neurons may help family members to connect emotionally with each other, everyone has unique conscious experiences that may not be easily shared with others. A concept relevant to the unique personal experiences of individuals and to the study of emotions in developmental neurobiology is the idea of ***qualia***. Qualia are "the 'raw feels' of conscious experience: the painfulness of pain, the redness of red. Qualia give human conscious experience the particular character that it has" (Ramachandran & Hirstein, 1997, p. 430). There are three primary "laws" of qualia as proposed by Ramachandran and Hirstein (1997). First, qualia are irrevocable perceptions and *input*; they cannot be revoked or second-guessed, because we fill in any missing bits and pieces of perceptual information to make a complete percept. We are then sure of what we perceive. In addition, we deem what we perceive as not being just a belief, and we do this to confer certainty to our moment-by-moment decisions and actions. Second, qualia allow flexibility of choice in *output* and decisions once we experience the irrevocable perception. Third, to decide what to do given the many options, we must hold the experience in consciousness long enough to allow processing in working or short-term memory. Qualia are thought to have evolved to enable deliberate, voluntary, intentional decisions and planning to act (Ramachandran & Hirstein, 1997). For Ramachandran and his colleagues, problems involving consciousness and the concept of qualia and problems involving the concept of the self in relation to others are just different facets of the same idea.

Developmentally, the emergence of consciousness and the ability to make intentional decisions is linked to self-awareness and self-referential behaviour as studied by Michael Lewis and his colleagues. Consider the emerging free will and budding consciousness of a toddler who has a newly developed self-awareness of his or her own needs, wants and desires; the child perceives an attractive toy while shopping with parents, and clearly communicates verbally: "I want … mine." Lewis (2014) contends that we first see such self-referential behaviour in typically developing children between the ages of 15 and 30 months of age as evidenced in their self-recognition in a mirror, use of pronouns such as "I" and "me", and pretend play where both self and other are represented symbolically. As mentioned earlier, such behaviours are delayed, absent, or atypical in children with autism. Importantly, researchers comparing the brain functions of typically developing children to that of children with autism have found that brain maturation in the left temporal lobe, which is a brain region beneath and behind the left ear (Cornelius, 1996), is linked to the emergence of such self-representational behaviours. Lewis (2014) concludes that the social problems and interpersonal behaviours associated with autism are a function of the timing and maturation of specific brain regions related to self-representation and consciousness.

The developing human brain and the resulting changes in behaviours enable thinking ahead, planning, the conscious mental representation of self and others, and the intention to act and make decisions within family relationships. This process is part of a very complex flexible and dynamic system. While there are many models and approaches to understanding how neurobiology relates to conscious self-awareness and interpersonal behaviours, the approach that has recently gained favour among those interested in developmental neurobiology is the dynamic systems approach, to which we now turn.

## Self-Organizing Tendencies and the Dynamic Systems Approach to Emotions

The ***dynamic systems*** approach to cognition, emotion and action in psychology was derived from concepts in the fields of mathematics and physics (Thelen & Smith, 1994). The dynamic systems perspective can be thought of as an overarching meta-framework for the various models and theories that will be discussed in this book; although dynamic systems concepts are somewhat abstract, they seem to be readily applicable to general developmental phenomena as well as to emotional development (Camras, 2011).

In psychology, the structures of human functioning are viewed as biological, *open systems* that are capable of exchanging both energy (e.g., heat, movement) and physical mass (e.g., nutrients, waste) with their environments (Brent, 1984). These systems have what are called ***self-organizing tendencies***, which means that even though there are many possible states and configurations for the system, they self-organize and are *attracted* to stabilizing in one preferred mode given the current conditions and context (Thelen & Smith, 1994); the resulting state is called an *attractor state.*

Among the first to popularize such dynamic system concepts in developmental science were Thelen and Smith (1994) who described infant crawling and walking as examples of attractor states. Why does infant mobility usually exist in the sequence of crawling, walking, and then running? Why are not some other activities in some other sequence typical of human infants? For instance, why would it be an unusual pattern for newly mobile infants to first use rolling around on the ground to get somewhere, then use hopping or jumping to get from one place to another? In a dynamic systems approach, the answer to this question involves the various possible coordinated motor movements in visual space given human evolution and the anatomy, physiology and physical environment of the maturing infant who is attempting locomotion. There are various components or subsystems of the infant (visual, motor, neural, cognitive, emotional) that *synergistically* and somewhat spontaneously and randomly become coordinated and self-organized into a structured pattern that functions well (such as crawling); there are many false starts and errors and no two infants seem to learn to crawl in an identical manner. In other words, there is much room for individual differences.

Thelen and Smith (1994) and Camras (2011) have further described additional concepts important in a dynamic systems approach. With respect to infant mobility, infants first stabilize into a self-organized pattern of crawling (an attractor state) with several important parameters involved, such as body fat, muscle development and head control. The fat-to-muscle ratio changes as the baby matures and is a *control parameter.* A control parameter is a parameter that reaches a critical threshold in a quantitative measurable way, followed by a qualitative and non-linear change that occurs somewhat rapidly. The system first becomes unstable and then reorganizes into another new attractor state, a process called a *developmental phase shift.* In this case, crawling behaviours destabilize, the infant stands and steps, and the infant begins to walk, which is another higher-level attractor state! Interestingly, there are also *precursors* to infant walking, such as leg cycling while lying down, or stepping behaviours if infants are held upright with pressure on their feet (Camras, 2011; Thelen & Smith, 1994). Developmental scientists have also noted that behaviours that eventually become important in attractor states are ***heterochronic***, meaning that components do not necessarily develop all at once, but rather can occur early on involuntarily; thus, not all components of what will eventually be an attractor state develop or mature together as a unified whole (e.g., Camras, 2011; Fogel & Thelen, 1987; Thelen & Smith, 1994).

In the case of emotional development, components such as physiology, social context and cognitions stabilize into one form or pattern of an emotion. For instance, anger (an attractor state) in a young infant may be manifest in a facial expression and overt crying; in an older toddler, the anger may be evident in a full-fledged temper tantrum, while in an older preschool child the anger may entail some aggression (Camras, 2011). In each case, the anger is an attractor state with some of the components sharing a similarity and some of the components being unique and specific to both the person's level of maturity and the context. With each new level of the development of anger expression, a developmental phase shift would have occurred leading to a new attractor state. Camras (2011) has named her dynamic systems approach to emotional development the ***differentiation and dynamical integration (DDI)*** perspective. Camras (2011) integrates several major theoretical approaches into her views on the development of facial expressions using a dynamic systems approach (also see Chapter 7). Briefly, Camras highlights how facial expressions begin as relatively undifferentiated states of positive and negative emotional valence and become more differentiated into discrete emotional attractor states (i.e., anger, sadness, fear, happiness), with the various components of each attractor state becoming reorganized with development. Importantly, Camras (2011) considers consciousness or self-awareness to be one component of emotional attractor states (e.g., for anger, sadness, shame) that may develop heterochronically and become reorganized and integrated into the emotional attractor state. Such consciousness or self-awareness provides a window of opportunity for individuals to know and comprehend their own inner physiological states of emotional arousal.

## Consciousness and Inner Physiological States of Emotional Arousal

Many scholars have taken note of the important dynamic features and temporal qualities of emotions involving frequency, duration and intensity. Individuals and families vary in how easily they are emotionally aroused, and there are measurable differences in the frequency, duration and intensity of emotional episodes and expressiveness (e.g., Halberstadt & Eaton, 2002). Furthermore, as noted by Ekman (1994), the underlying functional neural circuitry likely differs depending on whether the experience involves an emotion, a *mood*, a *sentiment*, or an affective/emotional personality *trait*. Emotions involve episodes of a duration limited from seconds to minutes; whereas, if an emotion is perceived to last for hours, there may have been recurrent but separate emotional episodes. Alternatively, the long-lasting emotions could signal the onset of an emotional mood state that could last for hours or days (Ekman, 1994). Emotions are acute (i.e., they have a beginning and ending), are usually focused on specific objects, and have a limited duration; sentiments differ in that they are chronic, more enduring, and often involve a generalized class of objects (Frijda, 2008; Larsen et al., 2008). For example, a child may show the emotion of fear by displaying a fearful facial expression when the new family dog growls and barks; but this same child otherwise may not have a generalized sentiment of fear of dogs. Another child may have such a generalized ever-present underlying sentiment or chronic feeling of fear of dogs, but this would not be apparent until the child is faced with the presence of a dog ... any dog, growling, barking, or not. When mood states (such as depressed or anxious moods) last for weeks or months, it could be symptomatic of an affective or personality disorder. Similarly, frequently occurring and long-lasting aspects of personality involving emotions (such as a tendency towards social anxiety if a person is shy) are known as emotional or personality traits that could potentially last over the course of a lifetime (Oatley & Jenkins, 1996).

Variations in emotional arousal also occur based on a person's age, gender and cultural background. With respect to age, an immature sensitivity to becoming easily emotionally aroused has often been noted to occur in preschool children (e.g., tantrums) due to the ongoing changes in the developmental neurobiology of the brain, the rudimentary emergence of consciousness, and the developing ability to self-evaluate and reflect on emotions in self and others (Lewis, 2008a, 2008b). In adolescence, there are emerging interconnections in various brain systems (limbic system, prefrontal cortex) as well as increased myelination in various brain regions such as the corpus callosum, which allows for more efficient functioning of various brain circuits; the increases in the production of sex hormones also affect this developmental process (Arain et al., 2013). Because of the immaturity of the neural circuitry during adolescence, emotional arousal may be linked to a vulnerability to engage in a variety of risk-taking behaviours, some of which can further exacerbate problems in brain functioning later on in adulthood. In one study, adolescents who were at risk for emotional problems because they had a parent with a substance use disorder were also found to have greater amygdala reactivity when they were presented with emotional stimuli than adolescents who were not at risk (Lindsay et al., 2014). Such hyperresponsivity to emotional stimuli may further add to the risk of future substance abuse in these adolescents (Lindsay et al., 2014). In normative adult development, older adults are more skilled at emotion regulation depending on the social context, although the intensity and duration of emotions varies by gender (Magai, 2008), as well as by cultural norms (Shweder et al., 2008), a topic addressed in more detail in a later chapter.

Disabilities that are prominent at different points in the lifespan also involve deviations in emotional arousal, a topic that is addressed in greater detail in Chapter 11. During infancy and early childhood, the autism spectrum disorders affect emotional processing, consciousness and the young child's identity or sense of self (Lewis, 2014) as mentioned earlier in this chapter. In middle-aged and older adults, two forms of organic brain disorders or dementia can affect emotional processing. These are *frontotemporal dementia (FTD)*, which involves degeneration of the frontal and temporal lobes of the brain, and *Alzheimer's disease (AD)*, which is characterized by memory loss, a slower disease progression, and a later age of onset than FTD (Alzheimer's Association, 2014; UCSF Memory and Aging Center, 2016). Progressive neurological disorders such as these deeply affect the emotional lives of the affected person and his or her family members. Persons with dementia may be at least somewhat consciously aware of the losses they have incurred which affect their identities or sense of self, leading to any of a variety of emotional reactions. They may become increasingly emotional at times and need their caregivers to assist them in calming down and relaxing in a way that helps them to maintain self-esteem and dignity; caregivers too may need a support group and encouragement for their own self-care (Mace & Rabins, 2011).

## Summary of Chapter Key Points

The regions of the human brain that are functionally involved in emotion develop in accordance with the orthogenetic principle. The human brain has opposing tendencies to be flexible and to adapt to changing conditions (i.e., plasticity) as well as to remain stable (i.e., experiential canalization). This allows a person to have autobiographical memories and a sense of continuity of his or her past, present and planned future goals. Even though contemporary approaches that emphasize mirror neurons and body maps are controversial, they are nonetheless stimulating much research. Integrating the human mind, consciousness and the brain/body has remained of interest to scholars throughout recorded history. Being consciously aware of our sensations, perceptions and our own bodily experiences is important to our sense of self in relation to important others such as our family members. The dynamic systems approach to emotional development is appealing because it emphasizes how there are self-organizing tendencies in the individual that synergistically coordinate and synchronize various brain and physiological systems depending on the moment-to-moment real-time interactions that the individual is having with the social and physical environment (Granic, 2005). The dynamic systems approach also allows us to label our conscious yet diverse experiences of emotion so that we can communicate with each other what it is that we are feeling. The dynamic and temporal features of emotion that vary among individuals can extend in time, leading to moods, attitudes or sentiments, and emotional or affective personality traits. Core personality traits relate to the construct of temperament, a topic to which we turn in the next chapter.

## Further Reading

Damasio, A. (2010). *Self comes to mind: Constructing the conscious brain.* New York: Vintage Books.

In this readable book about the human brain, Damasio summarizes contemporary thinking about how the human brain is linked to our emotional lives and relationships with others, how the brain is linked to our thoughts and conscious reflections on ourselves, others and the world we perceive around us, and ultimately how the brain is linked to our sense of self. Damasio takes an evolutionary perspective and attempts to show how the brain's ability to map experiences through remembering patterns of sensations and perceptions connects to our consciousness and self-awareness.

Lewis, M. (2014). *The rise of consciousness and the development of emotional life.* New York: Guilford Press.

For serious students of emotional development, this recent book by the acclaimed emotion researcher, Michael Lewis, is a must-read. In a comprehensive and integrative manner, Lewis discusses how emotional development intertwines with identity and the development of consciousness in individuals. In addition, Lewis elaborates on the various forms of self-conscious emotions and their implications for atypical development. Exposed self-conscious emotions include empathy, embarrassment over exposure, and jealousy or envy, while evaluative self-conscious emotions include shame, guilt and pride. Emotional and personality disorders may emerge when these go awry.

# 4

# Variations in Temperament Among Family Members

*Observations of children in school settings often reveal differences in their activity levels and willingness to engage with each other during playtime. Some children are more outgoing, while others are more reserved. Four-year-old Kenny has just started a new preschool and has been having difficulty separating from his mother when it is time for her to leave and go to work. He stands close to her and hugs her legs tightly while strongly protesting her departure. To settle down, he puts his fingers in his mouth with his head bowed down, while carefully observing other children as if he would like to join them. Kenny's mother was concerned enough to take him to see a child psychologist for an evaluation. While the psychologist observed Kenny and played with him, Kenny's mother completed some paper-and-pencil measures. Though Kenny initially had a hard time adjusting to preschool, his evaluation did not reveal any clinically significant emotional problems. Shortly after a month at the preschool, Kenny started to talk and interact with an outgoing boy, especially when they were outdoors building a castle in the sandbox. Though his mother and teacher were initially quite concerned about his shy behaviour, they now think he seems happier and that he has started to adapt to his new peers and environment.*

## Differences in Children's Temperament

For many young children, attending a new day care centre or preschool is a major adjustment. Sometimes children who are merely more reserved by temperament are mistakenly viewed as having a disorder and as being emotionally insecure (Stein, Carey & Snyder, 2004).

Such ***slow-to-warm-up*** or temperamentally shy children were initially identified in the classic New York Longitudinal Study (NYLS) conducted by Alexander Thomas, Stella Chess and their colleagues (e.g., Chess & Thomas, 1977; Thomas et al., 1963). Normally developing children like Kenny who display a slow-to-warm-up pattern are not necessarily emotionally disordered; they may merely require more time than many of their peers to adjust to novelty, new surroundings and new people (Carey & McDevitt, 1995).

Based on their extensive interviews with parents and studies with children, Stella Chess and Alexander Thomas (1977) were among the first to note that children's *temperament* (which includes relatively stable patterns of positive and negative emotions) influences parenting behaviours. They identified the following nine temperament categories: *activity; rhythmicity of biological functions; adaptability; approach/withdrawal to novelty; sensory threshold; primarily positive or negative moods; mood intensity; distractibility; and persistence/attention span.* In addition to the slow-to-warm-up temperament pattern, they identified easy and difficult temperament patterns (Chess & Thomas, 1977). This chapter includes a consideration of various approaches to temperament. Consistent with the approach to temperament taken by Chess and Thomas, babies who display an ***easy-going temperament*** with primarily positive affect, alertness and attentiveness are more likely to have parents who are responsive to their needs and who display positive adaptive parenting behaviours (Kochanska et al., 2004). The review by Kochanska et al. also suggests that children with ***difficult temperaments***, a tendency to get angry and to display attentional problems, were more likely to have parents who showed more maladaptive and less responsive parenting. Others perceive infants and children with such difficult temperaments as having any of several potential risk factors in their disposition, because they are sometimes more challenging to parent, thus requiring parental efforts towards greater flexibility and responsive adjustment to the child's needs (Carey & McDevitt, 1995). Children with difficult temperaments may be overly active, show unpredictable hunger, sleeping and elimination patterns, display excessive wariness in approaching new situations, or show bold age-inappropriate approach behaviours. They may adapt slowly to new situations, and be either too sensitive or too unresponsive to stimulation compared to other typical children of the same age. Their moods may be frequently negative rather than positive, and they may react too intensely to provocation. Distractibility, poor attention span and task persistence may also be problematic.

As alluded to above, the concept of temperament is important in the study of emotional development because family members with difficult temperaments have a harder time achieving emotional competence themselves. In addition, they have a harder time than those with easy temperament patterns in effectively socializing emotions in others. In this chapter, I provide a summary of historical and current trends in thinking about the construct of temperament. As noted by Bates, Goodnight and Fite (2008), the construct of temperament provides a way to discuss many of the unique individual differences in people's emotional lives as they progress from infancy to older adulthood. While the constructs of emotion, temperament and personality share some commonalities, they are also distinguishable based on the quality and types of patterns formed, as discussed further below.

## Definitions of Temperament

Historically, the ancient Greeks (e.g., Galen), early personality theorists (e.g., Gordon Allport, James McKeen Cattell, Hans Eysenck), and early developmental psychologists (e.g., Arnold Gesell) have recognized the important role of temperament in social and emotional functioning (Goldsmith et al., 1987) (see History Feature Box 4). In 1985, Goldsmith and a group of key

**History Feature Box 4**

**Back Then and Now: Changing Views of Temperament and Personality**

Hippocrates (c. 460–377/359 BC) was a celebrated Greek physician and "father of medicine" (Rockwood, 2007). Like Galen did later, Hippocrates gathered information from his predecessors, and the result was a collection of writings composed by Hippocrates and his followers (Munger, 2003). As described by Hippocrates, the four fluids of the body, called *humours*, were blood, phlegm, yellow bile and black bile, and when these were imbalanced disease and disability resulted (Rockwood, 2007). The ancient Greeks and Romans often noted the importance of earth, wind, fire and water in their considerations of human functioning; in addition, geography and seasons (summer, autumn, winter, spring) played a role in disease according to Hippocrates, so that climate was considered important as a determinant of health (Kagan, 1994; Munger, 2003; Rockwood, 2007).

Claudius Galenus or "Galen" (c. 130–201 AD) was a Greek physician who collated and summarized much of the existing medical knowledge of his time including that of the Hippocratic writings (Rockwood, 2007). Galen emphasized that the three major organs of the body (the heart, liver and brain) were central to various life processes (Rockwood, 2007). Isidore of Seville (c. 560–636 AD) was a Spanish saint who wrote about the works of both Galen and Hippocrates, and discussed their ideas in relation to individual differences; Isidore's scholarly works were quite influential during the Middle Ages (Kagan, 1994; Rockwood, 2007; Sharpe & Isidore of Seville, 1964). Galen elaborated on nine temperamental types; the first ideal type was based on a balanced combination of hot–cool and dry–moist bodily conditions (Kagan, 1994). There were also four less ideal types that were dominated by either warm, cool, dry or moist (Sharpe & Isidore of Seville, 1964). Then, finally, there were four more temperaments called melancholic, sanguine, choleric and phlegmatic, each of which was dominated by a complementary pair of interactive qualities such that one pair dominated the remaining pair (e.g., warm and moist dominating cool and dry), and each of which resulted from an excess in one of the bodily humours. According to Kagan, Galen's view was that:

> The melancholic was cool and dry because of an excess of black bile; the sanguine was warm and moist because of an excess of blood; the choleric was warm and dry because of the excess of yellow bile, and the phlegmatic was cool and moist because of an excess of phlegm. (Kagan, 1994, p. 2)

Although these characteristics were thought to be inherent to each individual's physiology, Galen's view was that climate and diet could have an impact via the influence of seasonal changes: 1) the body became warmer and moister in the spring and people became more sanguine, 2) in autumn as the climate became cooler and dryer, people became more melancholic, 3) in winter, as it became more moist and cold, people were more phlegmatic, and 4) in summer, as the climate becomes hot and dry, people became more choleric (Kagan, 1994).

Galen's approach remained popular into the 19th century and remnants of his views have persisted into contemporary times in some regions of the world (Kagan, 1994). In the 19th and 20th centuries, the work of Franz Gall (1758–1828 AD), the German physician and founder of phrenology, was popular in attempts to understand differences in human intentions and emotion based on brain physiology as evidenced in observable bumps on the skull (Kagan, 1994; Rockwood, 2007). In addition, other attempts to link body types and facial features to specific personality traits persisted into the late 19th and 20th centuries (see Kagan, 1994). Today, a wide variety of scholars study individual differences in temperament and personality along different points of the lifespan. The idea of innate individual differences in temperament that influence emotional behaviour is currently widely accepted, along with the idea that such differences are subject to environmental influences and modifications over time (Lewis, 2014).

temperament researchers held a roundtable discussion at a child development conference about their respective views on temperament; from this discussion emerged a paper summarizing four major approaches to understanding temperament (Goldsmith et al., 1987). The four approaches represent the works of: (1) Stella Chess and Alexander Thomas, as described above, (2) Mary Rothbart and her colleagues John Bates and Samuel Putnam, (3) Arnold Buss and Robert Plomin, and (4) H. Hill Goldsmith and Joseph Campos. More recently, Shiner, Buss, McClowry, Putnam, Saudino and Zentner (2012) published a paper updating the research and definitions of temperament provided by these four groups of researchers. Zentner and Bates (2008) added a fifth major approach, that of Jerome Kagan (e.g., 1994), which is discussed later in this chapter. See Table 4.1 for a summary of the five approaches.

**Table 4.1** Summary Table of the Five Approaches to Temperament

| Alexander Thomas & Stella Chess | Mary Rothbart, John Bates & Samuel Putnam | Arnold Buss & Robert Plomin | H. Hill Goldsmith & Joseph Campos | Jerome Kagan & Nathan Fox |
|---|---|---|---|---|
| **Nine basic temperaments are:** | **Four basic temperaments are:** | **Four basic temperaments are:** | **Temperament is tied to emotion regulation** | **Infant reactivity is tied to later behavioural inhibition** |
| 1. activity | 1. surgency | 1. emotionality | | |
| 2. rhythmicity | 2. negative emotionality | 2. activity | | |
| 3. adaptability | 3. effortful control (called regulatory capacity in infants) | 3. sociability | | |
| 4. approach-withdrawal | 4. orienting sensitivity | 4. impulsivity | | |
| 5. sensory threshold | | | | |
| 6. positive-negative moods | | | | |
| 7. mood intensity | | | | |
| 8. distractibility | | | | |
| 9. persistence-attention span | | | | |
| **Three patterns:** | | | | |
| 1. easy | | | | |
| 2. difficult | | | | |
| 3. slow-to-warm-up | | | | |

In the late 20th century, there were many definitions of temperament proposed by scholars and these various viewpoints converged on several key components early on (Goldsmith et al., 1987; Kagan, 1994). Thus, temperament was thought to reflect "a quality that (1) varies among individuals, (2) is moderately stable over time and situation, (3) is under some genetic influence, and (4) appears early in life" (Kagan, 1994, pp. 41–42). Rothbart and Bates (1998) view temperament as the essential core of personality that develops over the course of the lifespan. While this core is somewhat stable, it is nonetheless dynamic and interacts with features of the environment. As described by Bates et al. (2008), it consists of three levels of stability, each of which contributes to the temperament phenotype. For example, at the genetic level, there are biomarkers for physiological reactivity, responsivity to novelty and sensitivity to distress. At the neural level, synaptic plasticity may lead to changes in specific neural regions such as the amygdala and hippocampus, and at the behavioural level, patterns of behaviour may vary depending on the informant and the individual's life circumstances (Bates et al., 2008).

Currently, researchers are expanding the early 21st-century definition of temperament to allow for the incorporation of new research findings into the construct (Shiner et al., 2012). Shiner et al. review recent studies that have led to the following conclusions. First, not all temperament traits are as stable in infancy as previously thought, and some, such as self-control and the ability to inhibit behaviours, may not emerge until later during the preschool or childhood periods. Second, maturation rates may vary across different domains of functioning, and the manifestation of what might be the same process may vary by the person's age (e.g., visual exploration in infants may be like novelty seeking in adolescents). Third, the affective and cognitive systems are more integrated than previously recognized, and thus cognitive processes such as attention and executive control are intricately involved in self-regulation and temperament traits. Finally, scholars used to maintain that infants begin life with a bias towards regulation by their underlying biological and genetic make-up, with increasing influences of the environment on development over time. While this idea makes intuitive sense, it is now being challenged by research findings demonstrating that environmental input affects gene expressions even before an infant is born; thus, genetics and environment are both critically intertwined components right from the beginning of development and much remains to be understood about their integration (Shiner et al., 2012).

Although Shiner et al. highlight the potential for additional amendments to the *temperament* construct in the future, they offer the following updated definition. "Temperament traits are early emerging basic dispositions in the domains of activity, affectivity, attention, and self-regulation, and these dispositions are the product of complex interactions among genetic, biological, and environmental factors across time" (Shiner et al., 2012, p. 437). As shown in Table 4.1 and described next, there have been five major approaches to the study of temperament, each of which have some overlap with others.

## Five Contemporary Approaches to Understanding Temperament in Infants and Children

The first major contemporary approach to understanding temperament was the *child psychiatric* approach of Chess and Thomas, summarized earlier, with nine basic temperament categories, and three constellation patterns (*easy, difficult, slow-to-warm-up*) (Zentner & Bates, 2008). A fourth *average* pattern of temperament with components that didn't quite fit into one of the other three was also identified; this early work of Chess and Thomas and their colleagues from the 1950s to 1970s on such individual differences in children served as the catalyst for much research that followed (Lamb, Ketterlinus & Fracasso, 1992).

A second approach is the *neurobiological developmental* approach of Mary Rothbart and her colleagues (Zentner & Bates, 2008). Based on their research and theoretical views using the original nine temperament dimensions identified in the New York Longitudinal Study (NYLS) by Thomas and Chess, Rothbart and her colleagues (e.g., Evans & Rothbart, 2007; Rothbart & Putnam, 2002) have described four broad temperament systems. These are ***surgency*** (which includes extraverted approach behaviours and positive emotionality), ***negative emotionality*** (which includes some aspects of fear, sadness and anger/frustration), ***effortful control*** (which includes the ability to inhibit behaviour and self-regulate in children) and ***orienting sensitivity*** (which includes various forms of perceptual/cognitive/affective sensitivity in attending to internal or external stimuli). In infants, effortful control is called ***regulatory capacity***, which includes the ability to focus attention and show satisfaction in low-intensity activities (Shiner et al., 2012). In addition, some form of surgency/positive emotionality and negative emotionality are present in early infancy and continue to be manifest throughout life, even though each also interacts with input from the physical and social environment – that is, with socialization by caregivers and by others such as teachers who interact with the developing child. They review evidence suggesting that the temperament systems of surgency, negative emotionality and effortful control map well onto the adult personality characteristics of extraversion, neuroticism and conscientiousness, respectively.

Rothbart and Putnam (2002) claim that their view of temperament differs from the earlier conceptualization of Thomas and Chess and their colleagues because their approach places more emphasis on the importance of *specific content* in the manifestation of a given temperament. As examples, they cite the two temperament dimensions of intensity and rhythmicity. For instance, in their research, children who were highly intense during smiling and laughter were not necessarily intense in fearfulness, and children who had regular, rhythmic bowel movements did not necessarily have regular, rhythmic sleep patterns. Thus, the original nine temperament factors from the NYLS did not appear to generalize across different content domains as they had expected. Instead, Rothbart and her colleagues (e.g., Derryberry & Rothbart, 2001; Rothbart & Putnam, 2002) prefer to focus on three (of their four) broad temperament systems – surgency/positive emotionality, negative emotionality and effortful control – because there is some evidence for their generalizability and long-term stability. Rothbart and her colleagues further propose that each of these three temperament systems interacts with aspects of the caregiving environment in producing various outcomes for children. For example, they highlight the research of Kochanska from the 1990s (e.g., Kochanska, 1997) as being prominent in showing how parenting practices interact with children's temperament to result in their moral development and in children's acquisition of a conscience that helps to regulate their behaviours.

Currently, based on the Rothbart, Bates and Putnam approach (see Rothbart, 2006), there are several temperament questionnaires in use by researchers studying large groups of individuals. The measures are available through Mary Rothbart's website. These are *The Infant Behavior Questionnaire (IBQ)* (3–12 months of age), *The Early Childhood Behavior Questionnaire (ECBQ)* (18–36 months of age), *The Children's Behavior Questionnaire (CBQ)* (3–7 years of age), *The Temperament in Middle Children Questionnaire (TMCQ)* (7–10 years of age), *The Early Adolescent Temperament Questionnaire – Revised (EATQ-R)* (9–15 years of age), and *The Adult Temperament Questionnaire (ATQ)* (adults). These questionnaires are for research purposes with typically developing individuals and are not for use in identifying clinical cases during assessments.

A third *criterial* approach to temperament is that of Arnold Buss and Robert Plomin, who have set criteria for *only* including as temperamental traits those characteristics with a clear underlying genetic basis (Zentner & Bates, 2008). Thus, they have focused on garnering empirical evidence for the underlying genetic basis of temperament and have come up with four possible temperament categories based on the results of studies in the field of behavioural genetics (Shiner et al., 2012). First, *emotionality*, is a dimension of distress that involves emotional arousal ranging from a stoic lack of emotion to out-of-control emotion. Second, *activity*, is tempo and vigour ranging from lethargy to highly energetic. Third, *sociability*, is the extent to which being with others and responsively sharing with them is a personal preference. Finally, *impulsivity*, is the extent to which a person has emotional and behavioural control, persistence and a tendency to be planful (Goldsmith et al., 1987; Shiner et al., 2012).

The fourth *functionalist* approach to the positive and negative emotionality of temperament is that of H. Hill Goldsmith, developed in collaboration with Joseph Campos (Goldsmith et al., 1987; Shiner et al., 2012). Their approach views temperament as variability in developing emotion systems and looks at the adaptive emotional functions of temperament (Zentner & Bates, 2008). Of critical importance are the individual differences in the specific basic emotion systems of anger, sadness, fear, joy/pleasure, disgust, interest and surprise. These systems show distinct patterns of features in the vocal, motoric and facial expression domains across a wide variety of cultures and settings; it is noteworthy that emotion regulation is an inherent function of these emotion systems and consequently intimately intertwined with the concept of temperament (Goldsmith et al., 1987; Shiner et al., 2012; Zentner & Bates, 2008).

Fifth and finally is the *biotypological* approach of Jerome Kagan, who has taken an inductive perspective rather than a theoretically based one in describing the temperament pattern of ***behavioural inhibition***; Kagan's inductive approach involves carefully and systematically conducting studies of early temperamental *reactivity* biases in infants and then linking the results to later inhibition of behaviour (Zentner & Bates, 2008). In this approach, reactivity biases involve how motorically and physiologically reactive the infant is when presented with something new or unfamiliar. Although Kagan's programme of research began in the late 1950s, it has progressively expanded over time and contemporary longitudinal studies continue to make advances using his approach in which high and low reactivity in infancy is examined longitudinally by scholars such as Nathan Fox and his colleagues (e.g., Fox et al., 2015). For example, in the publication by Fox et al. (2015), low and high reactivity in infants at 4 months of age predicted behavioural inhibition at the age of 2 years old. In the three longitudinal studies conducted in two labs, low and high reactivity were specifically operationalized as variations in infant motor activity (arms, legs, trunk) and distress (fretting, crying) when they were exposed to unfamiliar and novel stimulation such as nonsense syllables spoken by multiple voices or unfamiliar mobiles placed within their field of vision (Fox et al., 2015). Behavioural inhibition in 2 year olds who had previously been classified as high or low in reactivity during infancy was assessed by examining their avoidant and approach behaviours to a battery of unfamiliar stimuli (e.g., a person dressed as a clown) in an unfamiliar setting such as a lab room. The results confirmed that reactivity in infancy predicts behavioural inhibition later in childhood; in addition, boys with high reactivity in infancy were more likely to display later behavioural inhibition than girls, although the authors note that additional research on parent socialization is needed to assist in clarifying the reasons for early gender differences (Fox et al., 2015).

## Temperament and Personality Development

As stated by Rothbart, "temperament and experience together 'grow' a personality, which will include the child's developing cognitions about self, others, and the physical and social world, as well as his or her values, attitudes, and coping strategies" (Rothbart, 2007, p. 207). Thus, temperament is a narrower foundational construct than "personality", which changes holistically and dynamically over time and eventually will include new emerging traits that become integrated with temperament characteristics as the person develops and interacts with others. Overall, the bidirectional interactive experiences of both parents and their children as they communicate with each other over time and across various situations has the potential to affect the links between their temperament and personality development as some studies reviewed below show.

Gender is an important consideration in the temperament and personality development of both children and their parents (e.g., Brody & Hall, 2008). Using multiple methods of assessment, Gagne, Miller and Goldsmith (2013) have found differences in the early temperament patterns of 3-year-old boys and girls, with boys showing a higher activity level than girls, and girls showing greater shyness and inhibitory control than boys. Furthermore, a pattern of findings emerged regardless of gender; that is, activity level, shyness and inhibitory control were related to each other such that greater shyness was related to less activity and more inhibitory control, and more activity was related to less inhibitory control. As reviewed by Brody and Hall (2008), these early components of young children's temperament may be related to later personality and emotional development in which researchers find that girls are more agreeable, sociable and attentive to relationship issues than boys. In socializing emotion, mothers and fathers take somewhat different approaches due to differences in their own personality structures as discussed further below.

Kochanska et al. (2004) conducted research that examined parents' personality (i.e., parental empathy and Big Five personality traits), young children's temperament, and their relation to the emerging parent–child relationship. Parents in the study completed standardized personality tests that resulted in the Big Five scores for personality along the dimensions of

*Openness, Conscientiousness, Extraversion, Agreeableness and Neuroticism,* the so-called *OCEAN* acronym of personality dimensions (John & Srivastava, 1999). Kochanska et al. (2004) observed infants in several laboratory situations to assess their temperaments, and observed the parents and children interacting with each other at home. They found that infants' temperament (operationalized as frequency of behavioural displays of joy, fear, anger and focused attentiveness) was clearly related to the parent–child relationship when the infants were 7 months old. That is, the child's temperamental proneness to joy and fear, and lack of tendency to anger predicted a positive emotional ambience at home (i.e., positive relationship between mother and child). For instance, the child's displays of joy predicted maternal responsiveness and her consistent tracking and monitoring of the child. The pattern was somewhat different for fathers with the child's proneness to joy predicting shared positive ambience, and the child's lack of tendency to anger predicting a positive emotional relationship and paternal responsiveness to the child. Parental personality also predicted the parent–child relationship and again the pattern differed for mothers and fathers. Low neuroticism in mothers predicted a positive emotional relationship in the home, while for fathers, high agreeableness and openness did so. High empathy predicted maternal responsiveness, while high conscientiousness predicted responsiveness in fathers. High conscientiousness predicted maternal tracking/monitoring of the child while low extraversion predicted paternal tracking/monitoring. Thus, parent gender moderated the quality of the relation between parents' personalities and the parent–child relationship.

Kochanska et al. (2004) also conducted a longitudinal study in which they assessed the personality of mothers and the temperament of their children at 9 months of age and then assessed their relationship five times between the ages of 9 months and 45 months. Some aspects of mothers' interpersonal personality traits, but not child temperament, predicted the quality of the mother–child relationship. Maternal personality assessment used an approach that assumes continuity between normal individual differences in personality and the extremes associated with personality disorders. Kochanska et al. found that maternal mistrust was associated with less positive relationships, while maternal manipulativeness and mistrust were associated with a less responsive mother–child relationship. Maternal workaholism (a trait that involves being well-organized and with a conscientious need to achieve) was related to a more positive emotional relationship between mother and child and to more maternal responsiveness. Maternal dependency, which involves a sensitivity to and concern with the views and opinions of others, was also related to greater maternal responsiveness to their children. The two positive aspects of the parent–child relationship that were studied by Kochanska et al., namely the positive emotional ambience in the home and parental responsiveness to the child's behaviours and needs, are both critically important for the development of emotional competence in the family. The seminal research by Kochanska and her colleagues demonstrates how child and parental personality, both of which have temperament as the core foundation, are related to the quality of the emotional socialization environment at home.

## Psychopathology: The Role of Temperament, Optimal Arousal and Self-Regulation

Temperament is important in helping to understand just what the optimal level of emotional arousal is for a given person, and being able to self-regulate by actively controlling arousal, attention and emotional responses is important in processes leading to psychopathology (e.g., Derryberry & Rothbart, 1988). A well-known finding in the psychological literature is that motivation and performance on tasks are enhanced when there is a moderate or optimal level of arousal for a person. If a person is not aroused enough, he or she will not care and will be unmotivated, whereas if the person is too aroused and anxious, his or her performance will suffer (sometimes called the Yerkes–Dodson law; see Teigen, 1994). Nevertheless, just what is optimal for each of us seems to vary in accordance with our temperament and personal history of experiences. As discussed by Derryberry and Rothbart (1988), this idea of the importance of level of arousal in individual differences has been noted historically by many researchers such as Hans Eysenck and Donald Hebb. Such researchers proposed that for some people with more shy, introverted personalities, milder forms of stimulation are optimal and preferred as compared to others who are more outgoing and extraverted who may need and prefer higher levels of stimulation. Within families, the quality and extent of such stimulation provided by family members to each other may be either too little, too much or optimal (i.e., just right) in terms of the physiological arousal that results – and this may have implications for the person's adjustment or the development of psychopathology.

During infancy and early childhood especially, caregivers provide both the social and physical environments that provide stimulation. The consistent presence of a warm, nurturing, loving adult in the life of the infant, toddler and young child is linked to specific *neurobiological patterns* that affect hormone production in the child and affect the developing child's successful interactions and social relationships with others later (e.g., Tops et al., 2007).

Specifically, parenting socialization behaviours such as comforting (rather than scolding) a distressed child affects the child's physiological arousal, emotional states, and the degree of sweating, heart rate levels and hormone production (Eisenberg et al., 1998a; Eisenberg, Spinrad & Cumberland 1998b). A wide variety of child outcomes can then result.

Adults as well as children are affected physiologically when stimulated and aroused. For example, researchers have found that how couples talk with each other in their everyday interactions is related to their physiological arousal, emotional states and the physical health of the partners as well as that of family members who witness their communication (e.g., Gottman, Katz & Hooven, 1997). Eisenberg et al. (1998a) have found that the child's emotion knowledge and ability to regulate or control emotions in socially acceptable ways is enhanced when the child is physiologically aroused in a manner that is optimal for learning (not too little and not too much in accordance with the child's temperament), and if the socializers in the child's life (parents, siblings, among others) are emotionally competent themselves.

As reviewed by Eisenberg et al. (1998a, 1998b), the child's physiological arousal is affected by the child's temperament as well as by the relative amounts of positive and negative emotional expressiveness in their families. These influences are bidirectional. A relatively high amount of positive emotional expression (e.g., shared joy and interest, praise) in the family relative to non-hostile negative expressions (e.g., anger, disgust) appears to be related to better child outcomes involving their emotional and social functioning. This is especially so if the negative expressions that occur within the family context are not angry hostile criticisms specifically directed at the child and if competent and successful management of negative emotions occurs. When parents and other family members, on the other hand, engage in hostile negative emotional expressions that are in direct reaction to the child's misbehaviours and self-assertive emotional expressions, there is a greater risk. That is, the child is at risk of also being high in negative emotionality and of having an ***internalizing disorder*** such as anxiety or depression, or an ***externalizing disorder*** that includes behavioural misconduct and angry temper outbursts. In such cases, children may not be able to effectively regulate or control the intensity, duration or frequency of their emotional arousal and this may interfere with their ability to learn about emotions.

In the model presented by Eisenberg and her colleagues, when children are physiologically well-regulated and able to maintain an optimal level of emotional arousal (i.e., alert and interested), they are better able to attend to the social environment and listen. This then allows them to process what their parents or other adults and children are communicating about emotions (rather than trying to soothe themselves and alleviate their own emotional pain). They are thus better able to comprehend and process emotional information when they are physiologically at an optimal level of arousal based on their temperament.

It is increasingly clear to researchers around the world that self-regulation is an important feature of temperament and developing personalities (e.g., Denissen et al., 2013). As described by Denissen et al., infants' temperamental physiological reactivity to the environment is supplemented over time by self-regulation processes and behaviours directed towards ***reference values*** (personal goals, standards to which the person is held, and social norms). In Denissen et al.'s theoretical framework, self-regulation underlies temperament and personality. Reference values change developmentally and individuals need to have sufficient regulatory resources (help and support from others and the environment) as well as sufficient practice in order to effectively self-regulate in accordance with a particular reference value. For example, Denissen et al. report that they have found that by late adolescence there is an increase in the personality characteristic known as conscientiousness as compared to middle childhood. However, this increase is preceded by a brief decrease in conscientiousness in early adolescence, presumably due to the shifting reference values from childhood to adolescence, and the adolescent's need for different regulatory resources and more practice in demonstrating their increased conscientiousness. It is also possible that the regulatory resources and supports from family and others in the adolescent's social world may fail (at least temporarily) to assist the individual effectively when reference values change, and/or there may be insufficient opportunities for the adolescent to practise the newly emerging skills. Researchers in the future will need to be attuned to providing additional evidence for how self-regulation maps onto the development of temperament and personality.

## Applications: Adapting to Temperament in Family Life

Parents and family members must adapt to each other's temperaments and personalities over time. In the opening example given with Kenny, Kenny's mother and teacher discovered that he was taking more time to adjust to his preschool than expected. Under such conditions, parents have the onus of responsibility to help regulate the external circumstances for their children. The physical and social environment that parents place their children in needs to be a good match for the child's underlying temperament and developing personality. In Kenny's case, his mother sought outside assistance from a psychologist to try to determine why he was not making the transition to preschool in the same way as his peers.

Carey and McDevitt (1995) discuss the importance of the *goodness of fit* concept proposed by Chess and Thomas. This concept involves how well the environment matches the motivations and needs of the child, and how flexibly the environment can adjust to the child. Caregivers need to be cognizant of how well the social and physical environment of the child matches his or her temperament. Sometimes, there is a poor fit between the caregiver's parenting style or the child's environment and the child's temperament. When this is the case, caregivers need to adapt and make environmental changes accordingly to facilitate the child's development. There are several steps to fulfilling this goal.

As a first step, when temperament is implicated in family interaction difficulties, it may be important for temperament to be assessed by a professional. The outcome of such an assessment will depend on which approach to temperament is adopted. While research on the various approaches and how best to assess temperament is ongoing, there are a number of questionnaires that can be completed by parents that may help to identify a child's profile pattern (see Rothbart, Chew & Gartstein, 2001). It is important that multiple methods (e.g., questionnaires, observations) and informants (e.g., mother, father, teacher, clinician) are utilized as part of the assessment process.

Carey and McDevitt (1995) summarize the guidelines provided by Chess and Thomas for parents and clinicians on how best to cope with children when their temperament styles are not a good match to that of the environment or their caregivers. First, parents and other caregivers in a child's environment should have a good working knowledge of possible temperament categories and patterns both within themselves and within their children. Second, adaptation to a child's temperament should be embedded in the basic parent management structure for how to socialize the child in accordance with his or her needs. This includes acknowledging that the child needs:

> (1) guidance in the form of discipline and approval – that is, the enforcement of firm, consistent rules with an avoidance of physical punishment, with praise for good behavior, and with little attention to behavior that is only annoying; (2) affection, which includes acceptance and intimacy; (3) stimulation in the developmental and cognitive spheres; and (4) intrafamilial and extrafamilial socialization. (Carey & McDevitt, 1995, p. 41)

It is noteworthy that some temperament characteristics that present as a risk factor at one point in the lifespan may turn out to be a protective factor at another point of the lifespan; as well, it is worth noting that how caregivers manage the child's temperament can make a difference (Carey & McDevitt, 1995). Consider the following case of a child who is high in the temperament characteristic called "task persistence" identified by Chess and Thomas (1977). A preschool child high in persistence may ignore others while engaged in an activity until he or she accomplishes the originally intended goal. In such cases, the child's attention seems to be hyper-focused on the one task or activity, and the child may be very inflexible about task interruption. The child may be oppositional when parents try to redirect attention away from the activity to do something else (go to bed, stop to have dinner, etc.). Given the child's age and immature ability to self-control, the result is that the child may have temper tantrums when not allowed to complete what he or she started. While managing this persistence in the preschool years can be quite difficult for parents, parents can learn to adopt some helpful strategies originally proposed by Chess and Thomas (as cited in Carey & McDevitt, 1995). For example, first give the child warning about the need to interrupt a task. Second, teach the child to estimate accurately how long tasks will take. Third, prevent the child from even starting a lengthy task if the time is short, unless the child acknowledges the reality and agrees to stop when required. To fulfil these, caregivers need to be effective at monitoring and tracking their child's moment-to-moment tasks and activities. Interestingly, it is possible that children who enjoy persisting at tasks to completion and who may have seemed to be at risk for doing so during the preschool years might (depending on other temperament and situational factors) later thrive in a school setting where they are presented with projects and tasks to work on and where completion is mandatory to succeed. Thus, persistence may be a protective factor in some school-age children where it could be linked to higher achievement goals and good school performance (Carey & McDevitt, 1995).

## Summary of Chapter Key Points

Throughout history, scholars have noted individual differences in humans that appear at an early age and seem to persist over time. Early longitudinal and interview studies, such as that conducted by Alexander Thomas, Stella Chess and their colleagues, confirmed that caregivers tend to notice some emotional and behavioural differences in children quite early. Although there are many definitions of "temperament", the concept typically involves emotional and behavioural features that form the core of later personality and are at least somewhat stable over time. Today, many researchers have begun to link the concept of temperament to emotional and personality development as well as to self-regulation, although they agree that additional work is needed before there are conclusive evidence-based strategies for prevention and intervention. Five major approaches are prominent in the literature on temperament and are summarized within this chapter. Many of the contemporary models of early temperament involve individual and gender differences in emotionality and physiological reactivity to the environment, especially when the environmental stimulation is novel or unfamiliar to the individual. The early temperament of parents and their children are modified over the course of development as they interact. Temperament integrates with general personality characteristics over time, thus providing the foundation of the developing person's self-regulation ability. Optimal arousal enhances an individual's ability to learn but this varies by an individual's temperament and their family's expressiveness that varies along a continuum from high to low. When negative expressiveness is high, family members are at increased risk for developing internalizing or externalizing disorders. The family social environment needs to be a good fit for each individual's temperament to prevent such disorders from developing. The use of multiple informants and methods can increase the validity of temperament assessments. Parents and those who work with children and families need to understand temperament patterns and the various strategies for how best to socialize children in accordance with their needs and the family's values. As described in the framework of Denissen et al. (2013), self-regulatory efforts are guided by reference values, which are composed of personal goals, standards of behaviour set by others, and social norms which are influenced by the person's background ethnicity and culture, as well as the more proximal everyday culture in which the person currently lives. The influence of social norms that vary by culture and have an influence on emotion socialization within the family is the topic of the next chapter.

## Further Reading

Carey, W. B. & McDevitt, S. C. (1995). *Coping with children's temperament: A guide for professionals*. New York: Basic Books.

This excellent, readable book introduces understanding temperament from the approach of Stella Chess and Alexander Thomas who wrote the foreword to the book. Dr William Carey, professor of paediatrics, and Sean McDevitt, a child and adolescent clinical psychologist, combined their expertise to review the research literature up to the point that the book was written. They demonstrate how certain temperament characteristics and patterns may be viewed as risk factors in one context and as protective factors in another. Most importantly, they provide many clinically relevant examples of how parents and professionals can try to modify their management strategies as they attempt to cope with children with different temperament characteristics and patterns. Such clinically based recommendations for how to apply knowledge about children's temperament may have to suffice until additional studies are conducted on evidence-based prevention and intervention involving temperament management.

# 5

# Culture and Emotion in Families

*Trinh is the son of Vietnamese immigrants to the United States, and a college sophomore majoring in business administration. He had high hopes for his future in the business world and he wished to attend graduate school to obtain a Master's degree in Business Administration. However, Trinh had this dream before his father informed him that he wanted Trinh, as his eldest son, to become a doctor because this would bring such great honour to the family. Trinh felt conflicted about this, but also obligated to switch careers even after discussing it at length with his college counsellors and church leader. Thus, he eventually graduated from medical school and became a successful medical practitioner in his family's community. However, Trinh often still dreamed of having a chance to go back to school to get the business degree that he had to abandon to fulfil his father's wish for the sake of the family honour.* (Case study summary from Leung & Boehnien, 1996, p. 299.)

Source: *Ethnicity and Family Therapy (2nd ed.),* M. McGoldrick, J. Giordano and J. K. Pearce (Eds.), 1996. 

## The Importance of Culture to Family Emotional Life

Broadly conceptualized, culture involves six social constructs or categories: ethnicity, race, class or socio-economic status, gender, sexual orientation, and religion/spirituality (McAuliffe, 2008a). As can be understood in considering the case example of Trinh and his family, cultures transmit which focal emotional events within these categories are the most important ones to highlight in everyday daily communication among family members (Frijda & Mesquita, 1994). Trinh's understanding that great family pride and happiness would result if he followed his father's wishes affected his life path. In addition, traditionally and historically in

Vietnamese culture, children have been viewed as parental property; thus, they were often pressured to follow parental advice regarding important life decisions, especially those involving marriage and career selection as was the case for Trinh (e.g., Leung & Boehnien, 1996). In many cultures around the world, such traditional values are actively changing over time and reflect changes in technology and advances in cross-cultural communications and influences with the advent of cellphones and the internet (e.g., Akyil et al., 2014).

Despite technological changes, cultures still vary in their emphasis on the ethics of what they value as meaningful and important in living a good and happy life. For example, consider what happens in Anglophone (i.e., English speaking) North American families at the end of a typical day. Family members commonly ask each other the question, "How was your day?", and expect responses that involve feelings of happiness and pride involving success and personal achievements, or feelings of disappointment or regret involving failed efforts at home, school or work regarding specific individualized goals. This focus on success and personal achievements towards one's own goals would be more likely to occur in ***individualistic*** Western cultures, such as exist in Canada, Australia, the United States, the United Kingdom and many Western European countries as compared to the more ***collectivistic*** cultures, such as those in the regions of Indonesia, Asia, the Mediterranean, and the Middle East (e.g., Triandis, 1994). Eastern cultures often emphasize family members' sense of contentment and well-being, upheld by maintaining family honour in the watchful public eye and by following traditional norms and conventions (e.g., sanctioned marriages, care of elderly) (e.g., Frijda & Mesquita, 1994; Hakim-Larson & Nassar-McMillan, 2008). Family members with Asian backgrounds, such as Trinh's, tend to be more collectivistic in their approach. Likewise, violating family honour in public situations by social acts that are viewed as rude or shameful (e.g., offending another person publicly among peers) may affect the whole extended family and emotional reverberations and gossip about the event in the collective community may take time to settle down (e.g., Ajrouch, 1999, 2000).

While the individualistic–collectivistic dichotomy that classifies cultures is clearly an oversimplification in considering the many unique patterns displayed by individuals with their family members, the terms help to clarify some general values promoted within ethnic groups. McAuliffe (2008a) notes that individualistic values include respect for the autonomy/independence, rights and freedom of each family member, while collectivistic values reflect a hierarchy of power in terms of who should defer to whom with elders, religious figures or adult males often at the top of the hierarchy.

There is some evidence that people of different ethnic backgrounds also differ in the quantity, quality and duration of their emotional states because some events are more likely to provoke emotion in some cultures than in others. Culture allows for the values of the past in the form of rituals, beliefs and attitudes to be carried forth into future generations by identifying for them what is acceptable in terms of feelings, emotional expression and emotional regulation (e.g., Boyer, 2013). While primary or basic emotional facial expressions (e.g., a smile for happiness) are considered by some to be universal and occur cross-culturally, more complex emotional expressions have been discussed as reflecting idiosyncrasies that are culture or family specific in terms of the meanings they convey (e.g., Ekman & Friesen, 1975; Izard & Ackerman, 2000; Malatesta & Izard, 1984). Such non-verbal emotion socialization is addressed in Chapter 7 of this book. People from different cultures and subcultures vary in which experiences they find to be emotionally meaningful (Frijda & Mesquita, 1994; Shweder, 1993; Shweder et al., 2008), and in the extent to which they experience psychosocial stressors such as poverty and economic deprivation (e.g., Gump, Matthews & Raukkonen, 1999). Because of these variations, the level of physiological arousal and emotional states in family members may also vary from culture to culture and by regions within cultures.

In this chapter, I review ways to enhance our understanding of emotional development in families by considering their cultures by using as a point of departure current research findings on European, First Nations/Native/Aboriginal, Asian/Pacific Islander, African/Caribbean, Hispanic and Arab/Middle Eastern families. Wherever possible, I attempt to avoid ethnic gloss, which often occurs in the literature for each of the broad cultural groups described in this chapter. ***Ethnic gloss*** occurs when these categorical labels for cultures are used in an overgeneralized way to identify features and characteristics of individuals who vary considerably within the category; it is preferable instead to give background details such as the name of the specific region and country represented wherever possible (Trimble & Dickson, 2005). While much of the research on culture and emotion in families is still in its early stages, the preliminary findings are intriguing and reflect the great diversity in the expression and experience of emotions in families around the world. This chapter concludes with an introduction to the use of genograms as a useful way to clarify the potential influence of a family's cultural background on emotion socialization within the family.

## European Families

In the social sciences literature, European families have been subjected to ethnic gloss and have often been described as simply White or Caucasian, even though there are both differences as well as similarities in individuals from the over 50 countries listed as part of the European continent by the United Nations Statistics Division (31 October 2013). The four major regions of Europe are: (1) Northern Europe (e.g., Scandinavia, United Kingdom, Ireland, Latvia, Lithuania), (2) Western Europe (e.g., France, Germany, Netherlands, Switzerland, Austria, Belgium), (3) Southern Europe (e.g., Greece, Italy, Cyprus, Spain, Portugal, Serbia), and (4) Eastern Europe (e.g., Hungary, Romania, Ukraine, Poland, Russia, Czech Republic) (United Nations Statistics Division, 31 October 2013). While Europeans share many Western philosophical values (e.g., Russell, 2004), regional differences also have been found in large-scale studies polling people across the various countries within Europe.

The European Centre for Social Welfare Policy and Research has collected data on social participation and social isolation, and has found that one in 14 Europeans (about 7 per cent) are socially isolated. They do not meet regularly with either family or friends, leaving them without sources of support or assistance if needed; such social isolation was associated with increased age and with poverty, while social participation was associated with increased happiness (European Union, 2013; Lelkes, 2010). In general, Europeans were more likely to maintain close contact with friends as compared to family members, although at least three-quarters of Europeans had at least monthly contact with a family member. However, the most intense social contacts reported were in the Mediterranean countries of Cyprus, Portugal and Greece, suggesting that regional and national differences are important considerations.

Families with a European ethnic background are also considered to be the mainstream in North America and share a number of characteristics related to emotional development and socialization with their overseas relatives on the European continent, although again (to avoid ethnic gloss) it is important to be cognizant that quite a wide range of differences exist (Richmond & Guindon, 2013). For instance, these differences are based on religion (e.g., Protestant, Catholic, Jewish, Muslim) and country of origin (e.g., Irish Catholic, Swedish Lutheran, Greek Orthodox, Italian Jewish, Bosnian Muslim), historical time period of family immigration (anywhere from the 17th to 21st centuries), and region of settlement in North America, from Northwestern Canada to Southeastern United States.

In addition to sharing values that emphasize individualism over collectivism, Northern European Americans' individualism and self-sufficiency has led to the perception that they are capable of courageous acts and individual heroic deeds, with the downside being a susceptibility to feelings of isolation (Richmond & Guindon, 2013). White European Americans may also suffer at times from unrealistic expectations involving privilege and entitlement; they may uphold a sense of intolerance of others who differ from the mainstream in their beliefs and cultural practices (Richmond & Guindon, 2013). In fact, many third- and later-generation European North American families simply think of themselves as White, Caucasian, Canadian or American and show little interest in better understanding their mixed family roots (Giordano & McGoldrick, 1996).

Interestingly, under times of emotional stress or crises, the usually self-sufficient person of European background will often seek out the comfort of whatever familiar leftover ethnic cultural practices exist from their family's ethnic heritage (Giordano & McGoldrick, 1996). For example, Anglo American families with English ancestors may resort to an emotionally stoic, logical problem-solving approach to clarifying a difficult situation (McGill & Pearce, 1996), while Irish American families may be more likely to engage in humour, intuitive thinking and creative endeavours or fantasy such as through poetry and music as they attempt to cope with difficulties (McGoldrick, 1996). Nordic families with a Scandinavian heritage tend to value a philosophy that individuals can figure out emotional problems and their consequent solutions on their own (Erickson, 2005). Therefore, they tend to believe that it should not be necessary to draw attention to yourself by seeking help or support from others; in other words, under times of crisis, they may withdraw while also feeling lonely (Erickson, 2005).

## Native, First Nations and Aboriginal Families

Among the Native Americans of the United States, the First Nations people of Canada, or the Aboriginal families of Australia, tribal clan traditions and intergenerational extended family communication through rituals often provide the foundation for emotional socialization and the creation of meaning. Within the United States, there are 566 federally recognized American Indian and Alaskan Native tribes, many of whom live on reservations segregated and apart from the mainstream American communities (U.S. Department of the Interior, Indian Affairs, 2015). The elders of these tribes in Native American culture are the keepers of wisdom, and demonstrate caring and mutual respect for the next generation by connecting emotionally with them and passing on their spiritual and worldly knowledge and traditions through rituals and storytelling (Garrett et al., 2013).

In Canada, the Aboriginal peoples make up three primary groups – First Nations, Inuit and Métis – and total well over one million people (Statistics Canada, 2008). Among the First Nations people (who used to be called Indians), there are 617 communities (Government of Canada, Aboriginal Affairs and Northern Development, Canada, 2014). Like the Aboriginal peoples of Australia and New Zealand, Canadian First Nations peoples share a history of colonialism and interventions from government programmes, such as residential schools and out-adoptions; the history of these Canadian families includes emotional suffering from various forms of abuses, and high rates of health problems (Kirmayer, Simpson & Cargo, 2003).

The crucial need for an alternative focus on the strengths and well-being of Canadian Aboriginal peoples as well as their problems has become increasingly apparent given that much of the currently available literature emphasizes their susceptibility to risks and problems. For example, McShane and Hastings (2004) highlight the fact that most children, youth and Aboriginal families in Canada do not have psychosocial problems, and that little is known about potential similarities and differences in family socialization patterns between the mainstream Anglophone Canadian population and the highly diverse Aboriginal population. Nonetheless, the evidence that they review suggests that Aboriginal children are likely to be raised in an extended family environment, where aunts, uncles and grandparents and other more distant kin may help to socialize and discipline children. Aboriginal children are encouraged to take on more adult-like tasks and responsibilities. In addition, there is adult acceptance of child autonomy and individuality, and an emphasis on transmitting the values of emotional restraint, sharing and cooperation instead of competition and conflict, and non-interference that allows for natural consequences (Brant, 1990; McShane & Hastings, 2004).

Stewart (2009), as a psychologist and member of the Yellowknife Dene band in Canada, describes the important family value of learning to help others and engage in peaceful practices of healing. She notes that although there are cultural differences between the Aboriginal and mainstream subgroups within Canada, there are also important shared values that place importance on family, faith/spirituality, group belongingness and health. In addition, Canadian Aboriginal people have various traditions that demonstrate the high value they place on their emotional connectedness to nature and to the ecology of their physical environments (e.g., Stewart, 2009).

Like their Canadian counterparts, Australian Aboriginal families maintain a deep connection to their ancestral lands and very ancient cultural and linguistic traditions; in contrast to their rich cultural past, many contemporary Aboriginal families have had to struggle with daily stresses and adversities such as poverty, unemployment, family violence, and child abuse and neglect (Hopkins et al., 2012). Resilient outcomes are nonetheless possible for some Australian Aboriginal children who do well emotionally and behaviourally despite the history of risks faced by their families and their community's history of colonization and dispossession (Hopkins et al., 2012).

## Asian/Pacific Island Families

As with the other broad ethnic categories discussed in this chapter, Asian/Pacific Islander families represent a wide range of nearly 50 countries and ethnicities (e.g., Asian Americans and Pacific Islanders, 2015; Asian American & Pacific Islanders Initiative (AAPI), 2015). These ethnic groups originate from the regions of Eastern Asia (e.g., China, Japan, Korea, Taiwan), South Eastern Asia (e.g., Cambodia, Indonesia, Malaysia, Philippines, Thailand, Vietnam), South Asia (e.g., India, Nepal, Pakistan), and the various Pacific Islands of Polynesia, Micronesia and Melonesia. Like Trinh and his Vietnamese American family, many Asian families seem to share some important cultural values, as identified by Kim and Park (2013) and listed in Table 5.1. Among these are

**Table 5.1** Asian Cultural Values (Summarized from Kim & Park, 2013)

- Avoidance of shame that would reflect on the whole family.
- Collectivistic goals of group belongingness and promoting the good of the group over individual interests.
- Conforming to the norms set forth by one's families and local society.
- Deference to anyone in a position of greater authority.
- Filial piety and obedience without question to parents.
- Obligation and sense of duty to promote family honour and well-being.
- Maintain harmony, avoid conflict with others and permit others to save face.
- Putting others' needs before one's own is viewed as a sign of social and emotional maturity.
- Allow for mutual reciprocity when favours are given or received.
- Elders and ancestors should be honoured and respected for their wisdom.
- Emotional control and restraint is commendable and is viewed as a sign of strength.
- Being humble and taking a self-effacing stance rather than drawing attention to one's own accomplishments is highly valued.
- Academic and occupational successes are top priorities.
- Resolution of psychological problems through inner resources is a sign of strength while seeking help from others is a sign of weakness.

many traditional values stemming from an agricultural history and the teachings from Confucianism and Buddhism; there is a holistic view of the family unit, where what happens to one reflects on everyone, and interdependency and obligations to others to maintain harmony is encouraged (Lee, 1996).

Individuals from East Asian families differ from American families in the value they place on different emotional experiences. In ***affect valuation theory,*** which forms the basis for Tsai's research (Tsai, 2007), *ideal affect* (the way a person would ideally like to feel under certain conditions) differs from *actual affect* (the way a person typically feels under certain conditions). Tsai and her colleagues have found that adults from East Asian countries tend to nominate low arousal positive affect states that involve calm, relaxed, peaceful states as ideal, whereas adults from America are more likely to view high arousal positive states that include overt happiness, excitement and enthusiasm as ideal (Tsai, Knutson & Fung, 2006; Tsai, 2007). Similar patterns emerged in their work with children. Even after controlling for differences in children's temperament, Tsai and her colleagues found that European American children were more likely to prefer excited emotional states to calm ones than Taiwanese Chinese children. In addition, their studies indicate that one mechanism for the cultural transmission of these affect values within families is through picture storybooks, since the emotional content (e.g., smiles) of popular children's storybooks differ in Taiwan as compared to the United States (Tsai et al., 2007).

## African/Caribbean Families

Families with African ethnic origins are widespread throughout the world and this diffuse settlement of people, sometimes called a *diaspora*, is quite heterogeneous. The continent of Africa has 54 countries within its five major regions: Northern (e.g., Egypt, Libya, Morocco, Sudan), Eastern (e.g., Ethiopia, Kenya, Somalia), Middle (e.g., Cameroon, Chad Congo), Western (e.g., Ghana, Nigeria, Sierra Leone), and Southern (e.g., Botswana, Namibia, South Africa), and there are many indigenous Africans whose families have never migrated overseas. Noteworthy is the fact that early classic research on parent–child attachment behaviours was conducted in Kampala, Uganda, Africa by Mary Ainsworth and her colleagues (see History Feature Box 5).

However, because of the historically accepted practice of utilizing slave labour for economic gain in past centuries, some people with ancestral origins

## History Feature Box 5

### Back Then and Now: The Study of Parent–Child Attachment Across Cultures

Is the emotional bond and the need for attachment security between a mother and her infant found universally across cultures? The early work of the British psychoanalyst, John Bowlby, and the Canadian psychologist, Mary Ainsworth, from the 1940s into the 1970s led many Western researchers to answer this question with a resounding *yes* at that time. Although cultural experiences were thought to play some role in the expression of attachment behaviours back then, little attention was given to just how and to what extent specific components of enculturation were involved (Quinn & Mageo, 2013). Rather, the formation of an attachment bond between mothers and their children was viewed as being universal, biologically based, and the culmination of species-wide human evolution and survival (for reviews, see Rothbaum et al., 2000; Fitton, 2012).

Historically, the advantage of using Ainsworth's Strange Situation procedure (see History Feature Box 1) as a method has been that it allows for comparisons of the distributions of the four attachment categories in various countries across Africa, Asia, the Middle East, Europe and North America (see van IJzendoorn & Sagi-Schwartz, 2008, for a review). Since the 1980s, researchers have made cross-cultural comparisons of the distributions of the four standard Strange Situation procedure categories. These studies have shown that about half to more than half of the infants studied showed a secure pattern with the remaining infants distributed among the insecure or unclassified categories. However, cultural differences have also been noted with infants from Western European countries (e.g., North Germany) being more likely to fall into the avoidant pattern, and infants from Japan and Israel being more likely to fall into the resistant pattern (for summaries and critiques, see Gaskins, 2013; Keller, 2013; Steele & Steele, 2014; van IJzendoorn & Sagi-Schwartz, 2008). These findings and other cultural differences have been interpreted by considering differences in values, parenting goals and everyday childrearing practices. For instance, Western European cultures tend to emphasize independence and self-reliance under stress, and thus an infant under stress may be more likely to take flight, and ignore or avoid the caregiver (Steele & Steele, 2014). In contrast, Japanese and Israeli cultures tend to emphasize group dependency and looking to others when distressed, and thus distressed infants may be more likely to fight and show ambivalent resistance towards the caregiver (Steele & Steele, 2014).

Cross-cultural work on attachment continues to be an active area of research among scholars from a wide variety of disciplines including but not limited to psychology, psychiatry, nursing, social work and anthropology. Some contemporary scholars and researchers claim that attachment theory and how it has typically been assessed in the West using Ainsworth's standardized Strange Situation procedure, or the attachment Q-sort method (Waters & Deane, 1985), may apply best to the population upon which these methods were developed (Western, North American, middle-class mothers living in the middle to latter half of the 20th century) (e.g., Quinn & Mageo, 2013). Rather than only use the predefined categories from Ainsworth's original classification system in cross-cultural studies, some have suggested that it may also be fruitful to conduct field observations to capture the cultural meaning of attachment patterns within everyday contexts (e.g., Gaskins, 2013; Quinn & Mageo, 2013).

Studies of attachment patterns between caregivers and infants in other cultures have revealed a number of areas of cultural variation that are worthy of further study. For example, in many non-Western cultures, infants have multiple caretakers and interact with a large number of extended family members routinely, with some people, such as the mother, being more important than others in the attachment system (e.g., Keller, 2013; van IJzendoorn & Sagi-Schwartz, 2008). In cultures with high infant mortality and poverty, it may be culturally accepted for stressed mothers to be emotionally detached and selectively neglectful if there is a good chance a particular child won't survive (Rogoff, 2003); survival for such a child may mean attaching to others instead. Some infants also may have more routine experience in separating from those they are attached to and this may affect their reactions to separation in the Strange Situation procedure (Cole & Tan, 2007). Depending on the cultural context, strangers may be welcomed or viewed neutrally and infants may not react with stranger anxiety; thus, even if there is a universal predisposition for infants to have separation or stranger anxiety, it may or may not be activated depending on the cultural context (Keller, 2013). Thus, there may be cultural variation in the nature of attachment security, depending on who raises an infant – the mother only, a handful of select adults and/or older children, or many caregivers in an extended network (e.g., van IJzendoorn & Sagi-Schwartz, 2008). Researchers now note the importance of examining attachment security within the entire network of caregivers – not just the mother (e.g., van IJzendoorn & Sagi-Schwartz, 2008). Furthermore, the meaning of separation anxiety and stranger anxiety in infants likely varies by specific parenting values and goals within their cultural context (e.g., Keller, 2013). Today, then, although the original claim to the universal validity of attachment theory has increasing evidence in its favour, it is also recognized that cultural differences and variations in the meaning of how caregivers (including but not restricted to mothers) and infants relate to each other is worthy of further exploration and study.

in Africa were forced to travel overseas into the Americas and throughout the Caribbean islands (e.g., Bahamas, Puerto Rico, Trinidad, Jamaica) (Sterns, 2008). Such slave trade began in the latter half of the 15th century and lasted into the 19th century before finally diminishing once slavery was abolished (e.g., Sterns, 2008). Because much remains to be discovered and understood about the emotional ramifications of the history of slavery through the study of historical documents and artefacts, we will focus here on what is currently known about the emotional lives of families with ancestries from Africa or the Caribbean based on contemporary research.

As reviewed by Evans and George (2013), the following four main ideas can assist in understanding the worldview and values of contemporary people with origins in Africa. First, Africans often take a holistic view of human nature meaning that they view the mind, body, emotions and spirituality as integrated, and this integration is evident in their cultural expressions of music, dance, art and language. Second, the individual and family unit exists within a broader cultural group or tribe. The well-being of this broader group or tribe is what is most highly valued. Third, time is conceptualized differently than it is in the West, and rather than being "on time" as set by a clock as in the Western world, being "in time" is valued according to the occurrence of life events (e.g., a birth, puberty) or natural cycles (e.g., day/night or seasons). Finally, Evans and George (2013) describe that the spoken word, oral histories and being responsive to others when they speak are highly valued traditions in African cultures.

The African worldview is sometimes still apparent in the emotion socialization behaviours of families with an African/Caribbean ethnic background. Although many individuals display resilience despite adversities, the legacy left by a history of enslavement has negatively affected the emotional lives of families with African heritage in many ways. These range from being the target of institutionalized racism and discrimination to the harmful psychological effects of false stereotypes on black identity; as an example, one such false notion is inherent in the stereotype that African Americans are intellectually inferior and come from black single female-headed family that are poor and on welfare (Evans & George, 2013). In the 1940s to 1950s in the United States, the famous doll studies conducted by the African American psychologist couple, Kenneth Clark and Mamie Phipps Clark, demonstrated that African American children preferred a "white" doll whom they viewed as being good and more attractive over a "coloured" doll, even when they identified themselves as looking more like the coloured doll (e.g., Clark & Clark, 1947, 1950; Goodwin, 2010). The harmful emotional effects implied by these findings on the overall well-being of black children's self-concept and identity were apparent to many (e.g., Goodwin, 2010). The seminal research of the Clarks helped to form the argument supporting racial desegregation in schools in the United States; Kenneth Clark used social science research to show how discrimination and stereotypical thinking about race in America had harmful effects on the identities and personality development of African American children (Keppel, 2002).

Contemporary psychological research on the emotion socialization behaviours of African American parents is consistent with the position taken by Kenneth and Mamie Clark on the potentially destructive consequences of discrimination on black families. To safeguard their children from the remnants of racial discrimination and prejudice that still percolate as an undercurrent and sometimes become overt in American society, African American parents often undertake ***racial socialization*** efforts as noted by Evans and George (2013). This includes instilling pride in their family's racial and ancestral African heritage, and increasing children's awareness of racism and social injustice. Such cultural socialization practices such as teaching children about important African American historical figures have been reported by African American parents (e.g., Hughes & Johnson, 2001). Parents also work to provide corrective messages to counteract racial stereotypes, and to teach children to use the extended family and friend network for emotional support when there is social injustice (Evans & George, 2013). They may try to prepare their children for bias in their encounters with others by teaching them, for instance, that they should work harder and be better than others to achieve their goals and get ahead; in some cases, they may encourage their children to mistrust others given the history of problems between racial groups (e.g., Hughes & Johnson, 2001). Finally, African American parents often share the goal of teaching their children to be emotionally tough or thick-skinned so that they can cope well with the racism they encounter; they tend to be strict in their discipline as they want to prevent their children from getting into trouble with law enforcement (Evans & George, 2013).

Many recent studies show the links between such racial socialization and the emotion socialization patterns utilized by African American parents (e.g., Dunbar et al., 2015). Dunbar and her colleagues found that higher income African American mothers engaged in educating and promoting cultural understanding in their children of what it means to be Black in America today, and provided responsive emotional feedback to their children about negative emotions. Likewise, for higher income fathers, there were similar results but at more moderate levels. Other patterns emerged as well in parents of relatively lower income levels where children's cultural socialization involved either high or moderate levels of preparation for bias, promoting mistrust of other groups, and providing non-supportive responses to negative emotions such as anger and depression; in addition, some parents were low in clearly engaging their children in racial and emotion socialization. Although additional research is warranted, these researchers suggest that some African American parents may be utilizing various forms of emotion socialization strategies (e.g., teaching their children how and when to regulate negative emotions) in the service of preparing them for likely encounters with prejudice and discrimination in the broader society in which they live (Dunbar et al., 2015).

## Hispanic/Latino/Latina Families

In the United States, the terms Hispanic and Latino/Latina are sometimes used interchangeably to refer to Spanish-speaking people with historical links to Spain, and those with origins in more than 20 countries dispersed throughout the Americas and Caribbean (U.S. Census Bureau, 2011). These countries include Mexico, Puerto Rico, Cuba and the Dominican Republic, as well as countries in Central America (e.g., Costa Rica, El Salvador, Honduras, Guatemala) and South America (e.g., Argentina, Columbia, Ecuador, Peru and Venezuela) (U.S. Census Bureau, 2011). However, according to Delgado-Romero, Nevels, Capielo, Galvan and Torres (2013), the term "Hispanic" is misleading when used as an overarching umbrella term, because it places emphasis on White European Spanish ancestry and the history of colonization in the Americas by Spain, when in fact racial-ethnic diversity is characteristic of the referenced groups. In contrast, the terms Latino (masculine and generic) or Latina (feminine) are regarded as being more inclusive of the various people from Latin America who have mixed backgrounds including European Spanish or Portuguese origins, African slave origins, and/or an indigenous heritage (e.g., Mayan) (Delgado-Romero et al., 2013). Delgado-Romero et al. note that the term Hispanic has resulted in pan ethnic gloss and does not apply to people from Brazil, who were colonized by the Portuguese rather than the Spanish. These authors prefer the use of the terms Latino/Latina as being more inclusive than the term Hispanic, and highlight the importance of considering how individuals prefer to identify themselves. Throughout this book, the critique given by Delgado-Romero et al. is kept in mind, but the terminology used in the primary sources will be retained.

As reviewed by Dingfelder (2005), the cultural values of Latinos/Latinas include *familismo* (close emotional ties of loyalty and support among family members), *simpatia* (maintenance of interpersonal harmony), *respeto* (affording greater respect and deference to people in positions of authority), and *personalismo* (close, intimate self-disclosure in interpersonal relationships). The use of the Spanish language is a commonality among the various ethnic-racial groups who self-identify as Hispanic or Latino/Latina, and the use of Spanish may be especially important in considering emotion socialization in the families. Dingfelder (2005) reviews some studies suggesting that emotional words and events are processed and accessed better in a person's first language, such as Spanish, in the case of Latino immigrants to the United States.

When considering any immigrant family's emotional well-being, both enculturation (being socialized into the heritage cultural background) and acculturation processes (adopting and adapting to the new host culture) are quite important (e.g., Yoon, Langrehr & Ong, 2011). Yoon et al. emphasize that enculturating and acculturating do not necessarily proceed at uniform rates across various dimensions involving learning values and behaviours. Interestingly, *behavioural* enculturation/acculturation (e.g., learning and speaking the words of a culture's language, preparing foods of a given culture, and participating in cultural traditions) may occur before the adoption of the deeper values that a family may attempt to socialize (e.g., familismo, simpatia) (Yoon et al., 2011). Thus, learning concrete behaviours and language may precede a deeper internalization of emotion-related understanding influenced by cultural attitudes and values.

Latina American mothers are more likely to focus on social interdependence and public, other-focused behaviours in the socialization of their children when compared to European American mothers, who tend to emphasize independence and self-confidence in the emotion socialization of their children (e.g., Harwood, 1992; Perez Rivera & Dunsmore, 2011). It has been suggested that there may be greater tolerance for ambiguity and uncertainty in European American mothers given their greater acceptance of multiple individualistic points of view. Because social harmony and cooperation are highly valued in Latino culture, Latina mothers may be more active in trying to guide their children towards emotions that will promote harmonious interactions, although additional studies are needed to understand the processes involved using culturally relevant and sensitive measurements (Perez Rivera & Dunsmore, 2011).

Using the Eisenberg et al. (1998a, 1998b) model introduced in Chapter 1, Perez Rivera and Dunsmore (2011) examined how Latina mothers' beliefs about emotions and cultural norms and values regarding emotions were related to parent–child discourse about emotions, which in turn was examined in relation to children's emotion understanding and social competence. They found that both maternal acculturation and enculturation were related to Latina mothers' emotion beliefs and to their children's emotion understanding. For example, mothers' Latino enculturation was positively related to the belief that it was important for them to guide children's emotions, which is consistent with the cultural value of promoting social harmony. Also, Latina mothers who were more highly Anglo acculturated were less likely to believe that emotions were dangerous as compared to mothers who were less acculturated. In this study, Latina mothers' beliefs about emotion were related to observations of their emotion-related socialization behaviours during interactions with their children.

When mothers interact with their children and attempt to gain their compliance, they are teaching their children about emotions directly as well as indirectly. Mexican American mothers' attempts to gain compliance from their 4-year-old children during actual observed interactions were studied by Livas-Dlott and colleagues (2010). They found that mothers initially used direct, clear verbal commands or non-verbal gestures, which were low in power assertion; if necessary, some mothers followed up with inductive explanations or reasons for the need to comply. Mothers were also likely to demonstrate *cariño* (warmth and responsiveness) rather than angry, negative affect expressed in loud commands. There were few incidences of high power assertion strategies (i.e., emotional harshness, shaming or inducing guilt in the child, or physical punishment) in the attempt to gain compliance. Mothers employed some culturally specific strategies as well, such as trying to trick the child into complying.

Studies on the socialization of children by Latino parents have also been conducted with adolescents and emerging adults. For example, in their studies of Latino ethnic identity socialization, Umaña-Taylor and her colleagues have examined ***ethnic identity affirmation***, which involves the emotional content of ethnic identity – that is, the extent to which children have positive or negative feelings about their ethnicity (e.g., Umaña-Taylor, 2013). Think of this as asking yourself the question: *Do I like who I am and the cultural background of my ancestors?* Influential and emotionally charged messages about how to feel about one's own ethnic background have two primary sources: *family ethnic socialization* which includes the messages one receives from parents, grandparents, aunts, uncles, cousins and siblings, and *discrimination*, which involves messages received from others and the broader cultural context in which one resides (Umaña-Taylor & Guimond, 2010). Such issues also have relevance for families of other ethnic backgrounds, such as Arab and Middle Eastern.

## Arab/Middle Eastern Families

The term *Arab* is often used to refer to the mainly Arabic-speaking people with ethnic origins from one of the 22 states of the Arab League of States. Arab countries range from various regions in South Western Asia (e.g., Lebanon, Syria, Palestine, Iraq, Jordan, Saudi Arabia, Yemen) to Northern Africa (e.g., Egypt, Sudan, Tunisia) and Eastern Africa (e.g., Somalia) (e.g., BBC News, 2011). The term *Middle Eastern* often includes many of the Arab countries as well as non-Arabic-speaking people in the nearby countries of Afghanistan, Armenia, Pakistan, Iran, Israel and Turkey (e.g., Nassar-McMillan, Ajrouch & Hakim-Larson, 2014). Arab and Middle Eastern families often share a background in one of the three major world religions (e.g., Judaism, Christianity and Islam) that traces ancestry back to Abraham (Esposito, 2003). In addition to religious diversity, Arab and Middle Eastern people are racially diverse. These variations point to the importance of differentiating ethnicity (country of origin), race and religious background in attempting to understand an Arab or Middle Eastern family's values and beliefs (e.g., Samhan, 2014), and consequently how they may be involved in emotion socialization within extended family kinship networks. In addition to ethnic origins, the country where the family currently resides (i.e., their national identity) also may influence the emotion socialization of successive generations.

The traditional core values of Arab and Middle Eastern families include *collectivism* and *paternalism*. In collectivism, higher value is placed on cooperation and group needs and goals than on competition and individual needs or goals (e.g., Triandis, 1994). With paternalism, men are viewed as having greater power than women, and women are viewed as having traditional roles and being dependent on men (Feather, 2004; Glick & Fiske, 2001; Hakim-Larson, Nassar-McMillan & Paterson, 2013). Nydell (2006) lists the following as being important Arab values. First, individuals should *always* create a good impression on others. Second, as in other collectivistic cultures, individuals should maintain family pride, honour and reputation and avoid shameful behaviours because they reflect on the extended family. Third, behaving loyally to the family is more important than an individual's personal concerns. Fourth, family background and social class determine status and take priority over individual characteristics such as achievements, and finally, standards of morality must be upheld, through legal means if necessary (Nydell, 2006).

Researchers have increasingly noticed that the traditional values and beliefs of families from the Arab world and Middle East are being challenged. This challenge is occurring on several fronts given the changing landscape due to socio-economic advances from the oil boon (e.g., Crabtree, 2007), ongoing wars, political conflicts and refugee/immigrant status (Beitin & Aprahamian, 2014), and global communication via the internet (e.g., Mohammad Bin Rashid School of Government, 2014). In the Muslim oil-producing regions of the world such as the United Arab Emirates, parental expectations for traditional gender roles persist even though education is highly valued for both boys and girls (Crabtree, 2007). Parents and the culture encourage and support unmarried girls in obtaining an education and career, but the message they get may be riddled with ambiguity and ambivalence given tradition (Crabtree, 2007). Though girls may appreciate the alleviation of boredom by being able to attend school, they may also worry about the gossip and social pressures to conform that may ensue if they stray too far from tradition; furthermore, unmarried girls have low status, with married women afforded greater status and married women with sons given the highest status (Crabtree, 2007). Parents afford sons much more freedom than daughters; the permissive attitude towards boys and cultural changes towards modernization may lead to boys being at greater risk for academic underachievement and subsequent behavioural problems than girls (Crabtree, 2007).

Changes in traditions have also been found among the previously nomadic Bedouin tribes currently settled in the Negev region of Israel (Al-Krenawi & Lightman, 2000), as well as in other regions of the Arab world. Although only a minority of Muslim marriages are polygamous and there are attempts to maintain fairness in resource distributions, polygamy nonetheless has been found to be associated with more jealousy and family conflict as reported by the children in the families (Al-Krenawi & Lightman, 2000; Crabtree, 2007).

Exposure to wars, violence and political unrest has led to over 10 million people from the Arab world and Middle East (e.g., Iraq, Palestine and Syria) being identified as being in need of help; they have been successively displaced in camps and for some, finally resettled as immigrants in various regions around the world (United Nations High Commissioner for Refugees, 2016). The emotional lives of Arab/Middle Eastern families are affected by ongoing world events as well as family ethnic socialization and issues of discrimination. Among Arab/Middle Eastern families who have immigrated to the United States, children and families face acculturation stresses, discrimination (especially post 9/11), and intergenerational conflicts since children tend to adapt and accept Western culture at a faster pace than their parents (Beitin & Aprahamian, 2014). As summarized by Beitin and Aprahamian in their literature review on Arab American families, there are many opportunities for emotional family conflicts given that parents who are attempting to negotiate two worlds are attempting to socialize youth. Parents are trying to preserve and maintain their specific heritage culture from their country of origin, while at the same time trying to adapt to the here-and-now everyday concerns of the mainstream American culture in which they now live; furthermore, their marital relationships must adapt to the changing roles and expectations. Family emotional support, such as nurturing and accepting parenting behaviours, seems to be instrumental in helping to protect children who have histories of wartime trauma (either directly or vicariously) from negative mental health outcomes, and in promoting their resilience (Beitin & Aprahamian, 2014).

## Cultural Genograms

In this chapter, I have introduced the values of various cultural groups to show how culture may influence parents' goals as they attempt to socialize emotions in their children – a topic that will be addressed further throughout the remainder of this book. The transmission of cultural and emotional frameworks of how to make meaning out of life and everyday social interactions takes place across generations. ***Cultural genograms*** are family trees that symbolize a person's cultural ancestry (Hardy & Laszloffy, 1995); they provide some hints as to what may be most emotionally meaningful to adults as they socialize children.

Figure 5.1 depicts three generations of a hypothetical British family. The rectangles represent the male members of the family and the circles represent the female members of the family. At the top of the diagram are the grandparents, in the middle of the diagram are the parents, and at the bottom of the diagram are two children – a brother and a sister. The extended family is not represented but could include all the siblings and their children within the parents' and grandparents' generations; this more complete but quite complex picture would then depict the aunts, uncles and cousins of the brother and sister in the diagram. The father of the children in this diagram comes from a

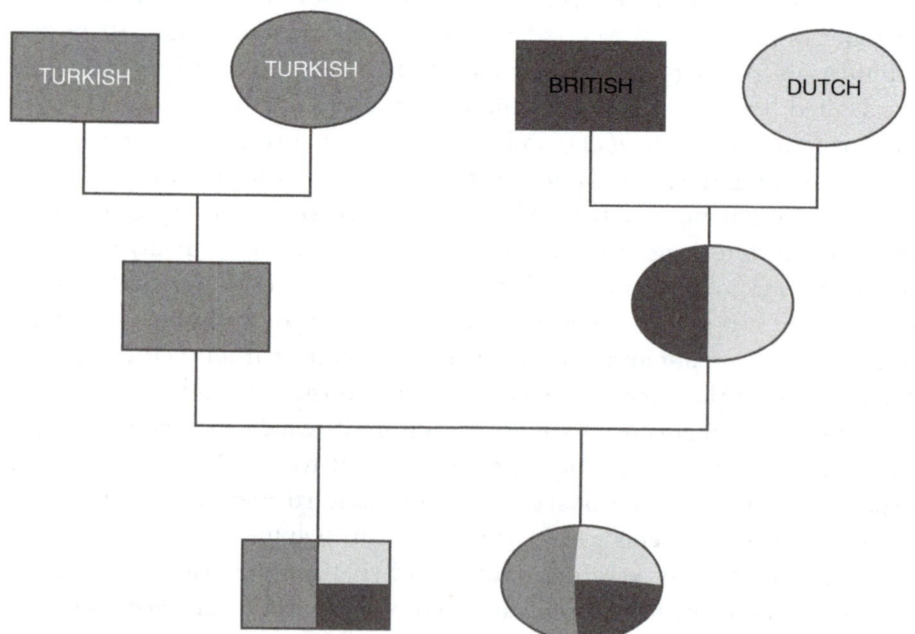


**Figure 5.1** Three Generation Cultural Genogram

Turkish Muslim family background, while the mother has a British Protestant background on her father's side and a Dutch Protestant ancestry on her mother's side. The father is a non-practising Muslim while the mother is a practising Protestant. The children thus have a national identity that is British and an ethnic identity that is half Turkish, one-quarter Dutch, and one-quarter British; they were raised as Protestants. One important function of cultural genograms is to show how the family's cultural values around emotions such as shame and pride might play into memories of emotional events that span from one generation to the next and laterally within the same generation (e.g., Hardy & Laszloffy, 1995; McAuliffe, 2008a, 2008b). For this Turkish father (whose parents are traditionally collectivistic and practising Muslims living in Turkey), we might ask, "What are the sources of shame and pride that he or his children might exhibit that could reflect upon the whole family's honour?" Even though contemporary values in Turkey are changing to be more democratic and less compulsory, educated Turkish parents currently continue to place high value on family emotional connectedness and may try to socialize this indirectly by modelling family interactions for their children such as having frequent phone conversations, visits, routines and rituals involving the extended family (Akyil et al., 2014). In this case example, we might wonder just how much contact the children have with their Turkish Muslim grandparents and their other relatives in Turkey. On the mother's side in the hypothetical example, the British influence on the children comes from both the mainstream culture in which they live and from her Protestant British father and Dutch mother; among the core values here are emotional restraint, strong work ethic and clear boundaries within a nuclear family (Richmond & Guindon, 2013). Marital happiness or satisfaction is related to the extent to which parents can resolve any differences they have on the values that they want to transmit to their children; also, parental tolerance of each other's values and good marital communication may be linked to the strength and success of value transmission to children (e.g., Akyil et al., 2014). Thus, in conducting a cultural genogram, it would be important to consider the extent to which the parents agree on the values to transmit, and the extent to which extended family is involved in emotion socialization.

## Summary of Chapter Key Points

This chapter provides a preliminary glance into the nature of how cultural values may be linked to emotion socialization behaviours in families. While being mindful to avoid ethnic gloss, it is important to understand how cultures might be contributing to emotion socialization. Cultures help to specify the positive (i.e., desirable) and negative (i.e., undesirable) social behaviours that family members may hold as goals for each other, although there are many other situational and biological factors at play; emotion socialization is important here as well because what family members do to regulate their emotions affects their social behaviours within the broader cultural context (Markus & Kitayama, 1991). In addition to individual and family differences in emotion socialization processes, differences may exist at the local, regional and national levels according to background ethnicity although much further research is needed. As reviewed in this chapter, researchers have started to identify emotion socialization processes in people from a variety of ethnic backgrounds including but not limited to European, Native/First Nations/ Aboriginal, Asian/Pacific Island, African/Caribbean, Hispanic/Latino/Latina and Arab/Middle Eastern families. In the next chapter, we turn to a consideration of how family beliefs, values and attitudes, including those that are informed by cultural values and norms, are related to various social and emotional behaviours.

## Further Reading

Matsumoto, D. & Hwang, H. S. (2012). Culture and emotion: The integration of biological and cultural contributions. *Journal of Cross-Cultural Psychology, 43(1)*, 91–118. doi: 10.1177/0022022111420147

Matsumoto and Hwang provide a useful framework for understanding the relative contributions of biology and culture along a continuum. Biology contributes more to priming (e.g., physiological responses) while culture contributes more to the role of emotion in values, attitudes and beliefs. Both biology and culture provide moderate contributions to subjective experiences. These authors recommend a classification system where some emotions are more biological and some more cultural. Biological emotions might include basic anger, disgust, fear, joy, sadness and surprise. It is not yet known what should qualify to be included under cultural emotions. However, culture provides meaning to our emotional experiences by prescribing norms and expectations. Cultures vary in how much attention they give to certain emotion words or concepts; some hypercognize (many variations) and some hypocognize (few variations).

van IJzendoorn, M. H. & Sagi-Schwartz, A. (2008). Cross-cultural patterns of attachment: Universal and contextual dimensions. In J. Cassidy & P. R. Shaver (Eds.), *Handbook of attachment: Theory, research, and clinical applications (2nd ed.)*, pp. 880–905. New York, NY: The Guilford Press.

van Ijzendoorn and Sagi-Schwarz make a compelling case based on research in non-Western societies for the universality and normality hypotheses stemming from attachment theory. They review studies showing that infants around the world have attachment systems that are activated particularly when they are in some danger or have needs potentially related to their survival. They also provide evidence from non-Western societies demonstrating that secure attachment is the normal (i.e., modal) type of attachment. Though additional research is needed, they claim that there is already considerable support for the cross-cultural validity of attachment theory as originally proposed by John Bowlby and Mary Ainsworth.

# 6

# Emotion-Related Parental Beliefs, Goals and Values

*Ann McGillicuddy-DeLisi is a developmental psychologist who has written about parental beliefs and how they relate to children's development. She is also a mother. One day, she was at a playground with her 4-year-old son who was busy on the swings. Ann began to observe two fathers of 3-year-old boys. The two fathers were playing frisbee with each other while their two sons were running around. One of the two boys who was very excited kicked the other boy in a karate-like movement. The boys continued to laugh and run around making physical contact occasionally, while the fathers continued to play frisbee with each other and the boys. Ann noticed that the boy who kicked was getting increasingly physical with the other child. She thought to herself, "That's the difference between mothers and fathers. A mother would see that this behavior is escalating and someone is bound to get hurt. She'd intervene now" (p. 115). After a while, there were sudden screams as the boy who kicked laughed as he sat on his friend while swinging his fists and hitting him. The father of the aggressive boy pulled him off his friend, spanked him hard three times, and reprimanded him telling him never to hit, and to apologize. Ann started to think that the father must not be aware of Albert Bandura's work on how children model, imitate and identify with others. Suddenly, a female neighbour who had also observed the episode said that she knew all along that the aggressive boy was going to go wild. Ann thought to herself that this woman understood her point of view – that is, that this father believed in using negative feedback to modify his son's behaviour and that he did not understand the role of imitation and identification in his son's misbehaviour. To validate her thoughts, Ann asked the female neighbour why she thought the boy acted as he did. Unexpectedly, the neighbour's response was that … "Boys are just so aggressive and physical. They can't help it"* (p. 116).

Source: Case study summary and excerpts from McGillicuddy-DeLisi, 1992, pp. 115–116.

## An Overview of Parental Beliefs

As illustrated in the example from McGillicuddy-DeLisi (1992), there are variations in parental beliefs about gender roles and/or inborn sex differences, as well as childrearing and discipline strategies. Parenting beliefs affect family members' emotional lives, as well as how they cognitively evaluate and appraise situations, their expectations for each other, and their behavioural responses. In addition, children and adolescents have belief systems about their parents, and spouses have beliefs about each other. Importantly, such beliefs may extend in a bidirectional manner across multiple generations. However, most of the currently available research that has been conducted has been on the influence of parental beliefs on child emotional and behavioural outcomes and so this topic in relation to family values and the socialization of emotions will be the primary focus of the current chapter.

***Parental beliefs*** are mental representations or schemas about children and parenting that are thought to originate from parents' own family and cultural backgrounds, as well as the setting and historical time frame in which they live (e.g., Sigel & McGillicuddy-DeLisi, 2002). Parental beliefs have been examined in various cultures and with reference to a wide variety of topics that may be related to parenting behaviours. Among these numerous topics are parents' thoughts and beliefs about food and eating behaviours, household chores, gender differences and roles, attributions or causal reasons for children's behaviours, childcare strategies, parental authority and discipline (e.g., Harkness & Super, 1996; Smetana, 1994), domains of personal choice for children, such as who gets to decide what clothing the child will wear on a given day (e.g., Nucci, 1994), and children's medical conditions and issues involving surgery (e.g., Miklósi et al., 2013) or immunizations (e.g., Johnson & Capdevila, 2014). While all of these domains of study involve family emotions and are worthy topics in their own right, most directly involved in the study of family emotion socialization are parents' beliefs about their own feeling of self-efficacy in their approach to parenting (e.g., Grusec, Hastings & Mammone, 1994), and parents' beliefs about emotions specifically in themselves and their children (e.g., Gottman, Katz & Hooven, 1996; Parker et al., 2012). Both areas of research are discussed next before addressing the topic of how values are related to parental beliefs, how parents may react intuitively in their emotion socialization attempts, and how parental beliefs may facilitate and enhance the development of prosocial behaviours.

## Parental Beliefs about Their Own Self-Efficacy

The study of parental self-efficacy emerges from the work of Albert Bandura (1977, 1982), who is also known for his emphasis on social learning through modelling and imitation. Bandura (1982) defined perceived self-efficacy as being "concerned with judgments of how well one can execute courses of action required to deal with prospective situations" (p. 122). More specifically, ***parental self-efficacy beliefs*** have been defined by Coleman and Karraker (1998) as entailing "an estimation of the degree to which parents perceive themselves to be capable of performing the varied tasks associated with this highly demanding role" (p. 47).

Parental self-efficacy involves having a good knowledge base and understanding of developmentally appropriate childcare tasks, self-confidence in the ability to engage in these tasks, belief in the child's ability to respond contingently to parental childcare efforts, and belief that a supportive network of family and friends is capable and willing to assist when needed (Coleman & Karraker, 1998). Parental self-efficacy can be thought of as originating from four main sources: (1) history of accumulated past experiences with parenting successes and failures, (2) vicarious (i.e., observed or having knowledge about) experiences of others around parenting issues, (3) verbal feedback from others regarding parenting behaviours, and (4) level of emotional arousal while parenting, whereby optimal level of physiological arousal may be linked to anticipations of success and higher than optimal levels of arousal to anticipations of failure (Bandura, 1989; Coleman & Karraker, 1998).

Parental self-efficacy and the associated feelings of confidence or uncertainty are tied to the emotional lives of parents and their attempts at emotion socialization in their children. For example, there are many important specific parental self-efficacy tasks involving the fostering of nurturance and children's emotional development as reviewed by Coleman and Karraker (1998). These include demonstrating parental competence in displaying emotional warmth and sensitivity to children's needs, being interested in and aware of children's feelings, expressing their own feelings, being a good listener especially as it involves children's feelings, and encouraging children's independence consistent with their level of development; the child outcomes associated with these behavioural competencies involve type of attachment security, predominant mood as positive or negative, ability to be affectionate, emotional regulation, self-esteem and capacity for empathy (Coleman & Karraker, 1998). Children are affected in two ways by the way their parents show self-efficacy: first, there is a *direct effect* in that children observe and may model the forms of parental self-efficacy displayed by their parents, and second, there may be *indirect effects* whereby parental self-efficacy affects parenting behaviours, which in turn affects child outcomes (Jones & Prinz, 2005).

Some studies have demonstrated that parenting self-efficacy is linked to challenging child behaviours as may occur with children who have developmental disabilities. Parents of children with disabilities have been known to experience less parenting self-efficacy than parents of children who are typically developing. Bugental (1992) suggests that parenting a difficult child can result in threats to parental confidence about engaging in caregiving activities and this appraised threat can result in defensive and negative emotional arousal and parenting behaviours. In such cases, it is possible that the accumulation of failed attempts at successfully meeting parenting goals erodes parental self-efficacy. As reviewed in the following section, parental uncertainty involving emotions is only one of several categories of parental beliefs about emotions in themselves and in their children.

## Emotion-Related Parental Beliefs: Views of Self and Child

Gottman, Katz and Hooven (1996) developed the concept of ***parental meta-emotion philosophy (PMEP)*** to refer to the thoughts and feelings parents have about the value and significance of their own emotions and those of their children. It has been noted by some researchers that both parental beliefs and parental behaviours regarding emotion are incorporated within the parental meta-emotion philosophy construct (e.g., Halberstadt et al., 2013). The concept of parental meta-emotion philosophy has inspired much research since its inception and these studies have been reviewed by Katz, Maliken and Stettler (2012). Some parents tend to engage in active emotion coaching behaviours with their children to teach them about emotions and their functions, while others tend to reject emotions by dismissing or disapproving of them because they believe they are not important. Still others may at times exhibit feelings of uncertainty about how they are socializing emotion in their children as mentioned earlier; such cases occur under some particularly challenging circumstances, such as raising a child with autism or another developmental disability (e.g., Bugental, 1992; Paterson et al., 2012). Fortunately, however, there is some evidence suggesting that parents of children with an autism spectrum disorder who nonetheless do engage in active emotion coaching may be providing a protective buffer for their children against the emergence of other disorders and behavioural problems (e.g., Wilson et al., 2013).

Katz et al. (2012) note that parents in general are teaching children about emotions whether deliberately or inadvertently in various ways. Parents model emotion-related behaviours for their children through their own emotional expressions and use of coping and regulation strategies. Both direct effects and indirect modelling effects on children may occur based on how parents react to children's emotions, and by whether and how they coach and discuss emotions with children. Parenting behaviours such as scaffolding, praising, validating and using self-disclosure are related to parent's meta-emotion philosophies. The component processes underlying parental meta-emotion philosophy are ***emotion acceptance, awareness and coaching***; although parental warmth is another relevant parenting variable, it is separate from the parental meta-emotion construct (Katz et al., 2012). As reviewed by Katz et al., parental emotion awareness, acceptance (versus rejection) and active emotion coaching (in contrast to a passive laissez-faire attitude) have been found to be related to children's emotional competence (i.e., their awareness, expression and regulation) and overall adjustment; the result is children with better physiological and behavioural self-regulation, fewer symptoms of disorders, higher feelings of self-worth and competence (i.e., self-esteem), and better social skills. Parent and child gender as well as child temperament may moderate the relation between parental meta-emotion philosophy and child adjustment; child age is a particularly important moderator for how parents socialize emotions in their children (Katz et al., 2012). That is, younger children in contrast to older ones may need to have emotions labelled and to be given direct guidance; thus, parental emotion awareness and coaching may be the most important component processes for this age group. In contrast, older children approaching puberty and adolescents may need a more indirect approach with relatively higher levels of parental acceptance and tolerance of their emotional ups and downs given the physiological changes occurring throughout their bodies and the ongoing maturation of their brains (e.g., Katz et al., 2012; Somerville & Casey, 2010; also see Chapter 3 of this book).

To operationalize concepts such as awareness, acceptance, coaching and regulation in the study of parental meta-emotion, Gottman and his colleagues developed the Meta-Emotion Interview (MEI) protocol in which parents were interviewed separately and audio-recorded as they responded to enquiries about anger, sadness and fear in themselves, their own parents and their children (e.g., Gottman, Katz & Hooven, 1997). Because of the time-intensive nature of the interview coding, questionnaire versions have been developed for use by parents (e.g., Gottman, 1997), and by researchers (e.g., Hakim-Larson et al., 2006; Lagacé-Séguin & Coplan, 2005; Paterson et al., 2012). More recently, because the parental meta-emotion construct incorporates both parental beliefs and behaviours regarding emotions (Halberstadt et al., 2013), qualitative methodology has been employed to study parental beliefs about emotions as a construct separate from parental behaviours (Parker et al., 2012).

Using focus groups and qualitative methods of analysis, Parker et al. (2012) studied parental beliefs about emotions in three different ethnic groups (African American, European American and Lumbee American Indian) living in the state of North Carolina. From their review of the literature, they identified three main themes that had been found in past studies and two new themes. The three themes expected based on past research were: (1) parental beliefs about the *value and acceptability* of children's negative and positive emotions, (2) parental beliefs that it is parents' role to *teach, guide and socialize* their children about emotions, and (3) parental beliefs regarding the *controllability* of emotions in children. Evidence for the importance of each of these themes was found in all three different ethnic groups by Parker et al. (2012). A few differences among the groups were found in some of the subthemes, however, such as whether parents should display negative emotion and have open conflicts with each other in front of children, the desirability or undesirability of the expression and control of specific emotions (e.g., love or pride), and whether children can and should learn to choose how they want to feel. Interestingly, some parents from each of the three ethnic groups singled out the need for boys to be more emotionally expressive than in the past, reflecting perhaps historical changes in gender roles. Two new themes that emerged from the focus groups were: (4) the role of emotions in the *relationship* between parents and their children, and (5) the *changeability* versus stability of emotions across time, generations and contexts. Some differences were found between the ethnic groups in the relational nature of emotions; for instance, European American and some African American parents felt it was acceptable for children to keep some of their feelings private, while other African American parents and the Lumbee American parents felt that it was important for parents to stay connected and know how their children were feeling all the time. Groups from each ethnicity discussed the value of emotional connectedness and the potential effects of emotional contagion in families. Focus group members from each ethnicity discussed how parental understanding of emotions can change over time as children develop, and from one generation to the next. As well, only focus group *fathers* from each ethnicity raised the idea that because emotions change and fluctuate, it was important not to be overly indulgent by dwelling on them with children; rather it was important to just experience the emotions and move on. Such differences found in qualitative data among the ethnic groups and between mothers and fathers raised questions for this group of researchers that led them to further explore parental beliefs using a questionnaire format and quantitative methods (Halberstadt et al., 2013).

Halberstadt et al. (2013) developed the *Parental Beliefs About Children's Emotions (PBACE)* questionnaire based on their own prior research and that of others studying parental meta-emotion and beliefs. They emphasized that parental beliefs are important precursors to parental actions and reactions with respect to their children; thus, to understand parental behaviours, their belief systems must first be clarified (e.g., Sigel, McGillicuddy-DeLisi & Goodnow, 1992). Furthermore, because such belief systems need to be understood by considering multiple ethnicities, parent gender (both mothers and fathers), and emotional valence (both positive and negative emotions), the PBACE was developed by carefully considering each of these variables as well as issues of reliability and validity. The resulting 33-item PBACE measure has the following seven subscales of parental beliefs: (1) beliefs that there is a cost or negative consequence to children showing intense positive emotions, (2) belief in the value of children experiencing and expressing anger, (3) belief that children use emotion to manipulate others or to get attention, (4) belief that children can control their emotional expressions, (5) beliefs about whether or not it is important for parents to know everything that their children are feeling, (6) belief about whether or not it is best for children to work out their emotions by themselves autonomously, and (7) belief in the stability of emotions and emotion styles over time (Halberstadt et al., 2013). An important consideration in the development of this measure involved the values about emotional experience and expression that were shared or that were disparate among parents from different ethnic groups living within the broader American culture, and how these may have affected their parental beliefs. Parents' own ethnic background then is related to their family values, emotion-related parental beliefs, and ultimately their caregiving behaviours.

## Emotion-Related Socialization Goals and Domains

When parents observe their children, they inevitably must make an appraisal of the external factors involved in the situation and make many cognitive inferences about their children's intentions, capabilities and age-related ability to self-control under the circumstances (Dix et al., 1986). The organization of parents' emotion lives and their emotional reactions to parenting in such circumstances is affected by their belief systems and the core values that guide the specific beliefs, as well as the outcomes they expect from their children and their own parenting behaviours (Dix, 1991). One socialization goal of parents may be to teach their children to believe in what they consider to be ethically right or wrong, good or bad, beautiful or ugly; emotions are involved whenever parents make and convey such evaluative judgements (Solomon, 2008). Parents are often emotionally invested in attempting to get their children to internalize or learn the values that they target as important; often these values include inhibiting antisocial behaviours, showing prosocial behaviours, and other non-moral values involving safety and health, having a work ethic, achievement-related goals, and social activities such as attending special events or dating (Vinik et al., 2013).

Parents' socialization goals have long been recognized as being important in children's ability to regulate their emotions (e.g., Goodnow & Collins, 1990). Goals, including those involving the internalization of values, are of importance in understanding how emotions are related to parental actions and children's responses (e.g., Carver & Scheier, 1990; Stein & Levine, 1990). Such goals may be anticipated, future-oriented end-states or ongoing processes, and may be short term or long term. Being motivated to move towards or away from something related to attaining the goal is clearly implied; such motivation and activation of goal-oriented behaviour involving approach and avoidance depends on the environmental situation, person variables, and where that goal fits in a hierarchy among various competing goals (e.g., Lazarus, 1991; Staub, 1989). Thus, at any given time, parents must balance and counterbalance many competing goals in their personal hierarchy. Interestingly, the competing goals may include those of others in the family system as well as that of the self.

Parental goals often include placing moral demands on children for competent prosocial behaviour as defined by their social group and culture, and demands on their children to acquire age-appropriate skills in everyday life (Kuczynski & Kochanska, 1995). Whether children fulfil their parents' expectations and internalize the desired values that parents intend them to learn may be related to the level of emotional arousal and the specific emotions experienced in both parents and children at the time of learning; the domain of socialization may also play a role as discussed further below (Vinik et al., 2013).

As shown in Table 6.1, Grusec and Davidov (2010, 2015) have described ***five domains of socialization*** relevant for understanding parent–child relationships and the parental behaviours that are directed at achieving parents' socialization goals. These domains broadly apply to parents' socialization of their children's cognitive, social and emotional skills, although what is emphasized within these different domains depends on just what specific skills are

**Table 6.1** Domains of Socialization: Parent–Child Relationships, Parental Behaviour and Mechanisms (Grusec & Davidov, 2010)

| Domain | Nature of parent–child relationship | Parental behavior that is required | Mechanism of socialization |
|---|---|---|---|
| Protection | Provider-recipient of protection | Alleviate child's distress | Confidence in protection |
| Reciprocity | Exchange/ equality | Comply with child's reasonable requests and influence attempts | Innate tendency to reciprocate |
| Control | Hierarchical | Use discipline method best suited for achieving parental goal | Acquired self-control |
| Guided Learning | Teacher–student | Match teaching to child's changing level of understanding | Internalization of language and approach used by the teacher |
| Group participation | Joint members of the same social group | Enable child to observe and take part in appropriate cultural practices | Firm sense of social identity |

Source: Grusec, J. E. & Davidov, M. Integrating different perspectives on socialization theory and research: A domain-specific approach. *Child Development, 81*(3), 687–709. doi:10.1111/j.1467-8624.2010.01426.x Wiley. 

the focus of parents' socialization goals. For our purposes in this chapter, the primary focus for these five domains will be on emotional skills as discussed in the literature review and synthesis by Grusec and Davidov (2010). In the Grusec and Davidov approach, the *protection domain* involves the parent as the provider of protection. The key activity of the parent is to be responsive to the child's distress and fears, and to help the child feel safe and secure; the outcome for the child, as apparent in many attachment studies, is that the child is better able to effectively cope with stress, and show empathy and trust in relating to others. The *reciprocity domain* involves mutual cooperative exchanges (e.g., in play) between parent and child, whereby the parent follows the child's lead and shows responsiveness to the child's reasonable requests for compliance. In addition to such receptive compliance by the parent which is reciprocated by the child, there is shared positive affect and emotional attunement with each other. The *control domain* involves parents exercising parental authority and power hierarchically over their children in their attempts to use discipline strategies that match their parental goals. The goals of parents and their children may conflict with each other in this domain, and thus may result in feelings of anger in all involved. However, when effective discipline is used, the outcome may be the development of self-control in the child and the internalization of the parents' values such that the child complies even when the parent is absent. The *guided learning domain* includes parents' active attempts to socialize their children by supporting them as they learn a wide variety of physical, academic, work-related, social and emotional skills, such as occurs during emotion coaching and what has been called scaffolding. The Russian psychologist, Lev Vygotsky, described the idea of the ***zone of proximal development*** in which a teacher helps a student with challenging learning material that is just beyond the student's current level of competence; the teacher effectively assists the learner by monitoring and maximizing engagement by providing appropriate structure, support and encouragement, known as ***scaffolding*** (e.g., Winsler, 2003). As applied to parental socialization, parents act as teachers for their children. By engaging in guided learning and scaffolding, parents may enhance their children's ability to adjust to their families, neighbourhoods, and to any other cultural subgroup and groups to which they belong by guiding them in learning complex skills; some examples would include how to prepare traditional ethnic foods or engage in valued artistic endeavours involving crafts, music, singing or dancing. Finally, in the *group participation domain* rather than direct guided learning, children learn by participation and observation of others in group-oriented activities that are imbued with the group's expectations, values and norms. Included here are family rituals, habits and routines such as at mealtimes or bedtimes, as well as gender-based activities or chores. Thus, the child develops a social identity and adopts some of the customs of his or her social group.

Grusec and Davidov (2010) also note that experiences and skills in one domain may conflict with those from another domain. For example, in the group participation domain, an extravagant over-the-top holiday party routinely experienced with the mother's side of the family can be quite pleasurable for a child. However, it is also possible that the child may experience conflicting, ambivalent or guilty feelings too if the father has been using guided learning at home to teach the child about the value of being frugal. Grusec and Davidov (2010, 2015) suggest that future studies may gain clarity from adopting an approach that incorporates specifying the domains of socialization in both the study design as well as in the interpretation of the study findings.

## Emotion-Related Family Values and the Role of Culture

As reviewed by Jonathan Haidt and Richard Schweder, among others, culture provides the moral context that helps individuals to make emotional meaning out of their everyday experiences, and cultures do so in accordance with ***three primary ethics*** that they use to varying degrees: autonomy, community and divinity (e.g., Shweder et al., 2008). For over 2000 years, the philosophical study of ethics has involved considerations of what is morally good and how to live a happy life (e.g., Robinson, 2004). However, cultures vary in what they consider to be morally good, and emotions are intricately involved. For example, as discussed by Shweder et al. (2008), when an *ethic of autonomy* is emphasized within a family and the family's culture, individual freedoms and rights are paramount and are highly valued. When individual rights are violated or freedoms restricted, the emotion of anger may be aroused directly or vicariously. In contrast, when an *ethic of community* is afforded relatively great value and meaning, protection of the collective extended family or community groups that the family belongs to is considered highly desirable, and this is achieved through expressions of loyalty, carrying out of one's duty and filial responsibilities, being respectful of others, maintaining group honour, and displaying restraint and self-control in physical appearance and behaviours. Thus, embarrassment and shame may occur when individual goals are successfully attained if they are not part of the collective's aims. Finally, Schweder et al. describe the *ethic of divinity* where people and sometimes animals are thought to have an inherent spiritual or god-like essence, with their physical bodies being a mere vessel or "temple" for their divinity. What is most valued then is a feeling of serenity and calmness that has moved beyond the experience of basic emotions. In Eastern traditions, a person may come to feel disgust at his or her own greediness for worldly desires and may try to move beyond the basic emotion of love, with its associated attachments to people and things, and hatred which binds the person to what is hated. Interestingly then, disgust as well as serenity and calmness are valued.

In Western philosophy and cultures, individual *virtues* are often idealized, considered highly desirable, and are woven throughout stories told to children. The highest virtues (e.g., love, hope and faith) were linked by medieval Christian scholars (e.g., Thomas Aquinas) to the mind and reason, while the desires or seven deadly sins (greed, lust, sloth, rage, gluttony, envy, pride/hubris) were linked to the body and emotions (e.g., Solomon, 2000). Parents' socialization goals are likely affected by their beliefs about virtues and what is needed to develop a child's character or personality. In Eastern cultures, as well, beliefs about virtues are linked to emotions. In Hindu thought, there are four basic worthwhile goals to aspire to in living a good life: (1) pleasure which is linked to sexual passion, (2) having control, autonomy or power which is linked to anger, (3) carrying out social duties and having moral virtue, linked to perseverance, and (4) attaining divinity through purity, sanctity and salvation which is linked to disgust or serenity (Shweder et al., 2008). Similarly, in Islam a Sufi Muslim mystic named al-Ghazali emphasized the virtues of wisdom, courage and temperance in the management of various emotional states (Shweder et al., 2008).

Given that the values adults hold vary by the culture within which they are embedded, parental beliefs too have been found to vary by culture. Harkness and Super (1996) note that cultures organize and give meaning to common parenting experiences; for example, tantrums in 2 year olds may be perceived as a temporary behaviour that occurs during a developmental stage in one culture, while in another it may be perceived as evidence of a stable personality characteristic that emerges early. Also, common parenting tasks that have been found to vary cross-culturally include how parents communicate with children, how they discipline them, and who parents turn to for help or advice in raising children. Such parenting cognitions that are thought to guide parents' behaviours and that vary by culture may be thought of as *parents' cultural belief systems* or *parental ethnotheories* which include folk theories of parenting beliefs (Harkness & Super, 1996). As described further in History Feature Box 6, variation in parental beliefs not only depend on the culture in which families live and the family's ethnic background, but also on the gender of the child and parent, and the historical period in which they live.

**History Feature Box 6**

**Back Then and Now: The History of Childhood and Parental Beliefs**

Throughout much of recorded world history, children have been perceived as the property of adults. The master of a household or parents were thought to have the ultimate say in major decisions affecting children, including whether they should be allowed to live or die. Among those children permitted to live, some were abandoned and only survived through their own resourcefulness or through the kindness of strangers or exploitation by others (Boswell, 1988). Children were historically expected to be obedient and respectfully deferential to their elders. The advent of individual children's rights is recent and is still being addressed in the worldwide arena (UNICEF, 2015). Today, there are many children, for example, who have had to sacrifice having an education so that they can engage in child labour for economic reasons benefiting their parents, families or other adults.

Consider this famous quote by the psychohistorian Lloyd DeMause (1974, p. 2), "The history of childhood is a nightmare from which we have only recently begun to awaken. The further back in history one goes, the lower the level of child care, and the more likely children are to be killed, abandoned, beaten, terrorized, and sexually abused." Throughout history as reviewed below, the evidence available to us summarized by Borstelmann (1983) suggests that conflicting parental beliefs often co-existed. On the one side, extreme parental strictness or even abusive discipline and control over children was highly valued along with children being obedient, respectful, and deferential to their elders and anyone in authority; on the other side, children's needs for love, affection, protection and playfulness were also at times acknowledged. Childrearing advice reflecting parental beliefs was given in ancient scriptures (e.g., the Bible) and in the writings of the ancient Greeks such as Plato and Aristotle; while the Greeks often emphasized nurture and education of the young, Roman fathers exercised their legal rights of life or death over their children even into their adult years (Borstelmann, 1983). Even though ideals about raising children consistent with Christian values emerged in the Middle Ages, these beliefs were not always reflected in practice, and infanticide as well as abandonment, child labour, and the sale of children persisted. Gradually, the education of middle and upper class boys increasingly took place in organized schools, but poor boys still had to work and forced child labour practices abounded (Borstelmann, 1983).

DeMause (1974) identified three major belief systems historically available to adults when they were presented with a child who had needs to be met: (1) *projection*, where the adult projects his or her own needs onto the child, (2) *reversal*, where the adult reverses roles with the child and uses the child as a substitute for an adult figure from his or her own childhood, and (3) *empathy*, where the adult empathizes with the child's wants and needs, and then acts accordingly in the attempt to nurture the child. Unsatisfied childhood needs of the parent may be acted out with projection; in reversal reactions, children may become "parentified" and take on inappropriate adult roles of responsibility. While parental affection and claims of parental love sometimes co-existed with abusive projection and reversal reactions to children throughout the historical records that he examined, DeMause describes finding occasional records of empathic reactions only during and after the 18th century. Thus, it appears that parental beliefs in socializing children by training them only began to appear in the 19th and 20th centuries. In addition, since the mid-20th century, some parental beliefs have emerged whereby it is considered optimal for parents to stay emotionally attuned to their children, empathize with each child's unique needs as expressed by the child himself or herself, and assist the child in attaining his or her own goals (DeMause, 1974).

Unfortunately, child labour and inadequate education of children has continued around the globe until the present day with numbers recently estimated at 168 million working children between the ages of 5 and 17 years (UNICEF, 2015). A gender disparity is especially clear among child domestic workers who are disproportionately female. These girls often live with their employers, are dependent upon them, and are quite vulnerable to being exploited and sexually abused (International Labour Organization, 2016). Fortunately, empathy for children and awareness of their rights are increasingly being promoted in the world arena with some positive results. That is, the statistics on child labour have shown a decline from 246 million child workers in 2000 to 168 million in 2012 with the sharpest decline in child labour among girls – a trend that will hopefully continue.

## Emotion-Related Parental Beliefs and the Enhancement of Prosocial Behaviour

Some researchers have taken the position that parental beliefs are modifiable and thus it is possible to enhance parents' knowledge base and train or educate them so that their beliefs and behaviours will result in more desirable and adaptive child outcomes such as prosocial behaviours (e.g., Ekmekci et al., 2015). *Parental sensitivity beliefs* involve the viewpoint that sensitive and responsive caregiving are ideal, desirable and important in promoting the welfare of children (e.g., Posada et al., 1995). Such parental sensitivity beliefs seem to be related to the protection domain of socialization (Grusec & Davidov, 2010). Some evidence suggests that these beliefs are held cross-culturally as ideals in a variety of ethnic groups within various countries, even when differences are found in actual parental sensitivity behaviours (e.g., emotional availability, responsiveness); notably, when such differences in parental sensitivity behaviours are found, it is low socio-economic status and family stresses, rather than cultural values per se, that seem to be the probable antecedent (e.g., Emmen et al., 2012).

An important facet of emotion socialization is to proactively promote prosocial emotional experiences rather than to merely be reactive in trying to prevent future emotional dysfunction and misbehaviours by disciplining the child via punishments or rewards (Padilla-Walker, 2014). Parents' underlying values and belief systems guide them in such proactive prosocial promotional efforts. As highlighted further below, Padilla-Walker (2014) describes the various ways that parents can potentially accomplish this. First, parents must be *self-aware* of just what prosocial values and beliefs they want their children to adopt; for example, these might include sympathetic and empathetic understanding, sharing of emotions and tangible materials, unsolicited displays of kindness and compassion, and helping others. Second, parents need to be able to convey these messages about their values and beliefs quite clearly to their children by being *consistent* in what they transmit across contexts and over time; the child must be able to perceive the messages as appropriate, acceptable and feasible given the world in which they live their daily lives, so that the child is then motivated to internalize and utilize parental beliefs as their own (e.g., Grusec, Goodnow & Kuczynski, 2000). Adolescents are attuned to what they perceive as hypocritical parental behaviour and discrepancies between what parents say they believe and how they behave. Here it is important to recognize that it is possible that some children may unwittingly or deliberately reject adopting their parents' values and beliefs for any number of possible reasons, a topic worthy of systematic research. Third, to optimize the adoption of prosocial parental beliefs, parents can monitor their children's activities including media exposure, proactively teach the child about the meaning of emotions in various situations as well as how to cope with emotions and how to respond to others; parents can also engage in inspiring conversations about parental beliefs that are neither preachy nor demanding in tone (Padilla-Walker, 2014). For instance, suppose a parent seizes an opportunity to teach a child about parental beliefs regarding a moral issue after the parent and child watch a movie together. ***Parental prearming*** would take place when the parent discusses the prosocial actions of the movie characters and highlights the possible positive and negative influences that may result, thus preparing the child in an anticipatory way for similar real-life situations (Padilla-Walker, 2014). Finally, parents can provide experiential learning opportunities for their children to encourage (but not demand) their voluntary participation in activities consistent with parental beliefs about prosocial values. Examples here would be helping with everyday household chores or donating time to volunteer at community or religious organizations. The bottom line is that parents must accurately convey their prosocial beliefs and children must be able to accurately perceive and accept them before these are adopted and translated into behaviours; cultures play a role since some cultures provide more cohesive organizational structures that allow children to observe at their own pace what is going on from the periphery and to participate in culturally sanctioned behaviours gradually over time (Padilla-Walker, 2014).

Because parents within different cultures vary in their beliefs, goals, values and emotion socialization, they are providing their children with specific motivations and expectations linked to how they express and control their emotions. Some researchers have utilized Edward T. Hall's (1976) constructs of low and high context cultures to better understand this issue (e.g., Crowe et al., 2012; Gudykunst et al., 1996). In *low context* cultures, there is direct, explicit, verbal communication of emotions, while in *high context* cultures, communication is indirect and implicit, and individuals verbally describe the situation and, based on what is said, expect others to infer underlying emotions. Gudykunst et al. (1996) compared individuals from several cultures that differed in individualism and collectivism and found that individual self-construal and individual values mediated the relation between cultural individualism–collectivism and the person's approach to communication behaviours. Consistent with this view, Crowe et al. (2012) compared emotional expression and control in young adults from the US and India. They found more self-focused motivations for controlling emotions, such as avoiding discomfort and a desire for privacy in the US, which is a low context society; individual needs, desires and emotions are communicated explicitly. In contrast, in India which is a high context society, the researchers found more relationship-focused motivations for controlling emotion involving prosocial reasons and maintaining social norms; being familiar with the cultural values and possible emotional outcomes was implicit and was expected to be understood based on the situation that was described. Vaishali Raval and her colleagues (e.g., McCord & Raval, 2016; Raval, Raval & Deo, 2014) have conducted a series of studies demonstrating that parental emotion socialization goals for both children and adolescents often differ within the US as compared to India.

While parental beliefs, goals and values form the basis for many individual differences in emotion socialization between parents and families in various cultures, there nonetheless are some similar ways in which parents socialize emotions across cultures. This is quite apparent especially in the non-verbal domain of emotional expressions as described further in the next chapter.

## Summary of Chapter Key Points

Although parents can hold beliefs about any aspect of their parenting role, the focus in this chapter was on parental self-efficacy beliefs and emotion-related parental beliefs, goals and values. Parental self-efficacy beliefs are linked to how certain and confident parents feel about themselves as parents. In general, emotion-related parental beliefs are important to understand because they may be linked to parental behaviours and ultimately to child outcomes. Important influences on such beliefs include both cultural values and the gender of the parent and child, which have gone through many changes over historical time. Parents often aspire to transmitting their own beliefs and values to their children, thus making the potential significance one that can last for more than one generation. It is important to note that parents' emotion socialization goals occur within various domains of socialization and that these may sometimes be in conflict with each other, making it necessary for goals to be prioritized. Emotion-related parental beliefs are potentially modifiable and thus interventions could start by assessing the emotion-related parental beliefs, goals and values that parents desire to pass on to their children. In addition to reviewing the reactive methods of disciplining and providing consequences for children, parents could be introduced to the various ways in which they might proactively promote their own prosocial beliefs, goals and values for their children. One promising method involves parents discussing and evaluating with their children media depictions of character beliefs, values and goals. This method allows parental prearming to occur in which children are better prepared to anticipate how they will react emotionally to real-life events. Researchers have begun identifying how the ethics promoted by cultures differentially influence parental beliefs, goals and values, and thus the emotion socialization of youth.

## Further Reading

Gottman, J. (with J. DeClaire) (1997). *The heart of parenting: Raising an emotionally intelligent child.* New York: Simon & Schuster.

This popular book by John Gottman is an excellent resource for parents and any adults who want to better understand their own current approach to socializing emotions in children. Gottman provides the reader with a way to self-assess the understanding and awareness of emotions in the self and in children. The book also explains the parenting emotion styles originally identified by Gottman and his colleagues based on their programme of research on parents interacting with their children. Some tips and strategies for how to be an effective emotion coach for children are also provided for readers.

Harkness, S. & Super, C. M. (Eds.) (1996). *Parents' cultural belief systems: Their origins, expressions, and consequences.* New York: Guilford Press.

As the title implies, this volume contains chapters examining the ways in which there are similarities and differences in parental belief systems as a function of parents' cultural origins. Both intracultural and cross-cultural variation are described and specific studies conducted in the Americas, Europe, Asia and Africa are reviewed. The focus in the chapters is on parental ethnotheories regarding the role of parenting. Links are made in some chapters between parental beliefs and practices, as well as between parental beliefs and the potential consequences of the beliefs for children's health and well-being. This book has served as a foundation for many later studies.

Sigel, I. E., McGillicuddy-DeLisi, A.V. & Goodnow, J. J. (Eds.) (1992) *Parental belief systems: The psychological consequences for children (2nd ed.)*. Hillsdale, NJ, England: Lawrence Erlbaum Associates.

This second edition book provides a useful introductory foundation for understanding the study of parental beliefs. It contains widely cited chapters on parent belief systems involving a variety of target groups including young children, adolescents, typically developing youth, and atypically developing youth. The book also contains chapters on conceptual and methodological issues that are important in trying to link parent cognitions to parent behaviours.

# 7

# Non-Verbal Emotional Expressions in the Family Context

*Anna is a typically developing girl who is small for her age. It's Anna's 9th birthday, and her family celebration this year included her immediate family as well as her aunts, uncles and cousins at a large family reunion picnic in a park on a sunny summer day. As to be expected in North American cultures, birthday parties are a happy occasion and the emotional tone and demeanour of everyone at this picnic was relaxed and positive. Anna smiled broadly as the time came for her to open her presents. Great Aunt Tillie, who had not seen Anna since she was a toddler, handed her a brightly wrapped package. Anna looked up and smiled just before she opened the gift, which was a box of sewing cards with drawings of circus animals meant for a much younger preschool-aged child. Anna's smile quickly disappeared momentarily as she grimaced and bit her bottom lip and touched her face and hair. Feeling disappointed, Anna then anxiously glanced back and forth between her mother and her great aunt, seeming to not know what to say or do. Her mother smiled and Anna then smiled again broadly, thanked her great aunt for the gift, and moved on to opening her next present.*

## The Human Face and Emotional Expressions

Paul Ekman and Wallace Friesen (1975) have described ***display rules*** as rules that we learn to manage our facial expressions of emotion within a given situation. Some *cultural display rules* are well-ingrained conventions or customs that are specific to a given culture, while others are more *personal display rules* that are idiosyncratic to a person's family upbringing. In a now classic psychology study, Carolyn Saarni (1984, 1999) identified such display rules in 6 to 11-year-old children who were given a task to perform and then given a disappointing baby toy gift for their efforts. She found that 6 year olds did not hide their disappointment, and made negative facial expressions such as frowning. Like Anna in the opening example, 8 and 9 year olds were aware of their dilemma; they were uncertain as to whether it was okay to show their disappointment or whether they should follow the cultural display rule to "look agreeable when you get a gift, even if you don't like it" (Saarni, 1999, p. 189). In North America, by the age of about 10 or 11, children seemed to understand the culturally sanctioned reasons for inhibiting negative facial expressions and showing positive expressions instead in certain social situations.

Thus, children learn rules of how, when and where to express their emotions non-verbally from both their families and their cultures. Paul Ekman, Wallace Friesen, Carroll Izard and Carol Malatesta/Magai view basic discrete emotional expressions such as angry, fearful, sad, happy, disgusted and surprised as inborn and universal across cultures; their work stems from the seminal ideas put forth by Charles Darwin and later elaborated upon by Silvan Tomkins (see History Feature Box 7).

**History Feature Box 7**

**Back Then and Now: Evolutionary Theory and Facial Expressions**

In addition to his seminal book on evolution, *The Origin of Species* (1909/1937), Charles Darwin is also known for writing about observations of emotions across species and cultures in another seminal volume called *The Expression of the Emotions in Man and Animals* (1872/2008). In this work, he describes *serviceable associated habits*, whereby facial movements occur to perform a function such as baring teeth to bite when angry; habits such as these then may show up in a weaker diluted form under similar conditions not only in the person who first experienced it, but in later generations as well. Thus, Darwin subscribed to Jean-Baptiste Lamarck's view of the *inheritance of acquired characteristics* (Pinker, 2008). While Lamarck's view fell out of favour for many decades (Pickren & Rutherford, 2010), it has been revived to some extent in the contemporary theorizing on *epigenetics*, which involves mutations and environmental effects on a person's genetic make-up which can then be transmitted across generations (Skinner, 2015). Theoretically (although evidence is lacking), what this means is that habitual expressions of anger, fear or depression, for example, could get encoded into a person's genetic make-up and transmitted to their offspring! This possibility has shed further controversy about the roles of nature and nurture in emotional expression.

Darwin's (1872/2008) writings on facial expressions reflecting the emotions of joy, anger, contempt, disgust, fear and surprise, among other emotions, formed the basis for the work of Silvan Tomkins in the mid-20th century (e.g., Tomkins, 1962). Tomkins' ideas include the ***facial feedback*** hypothesis, in which our experience of affect arises from conscious or unconscious feedback from our facial muscle movements (Tomkins & McCarter, 1964). Feedback from our skin (e.g., blushing, sweating or hair standing on end) amplifies the emotional experience and can make a good thing even better or a bad thing even worse (Tomkins, 1978). Tomkins (1981) proposed that emotions are the primary motivators of human behaviour (not drives) and this is because "without *affect amplification*, nothing else matters, and with its amplification, anything can matter" (p. 322, emphasis added). In other words, affects are very general and flexible across time and space, and can thus *co-assemble* with just about anything including memories, thoughts, perceptions and behaviours; one primary way that amplification occurs is by increasing the *urgency* of the matter at hand as reflected analogically in the associated neural firing patterns which vary in quality such as frequency and duration (Tomkins, 1981).

Both Darwin and Tomkins maintained that emotions were inborn and there was a cross-cultural or universal basis for some emotional expressions; this is not to say that they did not think experience played a role in other emotional expressions. This view has been adopted by two well-known contemporary emotion researchers, Paul Ekman and Carroll Izard, who were greatly influenced by Darwin and Tomkins. While Ekman and his colleague, Wallace Friesen, focused on developing a coding system for the specific muscle movements of the facial expressions of adults (Facial Action Coding System (FACS); Ekman & Friesen, 1975, 1978), Izard and his colleagues developed the MAX and AFFEX coding systems for the facial expressions of infants (cited in Camras & Fatani, 2008; see the film *Life's First Feelings* (NOVA/WGBH, 1986) for video footage using Izard's coding system).

In his *differential emotions theory (DET)*, Izard (1993) followed upon the work of Darwin and Tomkins in describing his discrete emotions approach whereby some (not all) emotional expressions are separate, unique biologically based core patterns of emotion that serve evolutionary adaptive functions and are universally recognized and acknowledged. These emotions include joy or happiness, sadness, disgust, anger, shame, interest, surprise and fear, and are readily observed in natural settings in the facial expressions of infants and young children (Izard, 1993; Izard in the film *Life's First Feelings* (NOVA/WGBH, 1986)). The coding of facial expressions by Izard and his colleagues makes use of the MAX facial affect coding system in which specific facial movements are translated into one or more discrete emotion verbal labels such as angry, sad, fearful or happy.

Although basic emotional expressions begin as innate, children learn ways to modify their emotional expressions depending on social and cultural circumstances. Children learn rules about emotions from their families and culture of how, when and where to express their feelings according to *display rules* (Ekman & Friesen, 1975). By the time we are adults, we have learned how to *minimize, maximize* or *exaggerate* expressions, *mask* them by putting on a neutral, poker face, and how to make *substitutions* by showing expressions that differ from how we feel. Research on facial expressions of adults by Ekman, Friesen and their colleagues makes use of Ekman's Facial Action Coding System (FACS) which, like Izard's coding system, identifies specific facial muscle movement patterns and assigns verbal labels to them.

As described by Ekman and Friesen (1975), facial deceit involves trying to modify or falsify facial expressions to conceal one's true underlying feelings; however, it is much more difficult to lie with facial expressions than it is to lie with words.

While people can often control the lower portion of their faces such as when they smile when they are upset, the upper part of the face around the eyes and forehead is harder to control and thus provides more clues as to how a person might feel. In his book on *Why Kids Lie: How Parents Can Encourage Truthfulness*, Ekman (1989) advises parents to attend to and address the underlying motivations for children's attempts to deceive in both their facial expressions and words. Lying is a violation of trust in communication, but occurs nonetheless in the workplace and within the family context among siblings, parents and children, and between spouses, such as in cases of marital infidelity. Contemporary interest in Ekman's approach to reading subtle facial cues to detect facial deceit has resulted in a popular television show, *Lie to Me*, that aired for three years, and in training packages for improving non-verbal decoding accuracy (see www.paulekman.com).

Even though the basic facial expressions have a biological basis, family and culture play a strong role in their management through the socialization of display rules. As a consequence, depending on the situation, infants may imitate emotions in others and young children learn how to reduce or exaggerate these inborn expressions; they also learn how to mask emotions by putting on a neutral, expressionless face, and how to make substitutions by replacing expressions of how they really feel (e.g., angry or afraid) with some other identifiable expression, such as smiling (Ekman & Friesen, 1975). Such dissemblance or facial deceit may be necessary in many family situations, such as when one family member is trying not to show an angry expression to another because it might escalate or fuel a conflict even further.

Interestingly, discrete emotional facial expressions continue to change and become modulated over time and with age due to the influence of family and cultural display rules across the lifespan as evidenced in studies comparing younger, middle-aged and older adults (Magai, 2008). Older women have been found to display more complex blends of emotions than younger women (Malatesta & Izard, 1984). In her review of the evidence for age-related changes in detecting emotions in others, Magai (2008) concludes that older adults are just as accurate as younger ones in recognizing emotions, except possibly for sadness.

In addition to the discrete emotion theories stemming from the work of Darwin, there are several other contemporary theories and approaches to the development of facial expressions and these are briefly described below (see Camras & Fatani, 2008 and Table 7.1 for a summary). The developmental *differentiation theory* of individual development was originally proposed by Katherine Bridges (1932) and then elaborated upon by Alan Sroufe (1996).

**Table 7.1** Summary Table of Theoretical Approaches to Facial Expressions of Emotion

| *Theoretical Approach* | *Key Proponents and Relevant Sample Ideas* | *Brief General Description* |
|---|---|---|
| **Discrete Emotions** | • Charles Darwin (serviceable associated habits)<br>• Silvan Tomkins (facial feedback, amplification, emotion co-assemblies)<br>• Carroll Izard (DET – differential emotions theory)<br>• Paul Ekman & Wallace Friesen (display rules)<br>• Carol Malatesta/Magai (adult masking, blending, fragmentation) | Evolutionary and biologically based individual patterns of facial emotions that are universally recognized across cultures. Includes anger, sadness, joy, fear, disgust, contempt, shame, interest and surprise. |
| **Differentiation Theories** | • Katherine Bridges (developmental process of differentiation and integration)<br>• Alan Sroufe (from pre-emotion reactions and precursor emotions to more mature emotions in the first year) | Emotion states are undifferentiated initially (excitement) and then differentiate to delight or distress and finally to more discrete individual emotions. |
| **Ontogenetic View of Expressive Development** | • Harriet Oster (the specific signal value and meaning of emotional states vary over time and situations) | Facial expressions are related to different adaptation demands in children and adults, and cover a wide variety of regulatory attempts. |
| **The Functionalist Approach** | • Joseph Campos and Karen Barrett (emotion expressions are linked to eliciting conditions that vary by the person's goals) | Functional attempts to obtain goals while interacting with some aspect of the environment. |
| **A Sociocultural Internalization Model** | • Manfred Holodynski and Wolfgang Friedlmeier (affect mirroring, parent–child co-regulative system) | Interactions with caregivers result in links between emotions and expressions that are internalized by children. |
| **Dynamical Systems or Differentiation and Dynamical Integration (DDI) Approaches** | • Esther Thelen, Alan Fogel, Linda Camras (principle of self-organization, attractor states) | The emotion system and facial expression system are not initially synchronized in development and the various components develop heterochronically (i.e., at different rates). |

Sources: Camras (2011); Camras & Fatani (2008); Holodynski & Friedlmeier (2006); Lazarus (1991); Malatesta & Izard (1984); Osofsky (1987); Sroufe (1996).

Undifferentiated emotional states of distress or excitement occur initially in the young infant; eventually, however, these states become differentiated and mature into more recognizable patterns of anger, fear, or pleasure and joy. Harriet Oster (2005) takes an *ontogenetic view of expressive development* noting that there are likely differences in the meaning and purpose of facial expressions in infants as compared to older children or adults. The *functionalist* approach of Joseph Campos and Karen Barrett (e.g., Barrett & Campos, 1987) views emotional responses as functional attempts to obtain an individual's desired goals; these emotional responses are not preprogrammed or predetermined by innate fixed patterns (Camras & Fatani, 2008). Rather, it is the *set of functional relationships* between the individual and the environment that determine the presence of any given emotion (Barrett & Campos, 1987). In the *sociocultural internalization model* of Manfred Holodynski and Wolfgang Friedlmeier (2006), infants mimic their parents' expressions during interactions; as well, parents engage in ***affect mirroring*** of their children's emotional states as part of the process that allows children to be socialized in their emotions. In this model, parents attempt to interpret their children's emotional and motivational states and expression signs, and try to confirm their interpretation by exaggerating the child's expression and mirroring it back to the child, who may then mimic it. As this happens, parents also attempt to show the child how to modulate and cope with the underlying emotion, all of which is part of the socialization process and the child's internalization of their parents' and culture's way of expressing emotion (Holodynski & Friedlmeier, 2006). The dynamical systems, or differentiation and dynamical integration (DDI) approach (e.g., Camras, 2011; Camras & Fatani, 2008) introduced and described more fully in Chapter 3, places emphasis on the multiple components involved in children being socialized in their emotional expressions; these components change heterochronically (i.e., they do not all develop at the same rate). In this approach, it is not simply maturation or socialization that leads to emotion patterns, but also the individual's own process of self-organization whereby there are attempts at coordination of the components (e.g., Camras & Fatani, 2008). Parental sensitivity to infant facial expressions and cues is integrated dynamically with the context (Mesman, Oster & Camras, 2012).

In this chapter, some of the growing body of research on non-verbal emotional expressions will be reviewed beginning with the early mother–child interactions, proceeding to school-age children and adolescents, and on to the non-verbal emotion communication among adults within families. Both emotional ***expression accuracy*** in sending emotional messages, as well as non-verbal ***decoding (judgement) accuracy*** while receiving and interpreting emotional messages are important in contemporary studies on emotional expression and thus both are addressed as well in this chapter.

## Mother–Child Non-Verbal Interactions

Developmentally, during infancy and the preschool years, non-verbal emotional expressions in the face and body precede verbal expressions of emotion and provide a powerful medium for the communication and socialization of emotions (e.g., Denham, 1998). For preverbal infants, there is a heavy reliance on non-verbal interactions with their caregivers and the adaptive synchrony that occurs in the give-and-take of their facial expressions and emotional vocalizations. Such face-to-face interactions between mothers and their infants have been found to be bidirectional in influence with mothers responding to infants and infants responding to mothers. Even as young as the newborn period, infants have been shown to engage in ***facial mimicry*** whereby they imitate the emotional expressions on the faces of others; if an adult looks disgusted and sticks out his tongue at a baby, the baby may do the same, or if an adult opens his or her mouth wide and looks surprised, the infant may do the same (Meltzoff & Moore, 1977). With such imitation, however, it seems unlikely that the newborn and the adult are sharing a similar inner subjective experience (Hess, Houde & Fischer, 2014).

In contrast, the earliest form of empathy may be a type of *emotion contagion* in which newborns or young infants not only mimic the emotional expression of others but also appear to be having the same inner subjective emotional experience; a good example of this is when a group of infants are in the same room and one begins to cry, followed by each of the others doing the same, all eventually demonstrating distress (Hess, Houde & Fischer, 2014; Saarni, 1999). However, when somewhat older infants are in an ambiguous social situation, they may scan and attempt to read the facial expressions of others, especially their caregivers, to tap into the emotional meaning of the situation; this ***social or affective referencing*** is a valuable strategy used over the course of the lifespan to better understand uncertain emotional situations (Saarni, 1999). In their classic study on such social or affective referencing, Sorce, Emde, Campos and Klinnert (1985) demonstrated that by 12 months of age, infants can use the emotional expressions of their caregivers to make emotional meaning out of ambiguous social situations and to guide their behaviour. Their study used visual cliff apparatus with a drop about the depth of a stairway step that an infant had to cross to obtain a desirable toy; infants who had just started to crawl perceived the drop as an ambiguous one and were uncertain about whether or not it was okay to cross. The experimenters trained the caregivers to display fake facial expressions as the child approached the drop off (e.g., a smile indicating that it was okay to cross, or a fearful expression, suggesting that it was not); as expected, they found that when the caregivers smiled, the infants were more likely to cross, and when caregivers showed a fearful facial expression, the infants were wary and much less likely to attempt to cross (for a demonstration from this study, see the film *Life's First Feelings* (NOVA/WGBH, 1986)). Thus, infants are especially attuned to receiving social signals from their caregivers' facial and bodily expressions and the caregivers in turn must be sensitive to the child's emotional needs.

Mechthild Papoušek and Hanuš Papoušek and their colleagues have conducted a series of studies in which they demonstrate the many measurable ways in which mothers are intuitively sensitive to the emotional needs of their preverbal developing infants; they have called this phenomenon ***intuitive parenting*** and suggest that these behaviours have evolved to facilitate infant learning (e.g., Papoušek, 2007; Papoušek & Papoušek, 1989). That is, in interactions with preverbal infants, mothers seem to intuitively make appropriate adjustments in their own behaviours for the goal of facilitating infant learning. They slow down, speed up, and exaggerate their non-verbal expressions, gestures and a variety of speech sound patterns; in addition, they intuitively read their infants' hand movements, gestures and vocalizations and respond to the infant contingently (Papoušek, 2007). Such interactions include the mother soothing her infant's negative affect and enhancing her infant's pleasurable affective experiences. Via their melodic speech contours which rise and fall, mothers intuitively encourage their infants' attention to facilitate turn-taking in interactions during play and imitation, while discouraging unpleasant emotional states including being hyperaroused (Papoušek, Papoušek & Symmes, 1991). These researchers have found intuitive parenting behaviours cross-culturally.

As noted in Chapter 1, mothers' non-verbal sensitivity and responsivity to their infants is especially important in socializing infant emotional behaviour. In the work by Cohn and Tronick (1988), for example, when mothers were responsive to changes in their infants' behaviours, the infants were more likely to attend to and respond to alterations in their mothers' emotional expressions as well; thus, it seems to be especially important for mothers to take the lead in maintaining the interactional give-and-take synchrony. While such adaptive outcomes are normative and typical of most families as demonstrated in the work of Edward Tronick, Mechthild Papoušek, Hanuš Papoušek and their colleagues as described above, maladaptive outcomes are possible as well.

As reviewed below, the study of maladaptive outcomes and depression in families has been linked to the quality of non-verbal emotional expressions.

## Non-Verbal Emotional Expressions and Depression in Families

One of the largest bodies of evidence that we currently have on non-verbal emotional expression and the socialization of emotional competence in the family comes from research on the influence of parental depression on the adaptation and well-being of children (e.g., Field et al., 1990; Reck et al., 2004). Tiffany Field and her colleagues (1990) have shown in a series of studies that mothers who are clinically depressed tend to show more neutral or flat emotion in their facial expressions, provide less stimulation to their infants, and are less responsive in their interactions with their infant than non-depressed mothers; the infants of depressed mothers, in turn, are more likely to be fussy and show evidence of fewer contented facial expressions. In addition, Field et al. found that depressed dyads were more likely than non-depressed ones to match negative emotional states (maternal anger and rough behaviours such as poking or pulling the infant, with infant fussiness, grimacing or crying) and less likely to match positive states (maternal smiling with infant positive facial expression or gaze directed at mother). In addition, Tronick and his colleagues have suggested that when there is a mismatch between the infants' and mothers' emotional states (e.g., infant smiles at mother but mother doesn't immediately respond), the infant is likely to show a negative emotional expression such as crying (Reck et al., 2004). Tronick and his colleagues, as well as other researchers, have used the ***still-face paradigm*** to experimentally show how infants react when their mothers act as if they are depressed. In normal, healthy interactions with mothers responding appropriately and sensitively to their infants, there is an attempt by the mother to repair the interaction and get the infant back to a positive emotional state when the infant becomes distressed; such interactive repair processes have been found to be impaired in depressed dyads (Reck et al., 2004).

Perhaps mothers who are depressed have difficulty in accurately interpreting the facial expressions of infants, as hypothesized by Broth, Goodman, Hall and Raynor (2004). In their research into this possibility, Broth et al. found that clinically depressed and non-depressed women did not differ in their ability to accurately identify and interpret the facial expressions of infants. They noted that infant expressions are usually easier to identify accurately because they are often intense and more like basic, prototypical emotional expressions than adult expressions. However, within the depressed sample that they studied, the mothers with the most severe depression were found to be less accurate at identifying positive infant emotional expressions. Broth et al. point out that while mothers' ability to accurately recognize emotion is a necessary component of being able to provide sensitive responses to infants, it is not sufficient in and of itself. Rather, as discussed in Chapter 6, mothers' beliefs about the parenting role are also likely mediators between maternal emotion accuracy and the quality of the mother–child interaction. As has been frequently studied from a cognitive-behavioural viewpoint, depressed adults tend to have distorted cognitions about themselves and their abilities. Even if depressed mothers do accurately perceive their infants' feelings, their lack of confidence in themselves and feelings of low self-worth and incompetence may interfere with their ability to respond appropriately to their children whether through non-verbal or verbal interactions.

Pine and his colleagues (2004) have found that children and adolescents with a history of childhood depression have selective difficulty in remembering fearful facial expressions, but not happy or angry expressions. These researchers hypothesize that this emotional memory bias may be linked to a dysfunction in the amygdala. Children and adolescents with histories of depression often come from families where one or both parents have also suffered from depression and/or anxiety. Such deficits in the processing of facial emotions can make family communication especially challenging. In addition, the selective processing of angry facial emotion has also been found to occur in physically abused children as compared to non-abused children; the abused children react more quickly to angry faces and take a longer time to disengage their attention away from them (Pollak & Tolley-Schell, 2003). Some evidence also suggests that the processing of emotional expressions such as anger differs by gender of both the sender and the receiver. It is to this topic that we turn next.

## Individual Differences, Gender and Non-Verbal Emotional Expressions

Individual differences exist in infants' emotional expressivity right from birth and this seems to be due to underlying temperamental characteristics such as how reactive the infants are to both social and nonsocial stimuli in their environments. There is considerable variation in such reactivity in both males and females (Field, 1982). Also, during observations of infants and children, various temperamental patterns and personality characteristics have been associated with specific non-verbal emotional expressions. For example, in the research by Kochanska et al. (2004) infant and child smiling and laughter were taken to indicate joy, kicking and banging were included in the non-verbal manifestations of anger, and twisting and looking away from a frightening stimulus was part of the complex of behaviours involving the child's voice, facial expressions and bodily reactions that indicated fear. During the ebb and flow of interpersonal interactions with others in the family, manifestations of temperament and personality include displays of such non-verbal emotional expressions that are involved in the socialization of emotional competence as well. As noted below, both gender and emotion socialization often converge in such family interactions.

It has long been known that infant boys and girls differ on average in temperamental reactivity to the environment with boys generally being more active and easily aroused than girls; infant girls, in contrast, often demonstrate earlier verbal skills and higher levels of effortful self-control involving inhibiting their behaviours and focusing their attention (Brody & Hall, 2008). Nonetheless, this changes over the course of childhood and by the age of 10 to 12 years, boys have adopted cultural display rules and sex role expectations; they have thus been socialized to inhibit their overt displays of emotion to a much greater extent than girls (Buck, 1977; Maccoby & Jacklin, 1974; Shennum & Bugental, 1982). How does this socialization process occur? Both family and culture seem to be implicated.

Parents' interaction styles with their infants are influenced both by how they react to their child's temperament and by the extent to which they have adopted cultural display rules that guide how they are supposed to differentially socialize their sons and daughters (e.g., boys don't cry or show fear; girls should smile and express their feelings) (Brody & Hall, 2008). Thus, even though infant boys and girls may start out being similarly expressive of their emotions, over time boys learn to dampen or inhibit their emotional expressions, while girls increasingly make gains in overtly expressing how they feel both non-verbally as well as verbally. In fact, boys' emotional suppression and inhibition of facial expressions has been called the *mask of masculinity* (Pollack, 2006). Brody (2000) reviews evidence that shows that parents may interact differently with their sons and daughters at least partially because their children differ in their level of activity and arousal, empathy for others and sociability, and language skills. She suggests that because boys are more active and may become more easily aroused or emotionally dysregulated, parents have a harder time with them, and thus take more time and put more effort into their attempts to get boys to inhibit or control their emotional behaviours. As reviewed by Brody (2000), the existing evidence also suggests that daughters are more responsive than sons to their mothers' facial expressions and are more likely to use their mothers as a social or affective reference; as a consequence, mothers may need to exaggerate their use of facial expressions (e.g., anger or fear) more with their sons to get them to pay attention and heed a warning than they do with their daughters.

While the term "sex differences" implies a strong underlying biological foundation based on a person's genotype, the term "gender differences" in contrast suggests that there is a strong socialization component as well as a biological one that involves learning gender roles for emotional expression (Chaplin & Aldao, 2013). Gender differences in the non-verbal communication of emotion have been found in: (1) *social smiles*, with females smiling more than males in emotionally appropriate contexts, (2) *emotional expressiveness*, with females showing more expressiveness than males in their faces and gestures, (3) *emotion expression accuracy*, with the non-verbal cues of females being judged as more accurate than that of males, and (4) *emotion decoding (judgement) accuracy*, with females scoring higher across various ages, the gender of the person being decoded, type of task and cultural context (see Hall, Carter & Horgan, 2000). However, with respect to emotion expression accuracy, Hall et al. note that gender differences may depend on the gender stereotype of the emotions studied with the female advantage minimized or eliminated for anger or disgust. Also, given that various raters judge the accuracy of facial expressions in males and females in different studies, *rater bias* and the ability to read others' emotions may play a role in some study findings. Finally, Hall et al. review studies that show that being skilled in the ability to express and decode emotions that are consistent with gender stereotypes is related to better social adjustment and acceptance; this would include the emotion of anger for boys and the emotions of happiness, sadness and fear for girls. In the next section, we turn to how families differ in how they socialize emotional expressiveness and emotion decoding.

## Family Expressiveness and Emotion Decoding

As described earlier in this chapter, some theoretical approaches to non-verbal emotional expressions focus on individual development while others emphasize family interactions and relationships. Halberstadt and Eaton (2002) suggest that the family unit is a "hotbed of emotion" with families varying in the frequency and intensity of their emotional expressions during interactions. Family members may encourage each other to either suppress or express emotions; they may provoke intense emotional reactions and expressions in each other, or actively try to discourage and dampen them. Thus, families seem to vary in their typical patterns of interacting and in their frequency of expressions and level of emotional intensity. Amy Halberstadt (1986) has created a *family expressiveness questionnaire (FEQ)* to assess the most predominant style of non-verbal and verbal emotion expression in a person's family for both positive (e.g., expressing exhilaration after an unexpected triumph) and negative (e.g., showing contempt for another's actions) family expressiveness. Based on the FEQ, Halberstadt, Cassidy, Stifter, Parke and Fox (1995) have created a *self-expressiveness in the family questionnaire (SEFQ)* to assess the frequency of positive and negative expressions by an individual within the family context.

While family expressiveness has been found to be positively related to self-expressiveness, they are not identical constructs, and thus it is possible for an emotionally expressive person to come from a family environment that is more reserved, or vice versa. In their meta-analyses of studies comparing family expressiveness to child self-expressiveness, Halberstadt and Eaton (2002) concluded that there is a moderate positive relation between family expressiveness and self-expressiveness. However, they point out that the relation between negative family expressiveness and negative self-expressiveness was strongest with very young children and young adult children, highlighting that older children and adolescents may be exploring styles of expressing themselves that originate outside of their families. Although all family members contribute to the family emotional climate and general construct of family expressiveness, at least initially, it is the parents and the adults in the household who set the emotional tone for family communication patterns, a topic which is covered next.

## Adult Communication of Non-Verbal Emotion

In addition to varying in family and self-expressiveness, individuals vary in the extent to which they internally experience the intensity of emotions, sometimes called affect intensity (e.g., Larsen, Diener & Emmons, 1986) or emotionality (e.g., Halberstadt, Dennis & Hess, 2011). Halberstadt et al. (2011) asked college students to decode facial expressions of anger, sadness, disgust and happiness that varied in the level of intensity displayed in posed photographs. They examined decoding accuracy for these photos along with each participant's self-report of their own family expressiveness, self-expressiveness, and their own level of emotionality. In addition, they asked participants to give ratings of their perception of others' emotional intensity as displayed in the photos. Consistent with previous studies that they reviewed, they found that family expressiveness was *negatively related* to emotion decoding accuracy, meaning that those from low expressiveness families were generally better at decoding emotions than those from high expressiveness families. One possible explanation offered for this finding is that children growing up in low expressiveness homes need to be more emotionally attuned and perceptive to facial expression nuances to understand their family's emotional climate and they thus learn to be better at emotion decoding (e.g., Halberstadt & Eaton, 2002). In the study by Halberstadt et al. (2011), this difference in emotion decoding skill between those from high and low expressiveness families increased as the level of emotional intensity displayed in the photos increased. In contrast to the negative relation between family expressiveness and decoding accuracy, a positive relation was found between self-expressiveness and emotion decoding accuracy with those having high self-expressiveness showing better emotion decoding accuracy than those showing low self-expressiveness. By examining individual's family expressiveness, self-expressiveness, emotionality, and variations in the intensity of emotions to be decoded, Halberstadt et al. demonstrated that even simple prototypical facial expressions displayed in still photos are interpreted differently depending on how individuals were socialized within their families. In addition to family socialization across generations involving parents and children, spouses socialize each other as well and the quality of their interactions are observed by others in the family.

Spouses have been found to be better at decoding each other non-verbally than an independent panel of judges (e.g., Sabatelli, Buck & Dreyer, 1982). Studies of the non-verbal communication of emotion between marital partners have shown that marital distress is more easily determined from non-verbal channels of communication in the face, voice intonation and sound patterns, and bodily gestures than from the content of words alone (e.g., Gottman, 1980). Gottman (1980) examined the consistency in the non-verbal communication of couples between high-conflict tasks, such as discussing situations involving sex or money, and low-conflict tasks, such as having a conversation about a fun shared activity. He also conducted sequential analyses on ***affect reciprocity*** whereby spouses' emotional reactions to each other were coded. Positive affect reciprocity is defined as positive behaviours followed by positive behaviours in the partner, while negative affect reciprocity involves negative behaviours followed by negative behaviours in the partner. Following are some examples of the non-verbal cues assessed by Gottman (1980): (1) *face*: positive cues include smiling and nodding and looking empathic, while negative cues include frowning, smirking, glaring, or expressions of disgust, fear, anger or sadness, (2) *voice:* positive cues include warm, soft, happy, empathic or satisfied voice tone, while negative cues were cold, sarcastic, whiny, accusatory, impatient, or mocking voice tones, and (3) *body:* positive cues were touching or reducing the distance between the partner, relaxed body, leaning forward, being attentive, while negative cues included putting arms on hips, showing rude gestures, throwing hands up in disgust, pointing or being inattentive. Gottman (1980) found that both consistency across tasks and affect reciprocity were higher for the negative cues than for the positive ones. Recall from Chapter 1 that the significance of Gottman's (2011) work is that even well-adjusted couples in long-term relationships have negative interactions, but these are outweighed by positive interactions by a ratio of about 5:1.

## Promoting Adaptive Emotional Development through Non-Verbal Skills in Family Members

One important component of adaptive emotional life in families includes the ability to accurately convey one's own feelings through non-verbal channels and accurately decode emotions expressed by others in the family. Peter Salovey, John Mayer and David Caruso (2002) contend that such adaptive non-verbal emotional skills are essential components of the construct that they call emotional intelligence. Ekman (2003/2007) specifies four goals for improving non-verbal emotion skills: (1) learning to consciously identify when we are starting to feel emotional even before trying to express it, (2) proactively choosing how to reveal our emotions to others so that we can both accomplish our own goals and do so without hurting others, (3) learning how to be more sensitive or attuned to how others are feeling by reading their facial expressions accurately, even their more subtle and fleeting micro-expressions, and (4) maintaining an awareness of how best to use the information we have about the emotions of others to readjust our own reactions and to make decisions.

What are some steps that family members can take to enhance non-verbal skills and promote adaptive functioning in themselves and in each other? Adults can work towards increasing their self-awareness of their own emotional expressions and feelings during their demonstration of non-verbal behaviours. Viewing your own facial expressions in a mirror as you think about an angry, sad, fearful, disgusting or happy event can sometimes aid in the process of increasing self-awareness (Ekman, 2003/2007). As described in the *facial feedback* hypothesis (Tomkins & McCarter, 1964), we have an underlying biological predisposition that links our bodily physiological sensations with feedback from the movements of facial muscles; thus, voluntary practice in making the expressions and feeling the accompanying muscle movements in the face and bodily sensations can be helpful in improving emotional self-awareness.

Some people have great difficulty in describing their own emotional states of arousal and their own emotional facial expressions; thus, they have difficulty in conveying how they feel both non-verbally and verbally to others. This maladaptive tendency in the extreme has been called ***alexithymia***; it is characterized by an externally oriented person who has trouble describing his or her own feelings and distinguishing feelings from bodily sensations of arousal (e.g., Taylor, Bagby & Luminet, 2000).

In families, parents can teach their children about non-verbal facial expressions by accurately labelling emotions for them and interpreting the emotional situations they observe in the child and in others when the child is a bystander. Such learning may be either direct or vicarious as the child may model what is observed. In addition, there are many other everyday contexts in which parents can teach their children about the meaning behind non-verbal expressions. These include parental interpretations of story character facial expressions while interacting with their children during storytelling; in such cases, a wordless picture storybook that depicts emotionally expressive story characters interacting with each other allows parents to freely convey their interpretations and emotional evaluations (e.g., Harkins, 1993). In such situations, parents may not only label the observed emotions for the child but may elaborate on them providing more specific and nuanced information, or prompt the child for his or her own interpretation and evaluation of the situation (e.g., Scott et al., 2014). Similar teachable moment opportunities arise for parents while their children are watching television and reacting to cartoon characters, television stars or movie actors/actresses. Communicating with children about how to read the non-verbal emotional messages they are exposed to daily is an important facet of the emotion socialization process. There are a number of products currently available to aid families in learning to improve non-verbal emotional understanding. Some children's picture books are now focused specifically on helping children to label and understand basic emotion expressions. Charts and posters have been created depicting facial expressions of emotion with verbal labels; for example, a quite popular poster of cartoon facial expressions with verbal labels called *"How are You Feeling Today?"* was illustrated by Pulitzer Prize-winning cartoonist Jim Borgman, and is available online in several languages in addition to English. Families can enhance their non-verbal emotion skills by playing games such as emotion charades (where emotions are enacted so that others can take guesses about the emotion or emotional situation), emotion bingo, and card games that use pictures of emotional facial expressions (e.g., www.creativetherapystore.com).

It is currently unclear what the effects are on family members of observing their everyday lives on social media websites where an ongoing record is often kept of non-verbal expressions of family members appearing in photos and videos with multiple interpretive comments by others. It is common now for both children and adults in families to record themselves and others on their computers, tablets and cellphones for immediate feedback and reviewing; thus, many are routinely exposed to perceiving their own non-verbal emotional expressions and those of others in their social network. These records can potentially be viewed repeatedly. Such means of sharing emotional expressions non-verbally among family members is worthy of future study.

## Summary of Chapter Key Points

Although channels of non-verbal communication of emotion include voice tone and bodily gestures, the study of facial expressions has been favoured in the research literature, primarily due to Darwin's influence that resulted in the discrete emotions approach of Tomkins, Ekman, Izard and Malatesta/Magai. While the discrete emotions approach emphasizes the evolutionary past of humans, other approaches focus more on the role of emotion socialization in the development of non-verbal emotional expressions and decoding behaviours. The complexity of emotional expressiveness and decoding behaviours is also revealed in studies that highlight the importance of gender and the nature of the relationship between interacting partners as they express and decode each other's emotions in the family context. The purpose of non-verbal interactions differs depending on whether it is a mother and her infant establishing a mutual affectionate bond, a brother and a sister engaged in mutual angry dirty looks in a rivalry over who will decide which show to watch on television, or an adult couple, where one partner glances knowingly over at the other desiring to leave a rather boring dinner party, and has the glance positively reciprocated with an affirmative brief nod. In addition to describing typical everyday non-verbal interactions, researchers have also begun to identify atypical ones, such as in individuals with alexithymia, or in depressed mother–infant dyads. Numerous opportunities exist in contemporary society for informally improving non-verbal emotion skills within the family, from playing emotion charades and other parlour games to labelling emotions in picture books, and discussing emotion displays by story characters in television or films.

## Relevant Films

NOVA/WGBH (Producer) (1986). *Life's first feelings [DVD].* Boston, MA: Public Broadcasting System.

This special documentary provides an invaluable look into the studies and perspectives of several of the researchers mentioned in this chapter. Of special interest is the work of Carroll Izard on infant emotion expressions, Joseph Campos and Mary Klinnert on affective or social referencing, and Edward Tronick on the use of the still-face paradigm. The film also depicts a number of other studies by prominent emotion scholars such as Rene Spitz and Robert Emde who studied neglected, institutionalized children, Stanley Greenspan who addresses early intervention and Michael Lewis who studies social emotions and young children's development of a concept of self.

ABC News-20/20 (1998). *The secret life of boys [DVD].* New York: Films Media Group.

This brief television show features the real lives of the Mazilli family members consisting of a father, mother, two daughters and one son. The father is absent from the family periodically and this has differential effects on the son's and the two daughters' emotional lives. The focus of the show is on gender differences in the socialization of emotional expressiveness in boys and girls, and the potentially detrimental effects on boys' adjustment. Dr William Pollock, whose work is mentioned in this chapter, illustrates ways to help boys to improve their emotional lives.

# 8

# Self-Esteem and the Self-Conscious Emotions

*Julie is 9 years old and her parents are recently separated. Julie's teacher was concerned about her tendency to withdraw from her peers and her mediocre academic performance. She thus decided to approach Julie about joining a children's separation and divorce counselling group at the school. The school counsellor met with Julie and learned that she felt ashamed about her parents getting a divorce. Even though some of her peers lived in single parent homes, Julie felt stigmatized and that she was being viewed as strange and weird. After being in the counselling group for a few weeks, Julie began to participate in role-playing skits that enabled the children to disclose, vent and enact their feelings. Julie was thus allowed to re-enact her feelings of shame. Eventually, she developed a close friendship with another girl and the two of them along with the help of the school counsellor created their own "crisis outreach team". If they noticed that another child felt rejected, or was unhappy or miserable, they would offer to listen and provide comfort. By the end of the school year, Julie told the school counsellor that she was still sad about her parents' divorce but enjoyed coming to school. Her teacher noticed the positive changes and Julie finished the year with excellent grades.* (Case study summary from Saarni, 1999, p. 7.)

Source: *The Development of Emotional Competence*, C. Saarni. Copyright © 1999. Guilford Press. Reprinted with permission of The Guilford Press.

## Emotional Self-Efficacy and Self-Esteem

In Saarni's (1999) vignette, 9-year-old Julie demonstrated ***emotional self-efficacy*** in coping with her parents' divorce after she participated in the counselling group and received support from her school counsellor and new friend. As noted in Chapter 6, the concept of self-efficacy comes from Albert Bandura (1982) and is closely related to the concept of self-esteem. Emotional self-efficacy refers to a person having the capacity and appropriate skills to achieve a desired *emotional* outcome (Saarni, 1999). In Julie's case, this meant finding the means to feel better about herself and her life, even though she still felt sad about her parents' divorce. It also involved having an acceptance of her experience of shame and being able to reconcile positive pride in her accomplishments with her shame (Saarni, 1999).

We begin this chapter by describing how the self-conscious emotions of shame and pride are implicated in self-esteem (also see History Feature Box 8) and how they develop during the childhood years. We then turn to the concept of self-esteem. Discussion of self-esteem has a long history in the field of psychology extending back to the work of William James and his writings on consciousness and the multiple forms of the self, including the self as related to the body and clothing (James, 1890/2013). When the construct of self-esteem is well-defined, it serves as a meaningful way to understand individuals' inner subjective emotional experiences (e.g., Mruk, 1995, 2006). Some scholars consider self-esteem globally, while others maintain that it is best thought of as having multiple domains (e.g., Guindon, 2002, 2010; Harter, 1985, 2012; Mruk, 2013). Self-esteem is an important construct internationally and researchers are now investigating how it is manifested differentially by culture (Harter, 2012; Mruk, 2006), although much work remains to be done. The emotions of shame and pride, which do seem to have some universal significance for humans, have been linked to self-esteem and are discussed next.

**History Feature Box 8**

**Back Then and Now: Shame, Pride and Self-Esteem**

Self-esteem issues within families involve both shame and pride. Shame was described by Charles Darwin (1872/2008) as including blushing in the face and efforts to hide or conceal one's face and/or body by turning away; the person may look away or look down to avoid gazing into another person's eyes. Darwin also noted ancient biblical references to these qualities of shame-based behaviours in his seminal book on emotions, covered in more detail in History Feature Box 7. He also described pride as involving a person who is exhibiting superiority over others by holding his or her head and body high and erect while simultaneously trying to appear as large and noticeable as possible. Furthermore, Darwin (1872/2008, p. 200) mentioned that some people are "affected by a monomania of pride" with perfect self-confidence in their decisions and that this stance is in stark contrast to humility.

The ancient Greek philosopher Aristotle (384–322 BC) also wrote about the emotion of pride and described it as being virtuous in moderation and essential to living an ethical or good life (Solomon, 2008). However, in the Middle Ages, pride (called hubris when exaggerated) was thought to be a sin linked to desires rather than virtues, even when it was experienced only in moderation; this viewpoint led the Enlightenment period philosopher David Hume (1711–1776) to later react by declaring pride, in contrast to the views held in the Middle Ages, to be a *good* emotion associated with the idea of accomplishment, and humility a *bad* emotion because it led to the idea of the self as being unworthy, flawed and inadequate (Solomon, 2008).

Today, in contemporary societies, self-esteem as reflected in the idea of feeling positive about the self is often thought of as desirable; low self-esteem is viewed as a mental health problem, and high self-esteem is therefore encouraged as a goal (e.g., Jongsma, Peterson & McInnis, 1996). As reviewed by Mruk (1995), the parents of children with high self-esteem are emotionally and behaviourally involved with their children. They demonstrate warmth and affection, yet have clear, consistently implemented expectations for their children with relevant limit-setting. They demonstrate and expect mutual respect for their children and other family members. Finally, they act as good role models for their children by showing them how to live out and handle self-esteem conflict issues. Parental attitudes towards children are potentially conducive or detrimental to a child's sense of healthy and adaptive self-esteem, construed as a balance in feelings of worthiness and competence (Mruk, 1995).

As emphasized by Leslie Greenberg (2008), feelings of self-esteem, including pride in one's competence and accomplishments, can be utilized in the efforts to overcome feelings of shame in response to a specific situation. That is, maladaptive shame can be transformed by encouraging a person to remember past accomplishments, access feelings of pride, and re-experience the feelings of pride as an antidote to the feeling of shame. In this way, emotional reprocessing can help to strengthen self-esteem.

## The Self-Conscious Emotions of Shame and Pride: Links to Self-Esteem

Shame occurs as a natural part of development but can become maladaptive (Harter, 2012). Erik Erikson (1963) developed a sequence of eight normative conflicts faced by the developing ego or self as individuals proceed through the lifespan: trust vs. mistrust (infancy), autonomy vs. shame/self-doubt (toddler), industry vs. inferiority (preschool), initiative vs. guilt (school age), identity vs. role confusion (adolescence), intimacy vs. isolation (early adulthood), generativity vs. stagnation/self-absorption (middle adulthood), and ego integrity vs. despair (older adulthood). Toddlers learn to counteract and balance their feelings of shame and self-doubt with their feelings of pride, autonomy and self-control. In Erikson's model, by about 2 or 3 years of age, the relevant urinary and anal muscles have matured enough to allow the child to have some self-control over his or her bladder and bowels, thus enabling toilet training. During training, caregivers often react with shame or pride which then is mirrored by the child. Children may feel a sense of autonomy and pride in knowing that they decided when and where to "go potty", and that they were successful in meeting others' standards in doing so. On the other hand, lack of success in this endeavour can lead to shame and a desire to hide, especially if caregivers are insensitive to the child. This shame and self-doubt in one's ability to have self-control, as noted by Darwin (1872/2008), may have to do with bodily functions and one's backside being exposed to others. Thus, 2 to 3 year olds have a newly emergent sense of self and conscious awareness of their bodies being viewed by others. They may be aware of who is watching their front sides, but become self-conscious that they may not always know who is looking at their backsides, especially when they are not able to control bodily functions (Erikson, 1963; Lewis, 2008b). Though this is the first time developmentally in which bodily appearance emerges as important, it is also very significant later on for self-esteem as reviewed later.

How do children develop such self-consciousness? According to Michael Lewis (2014), consciousness emerges largely through maturation of the brain between 15 and 30 months of age, as discussed in Chapter 3. He has studied what he calls the self-conscious emotions of embarrassment, shame, pride and guilt (Lewis, 2008b). Lewis and his colleagues noted that most children in this age range could recognize themselves in a mirror after a spot of rouge was surreptitiously placed on their noses; for a demonstration of children's reactions to having this done to them, see the film *Life's First Feelings* (NOVA/WGBH, 1986) described in Chapter 7. Children with the spot on their noses who have a sense of self and how they ought to look were placed in front of a mirror; they were often found to look away, then in the mirror a second time, touch their noses, then look up at the observer, and then down and away again while smiling. These behaviours indicate a sense of embarrassment (Lewis, 2008b), and the notion that "I am aware that you are aware of me" (Saarni, 1999, p. 32). Such self-recognition and understanding is a prerequisite for developing a sense of self-esteem; in other words, you must have conscious awareness of your own existence to evaluate yourself and feel good or bad about the outcome of your self-evaluation. Embarrassment is related to but also a little different from shame according to Lewis (2014), because it is specific to a situation, milder in intensity, involves exposure or the sense of being caught, and appears earlier in development; actual internalized shame emerges a bit later, does not necessarily involve being exposed or caught by others (but might), and is not accompanied by smiles as often occurs with embarrassment.

Shame, like pride, is one of the self-conscious *evaluative* emotions because the person has cognitions and makes attributions about himself or herself (Lewis, 2014). Feelings of shame are produced when people violate a standard, rule or goal, and they subsequently make global negative attributions about themselves involving their sense of failure (Lewis, 2008b). Corporal punishment, expressions of disappointment, and shaming of children by parents have been found to be related to anxiety in children (e.g., Gershoff et al., 2010). Feelings of shame have been linked to self-blame and stigma in people with *low self-esteem* and histories of various forms of neglect or abuse (Mruk, 2006).

Another self-conscious evaluative emotion linked to *high self-esteem* is pride. By the age of 4 years old, children can recognize the features of pride in others' expressions (Tracy, Robins & Lagatutta, 2005). High self-esteem can be broken down into two types: ***defensive self-esteem*** and ***authentic self-esteem*** (Mruk, 2006). Defensive self-esteem is apparent in individuals who display narcissistic traits and have an excessive sense of their own self-worth or in individuals who have an excessive sense of their own competence such as in those with antisocial or psychopathic traits (Mruk, 2006), as addressed in more detail later in this chapter. Pride takes the form of hubris in defensive self-esteem. The term "hubris" has been defined as "exaggerated pride or self-confidence often resulting in retribution" (Merriam-Webster, 1977, p. 556). Hubris is often used as a synonym for the "sinful", punishable version of pride and is related to defensive self-esteem.

Lewis (2008b) reviews evidence suggesting that parents who praise their children far too much and praise them for reasons that are not linked to actual specific successful task performances contribute to the development of hubris; the child develops a global sense of his or her own self-worth and when successful at meeting a goal focuses globally on the self (e.g., I'm great!), rather than on the specific characteristics of tasks (e.g., I did a really good job of putting that confusing puzzle together today!). Lewis also points out that children with such generalized self-worth that is not linked to specific accomplishments are particularly susceptible to feeling shame over their failures due to their being accustomed to making generalized attributions about themselves. It is not surprising that individuals who display hubris have interpersonal problems, are considered arrogant and haughty, and inspire feelings of disdain in others (Lewis, 2008b).

In contrast to defensive self-esteem, authentic self-esteem (stemming from Aristotle's focus on moderation) is reflected in feelings of pride that are a balance between the excesses of vanity and humility (Mruk, 2006). Such healthy moderate versions of pride involve making attributions about success and the self that are specific to the situation, the task at hand, and one's own actions or behaviours (Lewis, 2008b). Much of the remaining discussion in this chapter will focus on how feelings of competence and self-worth (i.e., worthiness) are related to self-esteem problems and how authentic self-esteem can be fostered in families.

## Self-Esteem: Feelings of Competence and Worthiness

Parents are often concerned about their children's self-esteem and there are a number of behavioural symptoms that indicate low self-esteem that can be targeted for intervention. These include the person not being able to accept compliments or identify his or her own positive characteristics, making self-disparaging remarks about feeling worthless or incompetent and avoiding social contacts; it also includes trying to excessively please others to get praise and attention from them, or having a fear of not being liked or of being rejected (Jongsma, Peterson & McInnis, 1996). As reflected in the problems apparent in those who are thought to have low self-esteem, there are two factors to consider in the self-esteem construct: (1) having a sense of *worthiness* or self-worth linked to feeling liked and loved by others, and (2) having a sense of *competence* which includes feeling skilled, capable of taking effective action and of being successful in reaching personal goals (Mruk, 2006). While some approaches to self-esteem consider either worthiness or competence, approaches that use both hold the most promise.

Christopher Mruk (1995, 2006, 2013) is an ardent proponent of an existentially based two-factor theory of self-esteem. He defines self-esteem as "the lived status of one's competence at dealing with the challenges of living in a worthy way over time" (Mruk, 2013, p. 27). Mruk's focus on an existential or phenomenological approach to the lived experiences of self-esteem is best reflected in the idea of what he has labelled ***self-esteem moments***. Self-esteem moments are critical experiential turning points in a person's self-esteem in either a positive or negative direction. This concept is based on the seminal work of Seymour Epstein on important transitions in self-esteem (Mruk, 2013). When faced with a critical life challenge that requires an impending decision, does the person face the challenge head on and do what is ethically just and morally right according to his or her standards in an authentic way, thus leading to a boost in self-esteem? Such a self-esteem moment can lead a person to strengthen positive, authentic self-esteem. Or, on the contrary, does the person shrink from and avoid the challenge and act in an inauthentic, compromising way that opposes his or her conscience, leading to a weakening sense of authentic self-esteem and a strengthening of defensive self-esteem? Such a defensive stance during a decisive self-esteem moment can exacerbate an already problematic sense of self rather than helping it to heal.

While the study of self-esteem moments and changes in self-esteem as a process is a relatively new focus of research, self-esteem worthiness and competence domains have been extensively studied. Self-esteem has been addressed in the context of a person's demographic status (e.g., socio-economic, gender, ethnicity), and over time during development (Mruk, 2013). In the following sections, studies of these various components of self-esteem are reviewed, beginning with childhood and adolescence and extending into adulthood.

## Competence and Worthiness in Children and Adolescents

In a study of changes in self-esteem following the transition from 6th to 7th grade (11–13 years of age), Lord, Eccles and McCarthy (1994) found that academic ability, physical attractiveness and peer social skills were positively related to self-esteem. Declines in self-esteem were related to an increase in worries and self-consciousness in both academic and social domains. Furthermore, Lord et al. (1994) found that decreases in self-esteem occurred when parents were not developmentally attuned to the changing needs of the early adolescent to be involved in democratic family decisions that affected the adolescent. For girls, a positive increase in their self-perception of physical attractiveness was found to feed into their sense of self-worth, while for boys a decline in self-esteem was related to feeling self-conscious about their academic competence, especially in more traditionally masculine fields such as mathematics (Lord et al., 1994).

According to Eccles (1999), the middle childhood to early adolescent years are especially noteworthy for the development of self-esteem for the following reasons. First, cognitive changes make it possible for children to reflect upon their own successes and failures, and they then begin to project and anticipate their future performance in many different domains of functioning. Second, the social world and activities of the child have begun to expand outside of the family to include friends in the neighbourhood, classmates and peers met during extracurricular activities, all of which also afford additional opportunities for self-esteem changes. Third, the exposure to a widening group of peers provides additional opportunities to compete, have successes or failures, and make social comparisons with others, all of which may influence self-esteem. Opportunities to develop enhanced self-esteem and self-confidence abound, as do social encounters that can erode self-esteem if protective factors are not in place.

## Prediction of suicidal ideation

Low self-esteem due to deficits in feelings of competence and/or worthiness is often associated with feelings of depression including suicidal thoughts in children and adolescents (e.g., Crocker & Hakim-Larson, 1997; Harter, Marold & Whitesell, 1992). In the Harter et al. (1992) model of risk factors that predict suicidality, feelings of competence are specific to the various life domains that may be considered important to the child or adolescent (see Table 8.1 for Harter's measures). These include physical appearance, peer likeability and athletic competence which together affect peer support, and scholastic competence and behavioural conduct which together affect parent support. This model takes into consideration how hopeless or hopeful youths feel about the domains they consider important to their self-concepts. Thus, if being athletically competent on a sports team is especially important to a male adolescent and he feels hopeless about accomplishing a targeted athletic goal (e.g., winning a championship game after sustaining a critical injury), this may have a negative impact on his perceived peer support. Similarly, a child might feel that it is important to gain parental approval by doing very well academically. If the child falls short of this goal and feels hopeless about being able to remedy the situation, this may have a negative impact on the perceived or actual parental support received.

Both peer and parent support along with any feelings of hopelessness about the support contribute to what Harter et al. (1992) call the depression composite. The ***depression composite*** consists of self-worth, affect and general hopelessness, all of which when taken together predict suicidal ideation in youth. Note that the domains of potential importance to youth in this model span the range of peers and parents as well as the home- and school-related contexts. Harter et al. (1992) found support for this model in a school-based sample of 12- to 15-year-old early adolescents, and support also has been found in a younger sample with some differences in the types of support considered most important (Crocker & Hakim-Larson, 1997). Both peer and parent support predicted the depression composite and were contributors to self-worth in the original sample of early adolescents (Harter et al., 1992). However, only parent support contributed to the depression composite in a younger sample of 9- to 12-year-old children (Crocker & Hakim-Larson, 1997). Thus, the powerfully significant influence of peers, classmates and friends on self-worth may not emerge fully until the early adolescent years. In addition, Colarossi and Eccles (2000) have provided some evidence that the positive spousal support and friend support that parents themselves receive within their own social network may have a beneficial effect on the self-esteem of their children.

**Table 8.1** Some Measures of Self-Esteem

| Measure | Author (Year) | Global Self-Esteem | Worthiness | Competence |
|---|---|---|---|---|
| Rosenberg Self-Esteem Scale (RSES) | Rosenberg (1965) | 10-item measure of global self-esteem for use with adolescents and adults | [some items emphasize worthiness] | [some items emphasize competence] |
| Coopersmith Self-Esteem Inventory (CSEI) | Coopersmith (1967b/1975/2002) | 58-item version for use with school- age children, and 25-item version for use with adults | [some items emphasize worthiness] | [some items emphasize competence] |
| Self-Perception Profile for Children (SPPC)<br><br>Self-Perception Profile for Adolescents (SPPA) | Harter* (1985, 2012)<br><br>Harter* (1988, 2012) | (Global self-worth used as measure of Global self-esteem) | -Physical appearance<br>-Social acceptance<br><br>*Additional scales for adolescents:*<br>-Romantic appeal<br>-Close friendships | -Athletic competence<br>-Scholastic competence<br>-Behavioural conduct<br><br>*Additional Scales for Adolescents:*<br>-Job performance |
| Multidimensional Self-Esteem Inventory (MSEI) | O'Brien & Epstein (1988) | -Global self-esteem<br>-Identity integration<br>-Defensiveness | -Lovability<br>-Likeability<br>-Moral self-approval<br>-Bodily appearance | -Competence<br>-Personal power<br>-Self-control<br>-Bodily functioning |
| Self-Liking/Self-Competence Scale-Revised (SLCS-R) | Tafarodi & Swann (2001) | [no global score recommended] | Self-liking | Self-competence |

* Susan Harter's *Life Span Battery of Self-Perception Profile* of tests and manuals are available online in their entirety at https://portfolio.du.edu/SusanHarter/page/44199; this includes tests for younger children, school-age children, children with learning disabilities, adults under 60 years of age, and adults over 60 years of age. She does not separate the domains of her tests into the worthiness and competence categories; I have separated them here to demonstrate that her measures do indeed assess both.

Interestingly, studies have repeatedly found that the domain consistently linked to inner global feelings of self-esteem is ***perceived physical appearance***; furthermore, this finding robustly applies to all of the social groups studied thus far (Harter, 2012). That is, Harter (2012) has reviewed evidence showing that the global self-esteem of older children, adolescents and young adults in the US, Canada, and 11 other countries is positively related to having a favourable perception of one's own external physical appearance. This finding is likely related to the concept of having a "***looking glass self***" as originally described in 1902 by Charles Horton Cooley (Franks & Gecas, 1992; Harter, 2012). The looking-glass self-concept involves the *reflected appraisals* of others. In other words, what other people think of us is reflected back to us and incorporated into our own views of ourselves. However, these appraisals are not just passively accepted as we move from one social context to another, but rather become integrated into our actively changing yet relatively stable self-concepts (Franks & Gecas, 1992). As humans interacting with other humans routinely, we are always on display in some way, shape or form and thus the potential for our perceived physical appearance to have an influence on our global self-esteem is rather frequent. According to O'Brien and Epstein (1988), our perceived bodily appearance feeds into our sense of self-worth or worthiness of being liked and loved, while our perceptions of how well our body functions feeds into our feelings of competence.

In contrast to our ever-present physical appearance, other domains of functioning linked to self-esteem such as athletic, scholastic or work competence, for example, are specific to certain contexts or activities, and thus afford fewer opportunities overall to have an impact on self-esteem (Harter, 2012). An important finding regarding perceived physical appearance and self-esteem is that individuals may be teased, bullied or harassed about their physical appearance for any number of reasons, such as disability, race/ethnicity, clothing, hair colour/style, etc., and as a consequence feelings of humiliation, anger and the urge for revenge may ensue (Harter, 2012). As described next, Harter and her colleagues have thus examined these and other potential risk factors that can lead to homicidal ideation in youth.

## Prediction of homicidal ideation

Harter, Low and Whitesell (2003) noted that sometimes youth with low self-worth and global self-esteem who were also high on the depression composite vacillated between suicidal and homicidal ideation. Thus, they expanded the original model of risk factors that predicted suicidal ideation (Harter et al., 1992) to include the prediction of homicidal ideation given the increasing number of youth involved in mass shootings of family members, teachers and schoolmates in the US. They sought an answer to the perplexing question of what could possibly account for such actions in young people. To address this question, Harter (2012) examined the media accounts of 12 case studies of White, male school shooters. She discovered that public humiliation with an audience who had hostile intentions was a root cause that fuelled revenge in each of them. She states:

> In every case, the shooters described how they had been ridiculed, taunted, teased, harassed, or bullied. The humiliation they experienced came at the hands of peers (who mocked their inadequate appearance and their lack of social skills or athletic behavior). A few had been spurned by someone in whom they were romantically interested. Still others were publicly humiliated in their classrooms by a teacher or school administrator. (Harter, 2012, p. 223)

Thus, Harter et al. (2003) added peer rejection, feelings of *humiliation*, and anger-induced physical aggression to the original model as contributors to the prediction of homicidal ideation; additional factors related to homicidal ideation were a preoccupation with violent media and an interest in and access to weapons or bombs.

It is important to note that feelings of humiliation are far more intense than mere embarrassment, although the humiliated person may feel embarrassment initially. Given that social comparison emerges in middle childhood to early adolescence (Eccles, 1999), the impact of peers as well as adults both within and outside of the family can be considerable. While researchers have focused on the school context to address self-esteem in youth, adult family members are also likely to be personally affected by what is happening with their peers or co-workers and engage in social comparison with them. In a meta-analysis conducted by Judge and Bono (2001), a positive relation was found between adults' job satisfaction or performance and their self-esteem, generalized self-efficacy, locus of control and emotional stability (low neuroticism).

While there is much in common regarding the self-esteem of youth and that of adults, there are also some unique aspects given the age-related differences in developmental tasks and the consolidation of personality characteristics related to feelings of competence and worthiness in adults, a topic to which we turn next.

## Competence and Worthiness in Adults

Adults and youth may have similar histories involving the antecedents of their self-esteem. For instance, Mruk (2013) summarizes the four key sources of self-esteem as originally described by Stanley Coopersmith (1967a), who is known for one of the earliest measures of self-esteem (see Table 8.1). These are: (1) *feeling accepted* versus rejected by our reference groups, which starts in childhood and expands during adulthood to include our friends, neighbours, spouses or partners, extended family, co-workers, colleagues, social and/or religious group members, (2) *upholding virtues*, including moral and ethical standards of what is believed to be just and right, versus feeling guilt for not doing so, (3) *having power or influence* over our social and physical environments versus having a sense of powerlessness, and (4) *having successful achievements* in domains of personal or collective importance versus having failures. Each of these holds importance and can be traced throughout the lifespan.

In contrast to children and adolescents, however, adults have a greater accumulation of past life experiences and more complex developmental histories. According to Mruk (2013), there are two primary self-esteem relevant pathways that adults have been found to take when they are faced with important self-esteem moments that require a decision. The first authentic self-esteem pathway leads to an expansion of the self in an emotionally positive way, while the second self-protective/defensive pathway may be a more familiar and easy path of least resistance, but is nonetheless inauthentic and maladaptive. In each case, the individual goes through a decision-making process of which fork in the road he or she will take. Will the decision be to accept the challenge to expand out of what has been a comfort zone and become freer of past conflicts, or to stay safe but remain in a defensive, constrained posture, retaining old conflicts that may inadvertently re-emerge again and again, perhaps never to be resolved?

How parents and other adults handle their self-esteem conflicts and the decisions they make during such self-esteem moments likely has some influence on the children observing them (e.g., Small, 1988). The few studies that have addressed the links between parent and adolescent self-esteem in families have shown a positive relation between them; this relation is thought of as bidirectional, meaning that how children interact with their parents also influences parental self-esteem (e.g., Demo et al., 1987). Demo et al. (1987) found that the quality of parent–adolescent interaction (e.g., supportive, controlling) was related to the self-esteem of both parents and their adolescent children; furthermore, during family interactions, reflected appraisals occurred in a bidirectional manner, with parents incorporating their adolescents' evaluations into their self-concepts and adolescents incorporating parental evaluations into theirs. Small (1988) found that in contrast to low self-esteem parents, high self-esteem parents were less likely to be punitive and more likely to have friendly discussions with their adolescents. Also, they allowed them to have more decision-making freedoms, an important developmental task for adolescents. One possible explanation offered by Small (1988) is that low self-esteem parents may feel relatively powerless to affect the course of their own lives and thus, they may be desperately trying to gain some areas of control as they contend with raising their not always compliant adolescents. Other studies as well have examined family communication patterns for links to self-esteem. For example, Reese, Bird and Tripp (2007) found that parents who referred to past events using positive emotional language and evaluations with their children were more likely to have children with high self-esteem than those who were less likely to do so. However, family discussions sometimes turn into parent–child conflicts or marital conflicts, including those that may result in family violence witnessed by children.

Family violence has the potential to affect the self-esteem of those involved and may include one or more types: between adult partners, parent to child, child to parent, and between siblings (Zeev, 2015). For example, Shen (2009) found that young adults in Taiwan with histories of both witnessing interparental violence and being the victim of abuse had lower self-esteem than those who experienced only one type of violence or none at all. Furthermore, male participants who experienced such dual family violence had lower self-esteem than did female participants; no gender differences were found for those experiencing one type or no family violence (Shen, 2009). Self-esteem problems also have been implicated as a background characteristic of both adolescent and adult male perpetrators of intimate partner violence in a study by Diaz-Aguado and Martinez (2015). Thus, an increasing number of studies have now shown that individuals who witness family violence or have histories of being a victim and/or the perpetrator of abusive behaviours are likely to have problems with self-esteem. Furthermore, family violence has been linked to perpetrator personality that develops in adolescence and adulthood. In particular, violent behaviour has been linked to deficiencies in self-control coupled with the personality characteristic of narcissism (Larson et al., 2015), a topic which is addressed next in the context of the hubristic form of pride.

## Personality and Self-Esteem: Narcissism, and Hubristic versus Authentic Pride

In addition to low self-control, perpetrators of violence have been shown to have overinflated self-esteem, and narcissistic personality traits characterized by grandiose fantasies or behaviours, a strong motivation and need to be admired, and a sense of being special and deserving of entitlement (American Psychiatric Association, 2013; Baumeister, Smart & Boden, 1996; Larson et al., 2015). This is noteworthy because intimate partner violence, especially by male perpetrators with female victim/survivors, has been recognized as a pressing problem around the world that needs to be better understood (e.g., Diaz-Aguado & Martinez, 2015).

Narcissism can be thought of as a maladaptive personality characteristic that involves hubristic pride and an *exaggerated sense of self-worth or worthiness* regardless of the person's level of competence (Mruk, 2013); thus, individuals with narcissism may or may not be competent in various domains of importance to them and/or others. When such narcissistic traits are below the clinical threshold, the person may merely strive for others' approval, perhaps underachieving in some areas of competence (e.g., work) while blaming other people, making excuses for themselves, or by bragging and looking to others for positive feedback; this has been called an acceptance-based form of self-esteem that involves unstable worthiness, and average to below average competence (Mruk, 2013). At the extreme, when such behaviours are inflexible and enduring over years, older adolescents and adults may form emotionally unstable narcissistic personalities. They are at significant risk for acting out aggressively towards themselves or others, especially when they are criticized, experience rejection, or are challenged or confronted; even mild or imaginary insults can threaten them and lead to what has been called a *narcissistic injury* with retaliatory actions (Mruk, 2013).

As noted earlier, individuals with hubristic pride make overgeneralized attributions about themselves; hubris feels good to the individual experiencing it in the moment, but the feeling is difficult to sustain in the normal course of everyday life, and therefore the individual may invent ways to repeat the feeling state including having contempt for others to whom they feel superior (Lewis, 2008b). Because others' needs, wishes and desires may be ignored, the individual with narcissism has serious interpersonal problems and may infringe on other people's rights as they enact ways to repeat positive feelings for themselves (Lewis, 2008b). Unstable narcissistic self-esteem has been hypothesized to begin in early childhood. Parents of those with narcissism may have overidealized their children leading them to feel hubristic pride and excessive worthiness; in addition, the parents may have held unrealistic expectations of perfection, thus leading to feelings of rejection, shame, or possible humiliation whenever expectations were not met (Tracy et al., 2009).

Defensive self-esteem that is based on excessive worthiness takes the form of narcissism at the extreme; however, defensive self-esteem can be achievement-based and may take the form of antisocial or psychopathic personality characteristics (Mruk, 2013). Thus, individuals who are relatively low in feelings of self-worth (i.e., not feeling liked or loved by others) may lack feelings of remorse or a conscience; in addition, they may have an excessive need to be competent and a need for perfectionism in domains that are important to them (Mruk, 2013). Thus, such individuals with antisocial or psychopathic tendencies may have excessive feelings of their own competence. Interestingly, because defensive self-esteem involves instability at the extreme in either worthiness or competence, clinical presentations of affected individuals may involve symptoms of either or both narcissistic and antisocial personality disorders; thus, a person with narcissism who displays hubris may at times use antisocial behaviours to achieve a given goal (American Psychiatric Association, 2013; Mruk, 2013). Thus, both forms of defensive self-esteem can co-occur within a person when there is unstable worthiness and competence.

In contrast, low self-esteem (low worthiness and competence) is relatively stable and occurs in people who self-handicap and are negativistic, or who at the extreme, are clinically depressed; authentic high self-esteem (high worthiness and competence) is stable and includes general feelings of adequacy at moderate levels, or at the extreme, active attempts to live out personally held values in an authentic way that is considerate of others (Mruk, 2013).

Feelings of pride can originate from such authentic self-esteem and are the consequence of feeling joy over positively evaluating specific actions meant to achieve specific goals (Lewis, 2008b). Because a person with authentic self-esteem has a balanced view of his or her own competence and worthiness, such evaluations are not as likely to be based on distorted perceptions and are more likely to be based on verifiable reality than those of individuals with low or defensive self-esteem. However, additional research is needed that clearly distinguishes between hubristic pride and pride from authentic self-esteem (Lewis, 2008b; Tracy et al., 2009).

Personality attributes and evaluations made about the self that are related to self-esteem have been addressed globally and specifically by domain. Harter and her colleagues have demonstrated the utility of examining the multiple selves associated with different roles and situational contexts (i.e., at home, school, work, with family, with schoolmates, with friends) that begin to emerge in adolescence (Harter et al., 1997; Harter, Waters & Whitesell, 1998). Harter et al. (1998) describe how the individual's sense of *relational self-worth* varies from one role and context to another, and that self-attributes may be in direct opposition with each other shifting from context to context, making it difficult to reconcile globally just how one feels about himself or herself. Being able to reconcile such inner conflict across multiple selves and contexts becomes a developmental task that first emerges in adolescence and continues into the adult years. The construct of multiple selves and self-worth that varies across relational contexts and in different domains (Harter et al., 1998) may be especially important in considering self-esteem as it varies by demographic characteristics (age, birth cohort, ethnicity) as well as culture, as briefly reviewed below.

## Self-Esteem Across Contexts: Demographic Characteristics and Culture

Self-esteem has been found to change ontogenetically within the same person over time. Using a revised version of Susan Harter's measure of self-esteem for adolescents (see Table 8.1), von Soest, Wichstrøm and Kvalem (2016) in Norway have reported the first comprehensive longitudinal study of both global self-worth and domain-specific self-esteem in six areas: physical appearance, social acceptance, close friendships, scholastic competence, romantic appeal and athletic competence. They studied adolescents in 1992 (13–18 years of age), and followed them for retesting at three additional points in time until 2005 (27–31 years of age). In general, they found increases in self-esteem scores from adolescence to the adult years. Also, they found that males reported higher self-esteem than females in many of the domains studied, except for the close friendship domain in which females were consistently higher. Similarly, in Germany, female adolescents and adults were found to have lower self-regard, and lower social, academic and physical self-esteem than males (Rentzsch, Wensler & Schutz, 2016). However, there are many inconsistencies in studies on gender and self-esteem that are likely due to the birth cohorts studied, the different ethnic or cultural groups assessed, and the variety of self-esteem measures utilized, some of which focus more on worthiness, some more on competence, and some on both in a global measure (Mruk, 2013; Rentzsch et al., 2016). Interestingly, von Soest et al. (2016) found in their longitudinal study that the gender gap in self-esteem narrowed over time with the difference in self-esteem between men and women nearly disappearing when physical appearance self-esteem was controlled. Thus, as noted earlier in this chapter, the contexts and roles that emphasize physical appearance are likely to be of relevance across the lifespan in self-esteem research.

In addition to age and gender considerations, self-esteem has been assessed across generations or birth cohorts. Twenge and Campbell (2008) reported on their comparison of self-esteem in large samples of American high school students in the 1970s and again in 2006. In addition to reporting higher grades and assessing themselves as more intelligent than the students in the 1970s, students in 2006 reported higher self-esteem in their general satisfaction with themselves, how well they liked themselves, and their perception of their futures as spouses, parents and workers. However, the 2006 sample also scored lower than those in the 1970s on items meant to assess their sense of competence. Thus, even though the later generation reported liking themselves more than the earlier generation, they did not necessarily feel like they were more competent. One potential explanation that was offered by the researchers is that the findings may be the consequence of the societal emphasis on the importance of self-esteem enhancement for children's overall well-being during the 1980s and 1990s.

Self-esteem has been examined in relation to race, ethnicity and socioeconomic status within North American samples, as well as across a variety of countries for cross-cultural comparisons. In a meta-analysis of global self-esteem in North America, Twenge and Crocker (2002) found differences by racial/ethnic group using the Rosenberg Self-Esteem Scale (RSES; 1965) with the highest global self-esteem reported by Blacks followed by that of Whites, Hispanic Americans, American Indians, and Asian Americans, in that order. As summarized below, differences in cultural expectations and self-concept were offered to explain the relatively lower self-esteem of Asian Americans. For instance, individualism and independent self-construal have been found to be associated with higher global self-esteem in Western samples. However, Asian Americans, especially first or second generation, may have a relatively higher interdependent self-construal style and maintain some collectivistic values such as a norm of modesty where it is desirable to engage in self-criticism to maintain social harmony (Twenge & Crocker, 2002). Consistent with this view, Harter (2012) also has reviewed evidence that shows that Asian children score relatively lower than Western children on her Self-Perception Profile for Children (see Table 8.1), which was designed for use in the US. Harter explains that Westerners have a more *self-enhancing* interpersonal style in comparison to that of Asians. In addition to having a more *self-effacing* interpersonal style, Asian American children are asked to engage in social comparisons to others while completing Harter's measure, which is discouraged in Asian cultures (Harter, 2012).

In addition, Twenge and Crocker (2002) note generational or birth cohort effects in that their findings show relatively greater increases in the self-esteem of Black Americans by the 1980s, right after the Civil Rights movement of the 1960s–1970s. In contrast to the studies conducted with White Americans showing greater male self-esteem, the opposite seems to hold among minority groups in studies reviewed by Twenge and Crocker; that is, Hispanic, Black, and Asian American females report higher self-esteem than males. Furthermore, Black and Hispanic American minority groups had higher self-esteem when their socio-economic status was higher (Twenge & Crocker, 2002). In many studies, self-esteem has been found to be positively associated with socio-economic status (Twenge & Campbell, 2002).

Cross-cultural comparisons of self-esteem show converging results with some of the findings reported in the West. Schmitt and Allik (2005) conducted a comparison of self-esteem in college students and community participants across 53 countries using the Rosenberg Self-Esteem Scale (RSES; 1965), which they broke down into two subscales: Self-Liking (worthiness dimension) and Self-Competence (competence dimension). Tafarodi and Swann (1996) have suggested a *trade-off hypothesis* whereby cultures that emphasize individualism will also promote relatively more self-competence than self-liking, while cultures that emphasize collectivism will be more likely to encourage self-liking. Schmitt and Allik (2005) tested and found some support for the trade-off hypothesis when they conducted analyses (controlling for covariates) comparing self-esteem in extreme cultural subgroupings of individualistic (e.g., United Kingdom, United States) versus collectivistic countries (e.g., Indonesia, South Korea).

To further study cultural influences, Tafarodi, Shaughnessy, Yamaguchi and Murakoshi (2011) conducted a study in which they experimentally manipulated self-esteem rating instructions to counteract cultural tendencies as they compared college students in Japan to those in Canada on self-liking and self-competence. They found that self-liking increased in Japanese students when they were specifically instructed to avoid being modest (i.e., self-effacing) in their ratings, while self-liking was lowered in Canadian students when they were instructed to avoid responding in self-inflationary (i.e., self-enhancing) ways; without the instructions, Canadian students had higher ratings than the Japanese students, but when the normative pressure was relieved, the self-liking scores did not differ. Also, the instructional manipulation changed self-competence ratings in the expected directions for the two groups, but self-competence continued to differ between Canadian and Japanese students even with the instructions (Tafarodi et al., 2011). This study shows that how research participants are instructed when they complete self-esteem measures can potentially influence their ratings.

Reviews of the literature show that self-esteem may vary by instructional conditions, socio-economic status, racial/ethnic background, birth cohort, immigration status, self-construals (more independent or interdependent) and cultural values (e.g., individualistic or collectivistic) (e.g., Harter, 2012; Mruk, 2013; Russell et al., 2008). Although numerous studies have examined these and other factors in the attempt to compare self-esteem across racial/ethnic groups or cultures, the task is a complex one in need of better links between self-esteem measures and theoretical constructs about ways to feel good about yourself that originate within the cultural symbols and meanings in the group(s) under study (Harter, 2012). At the very least, it is important for researchers to be cautious about how they interpret group differences in self-esteem, and changes that occur in groups over historical time. When the focus is on changes within an individual over time, the question arises as to how best to implement adaptive changes in self-esteem and protect the individual from self-esteem threats.

## Changing the Self-Esteem of Individual Children, Adolescents and Adults

Implementing change in the self-esteem of children, adolescents and adults can occur either reactively once a self-esteem problem has been identified, or proactively in the attempt to maintain and bolster an already well-functioning sense of self-worth and competence in an individual. In either case, it is important for the intervention or prevention approach to have some research support for its effectiveness in actual clinical settings (Kazdin, 1998). Although self-esteem is often mentioned in treatment planning and many studies have been conducted across the lifespan with multiple methods of measurement, few attempts have been made to demonstrate the effectiveness of self-esteem programmes (Guindon, 2002, 2010). The self-esteem enhancement programmes that currently exist utilize the humanistic framework and experiential activities to promote authentic growth and change, the behavioural or cognitive-behavioural approach to address connections between thoughts, feelings and actions, and the social cognitive developmental approach to reduce discrepancies between the ideal and real self while promoting appropriate social supports (see Mruk, 2013). As discussed below, both individual and group interventions currently exist to address self-esteem changes.

One way in which change in self-esteem has been addressed is to specifically target the processing of the self-conscious emotions (e.g., embarrassment, shame, humiliation and hubristic pride). As noted in the beginning of this chapter, emotional self-efficacy occurs when individuals feel good about how they cope with and process distressing emotions; this then contributes to their overall feelings of self-esteem, because they evaluate themselves as emotionally competent and successful in meeting their goals. In his therapeutic approach, Leslie Greenberg (2008) describes how shame and humiliation can be counteracted by self-soothing and meditative relaxation techniques or the practice of mindfulness. Self-soothing, self-empathy, and self-compassion have the potential to emerge after a child, for example, has been the recipient of empathic attunement during interpersonal encounters where empathic others, such as a parent, accept and validate the child's emotions and support adaptive emotional transformations (Greenberg, 2008; Sroufe, 1996). In clinical settings, the therapist would perform a similar function to the parent.

Another way to achieve change in self-esteem is to target changes separately on the basis of each of the multiple domains of self-esteem, which can be assessed with Harter's series of self-esteem tests that span the preschool years into older adulthood (see Table 8.1). Cognitive and cognitive-behavioural strategies hold promise as a way to improve the low self-esteem of children and adolescents because they focus on modifying inaccurate, distorted, inauthentic self-evaluations (Shirk, Burwell & Harter, 2003). For example, three of Harter's scales (social acceptance, athletic competence and global self-worth) were examined before and after a one-week summer camp intervention designed to improve the self-esteem of military children and adolescents, who often suffer from mental health consequences linked to a parent's military deployment; the focus of the targeted intervention was improving a feeling of social belongingness and skill at sports (Chawla & Wadsworth, 2012). Children in the study improved in their global self-worth, while adolescents improved in their perception of their social acceptance and athletic competence. This study is an example of how it is possible to have a beneficial effect on worthiness and competence through structured self-esteem programmes.

Similarly, Mruk's (2013) Competence and Worthiness Training (CWT) programme is an intervention for adults that targets the two factors of self-esteem and their domains as assessed by the Multidimensional Self-Esteem Inventory (MSEI) created by O'Brien and Epstein (1988). Because self-esteem ratings are often subject to socially desirable responses, the MSEI includes a defensiveness scale. As shown in Table 8.1, the MSEI has global, worthiness and competence scales. The CWT programme, even though it is usually offered in a group format, allows for an individualized assessment and treatment protocol for participants because participants assess their own self-esteem areas of strength and weakness by taking the empirically reliable and valid MSEI. These specific domains are then targeted for improvement; for instance, when individuals score low in the worthiness domain of moral self-approval, they might be encouraged to keep a diary of when they do act in ways that are consistent with their moral beliefs and to use cognitive restructuring to reassess their thinking related to this domain. At the end of the treatment programme and at follow-up, participants are retested. The manualized sequence of intervention strategies can be used in group or individual therapy (Mruk, 2013). Though additional research is needed, some evidence currently exists for the effectiveness of the CWT programme in both college students (Bartoletti, 2006) and community adults in a mental health setting (Hakim-Larson & Mruk, 1997). In both cases, the self-esteem of participants increased significantly after finishing the programme. Consistent with expectations in targeting healthy authentic self-esteem, it is noteworthy that Bartoletti (2006) also assessed narcissism and found that it did not increase in the post-testing of her participants.

## Summary of Chapter Key Points

The emotions of shame and pride and the construct of self-esteem have a long history of being discussed in philosophy and psychology. Emotional self-efficacy involves being skilled in achieved a desired emotional outcome, which thus enhances self-esteem. While some researchers emphasize the measurement of global self-esteem, others note the importance of considering the various facets and domains of self-esteem which can be subsumed under the categories of worthiness and competence. Contemporary studies have repeatedly found that the domain consistently linked to inner global feelings of self-esteem is perceived outer physical appearance, a domain that affects individuals across the lifespan. Simply put, people feel better about themselves if they like and feel good about how their bodies appear to others. Feelings of shame and pride also have been linked to self-esteem. Individuals who are prone to making global rather than specific attributions about themselves are prone to feeling shame for violating standards, rules, goals and expectations of important others. Authentic self-esteem is reflected in feelings of pride where there is a moderated balance beween vanity and humility. Unfortunately, imbalances in feelings of worthiness and competence can result in suicidal and/or homicidal ideation in children, adolescents and adults. As well, imbalances may result in defensive forms of self-esteem that have been linked to adult personality disorders. Parents and family members often strive for healthy, adaptive, authentic self-esteem, and clinicians often target self-esteem enhancement in their treatment planning. Additional research is needed to clarify our understanding of culture, self-esteem and emotional development in families.

## Further Reading

Harter, S. (2012). *The construction of the self (2nd ed.).* New York, NY: Guilford.

Harter covers the entire lifespan in her seminal volume on the construction of the self. She reviews and critiques the literature on the self-conscious emotions of pride, shame, guilt, embarrassment and humiliation. Causes, implications, roles of others, behavioural manifestations and adaptive functions of each of the negative emotions are described. Harter also provides an in-depth and careful review of the cross-cultural literature on the construction of the self. The interested reader can get a comprehensive overview and introduction to Harter's approach to self-esteem from this book and Harter's website: https://portfolio.du.edu/SusanHarter/page/44199

Mruk, C. (2013). *Self-esteem and positive psychology: Research, theory, and practice (4th ed.).* New York, NY: Springer.

In this fourth edition of this comprehensive book on self-esteem and positive psychology, the author reviews the history of self-esteem as a global construct and as an existentially based two-factor theory comprised of both worthiness and competence components. The construct of self-esteem moments and decisive process-oriented transitions that occur over time are described in detail. Methodological issues in defining and measuring self-esteem are addressed, as is the value of making use of both quantitative and qualitative assessment approaches. The author's Competence and Worthiness Training programme for adult groups is presented in a manual format and workshop handouts are included in the Appendices. The self-esteem programme can be adapted for use with individuals. Emotions linked to defensive self-esteem such as hubris and authentic self-esteem such as happiness and pride are discussed, as are a variety of positive emotions significant for the field of positive psychology.

# 9

# Verbal Emotional Expressions and Communication in the Family Context

Dorothy is a college student who has been regularly having unprotected sex with James, her boyfriend. She felt both exhilarated and scared after finding out she was pregnant. James was happy to hear the news. She called home to tell her mother privately, but instead had the phone passed around to her father and her brother, Cameron. So Dorothy waited and sent her mother an email:

> *"Mom, Okay. Here goes. So ... I didn't want to tell you this over email, but I couldn't get you alone on the phone just now, and it will take me a week to get up the courage again. I took a pregnancy test today and it came out positive. I'm happy and excited (and of course, scared). But more than anything, I'm scared that you won't be as happy about it as I am, or that 'people' will think that I'm throwing my life and education away. I should be much more worried than I am, but deep down I believe that this is what I am really here to do – be a mother ..." [email continues].*

Dorothy's mother responded back to her:

> *"I'm speechless. Cameron is very sad. Dad is going through the roof and blame [sic] it on me. My feelings are, as you might expect, mixed. There's a lot to think about and to grieve before being happy. And there's a lot to be angry or disbelieving about before thinking that you can actually deal with this. I'm sure I will be happy and excited for you. And for James. And I will be helpful. Count on that. But count on my saying that I knew you needed to do other things before this. Holy Shit (which may be a tiny bit better than just 'shit'). xxo m."*
>
> (Garrod et al., 2012, pp. 213–214)

## The Many Modes of Verbal Communication

Verbal emotional expressions among family members may be delivered orally in face-to-face interactions, over the phone or computer via audio or video-chatting, or via recorded messages such as voicemail. As in the vignette above, written verbal expressions of emotions also may occur in emails as well as in paper mail letters, in text or instant messages, or through various other forms of social media that are easily accessible in the second decade of the 21st century, such as Facebook, Twitter and Instagram. Social media affords the opportunity for *text-based paralanguage*, in which symbolic emotional meanings are attached to words that are deliberately presented or written in an exaggerated way (e.g., all caps or unusual punctuation), or symbolic pictographs which are consciously inserted into text to convey emotions (e.g., Luangrath, Peck & Barger, 2017). Family members are increasingly using the various forms of computer-mediated venues to express how they feel through pictures, verbalized text and pictographs such as emoticons and emoji, and researchers have begun to study these text-based expressions (e.g., Kaye, Malone & Wall, 2017; Vidal, Ares & Jaeger, 2016). *Emoticons* are emotion cues expressed as various ASCII-based keyboard characters, such as :-) or :-(, which indicate a happy and sad face respectively, or other pictograms, such as smiley faces ☺ or frowns ☹, that are increasingly being used in text to express emotions as a proxy for live non-verbal emotional expressions that take place during actual face-to-face communication (e.g., Riordan & Kreuz, 2010). Currently, *emoji*, which mean "picture words" in Japanese, are popular ways to express emotions in social media text communication (e.g., Vidal et al., 2016). Vidal et al. (2016) have conducted research that demonstrates links between food preferences, emoji and emotional expressions as assessed through Twitter data (e.g., "I love when my dad surprises me by making a huge dinner for me after work 😍❤", Vidal et al., 2016, p. 121). Riordan and Kreuz (2010) also describe other types of text-based paralanguage as *emotion cues* that exist in written verbal formats, such as repeating letters within a word, adding punctuation for emphasis, and capitalizing words to express intensity, urgency or speech volume (e.g., "Reeaally, I need HELP!!! NOW!!!").

Social context also makes a difference with respect to the function of emoticons/emoji. While emoticons/emoji are widely used among young people and in informal settings, they may be discouraged or even prohibited in some workplace settings; in other workplaces, emoticons are used sparingly and seem to provide additional information about the writer's attitudes, whether to interpret a statement as humorous/ironic, and to suggest hedging after a written comment (Skovholt, Grønning & Kankaanranta, 2014). Overall, the expression of emotions in our computer-mediated communication (CMC) is here to stay. As noted by Derks, Fischer and Bos in their review of the role of emotion in CMC, "CMC is crammed with emotions" (2008, p. 781), whether the focus is on emotion words and pictures or the use of emoticons/emoji.

In contemporary 21st-century life, family members may first learn about important life events such as births, marriages, separations, divorces and deaths over social media contacts with family members, rather than through audio phone calls or face-to-face communication. Thus, there is recognition among many scholars that in addition to researching traditional oral and written forms of verbal emotional communication in the family, it is now necessary to study CMC given that online users have made adaptations in the effort to express themselves emotionally (Riordan & Kreuz, 2010). In the following sections of this chapter, the various ways in which emotional communication can take place are reviewed along with the findings that are most relevant for direct verbal communication within contemporary families.

Although the focus of this chapter is on the linguistic aspects of face-to-face emotion communication, it is important to recognize that there are also in-person face-to-face ***paralinguistic features*** of emotion communication that are being socialized as well; paralinguistic features include voice intonation and sound patterns that convey emotional meaning and that may or may not be interpreted in a similar way cross-culturally (e.g., Scherer, Banse & Wallbott, 2001). For instance, *interjections* such as "Wow!", "Yuck!", or "Ugh!" convey emotion and often occur in everyday in-person interactions; some paralanguage, whether in-person or text-based, such as "Holy Shit", as used in the mother's email in this chapter's vignette, are emotional expressions with meanings that may vary by culture (Goddard, 2014; Wierzbicka, 1992). Keeping in mind that both linguistic and paralinguistic features of language are likely being socialized, this chapter begins with a description of the development of emotion language, and then proceeds to a discussion of how children are socialized into using emotion language through stories and narratives. Finally, we turn to the complexities of analysing emotion language in family communication. The chapter ends by exploring some possible ways to enhance emotion socialization by using emotion language.

## Emotion Words and Labels: The Development of Emotion Language

By 12–18 months of age, some children are using language to refer to their emotions (e.g., happy, sad, angry, scared), behavioural expressions of emotion (e.g., hug, smile, cry), and mental states (e.g., think, know, pretend);

thus, they have begun to create what has been called a ***theory of mind*** (e.g., Bretherton & Beeghly, 1982), which is a belief system about the internal states of both the self and other people. By 18–24 months, many can demonstrate self-awareness, first through expression of their own thoughts, beliefs, desires and emotions, and then eventually by commenting on these mental states in others (Harris, 1989). In a now classic study, Bretherton, Fritz, Zahn-Waxler and Ridgeway (1986) found that specific emotion words spoken by typically developing toddlers (1½ to 3 years) were uttered in socially appropriate contexts. Their findings suggested that these very young children understood and could express in simple language the underlying causality of the emotion in a logical sequence (e.g., "Doggy. I'm scared").

The acquisition of such basic emotion words and a comprehensive emotion vocabulary in appropriate causal and social contexts is an important developmental phenomenon that begins in infancy and continues to change and progress across the lifespan. In everyday communication, the most convenient access to our internal emotional states is through our verbal descriptions and language (Ortony, Clore & Foss, 1987). The corpus of possible words within a given language (e.g., English) that denotes emotional meaning is called the *emotion lexicon* and includes words that possess the following: "(a) they are internal, mental, as opposed to physical or external, conditions, (b) they are good examples of states, and (c) their predominant referential focus is on affect as opposed to behavior, cognition, or some combination of these" (Ortony et al., 1987, p. 358). Several emotion lexicons have been used in studies over the past few decades (e.g., Davitz, 1969; deRivera, 1984; Johnson-Laird & Oatley, 1989; Shaver, Schwartz, Kirson & O'Connor, 1987). In addition, researchers have also started to compile emotion lexicons of emoticons and emoji (e.g., see the Supplement for Luangrath et al., 2017, and Appendix A of Vidal et al., 2016).

In a review of how emotions are categorized in different cultures in verbal emotion lexicons and non-verbal emotional expressions, Russell (1991) concluded that there are both similarities and differences cross-culturally in emotion classifications. He raises the interesting question of the links between labelling one's emotional state and experiencing a given emotional state. That is, if your culture does not have a word or label for an emotional experience, is it possible or likely that you will experience the associated feeling? Theories of ***linguistic relativity*** (Lucy, 1997), stemming from the work of Edward Sapir and Benjamin Whorf, have proposed that language helps us to conceptualize, think and remember our experiences by providing yet another way in addition to our sensory perceptions for the experience to get encoded in our memories. Indeed, when a particular emotion is very important in a culture, it tends to be part of an elaborate schema or mental representation represented by a whole group of semantically related words. For example, as described by Levy (1982), the emotion of "anger" is *hypercognized* among Tahitians; that is, there are many specific well-defined words for the variations of this emotion, the conditions under which it may occur, and how it should be handled; in contrast, among Tahitians, sadness is *hypocognized*, and there are very few words to label the different forms of sadness or what to do about it. Sadness for Tahitians is linked more to bodily states (e.g., feeling fatigued) than to mental state concepts associated with emotion words.

Researchers interested in the study of emotion and culture have begun to catalogue and describe the similarities and differences in the meaning of specific emotion words such as anger and shame in various cultures (e.g., Shweder et al., 2008). Shweder et al. (2008) have reviewed the multidisciplinary literature on the cultural psychology of emotions and have concluded that while it is possible to understand the emotional meanings, experiences and mental states of people in cultures that are different from our own, the process is not simple and requires active consideration of various components on which cultures may be either alike or different. Shweder et al. (2008) cite Horton's research on the meaning of anger in Americans and Tibetans as an example. The expression *lung lang* in Tibetan translates to *anger* in English and refers to "a rising movement of the wind that animates consciousness, upward from the chest" (Shweder et al., 2008, p. 416). Both Americans and Tibetans were found to describe some similar bodily states (e.g., heat, shaking/nervousness) in reference to anger/*lung lang*, but were also found to differ in other ways. For instance, Tibetans were more likely to believe that *lung lang* could be prevented altogether and thus transcended, while Americans were more likely to doubt that anger could be avoided or that it would even be desirable to do so.

Children learn to adopt the specific emotion language and meanings of their cultures through interactions with family members, their peers and other members of their communities, and/or through various other technological media (e.g., television, videogames) and printed media (e.g., books) that they are exposed to either deliberately or inadvertently. As emphasized by Saarni (1998), emotions do not occur in a cultural vacuum and they are greatly influenced by interpersonal communication and relationships. Within cultures, individuals, including parents and other caregivers, vary their emphasis on emotion words and verbal expressions depending on the listener's gender and age. In a well-controlled study of emotion talk with preschoolers using cartoon facial expressions of basic emotions as the stimuli, van der Pol et al. (2015) found that fathers and mothers adjusted their language depending on the child's level of emotion understanding. In this task, both parents tended to use stereotypic gender labelling of the pictures such that anger was more likely to be interpreted as being linked to a boy character and sadness or happiness more with a girl character, even though the depictions were gender-neutral.

Girls and women tend to refer to more emotion words, both positive and negative, than do boys and men (Brody & Hall, 2008). William Pollack (2006) has proposed that boys are socialized into what he calls *the boy code* of emotionally silencing themselves; that is, they are put into a *gender straitjacket* to maintain strict consistency with cultural gender role expectations for masculinity which involve taking a somewhat stoic stance especially when it comes to the more vulnerable expressions of emotion. For boys in Western cultures to survive among their peers, they must avoid showing their feelings and engaging in behaviours that might lead them to feel shame and humiliation. Furthermore, he notes that because Western attitudes have become more egalitarian towards girls and women in the past few decades, boys may be confused about cultural expectations for their gender role. In addition to the emotional pain that boys undergo because of the boy code and gender straitjacket, there are other possible long-term negative consequences (e.g., mental disorders, suicide, homicide) that exist at greater rates for boys and men who have not found ways to openly express their emotions and counteract feelings of shame or humiliation (Pollack, 2006). This could potentially be linked to their acts of violence towards themselves or others.

Men who are more likely to endorse traditional masculinity have been found also to be more likely to have difficulty using words to communicate their own internal emotional state, a problem that has been historically labelled *alexithymia* (e.g., Levant, Allen & Lien, 2014; see Chapter 7). Taking into consideration the linguistic relativity hypothesis, do men who have such a deficiency in their emotion word vocabulary also have a deficit in their ability to experience certain emotions? Or is it possible, for at least some, that they do indeed experience the underlying emotions but actively suppress them and avoid expressing them at least in some situations? Both scenarios are likely possibilities. For instance, the goal of improving emotion vocabulary in psychotherapy is to enrich individuals' ability to self-report on their inner emotional experiences and to discuss them effectively (e.g., Greenberg, 2008). However, some evidence suggests that active suppression of using language to communicate emotions also occurs. For example, gender differences in the use of emotion language among couples is maximized and greater under conditions of high tension than it is under conditions of low stress in which the couple is relatively comfortable (Brody & Hall, 2008). That is, consistent with stereotypic gender roles, men are less likely than women to verbalize their feelings and they are more likely to stonewall, withdraw and actively suppress emotion expression when they are uncomfortable with the topic of discussion (Vogel et al., 2003).

In addition to gender, chronological age has been found to be related to the development of an emotion vocabulary. During normative language acquisition, children's emotion vocabulary increases greatly between the ages of 18 months and 6 years of age (Ridgeway, Waters & Kuczaj, 1985). Further changes in the quality of the use of emotion language continue to occur throughout the school years, the period of adolescence, and across young, middle and older adulthood as reviewed below and summarized in Table 9.1.

**Table 9.1** Summary of Emotion Language Development across the Lifespan

| Age/Developmental Level | Emotion Language (examples) | Source |
|---|---|---|
| Toddlers and Preschoolers | | See Ridgeway, Waters & Kuczaj (1985) for a comprehensive list of emotion language from 1½ to 6 years of age in children studied in the US. |
| 1½ to 2 years | At least half can comprehend the words *happy, sad.* | |
| 2 to 2½ years | At least half can comprehend the words *afraid, scared, angry, mad, loving* and produce the words *happy, sad, afraid, mad, scared.* | |
| 2½ to 3 years | At least half can comprehend the words *surprised, unhappy* and produce the word *angry.* | |
| 3 to 4 years | At least half can comprehend the word *worried* and produce the words *loving, surprised.* | |
| 4 to 5 years | At least half can comprehend the words *disgusted, ashamed, embarrassed.* | |
| 5 to 6 years | At least half can comprehend the word *jealous.* | |
| School-age Children (6 to 12 years) | Younger children can state having opposite valence feelings in *sequence* for different targets (e.g., sad that dog died, but happy about getting a present).<br>Older children can state opposite valence conflicting or *ambivalent* feelings that occur *simultaneously* involving the same situation or target (e.g., love dad but angry at him too). | See Saarni (1999) and Heubeck et al. (2016) for a review of literature on the development of understanding mixed emotions. |

*Continued*

**Table 9.1** *(Continued)*

| Age/Developmental Level | Emotion Language (examples) | Source |
|---|---|---|
| Adolescents (13 to 17 years) | Increases in understanding social emotions in appropriate social contexts from early puberty to post-puberty. | Burnett et al. (2011) |
| | Increases in producing conventional language to describe emotions and increases in ego development. | Labouvie-Vief et al. (1989)<br>Westenberg & Gjerde (1999) |
| Adulthood (18 + years) | Developmental changes in emotional/affect complexity that are not necessarily age-related. | Labouvie-Vief (2015) |
| | Increases in producing unconventional emotion language and increases in ego development that are not necessarily age-related. | Labouvie-Vief et al. (1989)<br>Lilgendahl, Helson & John (2013) |

Early emotion researchers noted that as children developed an emotion vocabulary, they began to use multiple words to describe their emotional experiences (Saarni, 1999). These words were either of the same valence (both positive such as happy and proud, or negative such as angry and sad) or of opposite valence indicating the potential for ambivalence, conflicting emotions, or what has come to be called *mixed emotions* towards a single target (e.g., Smith, Glass & Fireman, 2015). Because the experience of mixed emotions is common within family communication and relationships, it has become an important area of study (Heubeck et al., 2016). Harter and her colleagues found that 5-year-old children typically denied having opposite valence emotions in their experience (e.g., they could not love dad at the same time as being angry at him); in contrast, older children acknowledged the experience of opposite valence emotions sequentially in time, before finally recognizing by about the age of 11 or 12 years that opposite valence emotions towards the same target can be experienced simultaneously (e.g., Harter & Buddin, 1987; Harter & Whitesell, 1989). Tasks using story characters also found that it was not until children were about 10 or 11 years old that they were able to verbalize ambivalent feelings towards a single target or situation (e.g., Donaldson & Westerman, 1986). Smith et al. (2015) critiqued these early studies and have claimed that the cognitive task demands may have been too great for most preschool children to verbalize an understanding of mixed emotions. They conclude on the basis of their own research and that of others that even 3 to 5 year olds are capable of understanding and experiencing mixed emotions when the task demands are simple and age-appropriate. Thus, it is not until the preadolescent period of about 10–12 years of age that it is clear, based on what children say, that they can comprehend, experience and report on mixed feelings that interact and modify each other (Saarni, 1999); for instance, older children can describe how feeling sad at the same as feeling happy can dampen or alter their simultaneous feeling of happiness. However, some evidence nonetheless suggests that rudimentary comprehension and experience of mixed emotions occurs in children as young as 3 to 5 years old even before they are able to express it adequately in words (Smith et al., 2015).

Precisely what combination of mixed emotions are experienced and reported by children who are cognitively able to do so is dependent on their emotion lexicon. Different combinations of opposite valence emotions develop at different rates according to Heubeck et al. (2016), and additional research is needed to fully understand the development of mixed emotions. For example, because the words *happy* and *sad* emerge within the emotion lexicon in US samples before the words *mad* and *scared* (see Table 9.1), it is not surprising that the most frequently found combination of mixed emotion comprehension and use in children is *happy-sad*, and that this is followed by the combination *happy-mad* and then *happy-scared* (Harter & Buddin, 1987; Heubeck et al., 2016).

Emotion language development extends far beyond the basic emotions (e.g., happy, sad, angry, scared) to include the verbalized use of social emotion words (e.g., proud, jealous, ashamed, embarrassed, humiliated, guilty) which adds yet another layer of complexity given that inferring the mental states and evaluations of others is involved (e.g., Harter, 2012). In addition to verbalized use of the social emotions from childhood into adolescence, the development of mixed emotion comprehension and verbalized use continues. For instance, Burnett, Thompson, Bird and Blakemore (2011) found an increase from early puberty to post-puberty in the complexity of understanding multiple mixed emotions in situations that involve social emotions. They suggest that both brain development and hormonal changes coincide with these advances.

Emotion language continues to develop from adolescence into adulthood consistent with the orthogenetic principle (Lerner, 2002; Werner, 1957). Like biological development (see Chapter 3), language development involves growth (e.g., growth of emotion vocabulary) and increasing complexity (e.g., in emotion concepts and language use); it also goes from being relatively global and undifferentiated to being more differentiated and hierarchically organized and integrated over time. Researchers who study *emotional complexity* have incorporated the orthogenetic principle into how they describe the processes involved, although currently there is no one widely accepted definition by researchers regarding an acceptable way to operationalize the concept (Grühn et al., 2013). Lindquist and Barrett (2008) conceptualize emotional complexity as involving *dialecticism*, which includes the acceptance of emotional contradiction and the balance between positive and negative emotional experiences, and *granularity*, which includes the ability to use specific emotion words to convey precise, discrete and distinctively different emotional experiences. Consistent with the orthogenetic principle, dialecticism seems to involve the idea of integration, while granularity involves the idea of differentiation in the development of emotional complexity. Gisela Labouvie-Vief and her colleagues have found that affective complexity increases from adolescence through the middle adult years with a decline thereafter in the older adult years; the focus of their studies was on gains in insight into emotions, the differentiation of the perspectives of self and that of others, as well as the integrated use of positive and negative emotions (Labouvie-Vief, 2015). This decline has been replicated in both cross-sectional and longitudinal studies. However, it is important to recognize that the complexity of the older adults was still greater than that of the younger adults, and that older adults have been shown to have greater ***affect optimization*** than younger ones (i.e., a greater tendency to maximize positive emotions and dampen or minimize negative emotions to optimize overall well-being) (Grühn et al., 2013; Labouvie-Vief & Medler, 2002). Affect optimization is thought to interact with affect complexity during the process of emotional self-regulation, a topic that is described in greater detail in Chapter 10. However, with respect to the use of emotion language, it is noteworthy that future researchers will need to keep in mind that the interaction of emotional or affective complexity with affective optimization in adults is likely to be evident in how emotional experiences in adults are conveyed in their verbal descriptions and use of emotion language.

Studying the changes in the emotion lexicon from infancy to adulthood gives only a partial picture of the role of language in emotional development and family functioning. The ***pragmatics*** of communication are important as well. Pragmatics involve the underlying social intentions (e.g., being polite) and emotional meaning of the speaker in terms of what is being communicated within a given social context (e.g., Schnall, 2005). As described in the beginning of this chapter, the paralinguistic emotional cues such as voice tone, rhythm and speech rate also are involved in the communication of intended meanings. Morton and Trehub (2001) have found that even young preschool children can understand and interpret paralinguistic emotional cues such as voice tone and speech rate when there is a match between the words (what is said) and the voice tone and speech rate (how it is said). However, when there is a mismatch between what is said and how it is said, such as occurs with sarcasm (e.g., "I am so happy to see you", said in an exasperated, sad voice tone), children between 4 and 6 years old tend to interpret the emotion by considering the literal words spoken and not the paralinguistic cues (e.g., Morton & Trehub, 2001). Yet, some 6 year olds can effectively attend to paralinguistic cues if they are: (1) *primed* to be more aware of interpreting the paralinguistic cues, (2) given explicit *instructions* to do so combined with *feedback* about their accuracy in detecting the emotions, and (3) can describe the discrepancy between what is said and how it is said, which would indicate their ability to *mentally represent* and *reflect* on the conflicting emotional information (Morton, Trehub & Zelazo, 2003).

Children who grow up in families where there is bilingual communication may be learning about emotions and the intended communication of others in a different and more complex manner than children who grow up in monolingual environments. As a follow-up to the study conducted by Morton and Trehub (2001), Yow and Markman (2011) conducted a study comparing the ability to utilize paralinguistic cues that conflicted with content in monolingual and bilingual 4 year olds. Consistent with their expectations, they found that the 4-year-old bilingual children were better able to use paralinguistic cues than 4-year-old monolingual children when the emotional paralinguistic cues (i.e., voice tone) conflicted with the content of what was said. Yow and Markman (2011) attributed this finding to the adult-like necessity for children who live in a bilingual family to be attentive to the communicative demands of their everyday social environment. They must be more sensitive than those in a monolingual family to the intentions of others and they need to frequently make inferences about what others mean by what they say. These experiences are part of the emotion socialization of bilingual children.

Bilingual children of immigrants have been found to engage in linguistic *code-switching* whereby they alternate back and forth between languages depending on the setting, cultural norms, and their own communicative intentions. In an interesting study of code-switching in second-generation Lebanese youth living in London, Al-Khatib (2003) found that adolescents who were being defiant switched to using English in the middle of family conversations in Arabic! They seemed to be likely to do this when they wanted to convey feelings of Western autonomy and separation from their families at that moment during the interaction.

Thus, the development of emotion language in children who are bilingual or multilingual is likely to be different in some ways from children who grow up in households that are monolingual. To comprehend and successfully navigate whatever culture(s) they are exposed to, children need to make inferences about what others mean by what they say and they need to learn the meaning behind various cultural symbols, many of which involve emotions.

One specific way that cultures differ is in the meanings of the linguistic metaphors they use to describe emotional experiences, as discussed in the next section.

## Metaphors and Emotional Development

It is easier to describe our inner emotional experiences using language in some settings as compared to others. When internal emotional states are difficult to express verbally using the conventional emotion lexicon, they may be expressed in a compact and vivid manner via the use of metaphors; metaphors are more likely to be used for the expression of emotional states than for emotional behaviours, and more likely to be used for intense rather than mild emotions (Fainsilber & Ortony, 1987). Emotion metaphors take an internal experience and embody the affect involved in an external spatial representation; for instance, both positive and negative emotions are sometimes conveyed in metaphors that involve a substance-filled container such as "overflowing with sadness", "bursting with happiness", and "drained of all joy" (e.g., Crawford, 2009). Metaphoric language involving emotions may occur in the form of cultural proverbs; for example, an Arabic proverb that translates in English to "The hunter seethes and the bird preens" means "One is unaffected by the desperation of the other" (Arnander & Skipwith, 2007, p. 67).

Descriptive emotion language can be either *literal*, as in the development of a basic emotion vocabulary described earlier, or *figurative*, which consists of conceptual metaphors and metonymies (Kovecses, 2000). A ***conceptual metaphor*** involves the attempt to explain a domain or concept that is abstract (e.g., anger) by using another domain or concept that is more physical or concrete; for example, "boiling with anger" links anger (concept A) to a hot fluid (concept B) (e.g., Kovecses, 2000; Lakoff & Johnson, 1980). A related but different form of figurative language is a ***conceptual metonymy***, which involves a part or element of an emotion concept standing for another part or the whole emotion concept; for instance, a drop in body temperature is one element of fear, and the metonymy 'having cold feet' can stand for fear (Kovecses, 2000). Families socialize both descriptive language (i.e., emotion word vocabulary) and culturally relevant figurative language (i.e., metaphors and metonymies). Although most research presented in this chapter focuses on descriptive language, some research has been conducted on emotional development and the use of figurative language as discussed next.

Waggoner and Palermo (1989) compared comprehension of metaphors in children and adults; they found that even children as young as 5 years old can comprehend basic emotion metaphors (e.g., *a snorting bull* for anger) if the metaphor is concrete rather than abstract and is provided in an appropriate context. However, young children have difficulty explaining their interpretations. The ability to interpret more abstract metaphors for a greater variety of emotions and to make distinctions among same valence emotion metaphors (e.g., anger vs. fear) continues to improve throughout childhood into the adult years (Waggoner & Palermo, 1989). Waggoner (2010) also has compared the comprehension of metonymies in elementary schoolchildren to that of adults (e.g., heat standing for anger, as in "I'm really steamed"). He found that children were equally likely as adults to perceive fear as being related to the temperature of cold; for other emotions, there were some age differences in the interpretation of temperature and emotion between children and adults. Waggoner (2010) notes that children learn from their cultures about how to interpret metaphors and metonymies through emotion socialization in the family and through media, such as cartoons (e.g., an angry character with steam coming out of his ears). Consider the picture on the cover of the Disney PIXAR DVD movie about emotions entitled *Inside Out* (2015); the emotion-animated character of anger is shown as having *fire* coming out of his *red* head, while the *blue* sadness character is shown lying *down*, and the *yellow-tinged* happiness character is standing up with arms *up* in the air. Both the literal and the figurative content of films such as this one can be influential in the cultural process of emotion socialization.

While both children and adults can comprehend and utilize emotion metaphors and metonymies, researchers have noted some clear developmental differences. While childhood, adolescence and early adulthood are periods of *acquisition* in which emotion language and knowledge from familial and cultural sources are learned, the middle and later adulthood years can best be characterized as revealing an *inward emotional turn* with a primary focus on self-reflection, private inner experiences and autobiographical emotional memories (e.g., Neugarten, 1968; Labouvie-Vief, DeVoe & Bulka, 1989; Labouvie-Vief & Hakim-Larson, 1989). In a life-span study in which individuals between 10 and 77 years old were interviewed about their emotions, Labouvie-Vief and her colleagues found that younger individuals and those with less verbal skill and lower ego levels described their inner emotional experiences of anger, sadness, fear and happiness in a less complex manner using more conventional language with a focus on physical reactions and outer appearances; in contrast, more mature individuals (older, better verbal skills, higher ego levels) described their emotions by making greater use of complex, unique and vivid metaphorical language with a greater sensitivity to bodily sensations (Labouvie-Vief et al., 1989). For example, less mature statements included simple, conventionally descriptive metaphorical language such as "I was down" or "I felt empty", while more mature statements were complex and unconventional such as "Everything is like a cyclone going around", or, in a wedding context, "You have sunshine in your heart" (Labouvie-Vief et al., 1989, p. 429). As discussed in History Feature Box 9, Jane Loevinger's (1966, 1994) theory of ego development is one of the classic developmental theories that has been instrumental in demonstrating how cognitive-affective complexity is evident in the language and writing of individuals across the lifespan.

**History Feature Box 9**

**Back Then and Now: Integrating Thought, Language and Emotion**

Language involves both cognitive and affective processes, although most theorists and researchers have not historically addressed them together. Jean Piaget, Lev Vygotsky, Sigmund Freud, and Jane Loevinger are among those who have. Swiss psychologist Jean Piaget is known for his description of the *semiotic function*, which involves symbolic mental representations of play, dreams, imitation and language; the semiotic function shows rapid development between 1½ and 5 years of age (Piaget, 1962). Language development for Piaget proceeds from presocial to egocentric to social speech in the preschool years (e.g., Kohlberg, Yaeger & Hjertholm, 1968). With *egocentric speech*, young children engage in monologues (alone or collectively) and were thought by Piaget to have difficulty considering other perspectives; in Piaget's view, by about 7 years old, children could engage in social speech by taking others' points of view into account. The Russian psychologist, Lev Vygotsky, in contrast, challenged Piaget on the issue of social speech. He took the position that children's language is social from the beginning; it proceeds from being externalized and regulated by the sociocultural setting to becoming overt private speech said aloud to self-regulate actions, and then finally to covert private speech which becomes inner speech and silent verbal thoughts (Lidstone, Meins & Fernyhough, 2011; Vygotsky, 1962). For Vygotsky, this process of internalization characterizes the link between language and thought. Both views have spurred much research and are worthwhile with Piaget emphasizing the individual and Vygotsky the social and cultural environment (Cole & Wertsch, 1996).

For Piaget, thought is linked to actions prior to its symbolic representation as language; afterwards, this can take the form of ***affective schemas***, which he defined as "relatively stable modes of feeling or reacting" that continually involve attempts to assimilate and accommodate new situations to past ones to maintain an equilibrium (Piaget, 1962, p. 206). When such affective schemas are in an equilibrium, symbolic thought can reach conscious awareness, but when there is an unbalanced disequilibrium, assimilation may dominate, and the use of unconscious symbols as proposed by Freud may come to the foreground as they often do in preschoolers' play, earliest dreams and verbalized fantasies

(Piaget, 1962). Like Piaget, the Viennese physician and founder of psychoanalysis, Sigmund Freud, noted the rich symbolisms evident in language and dreams when a person unwittingly reveals disguised underlying emotional content that is below the threshold of conscious awareness (Freud, 1910). In his popular book *The Psychopathology of Everyday Life,* Freud (1914) gives examples of emotionally motivated mistakes and speech blunders that he calls *lapsus linguae* (Latin for "slip of the tongue"); today we often use the eponym *Freudian slip* instead.

Inspired by Freud and psychoanalytic theory, projective storytelling tests are still utilized to try to understand unconscious emotional themes. Historically, projective techniques involved the idea that if children or adults are asked to tell stories about characters with whom they identify rather than autobiographical stories, they would be less defensive and less likely to distort their feelings. In other words, they will project their own feelings onto those of the characters. The most well-known and widely utilized of these tests are perhaps the Thematic Apperception Test (Morgan & Murray, 1935; Murray & Bellak, 1973), the Children's Apperception Test (Bellak & Bellak, 1974) and the Roberts Apperception Test for Children (Roberts & McArthur, 1989). In these tests, children or adults are shown a picture on a card and instructed to tell a story about the characters and to elaborate on the situation, and on the thoughts and feelings of the characters. Zurbriggen and Sturman (2002) review research (e.g., McClelland, 1985; McClelland, Koestner & Weinberger, 1989; Morgan & Murray, 1935) in which the stories obtained are scored for the presence of themes involving three primary human motivations: *achievement, power and affiliation-intimacy.* They also find partial support in their own research for McClelland's (1985) hypothesis stating that emotions are linked to specific motivations. For example, there is some evidence to suggest that stories that involve anger are more likely to be linked to the power motivation than to other motivations, while stories involving love or sadness are more likely to be linked to the affiliation-intimacy motive.

Another projective test that is still widely used internationally was created by Jane Loevinger to assess ego development by asking individuals to finish incomplete sentences in any way they wish (e.g., Loevinger & Wessler, 1970). Using classic developmental theories as a foundation, Loevinger's theory of ego development describes changes over time in how deeply people think about their life experiences and how this is reflected in their language as they complete sentences such as "Raising a family ______" (Hy & Loevinger, 1996). As shown in Table 9.2, Loevinger proposed nine ego levels. Since its creation, numerous research findings using Loevinger's Sentence Completion Test (SCT) continue to show evidence for its reliability and validity as a construct separate from intellectual level, which may be a necessary but *insufficient* condition for ego development to advance (Cohn & Westenberg, 2004). Ego development change requires the processing of life experiences and incorporates the resulting advances in morality, conscience and the integration of multiple perspectives (Loevinger, 1994). Being open to new experiences as a young adult and being able to process difficult midlife experiences is related to advances in ego level across midlife (Lilgendahl, Helson & John, 2013). The contemporary significance of ego development is that it is evident in language and it shows links to some aspects of emotional maturity such as identity achievement (Jespersen, Kroger & Martinussen, 2013), adaptive coping (Labouvie-Vief, Hakim-Larson & Hobart, 1987), and conceptual exploration of major life growth goals (Bauer & McAdams, 2004).

**Table 9.2** Summary of Jane Loevinger's Ego Levels (Loevinger & Wessler, 1970; Hy & Loevinger, 1996)

| Ego Level | Description |
|---|---|
| E-1 Presocial | The ego is not yet formed and is in the process of emerging. |
| E-2 Impulsive | A limited number of emotions are impulsively expressed with an emphasis on sexual and aggressive content. |
| E-3 Self-Protective | There is a preoccupied interest in opportunism, hedonism and staying out of trouble.<br>The person is emotionally guarded and cautious, and may be manipulative or have an exploitive attitude towards others. |
| E-4 Conformist | There is a dualistic view of right and wrong, with an acceptance of social norms and traditional gender roles. Feelings of emotional security are linked to social approval and belonging to the social group. The person highly values appearance and attractiveness. |
| E-5 Self-Aware | Multiple points of view are considered by the person. Feelings of self-consciousness, loneliness and social embarrassment are characteristic. Interest in the appearance or well-being of self and and others is expressed in terms of feelings of being worried or concerned. |
| E-6 Conscientious | More conceptually complex thoughts and feelings emerge about self and others. The person tends to feel excessively responsible for influencing others. Values achievement, self-improvement, and mutuality and communication in relationships. Feels guilty over the actual consequences of wrongdoing. |
| E-7 Individualistic | The person has a psychologically complex process-oriented view of the relationships between self and others as changing over time. Internalized emotional conflicts are active and the person makes attempts to cope. Tolerates others but may not completely feel emotional acceptance towards them. |
| E-8 Autonomous | Rich diversity of topics show a toleration of emotional ambiguity. The person attempts to cope with or transcend inner conflicts that occur over time. Values and respects autonomy in both self and others with greater emotional acceptance than at earlier levels. Emotions are well-differentiated and clearly conveyed. Concern is expressed for broad social issues. |
| E-9 Integrated | The person gives vivid, poetic responses that integrate existential humour and paradox, inner psychological conflicts, role conflicts, respect for others' autonomy, social justice issues, sex and mutuality issues, and other unique topics. Conceptually complex identity issues for self and others are raised and addressed. |

As described next, one way in which the developing child's emotion language is learned within the family context is through everyday interactions involving parents, other caregivers and siblings during family storytelling (Nelson, 2014).

## Emotion Scripts, Stories and Narratives in Family Emotion Socialization

The meaning attached to the emotion words of young children changes over time. A number of researchers have described how children eventually develop ***emotion scripts*** for each basic emotion (e.g., sad) that includes a particular causal sequence of antecedent conditions (e.g., a loss) and consequent subevents that unfold over time (e.g., feel bad about the loss, cry, whine, or pout, move slowly, withdraw from others); these emotion scripts may differ from person to person, by family according to their typical routines, by the individual's age or developmental level, as well as by culture (e.g., Saarni, 1999; White, 2000; Widen & Russell, 2008). Emotion scripts are complex cognitive schemata involving cultural knowledge about emotions in self and others; they are used in ways that allow the individual to act (Lewis, 1989). Cultural emotion scripts are often embedded in naïve *folk theories* of emotion, which involve what members of a culture believe about how emotions operate (Saarni, 1999). A North American example would be the idea that you must have a way to vent your feelings and let them out or you will explode like a volcano (Saarni, 1999). As noted by Saarni, children need to learn their culture's folk theories of emotion to give them an overall working model of how emotions operate and to help them to make meaning out of their own and others' feelings and their social interactions.

Children in families can learn emotion scripts and folk theories of emotion by engaging in storytelling activities with their caregivers, listening to and producing narratives, and by engaging in give-and-take verbal discourse with their family members. The *content* of what is included can involve specific emotions, but as noted earlier the paralinguistic and pragmatic features of the interactions are also part of the socialization process. The stories involved include those that we read or make up in addition to real-life everyday stories or personal narratives that we write out or tell to each other. Saarni (1999) notes that stories are how we make meaning out of our interpersonal experiences. They help us to understand the *structure, form, function, content* and *processes* involved in our experiences and to comprehend what is missing and what needs elaboration and further understanding. By attending to and repeating stories, we come to an improved understanding of others, ourselves, our culture and the world around us.

Story structures in Western cultures involve a sequence of events that unfold over time with a beginning, middle and end (Crowley & Mills, 1989; Gardner, 1992; Mills & Crowley, 1986; Teglasi & Rothman, 2001). Thus, we may learn about the potential sequence of emotional change over time by attending to the emotional change of characters in stories. In the beginning, the setting and main characters are introduced along with how they feel now and what happened in the past leading up to the present. In the middle of the story, there is an elaboration of the events, thoughts, feelings, intentions and problems of the characters. The characters interact with each other in the story and situations and moral dilemmas arise, as well as problems that need a solution as the plot thickens. Finally, a good ending involves some resolution and integration of the various external circumstances with the inner emotional world of the characters in such a way that it seems to feel satisfactory to at least the main character. Sometimes, the lack of resolution of some aspects or some loose tie at the end can be the prologue to a follow-up story or sequel. Many well-constructed stories have a clear moral to the story underpinning as part of their structure – a moral theme that occurs throughout.

According to Debra Harkins (1993), there are many functions of reading fictional stories to children as reported by parents. In addition to academic reasons, parents also are trying to socialize the emotional life of children. For instance, they may use stories to: introduce emotionally difficult topics such as divorce or death, teach the child values and beliefs such as sharing, enchant the child by creating an imaginary world, relax socially with the child and converse during shared social time, and teach the child about social and cultural traditions (e.g., emotion scripts for birthday parties, weddings or holidays) (Harkins, 1993). With stories, parents enhance their children's emotion comprehension and management by asking their children questions and assisting in their recall of information about the content or characters.

Parents can also enhance children's recall and interpretation of everyday emotional situations by using what has been called an ***elaborative reminiscing style*** about real-life non-fictional events (e.g., Fivush & Nelson, 2004; Laible & Panfile, 2009). In studies of mother–child reminiscing about past emotional events, mothers have been found to vary in the extent to which they elaborate on and give details about the past situation and its relevance for the present; also, they vary in the extent to which they guide their children through making interpretations about what happened and what can potentially be done about it (Fivush & Nelson, 2004). Mothers who use an elaborative style give rich elaborations and interpretations with background details, make evaluative comments, and ask complex open-ended questions that spur further discussion; they encourage their children's participation in the conversation by confirming and praising them for their contributions to the discussion (e.g., Fivush, Haden & Reese, 2006). During such parent-guided elaborative reminiscing, parents linguistically scaffold the conversation consistent with Vygotsky's sociocultural approach (Fivush et al., 2006). In contrast, other mothers make use of a *repetitive style*, where they add little new information to what is being discussed and they ask yes/no questions that tend to stifle further discussion (Laible & Panfile, 2009).

Mothers with an elaborative reminiscing style are helping their children to develop a more complex understanding of their emotional lives by creating life stories situated in time that are linked to the child's ***autobiographical memories*** of their sense of self (Fivush & Nelson, 2004). Although most children have self-awareness by the time they are about 2 years old as evidenced in mirror self-recognition studies, it is not until they are closer to 4 years old that they seem to have a sense of self that exists across time, thus providing a firmer foundation for establishing such autobiographical memories. Evidence for having a continuous self across time comes from a *delayed* mirror self-recognition task conducted by Povinelli, Landau and Perilloux (1996). They videotaped children between 2 and 4 years old during a game in which a sticker was put on their heads without their awareness; a few minutes later when they were shown the sticker videotape, only the older children reached up to actually remove the stickers which were still on their heads. The study by Povinelli et al. (1996) shows that preschool children around 4 years of age have the ability to situate themselves at different points in time and to have a memory for the events, providing them with an enduring sense of a continuous self. Conversations about emotions and emotional events are crucial in assisting developing children to create enduring memories linked to their sense of having continuous but changing selves over time (Quas & Fivush, 2009).

By reminiscing with their children about past emotional events using an elaborative style, parents are encouraging their children to mentally represent themselves in the past and to reflect on any current or possible future thoughts, actions and emotions that might be related to the past; children thus learn to negotiate an understanding of past emotional situations (either those that were shared or those that were not) using such parent-guided reminiscing (Fivush & Nelson, 2006). Such reminiscing may involve narratives that are structured to show causes and effects and may include recurring *time markers* such as summer vacations, birthdays of family members, and special holidays that are linked to emotion scripts (Fivush & Nelson, 2004, 2006). Studies in a variety of cultures have shown that children of parents with an elaborative reminiscing style have better autobiographical memories and are better able to elaborate on their own personal narratives or life stories in a well-organized and coherent way (Fivush et al., 2006).

Many factors are associated with parental elaboration; among these are parent and child gender, whether the child has a secure attachment to the parent, and the quantity and quality of talk about the event prior to or during the emotional situation (Fivush et al., 2006). In their review of the literature on gender differences in narratives, emotion talk and autobiographical memories, Grysman and Hudson (2013) conclude that when gender differences are found, girls and women have been shown to use more emotion words than boys and men in their narratives and autobiographical memories; the source of this difference is thought to be the extent to which parents elaborate on emotions during their interactions with sons and daughters. In comparison to sons, parents who reminisce with daughters use more emotion words, a greater variety of emotion words, more elaboration and evaluative comments, and provide more background information, though this may differ by culture (Fivush, Haden & Reese, 2006). In their autobiographical memory narratives, girls and women tend to produce longer, more elaborate narratives with more emotion words than boys and men do, and this is not simply a function of greater verbosity (Grysman & Hudson, 2013).

Having a secure attachment with a parent also has been found to be related to more elaborative reminiscing given that a child who feels supported is more likely to be open and receptive to remembering and discussing negative emotions with that parent (Laible & Panfile, 2009). During such reminiscing, parents and securely attached children are co-creating a secondary mental representation (i.e., a new memory) of the primary mental representation or event that gets processed as part of the child's autobiographical memory (Laible & Panfile, 2009). While talking about an emotionally relevant event before or during the event might facilitate later elaborative reminiscing after the event occurs, it is possible that it might instead lead to difficulties; for example, preparatory talk in anticipation of emotional events such as the first day of school (e.g., "you might feel scared!") might not coincide with the child's experience of feeling happy or excited to go to school (Fivush et al., 2006; Thompson, 2009). Discrepancies in parent and child interpretations of emotional events as they unfold over time may escalate and lead to conflicts and the need to regulate emotions during the resulting family interactions, the topic of Chapter 10.

## Promoting Emotion Language Development in Family Members

Both children and adults can learn to improve their emotion communication by increasing their emotion vocabularies and by learning how to effectively communicate their feelings in a non-defensive manner. Children's picture storybooks, non-verbal facial expression flashcards, and games that focus on labelling emotions and improving emotion understanding and verbalization can be found online and in bookstores under the category of Feelings or Emotions (e.g., Creative Therapy Store, www.creativetherapystore.com, Magination Press, www.apa.org/pubs/magination/, and Amazon, www.amazon.com). A simple activity to improve emotion word vocabulary is to create a chart of emotion words that lists basic emotions along the left edge (e.g., *sad, angry, afraid, happy*) and three levels of intensity (low, medium and high) across the top edge (Oakland University Continuum Center, personal communication). For example, a low-intensity word for *sad* might be "down", a moderate intensity word might be "gloomy", and a high intensity word might be "despondent". These of course will vary from person to person. How many more words can you think of spontaneously for *sad, angry, afraid* or *happy*? This activity can be extended to include looking up words in dictionaries or just adding to the emotion vocabulary list whenever you hear or read a good word that fits. Another good exercise to spur practising emotion talk, as well as encouraging non-verbal skills as mentioned in Chapter 7, is playing a simple game of emotion charades with young children where the goal is to enact emotion scenarios while observers verbally guess and name the emotions the actor is trying to convey.

Having a good emotion vocabulary and being able to effectively label internal states in self and others is a preliminary step to effective communication. Using I-messages or what has come to be called *I-statements* to communicate feelings when parents own the problem and *active listening* in responding to a child when a child owns the problem was identified in 1975 by Thomas Gordon for use in his Parent Effectiveness Training programme (Hamner & Turner, 1996). Rather than making "you" statements where the other person is blamed for one's own emotional state, parents are taught to own their own problem and internal state by stating "I feel _____(emotion word of a specific intensity) when ____(description of the antecedent behaviours or causes)". For instance, instead of saying to a child "You are so lazy; this room is a mess", a parent could say "I get frustrated when I'm trying to keep the house clean and I see that you haven't done your share" (Hamner & Turner, 1996, p. 126).

The advantage to this approach is that the child learns how his or her behaviour affects the feelings of the parent and it places responsibility on the child to address modifying the behaviour.

Active (or reflective) listening involves attending to the other person's underlying emotional message, accepting it, and reflecting it back in a way that helps the other person feel that his or her emotions are confirmed and validated; this is accomplished by paraphrasing what the other person says, asking open-ended questions, checking on any assumptions made, and giving honest but sensitive feedback (Bodie et al., 2015; Fanning & McKay, 2000). In meta-analytic reviews of the literature, parents and their children have been shown to benefit significantly from parent emotion communication training in which parents practise specific communication skills, learn how to help their children label and cope with emotions, and learn how to decrease negative communication such as sarcasm or criticism (Kaminski et al., 2008).

Improving emotion vocabulary, making I-statements, and using active or reflective listening are all important skills needed for better family communication. Such basic training in emotion communication may be especially important for boys and men given that they are more likely than girls and women to have been socialized to suppress rather than express their emotions both verbally and non-verbally (e.g., Levant & Kopecky, 1995; Pollack, 2006; see Chapter 7). Parents can be trained to use more elaborative reminiscing with their children and this has benefits for family communication such as sharing emotional experiences (e.g., Reese & Newcombe, 2007; Salmon et al., 2009; Van Bergen et al., 2009).

The emotional lives of adults also can be enhanced by learning to elaborate on emotional causes and consequences in emotion talk as well as in their own attempts to improve self-awareness through *written* verbal expression. For example, James Pennebaker and his colleagues have conducted and reviewed studies that show that writing about feelings resulting from stressful or traumatic experiences has beneficial effects on the mental and physical health of adults (e.g., Pennebaker & Seagal, 1999). For Pennebaker, "writing to heal" over the course of a few days takes the form of written personal narratives that describe a specific episodic memory involving an important negative life event; by engaging in this activity, adults are able to process their emotions and alleviate potential health problems (e.g., Griffith, 2005). The ability to convey an autobiographical narrative in a coherent way is an important part of identity development and emotional competence in adults and has been found to be related to adults' psychological well-being (Waters & Fivush, 2015). For a vocalized or written narrative to show ***narrative coherence***, "it must be told in a way that clearly delineates the temporal order of actions (chronology), it must orient the event in time and place (context), and it must provide enough detail and elaboration to link component actions together in a meaningful way (theme)" (Waters & Fivush, 2015, p. 442).

One way that family members can enhance each other's emotional competence is by telling stories with emotional content that exemplify such narrative coherence. Barbara Fiese and her colleagues have studied such family storytelling in couples talking about their relationship or in families talking during their routines and rituals such as at dinnertime. Families socialize emotions in the next generation by the quality of the stories that get passed down. Family storytelling researchers have developed codes for narrative coherence that assess the story for how well it shows: *internal consistency* (complete, well-integrated), *organization* (orients the listener/reader), *flexibility* (consideration of alternative/multiple perspectives) and *congruence between affect and content* (match between the expressed emotion and the description – e.g., a sad story told with appropriate emotional expressions) (Fiese et al., 2001).

Family stories have been examined in several contexts. Family *identity* stories focus on the shared family experiences by birth, by cultural origins, or by common values and morals (Kellas, 2005). How parents tell and retell the adoption story to their adopted children is rich in emotion as parents try to prevent confusion, enhance their children's sense of self-worth, and convey a positive emotional tone and sense of family commitment to their adopted children (Harrigan, 2010). Parents sometimes give memorable messages and tell stories about how to succeed in college to their children (e.g., advice about what to do, warnings about what not to do, encouragement); it is possible for such stories to emotionally empower and motivate college-age children, although additional research is needed to clarify under which conditions this might happen (Kranstuber, Carr & Hosek, 2012). Adults may show a generative concern for the next generation by telling their children stories about values (Pratt et al., 1999). Parents who try to teach their adolescents moral values via stories, and who show hope and optimism in doing so, have been found to also grant more autonomy to their adolescents later on than parents who do not (Pratt et al., 2001). Family joint or conversational storytelling occurs when both the storyteller and the recipient contribute to the story, as often occurs in the retelling of stressful family arguments or disagreements (Kellas & Trees, 2006). In addition to narrative coherence in such joint family stories, other considerations are important such as engagement (i.e., warmth and involvement during storytelling), negotiation of taking turns to talk, and taking each other's perspectives into account (Kellas & Trees, 2006). Interestingly, the affective tone at the end of long-term intimate relationship stories told by couples has been shown to be related to the couple's actual relationship quality and mental health, with a positive tone being related to better adaptation (Frost, 2013).

Family storytelling involves the perspectives of each family member and thus the development of both individual and group identities; when family stories are told and retold, the perspectives of the family members differ based on gender or generation (e.g., grandparent, parent, grandchild) (Thorson et al., 2013). The quality of these retold family stories is related to the emotional satisfaction experienced by family members and to their ratings of how engaged they were in the storytelling (Thorson et al., 2013). Also, family stories are likely instrumental in helping emerging adults, midlife adults and older adults in later life to engage in a process of life review as they relay their own autobiographical memories (e.g., Fitzgerald, 1996; Fivush, 2011; McAdams, 2001).

## Summary of Chapter Key Points

There are many modes of verbal emotional communication within the family, some of which are face-to-face and some of which are text-based or online. Among the text-based paralinguistic forms of emotional communication are the use of emoticons and emoji; although there is currently limited research on how pictographs in online and social media communications are utilized by individuals, this line of research is likely to be more prominent in future research on emotion socialization in families. Family members can work to improve everyday emotion language development in themselves and in others in their families by improving their emotion vocabularies and enriching their verbal emotional expressions with their culture(s)' relevant figurative language, such as metaphors and metonymies. Parents can learn to communicate using I-statements and active listening and encourage their children to do the same. Processing emotionally difficult or traumatic life events by writing narratives and by orally telling stories about the events have long been used throughout history as a means of enhancing individual and group well-being; thus, writing to heal continues to be an important method of using emotion language constructively as shown in the work of Pennebaker and his colleagues. Stories serve many functions in families. Fictional stories in books, television and films can be used by parents as examples for family discussion about emotions, thoughts and behaviours in various contexts. Real-life stories told within the family context provide structure and emotional meaning to interpersonal experiences. Developmentally, the use of emotion-relevant language and complexity has been studied in the ego development of individuals, and in the autobiographical memories of both children and adults. Whether face-to-face or online, studies of the telling and retelling of joint family narratives in our computer-mediated communication era holds promise as a future method of improving our understanding of emotion socialization in families.

## Further Reading

Lindquist, K. A., MacCormack, J. K. & Shablack, H. (2015). The role of language in emotion: Predictions from psychological constructionism. *Frontiers in Psychology, 6,* Article ID 444.

These authors make a good case for the timely need to emphasize the crucial role of language in the study of emotion. They propose using a constructionist theoretical framework in which emotion language concepts provide the scaffold for the integration of the sensory, motor, neurological and physiological components of emotional functioning situated in context. In the view of the authors, language supports the emotion concept knowledge which is used to make meaning out of sensations and experiences within the moment. In this view, emotion language and concepts can help to shape emotional experiences.

## Relevant Film

Disney PIXAR (2015). *Inside Out.* Distributed by Buena Vista Home Entertainment, Inc.

This enjoyable full-length animated feature film depicts the thoughts, language and emotions integrated within the mind of an 11-year-old girl as she goes through her everyday life interacting with her family and coping with the challenges of growing up. Emotions are characterized "inside out" and are represented by the emotionally positive and optimistic Joy as she tries to work alongside and manage the consequences of Sadness, Disgust, Anger and Fear as they struggle for acknowledgement. Critics mostly seem to agree that this one is destined to be a classic. Also see Paul Ekman's video for parents about the film at www.paulekman.com/parentsguide

# 10

# Emotion Regulation and Coping in Families

> *Raymond DiGiuseppe is a psychotherapist who has worked with angry clients to address family violence. In one case that he describes, an angry father is asked to reflect on his own life and to have empathy for his family. The father is asked to describe who had treated him with such anger in the past. The man described his own father as being physically and verbally abusive to him. He also recalled that his father's parenting approach was effective in garnering his obedience. Yet the man further acknowledged feeling hatred for his father and a strong motivation to avoid him. Eventually, the man came to understand that he did not want to repeat the family pattern by using angry yelling when disciplining his own children. Rather, he expressed wanting a different kind of relationship to develop with his children, and was thus open to learning some alternative parenting strategies that did not involve yelling.* (Case study summary from DiGiuseppe, 1995, p. 146.)

## Setting the Family Emotional Tone

Actions speak louder than words or so the saying goes. In this example from DiGiuseppe (1995), the father was asked by his therapist to consider how modelling his own father's actions from the past was affecting his current behaviour, and then whether he wanted to repeat the family cycle of hate and estrangement from his children as a likely long-term consequence. Fortunately, this father was willing to learn new ways to regulate his own emotions in the service of learning how to obtain his children's obedience. Adaptive self-regulation and emotion regulation in parents are widely known as being crucial for family well-being and for the prevention of various disorders in children (e.g., Bariola, Gullone & Hughes, 2011; Bridgett et al., 2015). In this chapter, we consider the multidirectional influences of emotion regulation within the family system given that there is a growing body of literature on self-regulation, emotion regulation and coping strategy use among parents and their children. Many of these studies show that the emotional tone set and exemplified by parents and the emotional quality of the interactions in a family often reveal whether the family members will cope in an adaptive manner when the environment places stress on their functioning. Definitions of self-regulation, emotion regulation and coping with stress in families are described in this chapter before literature is reviewed that examines the development of coping and emotion regulation across the lifespan. A major focus of the chapter will be on the strategies family members can use to work towards effective regulation of emotion and constructive actions in themselves and others.

## Some Defining Features of Self-Regulation, Coping and Emotion Regulation

The constructs of self-regulation, coping and emotion regulation have overlapping meanings in the psychological literature and thus present a challenge to contemporary researchers as they attempt to unite theory with empirical evidence. Broadly speaking, Bridgett et al. (2015) describe *self-regulation* as the flexible regulation of cognition, emotion and behaviour in humans and animals. In their self-regulation model, both genetic/biological factors (e.g., prenatal exposures, temperament, maturation) and socialization (e.g., family context, bidirectional parent–child influences) work together in the transmission of self-regulation outcomes across generations. Furthermore, underlying neural processes (cortical, anterior cingulate cortex) account for effortful/executive control in a *top-down* manner resulting in behavioural and emotional self-regulation. Likewise, other underlying subcortical neural processes work in a *bottom-up* manner resulting in behavioural inhibition/fear (overcontrolled behaviour) or impulsivity (undercontrolled behaviour) (Bridgett et al., 2015). Thus, self-regulation covers a wide range of functioning, including physiological foundations, and seems to incorporate aspects of coping and emotion regulation, which are more narrowly defined. Coping and emotion regulation share many underlying features but also have some distinctions (Compas et al., 2014).

Richard Lazarus (1991) described *coping* as "cognitive or behavioral efforts to manage specific external or internal demands (and conflicts between them) that are appraised as taxing or exceeding the resources of the person" (p. 112). Coping thus is conceptualized as a clear response to stressful life circumstances. Ross Thompson (1994) gave the following definition of *emotion regulation* that continues to be used in many contemporary studies: “Emotion regulation consists of the extrinsic and intrinsic processes responsible for monitoring, evaluating, and modifying emotional reactions, especially their intensive and temporal features, to accomplish one’s goals” (pp. 27–28). In this case, modification of emotion intensity and duration to achieve goals are inherent in Thompson’s view of emotion regulation. Extrinsic emotion regulation refers to the notion that someone or something outside of the self may actively try to regulate a person’s emotions, which is often the case when parents try to regulate children’s emotions (Compas et al., 2014; Thompson, 1994, 2014). These are among the many well-known definitions of coping and emotion regulation; for others, see Compas et al. (2014).

As astutely recognized by Compas and his colleagues (2014), both coping and emotional regulation continue to grow in importance in the study of emotion socialization in families, even though currently there is no widespread consensus on either the structure of coping or that of emotion regulation. Nonetheless, there is considerable overlap in the constructs of coping and emotion regulation with a few key distinctions. For example, both utilize the constructs of *cognitive reappraisal/restructuring* and *emotional expression/suppression.* Compas et al. (2014) describe cognitive reappraisal/restructuring as “efforts to change one’s thoughts to address a stressor or one’s emotions” (p. 76).

> Emotional expression (e.g., letting someone know how you are feeling) and emotional modulation (e.g., keeping feelings under control until an appropriate time to express them) are constructs found in coping measures that are similar to emotional expression/suppression constructs found in emotion regulation measures. (Compas et al., 2014, p. 76)

Key distinctions noted are that the study of coping places specific emphasis on coping with *stressful* circumstances while the study of emotion regulation often involves *non-stressful* everyday circumstances as well as stressful ones. Thus, coping with stress can be viewed as a specific subset or type of emotion regulation. Compas and his colleagues also make a call for research addressing both coping and emotion regulation given that emotion regulation skills that have developed in the context of non-stressful circumstances may have implications for the ability to cope under stressful circumstances. They suggest that future research should examine emotion regulation before, during and after stressful events to better understand the links between emotion regulation and coping processes. As reviewed next, the study of coping strategies has a long history (Compas et al., 2014), while the study of emotional regulation in families is more recent but is expanding quite rapidly (Gross, 2014).

## Stress and Coping Strategies: Developmental Approaches

As introduced in Chapter 1, the cognitive-motivational-relational theory proposed by Richard Lazarus (1991) addresses thoughts, behaviours and emotions in relational contexts. For Lazarus, "the cognition of the emotions involves goals, plans, and beliefs and is about the stakes (active goals) and (coping) options a person has for managing the person–environment relationship" (Lazarus, 1991, p. 13). The relational part of the theory places emphasis on negotiations with both the physical and social environments. As a person negotiates with the environment, he or she engages in a process of *primary appraisal* and must determine the personal relevance or meaning of the situation. If it is not relevant or meaningful to one's goals, then nothing further happens. However, if it is *goal-relevant*, then whether the situation is *goal-congruent* (what the person wants) or *goal-incongruent* (thwarts what the person wants) is important for whether the person experiences a positive or negative emotion, respectively (Lazarus, 1991). In an earlier model, distinctions were made for situations being appraised as resulting in *harm* (current or in the past), a *threat* (an anticipation of harm in the future), a *challenge* (an opportunity or potential for mastery or gain), or a *benefit* (actual positive gain) (Lazarus & Folkman, 1984). Another component of primary appraisal is type of ego-identity (which incorporates self in relation to others and society); ego-identity is involved in many emotions, such as feeling anger when self-esteem or social group esteem are threatened (Lazarus, 1991, p. 101). After the process of primary appraisal, it becomes necessary to engage in *secondary appraisal* whereby the person must: (1) assign *blame or credit* for the situation, and acknowledge who or what to hold accountable or responsible as the cause, (2) assess *coping potential* and the various coping options that are feasible given the available resources, and (3) evaluate the *future expectancy* for the possibility of psychological changes in the goal congruence or incongruence of a situation (Lazarus, 1991).

To measure coping strategies, Richard Lazarus and Susan Folkman (1984) created the Ways of Coping Measure. The following eight scales were empirically constructed from this measure by Folkman, Lazarus, Dunkel-Schetter, DeLongis and Gruen (1986): *confrontive coping; distancing; self-controlling; seeking social support; accepting responsibility; escape-avoidance; planful problem solving*; and *positive reappraisal*. These strategies were further summarized into *problem-focused* coping (e.g., confrontive coping; planful problem solving), which involves overt action-oriented efforts to directly change the person–environment relationship, and *emotion-focused* coping (e.g., distancing, which is similar to denial; positive reappraisal) where there is an attempt to cognitively or emotionally change the response to the stress by modifying attention or interpretation (Folkman et al., 1986; Lazarus, 1991). Some coping strategies may not neatly fit into the problem-focused or emotion-focused categories (e.g., use of social support) and thus researchers have turned to refining specific strategies in their attempt to expand the study of coping. John and Eng (2014) provide a review and critique of these various coping scales and their link to affect regulation; they describe many of the unresolved difficulties that researchers have had in refining coping strategy scale items so that they do not confound regulatory processes with potential adjustment outcomes.

Gross (2014) notes that one way that coping differs from emotion regulation is that it tends to involve attempts to decrease negative affect and to do so over lengthier periods of time than emotion regulation. Over the course of time, a person might have to flexibly switch from one specific coping strategy to another depending on the controllability of the situation; Cheng (2001) has called this ***coping flexibility***. For instance, if a woman is using a problem-solving approach to cope with trying to find a medical cure for her terminally ill mother, she may at some point recognize the uncontrollability of the situation and switch to other more emotion-focused strategies such as positive reappraisal to cope with her negative emotional responses. Also, this woman may use social support to cope in different ways as she flexibly adapts her thinking; initially, she may seek others out for medical information about a cure, and later seek out other people for emotional support as she tries to accept her mother's terminal status.

Several early developmental studies examined some links between coping and emotion regulation. Labouvie-Vief, Hakim-Larson, DeVoe and Schoeberlein (1989) proposed four levels of emotional control based on interviews about personal experiences of anger, sadness and fear conducted with older children, adolescents, and young, middle-aged and older adults (aged 10–77 years). At the *presystemic* level, the child is not yet able to organize actions and states meant to control or regulate the self into a single abstract system; thus, there is a strong emotional dependence on others for help in regulation and to provide social support. At the *intrasystemic* level, organization into a single abstract system by adolescents is possible and attempts to mentally control emotions are thus made by trying to forget or ignore stressful incidents. At the *intersystemic* level, multiple systems (e.g., systems of social support) are acknowledged by adults, but are not yet well coordinated for motivating action. At the *integrated* level, the multiple systems are integrated and well coordinated with emotion serving as a constructive motivator for action. These levels correlated positively with age and ego level as assessed by Loevinger's Sentence Completion Test (e.g., Loevinger & Wessler, 1970; see Chapter 9 for a description of ego levels). As part of a second study with this sample conducted by Labouvie-Vief, Hakim-Larson and Hobart (1987), participants completed the Ways of Coping Measure (Lazarus & Folkman, 1984), as well as a measure of defence mechanism use (Gleser & Ihilevich, 1969). *Defence mechanisms* can be construed as unconscious attempts to manage intrapsychic conflicts resulting from stress, while coping involves conscious attempts to manage stress (Aldao, Sheppes & Gross, 2015). Before completing the measure of coping strategy use, participants wrote a narrative describing a recent stressful experience. These narratives were assessed for developmental variations in the sources of stress. A developmental composite consisting of age, ego level and source of stress level was created and predicted the use of some coping and defence strategies (Labouvie-Vief et al., 1987). That is, those who scored lower on the developmental composite were more likely to use defences such as turning against others and projection, and to use coping strategies such as escape/avoidance and distancing. In contrast, older and more developmentally mature individuals tended to use these to a lesser degree, and instead used more inner-focused strategies such as trying to accommodate to negative life events and reassess them in a more positive way. Consistent with other studies, females were more likely than males to use the defence of turning against the self and to cope by seeking social support or using escape/avoidance. In a similar follow-up study, Diehl, Coyle and Labouvie-Vief (1996) examined age-related differences in coping and defence mechanisms in adolescents and younger and older adults; using a developmental composite of age, verbal ability, and ego level, they found that older adults with higher verbal ability and ego level were more likely than adolescents and younger adults to use coping and defence strategies that implied better impulse control, less aggressive confrontation and a reinterpretation of conflict situations in a more positive way. Diehl et al. (1996) also found that females in the study were more likely than males to use empathy and to tolerate cognitive/affective complexities that were ambiguous; females were less likely to engage in reaction formation by turning unpleasant reactions into their opposites.

Few contemporary studies have attempted to address links between coping and emotion regulation (Compas et al., 2014). However, the family seems like an ideal context to examine both. In an early study of parental affect and coping using a time-specific and situation-specific approach, my colleagues and I asked an unrelated sample of mothers and fathers to write a narrative about a stressful incident with one of their children (ranging from < 1 to 27 years of age) and to complete questionnaires about their appraisal regarding causal attributions of the stressful event, their ratings of emotions before, during and after the event, and their consequent coping strategy use (Hakim-Larson et al., 1999). Sources of stress and the perceived causal attributions made by parents revealed two classes of stressful content: expectations for the child and expectations for the self as a parent. Several patterns of emotion and coping strategies were identified. Feelings of parental anger were positively related to *confrontive coping*, whereby a parent directly tried to socialize a child, and feelings of being afraid or guilty were positively associated with coping by *accepting responsibility.* Feelings of sadness and guilt in the stressful parenting situation were positively related to attempts to cope by *escape or avoidance*. It is not only important to study parental emotions and coping for the direct socialization effects such patterns may have on children, but also for the indirect socialization that occurs when parents act as models for how to engage in coping to make themselves feel better as they encounter stressful life events (Hakim-Larson et al., 1999).

To capture the various components associated with parenting stress, Richard Abidin (1990, 1992) created a parenting stress inventory; his measure was an early attempt to examine how parent and child characteristics as well as tangible resources are linked to parental stress and how this in turn influenced parenting behaviours and child outcomes. Abidin (1992) acknowledged the need for complex, testable models of parenting stress that incorporated such variables as parental cognitions, beliefs, cognitive coping, motivational systems, parenting skills and the parenting alliance, as well as social supports and material resources. Today, a reasonable addition to this comprehensive list might be the emotion regulation of both parent and child.

Some contemporary studies have addressed both coping and emotion regulation issues in families, though as noted by Compas et al. (2014), more comprehensive models incorporating both coping and emotion regulation are needed. In normal parenting, when parents attribute the cause of their stress to a child, their appraisals and angry affect may lead to the necessary motivation needed to confront a child with the goal of adaptive socialization; however, it is also possible that the confrontation that results from parents' attempts to cope may result in maladaptive responding such as child abuse (Hakim-Larson et al., 1999). For example, in a study comparing fathers with a known history of physical child abuse to those without such a history, Francis and Wolfe (2008) found that abusive fathers reported more parenting stress, more anger and aggression, more expression of negative affect, less empathy and understanding of the child's perspective, and more symptoms of psychopathology in the clinical range. As compared to the non-abusive fathers, the abusive fathers had a *hostile attribution bias* towards children's emotional expressions and were more likely to interpret child emotional expressions as showing disgust and anger than non-abusive fathers; abusive fathers were also less likely to notice expressions of interest and curiosity in children's faces, perhaps putting them at risk for overlooking opportunities to engage in a positive, constructive interactions with children. Abusive fathers in this study were more likely to have had histories of being severely abused and traumatized themselves as children (similar to the father in this chapter's opening vignette). In their discussion of interventions, Francis and Wolfe (2008) point to the need for such fathers to learn how to adaptively cope, accurately interpret and empathize with children's emotional signals, revise their cognitive distortions, and effectively regulate their own emotions.

In addition to parents' coping with stress, children's coping with stress has been addressed in the literature. Children's *coping competence theory* suggests ways that the life trajectories of children come to consist of prosocial, antisocial and asocial patterns of addressing life challenges (Blechman, Prinz & Dumas, 1995); in this theory, children's coping involves facing a multiplicity of life challenges in the *affective, social* and *achievement* domains, which are important for children's mastery of their age-related developmental tasks (Moreland & Dumas, 2008). A study based on coping competence theory has shown that perceived parental stress has a bidirectional relationship with children's coping competence; that is, parental stress predicted later child coping competence, while child coping competence predicted later parental stress, both at eight-week and one-year follow ups (Cappa, Begle, Conger, Dumas & Conger, 2011). In another study based on coping competence theory, Soltis, Davidson, Moreland, Felton and Dumas (2015) found that parental reports of child coping competence mediated the relationship between perceived parental stress and their preschool children's school readiness; thus:

> parents reporting higher levels of stress also reported lower levels of coping competence in their children (i.e., challenges with goal-oriented tasks; greater difficulty coping with interpersonal and social demands; and greater difficulty managing emotional situations), which, in turn, negatively influenced their child's academic performance. (p. 655)

Similarly, in a US sample of children and adolescents studied longitudinally (ages 7 to 17), Evans et al. (2015) found that the use of specific coping strategies mediated the relation between stress and depression, with less adaptive coping strategy use as a result of heightened stresses leading to increased depression. Thus, understanding stress and how to maximize optimal coping within the family may have important implications for long-term adjustment.

While the coping with stress approach to the study of affect regulation continues to have supporters, another increasingly influential approach to affect regulation involves the study of specific emotion regulation strategies (e.g., John & Eng, 2014), as described next.

## The Process Model of Emotion Regulation: A Contemporary Approach

Many contemporary researchers have focused on the construct of emotion regulation. Among the most widely influential of these is the ***process model of emotion regulation*** introduced by James Gross and his colleagues (e.g., Gross, 2008; Gross, 2014; Gross & Thompson, 2007; John & Eng, 2014). This model is based on past theory and research in developmental psychology including work on emotions, stress/coping, defence mechanisms and attachment theory. Gross (2014) describes three core features of emotion regulation: the *goal* that the person is trying to achieve, the *strategies* they use to try and achieve it, and the *outcome* of using a strategy to achieve a goal. As shown in Table 10.1, Gross highlights eight different possible emotion regulation goals based on whether the goal is to decrease or down-regulate an emotion,

**Table 10.1** Defining Features of Emotion Regulation Goals (Summarized from Gross, 2014)

| Focus is on Self or Other(s) | Emotion Valence is Negative or Positive | Goal is to Decrease Emotion Magnitude or Duration | Goal is to Increase Emotion Magnitude or Duration |
|---|---|---|---|
| **SELF** | Negative emotions | Focus on decreasing negative emotion in self | Focus on increasing negative emotion in self |
| | Positive emotions | Focus on decreasing positive emotion in self | Focus on increasing positive emotion in self |
| **OTHER(S)** | Negative emotions | Focus on decreasing negative emotion in other(s) | Focus on increasing negative emotion in other(s) |
| | Positive emotions | Focus on decreasing positive emotion in other(s) | Focus on increasing positive emotion in other(s) |

or to increase or up-regulate an emotion. The emotions can be of either a positive valence or a negative valence, and the regulatory focus can be either on the self or on another person. For instance, a mother who tries to calm her angry, distressed child after he gets a shot at the doctor's office is an example involving a negative valence with the extrinsic maternal goal of decreasing her child's anger and distress. Another example might be of a young man who tries to talk himself into feeling much happier than he does just before standing up as best man in his friend's wedding; this would entail an intrinsic goal of increasing a positive emotion within himself. Can you come up with other examples for each cell in Table 10.1?

The process model of emotion regulation (Gross, 2008, 2014; John & Eng, 2014) consists of five categories of emotion regulation *strategies* that occur in the following sequence:

1) *Situation selection* – Emotions arise within situational contexts. Initial *selection* of a situation provides the opportunity to regulate emotions by choosing an environment that is likely to promote obtaining goals. A specific emotion regulation strategy that might be used here is *avoidance* as individuals tend to stay away from situations that do not promote the possibility of goal attainment.
2) *Situation modification* – External physical situations may be modified or rearranged in the effort to regulate emotions in the self or others. An example of emotion regulation strategies that might be involved here would be taking a *problem-focused* approach to alter the physical environment, as a parent might do in scaffolding the materials a child needs to solve a problem.
3) *Attentional deployment* – While situation selection and modification involve regulating emotions through altering aspects of the environment, attentional deployment takes place within a situation and involves the person redirecting attention to manage the emotions experienced. Some examples are *withdrawal of attention*, such as would occur by covering one's eyes or using earplugs, *distraction*, where attention is turned away and focused on something else, and finally *rumination*, where attentional deployment is sustained for a period of time on an emotion-eliciting stimulus, often resulting in an increase in the emotion.
4) *Cognitive change* – As noted in the stress/coping and general emotion literatures, individuals use cognitive appraisal to assign meaning to the situations that they are in. Cognitive change with the goal of altering the situation's emotional significance occurs when one or more appraisals is changed. This is accomplished by means of the emotion regulation strategy

of *reappraisal*, whereby the meaning of the situation is altered such that a person's emotional response to the situation changes.

5) *Response modulation* – Finally, the last category of emotion regulation strategies in this recurring sequence proposed by Gross and his colleagues is response modulation, whereby rather direct changes are made to the physiological, behavioural, or experiential responses. One example here would include using muscle relaxation exercises to alter the physiological and experiential aspects of a negative emotion. The emotion regulation strategy of *expressive suppression* is another example and includes attempts to inhibit or reduce either ongoing negative or positive emotions depending on the situational context.

Gross (2014) makes it clear that this proposed sequence is one in which there are feedback loops that can occur at any of the multiple points in the process. In addition to the goals and strategies of emotion regulation, the affective, cognitive and social *outcomes* of emotion regulation are important to consider (Gross, 2014). Thus, Gross reviews the outcomes for two strategies that have been frequently researched: expressive *suppression*, which is behavioural and a type of response modulation, and *reappraisal* which is a cognitive change type of strategy. In brief, the research reviewed by Gross shows that suppression leads to worse memory for emotional interactions and to a decrease in positive emotion experience, with some studies also showing an increase in negative emotions. For reappraisal, either there is no effect on memory or memory is enhanced, there is a decrease in negative emotions, and/or an increase in positive emotions. Socially, suppression but not reappraisal has been found to be related to difficulties within relationships. Although reappraisal seems to be preferable as a strategy when compared to suppression, the research findings may vary for reappraisal depending on the emotional intensity experienced and may vary for suppression depending on the cultural context (Gross, 2014).

## Developmental Approaches to Emotion Regulation in Families

While future research will demonstrate how a developmental approach can best be utilized within the process model of emotion regulation, there are many researchers who have taken a general developmental approach to emotion regulation issues in families. Using their ***internalization theory***, which addresses culture and development, Holodynski and Friedlmeier (2005) trace the ontogenesis of emotion regulation from infancy to adulthood. Table 10.2

**Table 10.2** Summary of the Internalization Model (Holodynski & Friedlmeier, 2005)

| Developmental Phase | Form(s) of Emotional Regulation |
|---|---|
| Phase 1 – infancy to 2 years | Components of the emotion system are present in precursor form.<br>Interpersonal form of co-regulation shared between infant and caregiver.<br>Unable to control emotions linked to motives.<br>Unable to delay gratification. |
| Phase 2 – 3 to 6 years | Reduced caregiver support.<br>Child makes use of physical emotional expression and speech signs.<br>Intrapersonal action and reflective regulation commences.<br>Emotion regulation comes under the influence of the child's will to some extent.<br>Can delay or suppress gratification of motives. |
| Phase 3 – childhood | Expression and speech signs become internalized.<br>Mental level of expression, speech and action regulates emotion action readiness.<br>Able to distinguish mental expression signs from actual emotion expressions and from other bodily reactions. |
| Phase 4 – adolescence | Able to anticipate and regulate actions and emotions now and in the near future.<br>Develops ability to extend regulation into the distant future.<br>Fine tuning of reactions depending on interaction partner and context. |
| Phase 5 – adulthood | Advances that occur in emotional action regulation and reflective emotion regulation continue throughout adulthood. |

provides a summary. In this model, *signs* (whether expressive or verbal or some other culturally conventional type) can be defined as "a special group of artificial means that humans have created and to which they have assigned conventionalized meanings and functions" (Holodynski, 2013, p. 15). Based on the work of Lev Vygotsky and Aleksei Leont'ev, internalization theory proposes that emotional expressions act as signs for actions and are thus *required for the regulation of activities*; initially, these expression signs are co-constructed and co-regulated in the context of caregiver–infant interactions but later become mentally internalized and thus more under the volitional or wilful control of the young child and developing person (Holodynski, 2013). According to Holodynski (2013), "emotions are basically mediated by culturally coconstructed expression signs such as a pout, a smile, kneeling down, and only on an advanced level also by verbal signs when children start to talk about emotion" (p. 6); thus, in this model, expression signs (such as gestures, body posture and facial expressions), and verbal signs (such as speech and written language), mediate and help to coordinate the relation between the culture and the individual's internal mental actions. Various ontogenetic pathways of emotion regulation can occur over the course of development as the individual is co-regulated with others during social interactions which take place within a cultural context; during infancy, for example, the functions of emotions are shared and distributed across the activity of both infant and caregiver with each doing a part as affect mirroring takes place (Holodynski, 2013). In this model, an infant may go from unfocused crying which gets the caregiver's attention and attempts to regulate the infant's needs to a more specific expression sign with the function of an *appeal* – in this case, an older toddler may appeal to the caregiver for comfort while crying and holding his or her arms up in the air with the intended message of wanting the caregiver to "pick me up" and "hug me". This dependence on making appeals to others with signs attempting to convey the need for comfort eventually becomes internalized whereby the child can make appeals to the self for comfort during intrapersonal regulation. Expression signs can also become symbolized and used during interpersonal regulation (Holodynski, 2013).

Holodynski and Friedlmeier (2005) distinguish four levels of regulation processes – the first three are action regulation processes (automatic, volitional, emotional) and the fourth and highest level is reflective emotion regulation. *Automatic action regulation* involves actions that result automatically from learned routines, while *volitional action regulation* includes voluntary goal-directed actions that are mentally represented and manipulated through the use of symbols such as language. *Emotional action regulation* involves motives being fulfilled by emotions regulating actions. With *reflective emotion regulation*, it becomes possible for a person, such as a parent, to think about and mentally coordinate or transform automatic, volitional, and emotional forms of regulation for the purpose of planning or making decisions that may or may not take effect in actions involving the self or others (Holodynski & Friedlmeier, 2005).

During adolescence and adulthood, advances are made in the ability to engage in reflective emotion regulation. Such advances are linked to the ability to reflect upon and utilize social norms and rules of behaviour, as well as empathize with and take the perspective of others, a field of study that has historically been called social cognition. As described in History Feature Box 10, the field of social cognition integrates cognitive and socio-emotional development and includes concepts related to the contemporary study of emotion regulation.

Given that emotional regulation processes differ at various points in development, how do emotion regulation processes play out as family members interact? Both the co-regulation and self-regulation of emotions occur in moment-to-moment interactions, as discussed next.

### History Feature Box 10

### Back Then and Now: Social Cognition and Emotion Regulation in Self and Others

In 1975, Carolyn Shantz highlighted the important role of social cognition in child development by focusing attention on studies examining the ways that children think about the inner psychological lives of others, such as their thoughts, emotions, intentions and viewpoints or perspectives. She noted that children make causal inferences or attributions about others' behaviours during interactions with them based on their understanding of them, and that this had implications for the child's own social behaviours and reactions (Shantz, 1975). Later studies in social cognition addressed conflicts between children (e.g., Shantz, 1987), children's aggressive behaviours with peers (Dodge, 1980), children's interpersonal problem-solving skills (e.g., Shure & Spivack, 1982), and children's compliance with parental requests and adoption of rules as they learned to regulate their emotions (e.g., Gralinski & Kopp, 1993; Kopp, 1982). In the 1980s, other psychologists were transitioning from more cognitive developmental approaches focused on intellectual functioning to ones that incorporated social and emotional functioning as well. For example, Robert Selman (1980) wrote his seminal work on the growth of interpersonal understanding in children and adolescents in the domains of friendships, peer relationships and the parent–child relationship. Selman (1981) also focused on the integration of affect and cognition by conducting research on interpersonal negotiation strategies in children and adolescents; negotiation requires coordinating the thoughts, feelings and intentions of the self and others before engaging in social behaviours.

While early studies of social cognitive development focused on childhood and adolescence, but not adulthood, more recent studies on emotion regulation showed the importance of emotion understanding and social problem solving in the lives of adults as well. Carol Magai (2008) has summarized research on the regulation and expression of emotions during adulthood. In differential emotions theory, proposed by Carroll Izard and Carol Magai, emotional expression signals serve both self-motivational functions that promote actions or behaviours, and communicative functions with others in the social environment; while many of these functions are similar across the lifespan such as a sad facial expression reflecting a loss whether in an infant, child, adolescent or adult, other aspects of the emotion system change over time (Magai, 2008). For example, Silvan Tomkin's *ideo-affective structures* and Carroll Izard's *affective-cognitive structures* are relatively stable aspects of emotion and personality that have resulted from multiple experiences over the course of development and result in affective or ***emotional biases*** (Magai, 2008). Emotional biases are biases towards specific emotional experiences and expressions reflected in personality and can have an important influence on social interactions and relationships. However, personality change in these emotional biases in adulthood is possible. Magai and her colleagues have utilized dynamic systems theory (see Chapter 3) to propose that:

> when intense, unanticipated, or surprising emotional experiences of a positive or negative nature are encountered and are cognitively elaborated in the context of an interpersonally supportive environment, internal models

of affect and interpersonal process can be substantively reworked and result in personality change (Magai, 2008, p. 378).

In addition, Magai (2008) reviews the work of Powell Lawton, Laura Carstensen and Gisela Labouvie-Vief and their colleagues. Lawton has proposed *affective optimization* as being the primary goal of older adults as they become more skilled in regulating their emotions over time; affective optimization involves using self-regulation skills to proactively create and maintain social environments that optimize the emotions that older adults want to feel and minimize those they don't (Magai, 2008). Laura Carstensen's socio-emotional *selectivity theory* is based on the selective optimization with compensation model of successful ageing developed by Paul and Margaret Baltes. In Carstensen's model, there is a shift from younger to older adulthood, from the acquisition of information to the successful maintenance of select emotionally meaningful activities and social relationships (Magai, 2008). As discussed in Chapter 9, Gisela Labouvie-Vief has emphasized the development of affective complexity, which may or may not increase in adults beyond the period of middle age given that it is intimately integrated with cognitive complexity (Labouvie-Vief, 2015; Magai, 2008).

In her research on emotion regulation in younger and older adults, Fredda Blanchard-Fields (2009) demonstrated how the cognitive, affective and social domains of adult life interrelate. In her review of the studies she conducted along with her colleagues, Blanchard-Fields (2009) provides evidence that older adults, in contrast to younger ones, show more flexibility and adaptive responding when it comes to interpersonal socio-emotional problem solving. She studied three types of emotion regulation strategies: instrumental (e.g., actions to try to solve the problem), passive (e.g., suppression of feelings), and proactive (e.g., actively managing emotions). While older adults flexibly applied the use of these strategies depending on the context, younger adults were more likely to consistently use a similar approach across contexts. The research reviewed by Blanchard-Fields also indicated that older adults were more motivated than younger adults to down-regulate negative emotions such as anger. These findings and others from the work of Blanchard-Fields and her colleagues show that a positive developmental trajectory is possible for the cognitive-affective functioning of older adults when the context involves interpersonal problem solving.

## Emotion Regulation and Family Interactions: Harmony and Conflict

In this section, we consider emotion regulation in parents with children, among siblings, and in adult couples. Emotion regulation processes are important in both harmonious interactions (positive shared emotional interchanges) and in conflictual interactions that involve negative emotional expressions.

During parent–infant play interactions, infants show what are called background emotions while they are at play (Feldman, 2007). As described by

Antonio Damasio, ***background emotions*** are ongoing emotions that occur in real time and include momentary shifts that are observable in facial expression, gazing, muscle tone, gestures and body language; background emotions involve the contour of affect and the organizing of components of arousal and affect into broader patterns (Damasio, 2010; Feldman, 2007). Affective or ***vitality contours*** as described by Daniel Stern (1999) refer to feeling flow patterns that come from how sensations are experienced in the moment (e.g., accelerating or fading or explosive bursts of arousal). In a study of vitality contours in toddlers interacting separately with their mothers and fathers, Feldman (2007) coded parent–toddler interactions for interaction synchrony, emotion reciprocity, parental intrusiveness and the child's level of symbolic play with toys (e.g., dolls, tea set, cars, animals). Parents (mothers particularly) helped children to symbolize and to do so in synchrony with their interactions while the children were playing. The vitality contour with mothers involved a single positive arousal episode with social gazing, while the contour with fathers tended to have several peaks of positive arousal of shorter duration than that for mothers. Maternal reciprocity (i.e., matching the child's emotion) was sequentially linked to symbolic expansion in the child's play, while intrusiveness was linked to symbolic constriction. Finally, symbolic complexity in the child's play was predicted by the synchrony of the parent–child interaction and by how supportive the parent was of the child's play (Feldman, 2007).

Feldman (2007) points out that full-fledged positive emotions in infancy are almost exclusively observed during interactions rather than when infants are alone; thus, infants depend upon an emotionally attuned caregiver to co-construct and co-regulate positive experiences as they unfold. Social smiling, laughing, and experiencing and expressing positive emotions involves synchronizing and co-regulating shared pleasurable experiences in a harmonious way with other people. In contrast, unpleasant negative emotional states need to be regulated even when the infant is alone; thus, even very young infants begin to find ways to self-soothe and self-regulate when they are experiencing negative emotions in the absence of others (Feldman, 2007).

Feldman, Bamberger and Kanat-Maymon (2013) conducted a longitudinal study in which mother–child and father–child ***dyadic reciprocity*** were examined in infancy, preschool and adolescent periods. Dyadic reciprocity was operationalized as interactions in which:

> the dyad is moving in harmony, each is engaged and contributes to the mutual exchange, the interaction is the end product of the input of both partners, and the atmosphere is one of collaboration and joint activity, whether the activity

> is verbal or non-verbal, focuses on social give-and-receive or on object manipulation. (Feldman et al., 2013, p. 413)

Such reciprocity incorporates the notions of synchronicity and co-regulation in family interactions. Their findings show that reciprocity is relatively stable both within individuals from childhood to adolescence and within families; furthermore, reciprocity with mothers and fathers contributed uniquely to the prediction of preschool children's aggression and social competence, with higher reciprocity linked to lower aggression and higher social competence. Feldman et al. (2013) also studied *dialogical skills* in the adolescents as they communicated with their friends during a positive interaction and one involving a conflict. These skills included:

> acknowledgement of other's position and perspective; empathy to friend's feelings, hurts, emotions, or point of view; elaboration of suggestions/ideas suggested by partner; attention is focused on partner; maintaining positive affect, vocal clarity and warm tone of voice, reciprocity and give-and-receive mutuality; adaptation to content, expressed affect, or position of partner; and interactions are fluent and rhythmic. (Feldman et al., 2013, p. 414)

Interestingly, reciprocity with mothers predicted better dialogical skills in the adolescents with their friends during positive exchanges, while reciprocity with fathers predicted better dialogical skills when the friends were discussing a conflict. This study is one of a growing number that show that fathers, as well as mothers, play an important role in children's emotion regulation skills and that this has implications for their peer relations (e.g., Bocknek et al., 2014). Other family members, such as siblings, are also important in children's developing emotion co-regulation and self-regulation as described next.

The emotion of *jealousy* in particular is one that is likely to be experienced during sibling relationships according to Brenda Volling and her colleagues. Jealousy is experienced in a social triangle and thus research on sibling jealousy is best conducted in the context of a mother or father with two siblings – that is, in triads (Volling, McElwain & Miller, 2002). The ***jealousy complex*** refers to the complexity of the possible primary emotions that might underlie jealousy; when a child is feeling jealous of a sibling who is having fun interacting with a parent, the jealous child might feel sad due to feeling a loss, angry if there is a sense of betrayal or injustice, and/or fear if there is anxiety about being left alone and unattended (Volling et al., 2002). Volling et al. (2002) conducted a study in which toddlers and their older preschool-aged sibling interacted with one of their parents in a controlled laboratory triad setting.

In the *triadic jealousy paradigm*, one parent was given an attractive new toy and was instructed to play with one child at a time while excluding the other child, thus placing a challenge on the excluded child to find something else to do until it was his or her turn to play with the parent. Jealous reactions by the excluded child included such behaviours as making bids for the parent's attention, trying to distract parent and sibling away from playing with the new toy, trying to get on the parent's lap or grab the new toy, and facial and vocal expressions suggesting general distress (whining, crying) as well as specific emotions such as sadness, anger and fear/anxiety. For toddlers, the researchers found that temperament played a role in their reactions, while for the older preschool siblings, emotion understanding played a role. The emotional reactions of both younger and older siblings were affected by the session order (who played with the parent first). Younger siblings had stronger jealous reactions than older siblings did when they were challenged first, whether it was with their mothers or their fathers; older siblings had stronger reactions when they were challenged second with their fathers only, perhaps not wanting to give up valued time with the father. In addition, Volling et al. (2002) found that a positive marital quality predicted the older preschool-aged sibling's ability to regulate jealous reactions.

Additional research findings support the idea that a positive marital relationship is important for children's emotion regulation. Morris, Silk, Steinberg, Myers and Robinson (2007) suggest a *tripartite model* of how the family context is linked to emotion regulation in children. The three components of the model can be summarized as: 1) *modelling*, in which emotion regulation among and between family members is influenced by observational learning, emotion contagion and affective/social referencing processes; 2) *emotion-related parenting practices*, such as emotion coaching, acceptance of negative emotions, emotion talk, intentional teaching, cognitive reframing and niche-picking (similar to situation selection in the Gross process model described earlier in this chapter, whereby family members choose contexts for themselves or others); and 3) the *emotional climate* in the family.

As discussed by Morris et al. (2007), the emotional climate of the family is affected by family relationships as reflected in attachment, emotion-related parenting styles, attitudes and behaviours, and the marital/co-parent relationship. The importance of the *parent–child attachment* relationship was described in the History Feature Boxes for Chapters 1 and 5 while aspects of emotion-related *parenting styles, attitudes and behaviours* were described in Chapter 6 on parenting beliefs. Another way that family emotional climate is manifest is through positive and negative family emotional expressiveness (see the work of Halberstadt and colleagues in Chapter 7). For example, Garner (1995) conducted a study on emotion regulation in which toddlers were briefly left alone with their preschool-aged sibling or with the sibling and a stranger; positive family expressiveness in the home environment as reported by mothers was found to be positively related to self-soothing emotion regulation in the toddlers when they were left alone with their older siblings. In a US sample of 4th-grade children (approximately 10 years old), the family emotional climate was assessed and both negative family expressiveness and maternal acceptance of negative emotions predicted children's emotion regulation which in turn predicted children's level of aggression (Ramsden & Hubbard, 2002). That is, negative family expressiveness was negatively related to children's emotion regulation while maternal acceptance of negative emotions was positively related to children's emotion regulation; children's emotion regulation was negatively related to their level of aggression. These studies exemplify some ways that the emotional climate of the family is linked to emotional regulation in children.

A number of recent studies have shown links between positive or negative family emotional expressiveness and emotion regulation in children. For example, positive family expressiveness mediated the relation between cumulative family risks and children's emotion regulation in a study with parents of school-age children in China (Gao & Han, 2016). Similarly, Are and Shaffer (2015) found that positive family expressiveness mediated the relation between mothers' emotional dysregulation and children's emotion regulation; that is, mothers lower in emotion dysregulation were more likely to report higher positive family expressiveness which in turn predicted better child emotion regulation. In yet another study, Chen, Zhou, Main and Lee (2015) found that self-reported negative self-expressiveness and observed expressions of parental anger/frustration while completing a parent–child task were negatively related to parental reports of children's emotion regulation in a sample of Chinese-American immigrant parents with 5- to 9-year-old children. These examples show that there is an increasing body of literature on diverse families that demonstrate links between the emotional climate of the family (assessed by family expressiveness) and children's emotion regulation.

Family conflicts such as those between parents and their children and those between adult partners and married couples occur routinely within families and have the potential to lead to a more negative family emotional climate affecting children's emotion regulation. This possibility is well-reflected in a study by Lunkenheimer, Hollenstein, Wang and Shields (2012) in which verbal discussions in whole families with a school-age child were recorded as they talked about good and difficult past family interactions, as well as one in which there was child misbehaviour. Using a dynamic systems approach in their analyses (see Chapter 3), they found that child emotion regulation skills were related to greater *flexibility* in using discrete emotion words and switching among various emotion socialization functions (e.g., emotion coaching, dismissing, elaboration) while the family was discussing challenging topics; such flexibility may allow children to experience a wider range of emotional contexts, thus fostering their learning more about how to regulate emotions (Lunkenheimer et al., 2012). In another study using a family systems approach, Fosco and Grych (2013) found that the emotion regulation of 4th- and 5th-grade children (median age of 10 years, range from 8 to 12 years) was indirectly related to conflict beween parents. Parental conflict was found to influence the family's overall emotional climate (less positive, more negative) when the mother, father and child interacted with each other and to be related to the amount of warmth and emotional sensitivity of the mother; the family emotional climate and maternal warmth in turn were related to the child's emotion regulation (Fosco & Grych, 2013).

## Adaptive Emotion Regulation and Coping Strategies in the Everyday Life of Families

Adaptive regulation of emotions in everyday situations and under more stressful circumstances is affected by the developmental level and needs of each family member. There is currently no comprehensive life-span theory or model that addresses emotion regulation and coping. However, scholars seem to agree that improving adaptive emotion regulation and coping within the family requires that family members spend time together with the goal of building a strong emotional foundation for their relationships. Infants depend upon the co-regulated interactions with caregivers and other family members to enrich their positive emotional response repertoire as they co-construct meaning in their shared life experiences. Thus, sharing enjoyable interactive playtime with infants is a critical family activity needed on a routine daily basis. Through play, infants gain experience in engaging with others and exploring toys and the world around them in ways that are pleasurable and that promote learning about their sociocultural environment. Barbara Frederickson's ***broaden and build theory*** of positive emotions maintains that the experience of positive emotions broadens and expands possible options for thoughts, activities and ways of relating in the moment; this openness leads to the building up of personal resources (such as skills and knowledge) that can be utilized to promote future emotional well-being (e.g., Fredrickson & Cohn, 2008; see Chapter 12). As reviewed earlier, infants and young children depend on those they interact with to learn ways to regulate their emotions and to cope under stressful situations. The importance of building relationships through positive interactions and shared activities is one that continues throughout the lifespan and is also essential for school-age children, adolescents and adult couples or marital partners. More theoretical work and relevant research is needed to address emotion regulation within different age groups using some of the tenets of the broaden and build theory.

For school-age children, Gayle Macklem (2008) has provided some suggestions for strategies that parents and teachers can use to help children learn to strengthen their coping and emotion regulation skills given that children spend most of their waking time in school. Educational settings can be stressful, and academic, social and behavioural challenges to children's well-being abound. According to Macklem (2008), parents and teachers may need to: 1) learn ways to regulate their own emotions as they react to negative emotional outbursts in children, 2) consider children's temperaments and how the social and physical environments may need to be adjusted to make a better match to the child's emotion regulation needs, 3) offer children specific options for how to regulate themselves with elaborations on the possible consequences, 4) encourage emotion talk with children by using books, movies or writing tasks to explore how characters regulate their feelings, 5) engage in specific question-and-answer dialogues with children about how to handle difficult interpersonal situations, 6) engage in emotion coaching strategies, and 7) focus on teaching children and adolescents specific emotion regulation strategies when it is developmentally appropriate to do so. Features of emotion coaching strategies addressed in the literature include being attentive to and respecting the child's emotions, teaching the child how to calm down and self-soothe, showing the child how to stay engaged and cope when things are stressful, helping children to understand what caused their emotions, being responsive to the child's questions, and assisting children in managing specific feelings of sadness, anger or fear/anxiety (e.g., Gottman, 1997; Macklem, 2008).

For adolescents, much of the research on emotion regulation has focused on the risks for psychopathology given the vulnerability of the adolescent period; thus, emotion regulation issues relevant to adolescents and parent–adolescent conflict resolution are topics discussed in the next chapter, Chapter 11, which addresses psychopathology. However, as pointed out by Macklem (2008), emotion coaching is also appropriate and important for adult–adolescent interactions.

Adults need to expend time and energy on their own emotion regulation goals within their family relationships. More theoretical work and relevant research is needed to address how adults pursue such goals. There is often a need for adults to increase their repertoire and understanding of emotion regulation and coping strategies. Although learning how to make effective use of the emotion regulation and coping strategies reviewed earlier in this chapter is a reasonable goal for adults, many adults have now turned to using ***mindfulness*** approaches, as reflected in the expanding public interest in yoga, meditation and Buddhist psychology. Mindfulness has been defined as intentionally attending in a non-judgemental way to the here-and-now moment and is increasingly the focus of interventions to improve emotion regulation (e.g., Farb et al., 2014; Kabat-Zinn, 2015). Although many people are able to be mindfully aware in the here-and-now moment, remaining non-judgemental is difficult and requires a higher-level form of emotion regulation that has been called *equanimity* (Desbordes et al., 2015). Desbordes et al. (2015) state that: "Mindfulness emphasizes the ability to remain *consciously aware* of what is happening in the field of experience, while equanimity allows awareness to be *even and unbiased* by facilitating an attitude of non-attachment and nonresistance" (Desbordes et al., 2015, p. 358). Desbordes et al. (2015) view equanimity as a specific important, but often neglected, form of emotion regulation that alters the magnitude and quality of emotional responding.

It is interesting to note that Eastern approaches to emotion regulation in adults that involve mindfulness and equanimity emphasize transcending specific positive, negative and neutral emotional states. Western approaches such as the optimization and selectivity theories of emotion regulation in adults differ in that they emphasize ways to optimize and expand positive emotional states. Magai (2008) states that optimization and selectivity theories of emotional regulation imply that as adults age they need to focus more on emotional information, put a priority on their emotional relationships and work towards ways to minimize their negative affect while increasing their positive affect. This contrast in Eastern and Western perspectives is likely to be one that is addressed in future research involving cultural differences in emotion regulation.

## Summary of Chapter Key Points

The emotional tone of the family is set by how parents and other family members regulate their emotions and cope with stress as they interact with each other. The concepts of self-regulation, coping and emotion regulation are prominent in many contemporary studies on emotional development. Self-regulation broadly refers to cognitive, emotional and behavioural systems as well as neural processes that are activated during attempts at managing goal attainment; emotion regulation and coping can be subsumed under the concept of self-regulation. The concept of emotion regulation involves managing emotional reactions whether or not they involve stress, while the concept of coping specifically involves managing reactions to stress. Emotion regulation is important in understanding family interactions that promote harmony or result in conflict escalation or resolution. The rapidly expanding field involving the study of emotion regulation needs a comprehensive developmental theory to organize the plethora of research findings across the lifespan. Such a theory would need to generate hypotheses for linking the study of general emotion regulation processes to the study of stress and coping, a point made by Compas et al. (2014). Important avenues for future research involve the co-regulation of emotion in family interactions, which has most often been studied in normative family interactions during the period of infancy with fewer studies in childhood, and with parent–adolescent interactions often focused on conflicts rather than normative emotion socialization exchanges. In addition to co-regulation, emotional regulation also begins in infancy and has been studied in the context of predicting child emotion regulation on the basis of parent and child characteristics and marital quality. Additional directions for future theorizing and research on emotion regulation and coping will likely include the broaden and build theory, as well as the use of mindfulness strategies.

## Further Reading

Gross, J. J. (Ed.) (2014). *Handbook of emotion regulation (2nd ed.).* New York: Guilford Press.

James J. Gross, author of the process model of emotion regulation and editor of this comprehensive volume on emotion regulation, has brought together the collected works of many of the leading scholars in the field including a special section on developmental considerations. In addition, other sections include chapters on the biological bases of emotion regulation as well as cognitive, social and personality approaches to emotion regulation. Finally, chapters relevant for the study of health, psychopathology and intervention are included.

Macklem, G. L. (2008). *Practitioner's guide to emotion regulation in school-aged children.* New York: Springer.

Educational psychologist Gayle Macklem provides a readable and accessible account of the state of research on children's emotional regulation with an emphasis on practical applications for teachers and parents. The volume is replete with suggestions for how adults can work with children to assist them in emotion regulation. In addition, the author provides handouts and suggested coping strategies for children to use under specific stressful conditions, such as being the victim of bullying. Given that the largest proportion of time spent by children and adolescents is in school, family members must often accommodate and regulate their emotions around school-related social and academic stresses. Macklem's work provides an excellent guide to assist in this process.

# 11

# A Developmental Psychopathology Approach to Emotion in Families

*Dalia is a 15-year-old girl with above average academic functioning. She came to the attention of the school psychologist after she made a suicide threat. After evaluating Dalia, the psychologist learned that Dalia had suicidal thoughts about overdosing on her mother's medication. Dalia's parents were well-educated, recently divorced, and underemployed Iraqi Muslim refugees who had emigrated to the US with their family a few years earlier. Dalia had symptoms of depressed affect. She appeared clean but dishevelled, and was guarded in her interactions. She spoke about feeling isolated and not having very many friends. Also, she revealed that she felt especially desperate and hopeless when her parents engaged in heated arguments. Family conflicts that were upsetting to Dalia included her father's derogatory comments about her obese mother and arguments over her father's unwillingness to help pay for Dalia's college education. Although the school psychologist tried to make some helpful recommendations to Dalia and her custodial mother, she was unable to establish a working alliance with them possibly due to her having insufficient background knowledge about Middle Eastern cultures and inadequate information about resources to facilitate refugee mental health.* (Case study summary from Nassar-McMillan & Hakim-Larson, 2014, pp. 67–70.)

Source: In D.W. Sue, M. E. Gallardo and H. A. Neville (Eds.), *Case Studies in Multicultural Counseling*. Wiley. 

## Key Concepts in Developmental Psychopathology

The case of Dalia and her family illustrates many of the core constructs in a developmental psychopathology approach to emotional problems across the generations. These constructs include consideration of the interplay of *continuities* and *discontinuities, adaptive* and *maladaptive* functioning, and the *developmental pathways* that emerge as possibilities over time (e.g., Ross & Jennings, 1995; Rutter, 2013). The developmental psychopathology perspective differs from but is closely related to a clinical perspective, which usually focuses on diagnoses, treatment, and an age range such as childhood, adolescence or adulthood. Rather, the focus in developmental psychopathology is on various pathways or life-course trajectories extending from childhood to adulthood with less emphasis on diagnosis and treatment, but more emphasis on *preventive interventions* and fostering *resilience* (Masten, 2007; Ross & Jennings, 1995; see Chapter 12). Developmental psychopathology is not a theory, nor does it constitute a separate discipline according to its founders; rather, it is an interdisciplinary approach with proponents seeking to understand variations in both normal and abnormal development by examining the mechanisms and processes leading to individual differences in functioning (Rutter, 2013). Table 11.1 displays definitions of some key concepts utilized in a developmental psychopathology approach. Using a developmental psychopathology framework, this chapter highlights the role that emotions play in the developmental pathways of family members. While the emphasis in this chapter is on indicators of psychopathology along the pathways, the emphasis in the final chapter of this book, Chapter 12, is on resilience.

In the opening case vignette, among Dalia's adaptive strengths are her above-average intellectual ability and her motivation to someday attend college. Due to the Persian Gulf wars, the US invasion of Iraq and the ensuing insurrections and instability in the region, Dalia and her family suffered pre-migration traumas, traumas during multiple resettlements, and post-migration traumas similar to the typical readjustments of many refugees (e.g., Keyes, 2000; Kira, Amer & Wrobel, 2014). In a developmental psychopathology framework, the multiple risk factors that accumulate during wars, natural disasters and other traumatic life events cut across ethnicities and generations at multiple levels of analysis, including the biological and socio-emotional levels (Masten & Narayan, 2012). The growing number of studies on immigrants from the Middle East has found that among clinical samples, refugees who came from Iraq who sought medical help had a relatively high rate of depression and anxiety (e.g., Jamil et al., 2002). However, it is important to note that most Middle Eastern immigrants and refugees show evidence of resilience and adaptive functioning despite the hardships they have endured (e.g., Kira et al., 2014). In the case of Dalia, both of her parents had professional positions prior to the upheaval in their country of origin, but both lost their professional status and credentials after their relocation and did not recover them after migration. Pre-migration functioning, the stresses related to acculturation (e.g., Amer, 2014), and the accumulation

**Table 11.1** Developmental Psychopathology: Some Key Concepts and Definitions

| Concepts | Definitions and Sources |
|---|---|
| Risk factors | "[E]stablished predictors of undesirable outcomes where there is evidence suggesting a higher than usual probability of a future problem" (Masten, 2014, p. 13). |
| Protective factors | Variables that operate in stressful life circumstances that seem to enable the person to circumvent the adverse effects of the stress (Garmezy, 1991).<br>May act as mediators or moderators of the stress/adversity and a more adaptive or resilient outcome (Masten, 2007). |
| Vulnerability | Process by which individuals who are high on some variable are more susceptible/vulnerable to risks than those who are low on the variable (Luthar, 1991). Vulnerability varies over time within individuals as a result of age (Rutter & Sroufe, 2000) and as a result of genetic-environment interactions (Rutter, 1999). |
| Equifinality | A diversity of initial developmental processes and pathways may lead to the *same* outcome or end-state (Cicchetti & Rogosch, 1996). |
| Multifinality | The same initial developmental processes and pathway may lead to quite *different* adaptive or maladaptive outcomes or end-states, depending on the choices made or the circumstances encountered along the way (Cicchetti & Rogosch, 1996). |
| Developmental cascades | Refers to the cumulative consequences of interactions and transactions that result in *spreading* effects across multiple levels, within domains at the same level, across different systems of development, and across generations; the effects can be direct or indirect, uni- or bidirectional and may significantly alter the course of development (Masten & Cicchetti, 2010). |
| Resilience | "[R]elative resistance to psychosocial risk experiences" (Rutter, 1999, p. 119).<br>Entails three types of experiences: (1) overcoming the odds against adaptive development, (2) functioning well despite adversity which is sometimes called being stress-resistant, and (3) demonstrating normal or adaptive functioning after a traumatic experience or extreme adversity (Masten & Obradović, 2008). |

of these and other major life stressors likely contributed to the marital conflicts that ensued, leading to their eventual divorce. While some children and adolescents faced with trauma show internalizing symptoms (i.e., depression, anxiety), such as occurred in Dalia, others tend to act out and externalize their anger and frustration. It is also possible for internalizing and externalizing disorders to be comorbid (i.e., occurring at the same time) or to be comorbid with personality disorders, eating disorders, substance use disorders and psychotic disorders such as schizophrenia (American Psychiatric Association, 2013). Emotion dysregulation is often apparent in such disorders as is discussed throughout this chapter.

## Emotion Dysregulation: Defining Abnormality and Disorders

Emotions are well-known to be involved in one way or another in abnormal or psychopathological functioning. *Emotion dysregulation* occurs when patterns of emotional functioning disrupt cognitive or social processes or interfere with the ability to flexibly regulate attention and experiences (Cole, Michel & Teti, 1994). Cole et al. (1994) review literature that suggests that emotion dysregulation involves the failure to achieve normal emotional developmental tasks with the person having trouble processing or integrating information, and controlling emotional experiences or their expressions.

Several criteria have been identified by which to judge whether or not emotional and behavioural problems can be considered abnormal or atypical, and thus warrant the label of psychopathological. These criteria were summarized by Garber (1984) and Ross and Jennings (1995) as follows. First, behaviours can be considered to be abnormal if there is a *significant deviation* from what is considered to be age-appropriate and developmentally typical under the given conditions. Second, an *exaggerated normal developmental trend*, such as extreme adolescent rebellion, may warrant consideration as being atypical; for example, a young teen who "accidently on purpose" forgets to let his parents know his whereabouts after school and into the late evening may be displaying some "normal" rebellion and withdrawal from parents. However, a young teen who repeatedly runs off with deviant peers and is absent for days at a time without parental knowledge of his whereabouts would be showing an atypical pattern. Third, some emotional behaviours are considered abnormal because they *interfere with normal developmental tasks*; for example, extreme angry outbursts accompanied by aggressive acting out can interfere with the development of friendships. Finally, the *intensity, frequency and chronicity* of the emotional and behavioural problems need to be considered in interaction with a person's age and developmental level (Garber, 1984; Ross & Jennings, 1995). Such clinically significant abnormality has resulted in different methods of classifying and studying disorders throughout history, as described further in History Feature Box 11.

### History Feature Box 11

### Back Then and Now: The Classification and Study of Mental Disorders

The need to understand and classify mental disorders was recognized early in the history of psychology. In the 1840 census in the United States, there was a need to know the number of people with mental disorders (called *idiocy/insanity* at that time); by the 1880 census, there were seven categories of mental disorders: *mania, melancholia, monomania, paresis, dementia, dipsomania* and *epilepsy* (American Psychiatric Association, 2016). In 1883, the German physician Emil Kraepelin (1856–1926) began to create a classification scheme for disorders and published nine editions of his work; the sixth edition (1899) was the most popular and contained 13 disorders ranging from mild with a promising prognosis (e.g., *fright neurosis*) to more serious disorders with poor prognoses such as *manic-depressive psychosis* (bipolar disorder) and *dementia praecox* (schizophrenia) (see Goodwin, 2015). While additional classification schemes were created after Kraepelin's volumes, they were created to gather data from mental hospitals or to assist in the medical diagnosis of mental disorders in servicemen and veterans after World War II (American Psychiatric Association, 2016).

In 1952, the sixth version of the *International Classification of Diseases* (ICD-6) formed the basis for the *Diagnostic and Statistical Manual of Mental Disorders* (DSM-I), which was the first official manual developed for general clinical use; revisions were made in the DSM-II and DSM-III to be consistent with revisions made to the ICD classification system (American Psychiatric Association, 2016). By 1980 with the DSM-III, attempts were made to be more neutral about possible causes and to provide clear definitions for clinical and research purposes; subsequent revisions to the DSM-IV and DSM-5 continued to coordinate changes with those made to the ICD system (American Psychiatric Association, 2016).

While the DSM-5 (American Psychiatric Association, 2013) remains a valuable clinical tool for use by mental health professionals enabling psychiatric diagnoses and a common language for communication, its validity for understanding the underlying neurological foundation of mental disorders has been questioned by those adopting the perspective of the Research Domain Criteria (RDoC) Project initiated by the National Institute of Mental Health (NIMH) in the US (e.g., Kaufman et al., 2015). While the DSM-5 identifies and describes symptoms and categories of disorders for clinical diagnoses and application, the RDoC emphasizes a research framework, takes a dimensional rather than categorical approach to features of disorders, and has a primary focus on genetics and the role of neural circuits (fear circuitry, emotion processing, reward circuitry, executive function and memory) in behaviours (Kaufman et al., 2015). Multiple levels of analyses are considered in the RDoC approach (genetic, molecular, cellular, circuits, physiological, behavioural, self-reports and treatment paradigms) with five constructs proposed for study: 1) negative valence systems (e.g., acute fear, loss), 2) positive valence systems (e.g., approach motivation, reward responsiveness), 3) cognitive systems (e.g., attention, perception, memory, effortful control), 4) systems for social processes (e.g., affiliation and attachment, social communication), and 5) arousal/regulatory systems (e.g., arousal, biological rhythms, sleep/wake cycles) (Kaufman et al., 2015). In their review of RDoC papers, Kaufman et al. (2015) utilize developmental psychopathology constructs such as *risk* and *resilience* in their application and interpretation of RDoC studies of children with maltreatment histories and their families.

Franklin, Jamieson, Glenn and Nock (2015) agree that there are many benefits to the RDoC system given that there are still many comorbidities, classification uncertainties and boundary confusions in the DSM-5 categorical approach. However, Franklin et al. (2015) also recommend that researchers using the RDoC approach better articulate and fully utilize developmental psychopathology constructs to inform their work. In their critique, they note that *psychopathology* has been reframed to be *pathophysiology* given the emphasis on neurological processes. They caution that proponents of the RDoC approach must avoid biological reductionism by incorporating a more clearly transactional (heredity by environment) and developmental approach into their models and interpretations of research findings. Franklin et al. (2015) note that the initial constructs chosen for study in RDoC include several that are relevant for emotion regulation/dysregulation such as negative valence and positive valence systems. However, approach motivation was only included under positive valence (e.g., attachment love). They claim that approach motivation can be either positive or negative in valence (e.g., aggressive anger), and therefore a separate *motivation* domain of study is needed. Franklin et al. (2015) conclude that the RDoC project is promising, but would benefit from explicit incorporation of a developmental psychopathology perspective. Important additions would be to add motivation to the constructs under study, and to consider social context, developmental changes over time, and normative processes as well as pathological ones. Also, they suggest that the transdiagnostic dimensional approach of RDoC can be instrumental in informing research in developmental psychopathology by helping to identify common developmental pathways and their causal mechanisms.

Outcomes along possible adaptive and maladaptive developmental pathways that are often studied and widely agreed upon as a way to classify disorders are internalizing disorders and externalizing disorders (Achenbach, 2014; Cicchetti & Natsuaki, 2014). Emotion-related internalizing and externalizing symptoms characterize a variety of disorders that are classified in the *Diagnostic and Statistical Manual of Mental Disorders* (e.g., DSM-5) and the *International Classification of Diseases* (e.g., ICD-11) (American Psychiatric Association, 2013). Among the internalizing disorders are anxiety, depressed mood and related physiological and cognitive symptoms; among the externalizing disorders are symptoms that are impulsive, antisocial, and involve disruptive conduct, substance use or addiction (DSM-5; American Psychiatric Association, 2013). In addition, other disorders that involve emotion dysregulation have been studied using a developmental psychopathology approach; among these are personality disorders (Cicchetti, 2014), bipolar disorder

(Miklowitz & Cicchetti, 2006), autism spectrum disorders, schizophrenia and psychoses, and disorders involving intellectual or learning disabilities (Rutter & Sroufe, 2000). While a comprehensive review of these disorders and their link to emotion dysregulation is beyond the scope of this chapter, some illustrative studies on emotion dysregulation in families and how it is manifest in internalizing and externalizing disorders are reviewed next.

## Emotion Dysregulation and Internalizing Disorders

It is important to study emotion socialization in non-normative contexts as well as normative ones. For example, children are socialized in families in which there is maternal incarceration (e.g., Zeman, Dellaire & Borowski, 2016), parental mental illness (e.g., Cuijpers et al., 2015), intimate partner violence (Katz, Stettler & Gurtovenko, 2016), family poverty (e.g., Garmezy, 1991), and homelessness (e.g., Labella, Narayan & Masten, 2015). These and other risk factors have often been linked to emotion dysregulation and internalizing disorders in children. For example, Labella et al. (2015) studied homeless families with children living in temporary shelters and found that higher expressions of parental negativity and distress predicted negative affect and lower prosocial behaviours in the children; in contrast, higher parental warmth was linked to greater positive affect in the children. Labella et al. (2015) recommend that interventions in shelters occur at the level of addressing parent's internalizing symptoms and distress since helping parents to modulate their emotional reactions could be beneficial for the socio-emotional development of their children.

In a study of mothers with a history of multiple risks (childhood maltreatment, postpartum depression, single parenthood, low income), Martinez-Torteya et al. (2014) found that positive parenting strategies such as displaying warmth, positive affect, and engaged, sensitive behaviours during interactions with infants predicted better infant behavioural/emotional regulation and less cortisol reactivity to stress during the still-face paradigm. This study demonstrates the value in using multiple methods (observational, self-report and biobehavioural markers); importantly, mothers' own childhood history of maltreatment alone did not directly relate to the outcomes for the child. Rather, mothers with a history of maltreatment were more likely to report being depressed and it was maternal depression in turn that was related to less positive and more negative parent–infant interactions.

The study of maternal depression and treating it effectively seems to be critically important to improving understanding of major contributors to infant mental health. It is via interactions with caregivers that infants make meaning out of their experiences and develop the cognitive-affective schemas or mental representations that allow them later on to symbolize their relationships with others in accordance with their cultures and to develop internal working models based on their own individual pattern of interactions with their caregivers (e.g., Greenspan & Porges, 1984; Tronick & Beeghly, 2011). However, when mothers are depressed, the normal mother–infant interactions that involve matching or mismatching meanings and intentions, and making attempts to repair failed emotional connections are likely to get derailed and go awry (Tronick & Beeghly, 2011). Occasional failed attempts to connect are likely in normal mother–infant interactions but when failures are chronic over time, as can happen with depressed caregivers, there is evidence that psychopathology is the outcome for children. Varga and Krueger (2013) describe depression as a background emotion characterized by a felt inability to connect and thus the depressed person is experientially constrained. Depressed caregivers are thus unable to provide the emotional co-regulation that is vital to their children's adaptive functioning. Fortunately, a meta-analysis of studies of psychotherapy with depressed mothers has shown that treatment for depression not only had positive effects on the mothers, but also on their parenting and marital distress, and on their children's well-being (Cuijpers et al., 2015).

Parents' own emotion regulation understanding and ability to coach emotions in their children may serve as a protective factor against behavioural/emotional disorders in their children under conditions of traumatic stress such as domestic violence (e.g., Katz & Windecker-Nelson, 2006). Katz et al. (2016) conducted the parental meta-emotion philosophy interview (see Chapter 6) with mothers of 6- to 12-year-old children who had been exposed to intimate partner violence. They found that there were specific pathways in which maternal emotion awareness, acceptance and coaching were linked to better emotion regulation in children, which in turn was related to fewer depression and post-traumatic stress symptoms in children.

Although depression occurs throughout the lifespan, adolescents are at a particularly high risk for depression (e.g., Bellamy & Hardy, 2015). Shortt et al. (2016) summarize a series of studies that they and others have conducted that show that how both mothers and fathers socialize sadness and anger in their adolescent children is related to parent–adolescent interactions and adolescent depression. In particular, the parents of depressed adolescents were less emotionally supportive and more non-supportive than the parents of non-depressed adolescents; parent and child gender moderated the findings. Shortt et al. (2016) also highlighted possible bidirectional effects, with the behaviours of the depressed adolescent also affecting the quality of parental responses.

As has been found with the study of parental depression and its relation to children's psychopathology, parental anxiety also has been examined for links to child dysfunction. Laskey and Cartwright-Hatton (2009) studied anxiety in the parents of 4- to 10-year-old children and found links to children's internalizing disorders. In this study, parents' anxiety was linked to their beliefs about parenting which in turn was linked to their use of harsh discipline; the use of harsh discipline then predicted children's internalizing disorders.

In another study of the link between parent and child anxiety, Murray and her colleagues (2014) studied mothers with social anxiety disorder as they interacted with their 4- to 5-year-old children around a story with potentially socially threatening story content – the experiences of a child who is starting school. The storytelling responses of the mothers with anxiety were compared to those of mothers without anxiety. In contrast to mothers without anxiety, socially anxious mothers were more likely to make threat attributions about the environment and focus on the child's vulnerability in the new situation; they were also less likely to make encouraging positive statements meant to promote the child's ability to handle the transition (Murray et al., 2014). The authors suggest that it might be beneficial to target interventions at the level of maternal narratives and how they make meaning out of the stories that they tell to their children.

Thus, the way that mothers and fathers discuss a child's emotions with the child has implications for the child's anxiety symptoms. Consistent with this notion, Suveg et al. (2008) studied parent–child communication about real-life emotion situations in a sample of 8- to 12-year-old children with and without an anxiety disorder. Evidence for gender-related emotion socialization differences were found with fathers overall speaking more with sons than daughters. However, fathers of children with anxiety spent less time explaining emotions to their children than did fathers of children without anxiety, and were more likely to display negative affect and less likely to display positive affect in the interaction. Mothers overall tended to discourage discussion of anger especially with their daughters. Parents of children with an anxiety disorder were found to provide less explanatory descriptions of emotion, to be more discouraging of emotion discussion, and to show less positive affect than parents of children with no diagnoses (Suveg et al., 2008). The children with anxiety disorders made less use of problem solving and more use of maladaptive strategies in the discussions about emotion with their parents. Thus, as for depression, emotion-related deficits have been found in children with anxiety disorders and these deficits are linked to interaction patterns with their caregivers.

It is noteworthy that children's susceptibility or vulnerability to different forms of anxiety disorders (e.g., separation anxiety disorder, social anxiety disorder) may vary depending on the context in which the disorder develops and the person's level of psychosocial maturity. Westenberg, Siebelink, Warmenhoven and Treffers (1999) found that separation anxiety disorder, which was more likely to be diagnosed in children than adolescents, was associated with an impulsive ego level. However, overanxious disorder (from DSM-III-R; later called generalized anxiety disorder in DSM-IV and DSM-5) was more likely to occur in adolescents and was linked to a conformist level of ego functioning. Westenberg et al. (1999) found that ego level rather than age alone was related to this shift, acknowledging that many other factors in addition to psychosocial maturity are likely implicated. In another study, Westenberg, Drewes, Goedhart, Siebelink and Treffers (2004) suggest that there is evidence that children, in contrast to adolescents, have more fears related to physical dangers, but this decreases with age; however, adolescents have an increase in fears related to social evaluation, which amplifies their susceptibility and vulnerability to developing social anxiety disorder.

In addition to being vulnerable to more fears related to social evaluation in adolescence and early adulthood (Westenberg et al., 2004), adults with childhood histories of insecure or disorganized attachment are also vulnerable to the development of any of the anxiety disorders with the possible exception of some phobias (Dozier, Stovall-McClough & Albus, 2008). In a study by Seedall and Wampler (2016), attachment anxiety in adult couples was studied in relation to their psychophysiological reactions during videotaped interactions with each other under two therapy-like conditions. After a warm-up session in which the couple discussed how they met, the couple was instructed to talk about relationship topics in which they felt angry or hurt – first, while a therapist was present but inactive (low structure condition), and second, while a therapist was present but actively involved in guiding, structuring and coaching the partners to listen to and validate each other's emotions in a softer and more conciliatory way than they had previously (high structure condition) (Seedall & Wampler, 2016). The partners then independently watched and rated the videotape of their interaction for how negatively or positively they felt about it from moment to moment. The researchers found that men and women with high attachment anxiety had more positive feelings towards their partner when viewing the videotaped interaction in the high structure condition (as compared to low); thus, those with high attachment anxiety seemed to benefit from the therapist buffering and containing the emotions expressed, acting as a filter, and scaffolding the partners' responses to each other in a more adaptive way (Seedall & Wampler, 2016). Much in the same way that parents with internalizing symptoms can be trained to co-regulate emotions in a more adaptive way with their children, adults with internalizing symptoms can be trained to do so with their partners.

In the following section, we turn to the literature on emotion dysregulation that involves antisocial pathways and symptoms of externalizing disorders such as impulsive acting out, anger and aggression, and disruptive behaviours.

## Emotion Dysregulation and Externalizing Disorders

The most common problems referred for treatment involve emotion dysregulation and externalizing disorders; the most likely reason for this relatively high prevalence rate is because the symptoms are often disturbing and disruptive to others in the social network of the child, adolescent or adult (e.g., Kazdin & Weisz, 1998). These symptoms interfere with the individual's development and may include interference with the rights of others; among the defining features are symptoms that are *cognitive* (poor attention and planning), *behavioural* (disruptive, antisocial activities), and *affective* (angry, explosive, defiant outbursts) (Mullin & Hinshaw, 2007). Categorical designations of externalizing disorders include: (1) attention deficit hyperactivity disorder (ADHD), characterized by various patterns of inattention, impulsivity and hyperactivity, (2) oppositional defiant disorder (ODD), characterized by an angry/irritable mood, argumentative/defiant behaviour and vindictiveness, and (3) conduct disorder (CD), which involves aggression to animals or people, property destruction, theft, deceitfulness and serious violation of rules and other people's rights (DSM-5; American Psychiatric Association, 2013). Several externalizing developmental pathways have been identified as extending from childhood to adulthood.

Due to an underlying genetic and temperamental predisposition that may be exacerbated by environmental risks, individuals with ADHD have difficulties with attention, impulse control, executive functions and academic achievement (Mullin & Hinshaw, 2007). Barkley (2013) describes another distinct disorder that involves symptoms of what has been called *sluggish cognitive tempo* (SCT; daydreaming, mental fogginess, sleepiness, lethargy) that may overlap with ADHD symptoms in some cases, although further study is needed. While it has been suggested that some individuals with ADHD may not display significant emotion regulation problems (Mullin & Hinshaw, 2007), these cases may be ones that include individuals with overlapping SCT symptoms. Russell Barkley (2015) provides compelling evidence that emotional impulsivity and deficient emotional self-regulation (EI-DESR) are *major* contributors to the lifelong difficulties encountered by individuals with an ADHD diagnosis. Indeed, some individuals with ADHD show internalizing symptoms and thus meet the criteria for comorbid anxiety and/or depression (Steinberg & Drabick, 2015). In addition, emotion dysregulation in individuals with ADHD can result in angry, hostile and aggressive symptoms; the person may then meet criteria for a comorbid diagnosis of ODD, CD, or antisocial personality disorder (American Psychiatric Association, 2013; Mullin & Hinshaw, 2007).

Thus, a possible path for some children with ADHD leads to the development of ODD symptoms. But even within ODD, there are different possible pathways. Individuals with ODD vary in their symptoms of aggression, with some displaying relatively more *reactive* forms and others more *proactive* forms although multiple forms of aggression are possible within the same person (Greene & Doyle, 1999; see Table 11.2). ODD involves non-compliant behaviours and defiance to people in authority which becomes evident at home with family, at school with teachers, or outside the home in the workplace. Studies of individuals with ODD show that it is characterized by a temperamental pattern of negative emotion, low effortful control, low agreeableness, and relatively high anger, irritability, emotion lability/instability and aggression (Steinberg & Drabick, 2015). In addition to temperament, maternal emotion socialization plays a role in the eventual outcome of ODD as illustrated in a study by Dunsmore, Booker, Ollendick and Greene (2016). Dunsmore et al. (2016) found that pretreatment maternal emotion coaching predicted a reduction in posttreatment

**Table 11.2** Emotion Dysregulation and Different Forms of Aggression

| Aggression Type | Description (Mullin & Hinshaw, 2007) |
|---|---|
| Overt aggression | Verbal assaults or physical fights and confrontations |
| Covert aggression | Theft, property destruction, lying, cheating |
| Indirect aggression | Indirectly causing harm to another person's reputation by talking about a person<br>Similar to relational aggression observed in those who gossip and form alliances meant to exclude specific others |
| Reactive aggression | Characterized by emotional overarousal, and angry, explosive, volatile reactions to frustration and threat<br>Negative affect is heightened |
| Proactive aggression | Characterized by planful, instrumental, proactive means of obtaining desired goals<br>Emotional underarousal |

ODD symptoms in 7- to 14-year-old children; however, this beneficial effect of emotion coaching was found only for those ODD children who were high in negative emotionality and emotion lability. The authors conclude that mothers and their children with ODD who are at high risk due to their emotion dysregulation will benefit the most from parent training if the mothers begin treatment already using some emotion coaching strategies based on their previous background experiences.

Unfortunately, approximately one-third of those with ODD later develop more serious antisocial behaviours that may qualify as CD or antisocial personality disorder (Biederman et al., 1996; Mullin & Hinshaw, 2007). Both overt and covert forms of aggression may be involved. Two developmental pathways that involve emotion dysregulation for CD have been suggested by the literature and research and involve ***callous-unemotional traits***. These are: (1) *CD without callous-unemotional traits*, where there is reactive aggression, high fear and negative emotionality, and (2) *CD with callous-unemotional traits*, where there is low fear, low anger, low emotional distress in general, a lack of empathy or remorse for wrongdoing, and high motivation to attain rewards (such as through sensation seeking), but a lack of emotional arousal or influence by punishment or other forms of negative evaluation (Mullin & Hinshaw, 2007; Steinberg & Drabick, 2015). In the DSM-5, callous-unemotional traits are given the specifier label "with limited prosocial emotions", where there is a lack of remorse, guilt or empathy for others, a lack of concern about performance and shallow or deficient affect; conduct disorder may have a childhood or adolescent onset, may vary in severity, and may or may not persist into adulthood and result in a personality disorder (DSM-5; American Psychiatric Association, 2013).

Conduct disorder has been described as having a *life course persistent (LCP) antisocial pathway* or an *adolescence-limited (AL) antisocial pathway* which occur in a similar manner in both males and females, although the sex ratio has been found to favour boys to girls 10:1 for LCP, but only 1.5:1 for AL (e.g., Moffitt & Caspi, 2001). Children who start on the LCP pathway have a family and individual history of multiple psychosocial and neurocognitive risks that begin in early childhood and persist over time; the AL group as a whole do not show the same high level of risks, but seem to get involved in antisocial behaviours through their association with delinquent peers during adolescence (Moffitt & Caspi, 2001).

As noted in the above review, there are a number of pathways that are possible when a child begins life with an inherited vulnerability, such as occurs with ADHD symptomatology. Theodore Beauchaine (2015) provides the following example of *multifinality* and outlines the results of three divergent pathways. Common to the three pathways are children born with the same genetically acquired, inherited, biological predisposition to impulsivity, reactivity and oppositionality. The first pathway described by Beauchaine (2015) involves a *protective* family environment, where the parents avoid power struggles with the child, remain calm while helping the child to deescalate emotional arousal, and set firm limits as well as consequences for aggression. Such parents are likely to show a pattern of deescalating conflict with their child while positively encouraging and reinforcing prosocial behaviours. With competent emotion socialization by parents, the child may learn strong emotion regulation skills, which in turn may make the child more attractive as a potential friend within a normative peer group. Healthy peer group affiliations and neighbourhood cohesion are additional protective factors that may help to buffer the vulnerable child from developing emotion dysregulation; in this case, the developing individual may display socialized and regulated impulsivity. The second and third pathways described by Beauchaine (2015) begin in *high-risk* family environments where parents interact with their vulnerable children by engaging in ***coercive parenting***. The coercion theory of Gerald Patterson and his colleagues is characterized by a repetitive cycle of negative interactions between parent and child that are highly aversive, involve intrusive behaviours and negative emotion reciprocity, irritable commands, and negative attributions about the other person; this form of interaction has been associated with child non-compliance, deviancy and social incompetence (Patterson, Forgatch & DeGarmo, 2010). Thus, in Beauchaine's (2015) second and third pathways, the parents attempt to assert their power, control and authority over their non-compliant child. However, a repetitive pattern of conflict escalation develops with negative reinforcement facilitating the continuation of negative emotional arousal, anger and aggression. The child fails to develop appropriate emotion regulation skills and instead emotional lability and mood dysregulation become chronic as the child develops symptoms of ODD. At this point, the pathways may diverge for boys and girls given gender socialization and different life experiences (Beauchaine, 2015). In the second pathway (for boys), exposure to deviant peers, violence and criminal activity in their neighbourhoods, and drug use can put them at risk for CD and eventually, antisocial personality disorder. In the third pathway (for girls), exposure to deviant peers, engaging in self-injurious behaviours and relational aggression can put them at risk for CD and eventually borderline personality disorder. In these examples from Beauchaine (2015), we can see how one thing leads to another and how events accumulate to have an overall impact, ideas that are known as *developmental cascades*, and which are elaborated upon below.

## Mediators, Moderators and Developmental Cascades: How One Thing Leads to Another

The complexity of how vulnerability interacts with risks and protective factors to lead to adaptive and maladaptive outcomes is apparent in the field of developmental psychopathology through research that addresses *mediators* and *moderators* and developmental cascades over time. In mediational analyses, a predictor indirectly influences an outcome through a mediator or intervening variable; the predictor influences the mediator which then in turn influences the outcome; in this way, the potential influence of more distal variables can be examined in relation to more proximal variables and a complex chain of events can be examined that links risks and protective factors to outcomes (McCartney, Burchinal & Bub, 2006). McCartney et al. (2006) cite the example of a study in which maternal exposure to community violence predicted maternal depression which in turn predicted higher levels of distress in children (Farver et al., 2005). In studies that use moderation analyses, the relation between the predictor and the outcome shifts depending on the value of the moderator variable; thus, the predictor may only influence the outcome when the moderator variable alters the relation between the two (McCartney et al., 2006). McCartney et al. (2006) cite a study conducted by Jaffee, Moffitt, Caspi and Taylor (2003) that examined fathers' level of antisocial behaviour as a moderator of the relation between the amount of time the antisocial father spent in the home since the birth of his now 5-year-old child and the level of antisocial behaviour displayed by the child. Jaffee et al. (2003) found evidence for a link between the amount of time fathers spent in the home and their children's level of antisocial behaviour, but this was only if fathers' level of antisocial behaviour was high; the relation did not hold for fathers with low or moderate levels of antisocial behaviour, suggesting that this variable acted as a moderator.

Studies that examine developmental cascades demonstrate that the direct, indirect, moderating and mediating effects of risk and protective factors can have spreading effects over time and within and across family members and their domains of functioning. In longitudinal research extending from childhood to adolescence, Bellamy and Hardy (2015) identified a number of childhood risk factors that were linked to depressive symptoms in mid- to late adolescence. Childhood risk factors associated with later adolescent depression in both boys and girls included self-reported parental rejection and having a history of depression or anxiety symptoms. For boys, early risk factors also included low self-esteem, while for girls the risks included parent absence or loss by age 4 to 8 years, early aggression or conduct disorder symptoms, maternal history of depression, and low parental monitoring.

Garber and Cole (2010) found evidence for a ***launch and grow model*** of adolescent depression in a sample of children assessed six times from Grades 6 to 12 (approximately 12 to 18 years). In their longitudinal, developmental cascades study in the US, maternal depression experienced by children under 12 years old was found to launch a series of other risk factors for children such as increased family stresses, deficits in interpersonal interactions and cognitive vulnerabilities (self-blame, processing biases, negative attributions) that eventually led to the growth of adolescent depression.

Obradović, Burt and Masten (2010) conducted a dual cascade study by examining the long-term effects of dual failure in academic and social competence stemming from childhood to adulthood. Obradović et al. (2010) based their study on a comprehensive review of literature and several models of the cascading effects of earlier risks on the development of psychopathology. For example, Cole (1990, 1991) and Harter, Marold and Whitesell (1992) developed competency-based models of the development of depression suggesting that both *academic* and *social* competencies are critically important developmental tasks that contribute to children's self-esteem and overall well-being. Patterson and Stoolmiller (1991) describe a ***dual failure*** model in which young conduct disordered children show deficits in academic and social competency during their school years which sets in motion risk for further psychopathology such as depression. Obradović et al. (2010) found support for the notion that success or failure in academic and social domains has *spillover effects* on later internalizing symptoms, but this varied by developmental period studied. Thus, childhood externalizing symptoms led to lower academic competence by adolescence; academic failures led to social failures such as deviant peer associations, which in turn led to further social failures in emerging adulthood and internalizing symptoms in young adulthood (Obradović et al., 2010). Obradović et al. utilized data from the Project Competence Longitudinal Study (PCLS) started by Norman Garmezy (Masten & Tellegen, 2012). In another study using these data, children's externalizing behaviours that influenced their academic and social functioning also had links in adulthood to problems in work competence (Masten et al., 2010).

As can be seen in the studies reviewed above, the cascade of many mental health problems begins in early childhood. Among the many possible risk factors are variables arising from within the child (e.g., low birth weight, temperament, genetic anomalies), parenting and parent–child interaction patterns, parents' mental health, family functioning, and broader community and societal variables (Landy & Menna, 2006). These various multiple causal risk factors can lead to similar internalizing or externalizing behavioural problems and symptoms in young children (*equifinality*), but the nature of the symptoms may later diverge and consolidate into different patterns over time. For example, Okado and Bierman (2015) conducted a longitudinal study of high-risk children with externalizing symptoms in the Fast Track project randomly assigned control group (i.e., they did not receive prevention intervention services, but another group did); the children were followed from early childhood (5 to 7 years) to late adolescence (17 to 19 years). They proposed a *diathesis-stress* model in which a child's underlying predisposition (in this case, overt aggression or emotion dysregulation) interacted with environmental risks, thus leading to specific forms of psychopathology. Demonstrating multifinality, Okado and Bierman (2015) found three developmental pathways: (1) severe conduct disorder including criminal activity, (2) mood dysregulation including suicidality and reactive anger, and (3) low levels of conduct or mood difficulties. In another study from the Fast Track project, an attempt was made to intervene with a randomly assigned treatment group of high-risk schoolchildren by providing them with extra academic support and assistance at school (Bierman et al., 2013). Short-term academic gains were made for the high-risk children in the programme, but these gains dissipated over time; however, other studies of the long-term outcomes of children in the Fast Track intervention prevention programme show that the programme was effective in reducing antisocial outcomes such as conduct disorder and juvenile arrests (Bierman et al., 2013).

Next, we turn to a summary of how some other interventions with families have effectively addressed emotion dysregulation and the promotion of adaptive family functioning.

## Emotion Dysregulation and Interventions with Families: Future Directions

The purpose of this section is to provide examples of family interventions with a focus on future directions for research and practice. Clinicians have created and assessed numerous early intervention programmes in the effort to treat emotion dysregulation in multi-risk children and their families. Their effectiveness in preventing further dysfunction varies considerably and depends on targeted goals, as well as on how well the programme is able to integrate its methods with the unique and specific needs of family members (see Landy & Menna, 2006 for a review of these programmes). An important goal of intervention with families is to address the emotion regulation of parents;

this may be accomplished by helping parents to cope with their child's temperament and their own experiences of trauma, by enhancing their neurobiological functioning and parenting skills, and by improving the quality of their parenting beliefs and attributions (Landy & Menna, 2006). Consistent with this goal, Katz and Windecker-Nelson (2006) provide guidelines for an effective meta-emotion intervention programme to help parents learn how to effectively socialize emotions in their children. In addition to parent training for behavioural management, treatment for parents of children from high-risk backgrounds should include: (1) addressing parents' beliefs and attitudes about emotions, (2) teaching parents how to engage in emotion talk with their children, and (3) teaching parents how to have and show respect for children's experience of emotions. Also, addressing the nature of marital/interparental communication and conflict resolution is essential to enhancing the emotional security of family members and improving the emotion regulation skills of children (e.g., Cummings & Miller-Graff, 2015).

The *emotional security hypothesis* of Davies and Cummings (1994), which stems from attachment theory, has resulted in studies of marital/interparental conflict and child difficulties in emotion regulation for over 20 years (Cummings & Miller-Graff, 2015). Emotional insecurity may result from trauma exposure or interpersonal conflict; it promotes dysregulation, impairs physiological functioning (e.g., by affecting cortisol reactivity, sleep cycles, autonomic nervous system activity), and disrupts the ability to achieve developmental tasks (Cummings & Miller-Graff, 2015). Thus, Cummings and Miller-Graff (2015) suggest that for families that experience trauma (e.g., child maltreatment, interparental conflict or community violence) that results in emotion dysregulation, a critical intervention point and direction for future research is to address the emotional security of parents and their children.

One suggested way to intervene with high-risk mothers of infants and young children involves addressing parents' internal working models or mental representations of emotional security (Huth-Bocks et al., 2014). ***Mentalization***, or what also has been called self-reflectivity or the reflective function, develops when individuals synergistically interact with important others and reflect on their own and others' internal mental states (i.e., beliefs, thoughts, feelings, intentions, desires) (Fonagy, Gergely & Target, 2008). As noted in Chapter 9, the ability to verbalize internal states occurs once children have developed a theory of mind, but how does having an appropriate and attuned understanding about the internal mental states of self and others develop?

Following upon the work of Mary Ainsworth (see Chapters 1 and 2) who noticed more sensitive caregiving occurring in infant–mother dyads who were classified as secure in contrast to insecure, Elizabeth Meins and her colleagues

(Meins et al., 2002; Meins, 2013) have attempted to link attachment security to the development of a theory of mind. Meins (2002) suggested that some mothers tend to treat their infants as individuals who have a mind capable of making decisions and acting intentionally; she has called this tendency parental ***mind-mindedness***. According to Meins (2013), "mind-mindedness is defined as caregivers' tendency to treat their young children as individuals with minds of their own, and enables caregivers to 'tune in' to what their infants may be thinking or feeling" (p. 530). Mind-mindedness in caregivers can be operationalized as being either: (1) appropriately attuned statements about the infant's mental states based on the context and the interaction (e.g., commenting to a child that she really likes playing with a toy car while she is actively engaged with it and showing signs of pleasure), or (2) inappropriate non-attuned comments about the infant's mental states (e.g., commenting to a child that he is not interested in a toy car while he is actively engaged with it and showing signs of pleasure) (Meins, 2013); in the latter case, there is a mismatch between what is verbalized and what is observed. While mind-mindedness complements parental sensitivity in responding to children, it appears to be an independent predictor of the quality of attachment, with distinctions found for the secure, insecure-avoidant and insecure-ambivalent attachment types (Meins, 2013). Specifically, Meins (2013) found in her research that mothers who are relatively high in being appropriately attuned to their infants' internal states are more likely to have infants with secure attachments; also, Meins found that mothers in the two insecure groups did not differ in their relatively lower levels of appropriate mind-mindedness comments, but those in the insecure-resistant group had higher scores on inappropriate non-attuned mental state comments than did those in the insecure-avoidant group. These findings have important implications for intervention planning with at-risk families.

While the research and analysis of Meins and her colleagues (e.g., Meins et al., 2002; Meins, 2013) demonstrate the importance of attending to what parents say to a child about his or her mental activities (e.g., labelling the child's cognitive and affective states, motivations and intentions), that is not the complete picture. For Shai and Belsky (2011a, 2011b), mind-mindedness as studied by Meins involves studying parent–infant interaction in conjunction primarily with the parent's *verbalized explicit comments* made to a child within a given context. Shai and Belsky (2011a, 2011b) highlight that, in addition, there are *automatic implicit kinaesthetic actions* occurring in the nonverbal muscle movements of the faces and bodies of the parent–infant dyad; for these researchers, ***parental embodied mentalization (PEM)*** involves the parent's capacity to view the infant as a mentalistic partner during the kinaesthetic dialogue or process of interaction. According to Shai and Belsky

(2011a), "PEM is the parental capacity to (a) implicitly conceive, comprehend, and extrapolate the infant's mental states (such as wishes, desires, or preferences) from the infant's whole body kinesthetic expressions, and (b) adjust one's own kinesthetic patterns accordingly" (p. 175). An example here would be a parent who appropriately makes bodily contact by picking up, holding close, and hugging the infant after the infant signals the need and shows receptivity; in contrast, a parent might inappropriately insist on bodily contact while an infant is actively protesting and resisting. Even in functional families with healthy emotional regulation, miscoordination likely occurs at times, such as in the latter case, but caregivers then often make an attempt to repair the interaction (e.g., Tronick & Beeghly, 2011). When miscoordination is frequent and reparative actions are deficient, emotional dysregulation is more likely in interactions. Shai and Belsky (2011a) have created a coding scheme for PEM where video recordings are examined with the sound muted; they emphasize the importance of considering dyadic interpersonal sensory and kinaesthetic experiences during the emotion socialization process. Thus, although mentalization is typically studied using verbal data (as described further below), future directions for intervention research are likely to include more full body non-verbal and kinaesthetic features as well.

The verbal features of mentalization have been assessed via attachment narratives using a variety of methods. One method is the use of secure base scripts in semi-projective tasks involving the creation of attachment-relevant stories (Bretherton & Munholland, 2008; Huth-Bocks et al., 2014; Waters & Rodrigues-Doolabh, 2001). By examining a variety of attachment-relevant scripts within different relationships (e.g., child–mother, child–father, adult partners, etc.), it may thus be possible to understand a person's overall sense of emotional security. The ***secure base script*** is a research paradigm in which participants are asked to tell a story using the words in a series of word prompts that suggest a story when read from left to right (Waters & Rodrigues-Doolabh, 2001; Waters & Waters, 2006). Table 11.3 displays one such series of word prompts (Baby's Morning), which is meant to stimulate an attachment-relevant story from adults. The table also displays an example of a response with a secure base structure and one lacking such a structure. The scripts generated by individuals with insecure attachment behaviours have been found to differ from the scripts of those who are emotionally secure; that is, they have fewer and/or more distorted secure base components (Waters & Waters, 2006). Scripts vary in terms of organization, coherence and the quality of the content in this paradigm. Scripts indicative of emotional security are interpersonally and emotionally rich with interactions, secure base content, and descriptions of the mental states of the story characters; a variety of such

**Table 11.3** Secure Base Script and Narrative Examples from *Baby's Morning* (Waters & Waters, 2006)

| | | |
|---|---|---|
| mother | hug | teddy bear |
| baby | smile | lost |
| play | story | found |
| blanket | pretend | nap |

**Narrative with clear secure base script structure**

A mother and baby were playing one morning. Mother would hide under a blanket and then jump out and the baby would smile and hug her and then do the same thing. Then they read a story. And then the baby wanted to play with his teddy bear but it was lost and he got upset. But Mother found it and said "Here it is. He's ok." And the baby was happy and they played some more and then the baby took a nap.

**Narrative lacking secure base script structure**

A mother was watching her baby play with a blanket in his crib. He would smile and hug the blanket. After a while, the mother wanted to read him a story. She knew he was too little to understand but she liked sitting with him and his teddy bear and pretending to read to them. But today the teddy bear was lost. And by the time she found it, the baby was already taking a nap. So they didn't have a story today.

Source: Waters & Waters (2006). The attachment working models concept: Among other things, we build script-like representations of secure base experiences. *Attachment & Human Development, 8(3)*, 185–197. Table II., p. 190. Routledge © 2006 Taylor & Francis. Reprinted by permission of the publisher (Taylor & Francis Ltd, www.tandfonline.com).

secure base scripts have been studied in other countries and have focused on early and middle childhood, adolescence and adulthood (including couples, parents and caregivers of the elderly); also, secure base scripts have been validated by showing links to attachment-relevant behaviours (see Waters et al., 2015). In their research on secure base script knowledge in parents and their school-age children, Waters et al. (2015) found evidence for a positive association between the independently assessed secure base script knowledge of mothers and children, suggesting intergenerational transmission of an internal working model of emotional security; they also found a negative association between children's secure base script knowledge and mothers' reports of their children's internalizing and externalizing symptoms.

While mentalization abilities may develop adaptively in typically developing children with secure attachments, Fonagy et al. (2008) note that this process is likely to be disrupted in children with histories of maltreatment for a variety of possible reasons – such as hyperarousal and child avoidance of open, reflective communication with their maltreating caregivers given that the content of such communication might include overt emotional verbal abuse. Thus, treatment to foster mentalization skills or self-reflectivity is needed for high-risk families in addition to child protection from abuse and the provision of parenting skills training; Landy and Menna (2006) outline the specific self-reflectivity skills for therapists to target with parents based on the age/developmental level of the preschool child (e.g., with infants, the therapist focuses on empathizing with and mirroring parental affect to serve as a model; once the child develops verbal skills, the parent can be supported in helping the child to label and express emotions; once the child has a theory of mind, the therapist can encourage the parent to imagine how the child thinks and feels).

Dante Cicchetti and his colleagues are among those who have emphasized the importance of studying and providing resources for interventions with families with maltreatment histories given the potential for negative cascading effects over time and the prominence of maltreatment (emotional, educational and physical neglect; emotional, physical and sexual abuse; exposure to family violence) in the aetiology of many forms of developmental psychopathology (e.g., Cicchetti & Banny, 2014). Cicchetti and his colleagues have studied interventions with children and families with multiple risks and histories of maltreatment by making use of ***randomized control trial (RCT) interventions*** in which children and their families are randomly assigned to interventions or a comparison group; the interventions are manualized and involve therapists who receive regular supervision and fidelity checks to make sure that they are following the manual (Cicchetti, 2016; Cicchetti, Rogosch & Toth, 2006; Toth et al., 2013). Using a RCT design, Cicchetti et al. (2006) conducted a study of high-risk mothers with histories of maltreatment and their 1-year-old infants who were randomly assigned to one of three groups: intensive child-parent psychotherapy (CPP), psychoeducational parenting intervention (PPI) or a community standard (CS) control group. A fourth group was also assessed which was comprised of a low-income but non-maltreating comparison (NC) group of mothers with their infants. Preintervention, the mothers with a history of maltreatment were more likely to have 13-month-old infants with disorganized attachment than the comparison group; they were also more likely to have abuse/neglect childhood histories, insecure relationships with their own mothers, maladaptive parenting attitudes and parenting stress, and less likely to have family support and show maternal sensitivity. After intervention, when the infants were about 26 months old, significant increases in secure attachment were found for both the CPP and the PPI groups in contrast to the CS and NC groups (Cicchetti et al., 2006). In a follow-up to the Cicchetti et al. (2006) study occurring when the children were about 38 months old, only the CPP group were able to maintain the gains made in attachment security; while the PPI programme involved a focus on the mother's parenting understanding and skills, the CPP is a ***relational intervention*** approach that places emphasis on empathically helping mothers to gain insight into reasons for their reactions to their infant, on modifying how mothers and infants interact, and on improving the quality of their emotional relationship (Stronach et al., 2013).

Toth et al. (2013) note that there are a wide variety of relational parenting interventions that have a growing body of support for their effectiveness, although much more research is needed for the programmes to be considered well-established. The premise behind attachment-based relational interventions is that it is the emotional quality of family relationships and interactions across the lifespan which ultimately impacts the developmental trajectory of both children and adults from maltreating family environments. Thus, relational interventions have not only been used with parents and children, but also in programmes that address adolescents and adults with histories of abuse, trauma and depression (Toth et al., 2013).

## Summary of Chapter Key Points

This chapter introduces emotion dysregulation and the key concepts in a developmental psychopathology approach. Historically, the classification of mental disorders has gone through many revisions; scholars are currently incorporating research findings into their refinement of the classification of disorders and are increasingly taking a developmental psychopathology perspective. In this chapter, risk and protective factors were discussed along with various developmental pathways leading to internalizing and externalizing disorders. Researchers examining emotion dysregulation and psychopathology often take into consideration mediator and moderator variables in their models in the effort to better understand the underlying developmental processes. The concept of developmental cascades is especially important in understanding how one thing leads to another over time and sometimes even across generations. Numerous interventions exist for treating disorders and their effects on families; thus, the scope of what was covered in this chapter was limited to some recent interventions that involve addressing psychopathology in the family by improving emotional security, emotion understanding and emotion regulation of family members. Future research will need to use randomized control trial interventions to help in establishing effective interventions for families with histories of maltreatment.

## Further Reading

Landy, S. & Menna, R. (2006). *Early intervention with multi-risk families: An integrative approach.* Baltimore: Paul H Brookes Publishing.

Landy and Menna provide readers with an excellent introduction to the many risk and protective factors that are characteristic of multi-risk families. Both individual and family factors are utilized in providing the reader with a guideline for ascertaining the level of family risk as being low, moderate or high. Comprehensive, detailed summaries of assessment instruments for use with parents and children include measures of parental self-reflectivity and empathy for the child, maternal competence and self-confidence, unresolved loss and trauma, parent–infant–child interactions, emotion regulation, parent cognitions, and parent planning and problem solving. The authors review early intervention programmes and their effectiveness, and introduce an integrative theoretical framework for conducting early intervention with multi-risk families. They highlight specific therapeutic techniques that can be individually tailored to meet the needs of specific families. Noteworthy is the focus on ways to engage and support parents in an effective and sensitive manner.

# 12

# Emotional Resilience in Families: From Research to Prevention and Everyday Life

*Mimi and Doug have two sons, Reilly (age 7) and Keegan (age 5), and an infant daughter, Tierney, diagnosed at birth with a genetic disorder. Because survival rarely extends beyond 1 year for those with this disorder, Mimi wanted to make sure that her daughter's life was as meaningful as possible. She explained to her sons that their little sister would probably die before her first birthday. It was hard for the brothers to imagine that their sister might not ever have a birthday party. So, the boys wanted to celebrate Tierney's birthday early, and the family arranged to have elaborate, well-planned, monthly birthday parties for her. Reilly and Keegan helped to plan the decorations, candy, and scheduled birthday events with the family members and friends they invited to be in attendance. Though they hoped she would make it to one year, they all thought it was unlikely. To mark that occasion when it did occur, the family and others in attendance wrote letters of appreciation and sent them up to heaven in helium balloons. Mimi and her sister started to make the funeral plans a short time after the diagnosis. Their plans included concert-quality music and a home-made quilted casket covering. The quilt squares were prepared by family members and depicted the major events of Tierney's short but emotionally meaningful life. Her brothers even imagined her to have superpowers as an angel in heaven. Mimi accomplished what she set out to do: help her family and friends see Tierney's life as beautiful rather than tragic. Years after her daughter's death, Mimi continued to cherish and display the quilt, and planned to continue to work on it in the future* (Hochberg, 2010; Hooghe & Neimeyer, 2013).

Source: Case summary from *Other Rituals: Parents Stories of Meaning Making*, a film by Todd Hochberg. 

## Resilience and Bouncing Back from Adversity

Death and grieving over the loss of loved ones is part of the stark reality of everyday life; yet as noted by those who study family resilience, such losses, inevitable as they are, also present families with opportunities for demonstrating their strengths and stability, and even possibly emotional growth and positive change. In his interviews, photos and filming, Hochberg (2010) captures the creative ways that families use rituals to help them to make meaning out of the short lives of their ill and dying children. In the heart-wrenching example in the opening vignette, the emotional needs of family members were addressed by how they related to each other during their interactions around making meaning out of Tierney's brief life, and by actively planning memorable events that they could share at the time as well as in the future (Hochberg, 2010; Hooghe & Neimeyer, 2013). These emotionally imbued moments were also represented in the jointly created quilt. Both the knowledge of an impending death of a loved one and the unexpected death of a loved one present families with deeply significant life challenges that may test their ability to cope. Hooghe and Neimeyer (2013) highlight that cultures vary in what they consider to be an adaptive reaction to the loss of family members; given the cultural context in which the family lives, both at the individual and family level, family members need to be able to flexibly integrate the meaning of the loss into their own ongoing family life story. Family members can emotionally support each other during this process and can co-regulate their emotions as they interact during such grieving processes by soothing each other's pain and by engaging in joint problem-solving activities.

In trying to understand emotional resilience in families, it is important to adopt a strengths-based approach that focuses on what the family did well together in the past and what they do well together now to foster an adaptive developmental pathway for the family's future (Hawley & DeHaan, 1996). Like individuals who encounter stumbling blocks over time along their developmental pathways, families can be viewed as systems that change and adapt along developmental pathways that are relatively more maladaptive and dysfunctional within specific contexts, or relatively more adaptive and resilient with episodes of bouncing back from adversities when they stumble along the way (e.g., Hawley, 2000).

In this chapter, the primary focus is on resilience in family systems as well as resilience in individuals within families, such as parents and their children, in the context of attempts to foster their emotional development. Basic emotions (e.g., sadness, anger, fear and happiness), prosocial emotions (e.g., empathy), antisocial emotions (e.g., vengefulness leading to violence), and self-conscious emotions (e.g., pride, shame, embarrassment) are all implicated in individual and family resilience. The concept of resilience was introduced in Chapter 11. Masten (2014) defines resilience as the "capacity (potential or manifested) of a dynamic system to adapt successfully to disturbances that threaten system function, viability, or development" or as "positive adaptation or development in the context of significant adversity exposure" (p. 308). According to Masten (2014), to foster resilience it is crucially important to restore, harness and mobilize the power in the basic human adaptive systems (e.g., loving and warm parents/caregivers/family, individual executive functions such as self-regulation or effortful control, mastering areas of competence and self-efficacy, and building and strengthening community supports). By living in ways that foster resilience, individuals, families, communities and societies can be better prepared to face the inevitable adversities that can emerge and challenge emotional well-being over the course of the lifespan (e.g., Masten & Narayan, 2012; Masten & Obradović, 2006).

It is important to consider that resilience has been studied in many ways and at various levels of analysis such as within individuals, families, communities (e.g., neighbourhoods, schools), and the broader culture or society at a given point in time (Masten, 2014; Walsh, 1996). In the study of resilience at the family level, enhancing family strengths rather than just reducing deficits or weaknesses are targeted domains in the prevention of later problems (e.g., Hawley & DeHaan, 1996).

Masten (2014) has described four waves of research involving the study of resilience, which are summarized next. We begin with research on resilience in the following sections and proceed to a discussion of clinical practice and preventive interventions. Finally, the chapter ends with a discussion of the relevance of resilience for the everyday emotional life of families.

## Resilience Research in Four Waves

Research on resilience initially came from the study of risk factors that led to psychopathology. The goal of early risk and psychopathology researchers, such as Norman Garmezy, Irving Gottesman, Lois Murphy, Michael Rutter, Arnold Sameroff, Alan Sroufe, Emmy Werner, and that of their students was to understand and identify the causes of mental illness and any potential threats posed to adaptive individual development (Masten, 2007). However, once studies showed that both quality and quantity of risk factors were linked to psychopathology, it became apparent that not all outcomes were adverse, and that some individuals thrived instead of being harmed; the question was, "Why?" (Masten, 2014). This led to resilience research which has occurred in four waves according to Masten (2007, 2014): Wave 1 involved defining and measuring resilience, Wave 2 addressed understanding the processes through which resilience works, Wave 3 focused on determining whether resilience can be promoted through interventions, and Wave 4, which is currently ongoing, places emphasis on utilizing technological advances in genetics and neuroscience to address the multiple levels of analysis involved in resilience, thus taking a dynamic systems approach to interpreting intervention outcomes.

In terms of Wave 1, deficit models of psychopathology were replaced with a focus on assets, strengths and protective factors; the measurement of an accumulation of risks became important along with ways to measure adaptive outcomes (both internal well-being and external achievements) (Masten, 2014). Wave 1 research resulted in what was called the "short list" of factors associated with resilience, which has since expanded (see Masten & Coatsworth, 1998; Masten et al., 1999; and Masten, 2014). The short list includes: (1) effective parenting, healthy attachments and social relationships, (2) a healthy brain and adaptive self-regulation (as assessed cognitively, emotionally and behaviourally), (3) healthy immune and stress systems, (4) the motivation to succeed and demonstrate self-efficacy, (5) faith, a hopeful outlook and spiritual beliefs in the meaningfulness of the future, and (6) effective school, neighbourhood, and broader community functioning (Masten, 2007, 2014). In Wave 2, this short list was examined further by those with an interest in developmental psychopathology. Several important developmental processes were identified as important *moderators* of resilience and adaptive outcomes; these included emotional security processes and the attachment system, stress reactivity and hormonal systems, and self-regulatory processes; in addition, these protective moderators of development were also found to act as *mediators* in early development because they too can be affected directly by adversity (e.g., under adverse conditions, insecure attachments can develop, which then can lead to maladaptive outcomes) (Masten, 2007). As noted above, Wave 3 went on to address the development of preventive interventions, while in Wave 4 researchers are currently attempting to understand and promote resilience through multi-level analyses across dynamic systems with interdisciplinary research. Some of the findings from Waves 3 and 4 are reviewed next in the following section on resilience and preventive interventions.

## Preventive Intervention Research and Promoting Resilience in Clinical Practice

Both resilience science and preventive intervention research reflect the goals of developmental psychopathology, which are to study both adaptive and maladaptive developmental pathways to address how to reduce the impact of risks and promote or facilitate protections; however, they are also different in that prevention science addresses attempts to avoid psychopathology, while resilience research attends to the adaptive benefits of positive outcomes (not just the absence of psychopathology) (e.g., Luthar, Cicchetti & Becker, 2000).

Family therapists and researchers who focus on resilience have examined the various developmental pathways that occur when families experience similar traumatic backgrounds via their interactions within their close social kinship network (e.g., violence, alcoholism, mental or physical illness), or within the broader culture within which they live, such as occurs during wars or in natural disasters (e.g., Hawley, 2000; Masten & Narayan, 2012). During wars, the resilience of affected civilians as well as military families has been studied (e.g., Saltzman et al., 2013). In spite of experiencing adversities and cumulative risks, it is possible for ***cumulative protections*** to pile up and to counteract the risks, and this is where preventive interventions have the potential to make a difference by adding to the protections (e.g., Yoshikawa, 1994).

In his review of studies of early interventions to prevent delinquency, Yoshikawa (1994) identified two key domains where protective effects can be nurtured early in development for the long-term prevention of later delinquent behaviours. These are: (1) providing family support that addresses the emotional and tangible needs of the caregivers, as well as their parenting skills, and (2) the education of the child to foster cognitive and academic skills. As discussed in Chapter 11, these and other key targeted domains have been incorporated into the many early intervention programmes that have been implemented over the last several decades. The goal of some of these prevention and early intervention programmes is to address the needs of relatively less at-risk families and to help them to re-orient or stabilize along an adaptive developmental pathway, thus promoting their resilience; however, for other high-risk families, the primary goal may be to provide intensive interventions to change or switch the ongoing developmental course and to implement appropriate mental health supports for longer-term stability and management of problems (Landy & Menna, 2006).

Contemporary intervention researchers are continuing to conduct and publish studies on the outcomes of preventive intervention programmes and to refine some conclusions. For example, Pasalich, Witkiewitz, McMahon, Pinderhughes and The Conduct Problems Prevention Research Group (2016) in the US reported the results of the Fast Track 10-year programme that assessed interventions with high-risk school-age children from Grades 1 through 10 (approximately 6 to 15 years) and their parents. In brief, they found that the interventions (which consisted of home visits and skills training for both children and their parents) had indirect effects on the children's targeted conduct disorder symptoms and callous-unemotional traits. Specifically, the Fast Track programme resulted in lower levels of harsh parental discipline which in turn was linked to lower child conduct disorder symptoms; the programme also resulted in higher levels of parental warmth, which in turn was associated with lower levels of child callous-unemotional traits (Pasalich et al., 2016). Thus, intervening with parents to address their disciplinary approaches and to support them in relating to their children in an emotionally warm manner contributed to lower levels of externalizing child symptoms. The strengthening of parenting skills and emotional warmth between parents and their children may thus serve as protective factors and promote childhood resilience over time. For example, some children who are victimized by bullying at school are also aggressive, victimize others, and have problematic psychosocial outcomes; however, family connectedness has been found to be protective against aggressive behaviours among children and youth who were victimized by bullying (e.g., Duggins et al., 2016). While they note the important role of schools and teachers in providing a safe and emotionally supportive environment, Duggins et al. (2016) highlight the significant value of providing interventions for the families of victimized youth. As noted earlier by researchers (e.g., Landy & Menna, 2006; Yoshikawa, 1994), the provision of both emotional and tangible, instrumental family support in preventive interventions, especially to key caregivers such as mothers (e.g., Luthar, 2015; Luthar & Suchman, 2000) and fathers (e.g., Carr, 1998; Kaslow, 2013), is critically important to facilitate their roles as providers of protection and promoters of resilience for their children.

Another protective domain to foster resilience that was identified early on involves childhood education and the fostering of cognitive skills (e.g., Yoshikawa, 1994). Currently, these cognitive skills are perhaps best represented in what have been called ***executive functions*** (EF) (also see Chapter 3). As defined by Obradović (2016):

> Executive functions (EF) are a set of higher order cognitive skills (i.e., inhibitory control, working memory, and cognitive flexibility) that help children

> regulate their own attention, behavior, and emotions. As the building blocks of various salient competencies, EF's affect children's social, emotional, and cognitive development. (p. 66)

The implication here is that preventing psychopathology and promoting resilience may involve attempting to intervene where necessary to improve age-appropriate inhibitory control, working memory and cognitive flexibility. While many studies, especially with adolescents, have shown links between executive dysfunction (e.g., excessive reward seeking) and externalizing problems and risk-taking, fewer studies have as yet addressed the link between EFs and regulatory processes related to internalizing symptoms, such as depression (Luciana, 2016). Nonetheless, recent neuropsychological evidence does indeed suggest that there are problems in regulatory control and with EFs in youths who are depressed (Klimes-Dougan & Garber, 2016).

One important way that EFs can promote adaptive functioning and resilience is through their association with coping skills (e.g., Evans et al., 2016). Evans et al. (2016) studied depression in 9- to 15-year-old children and found that EFs, such as working memory and cognitive flexibility, were indirectly linked to depression through the coping strategies used in reaction to stresses. That is, children with better working memories and greater cognitive flexibility were more likely to engage in coping strategies that modified their reactions to stressors and that protected them from depressive symptoms.

In the past, diathesis-stress models of depression were the dominant models used to interpret the interaction of nature (the diathesis as personal biological vulnerability) with nurture (stressful life experiences and adverse environments); currently, a new paradigm has arisen in the form of ***differential susceptibility*** models that challenge diathesis-stress models (e.g., Boyce & Ellis, 2005; Ellis et al., 2011). In contrast to diathesis-stress models which emphasize how the diathesis makes a person vulnerable and susceptible to environmental risks, differential susceptibility models propose that the same biological susceptibility to environmental influences may either increase the impact of risks in adverse environments or enhance development in enriched environments (Ellis et al., 2011).

Differential susceptibility models allow researchers to conduct sophisticated analyses that involve the testing of mediator and moderator variables within a variety of contexts (Obradović, 2016; Roisman et al., 2012). For example, some children may be more susceptible to being physiologically aroused by environmental stimulation whether it is positive and nurturing, or whether it is negative and involves maltreatment; these children would be more likely than others to have a low threshold for reacting to the environment in either case (Obradović, 2016). Resilience would be apparent when a child has such a susceptibility to being easily physiologically aroused in reaction to stressful environments, but also has an enhanced ability to cope, recover and regulate his or her reactions (Obradović, 2016). Differential susceptibility research would involve testing and comparing individuals with the same underlying biological susceptibility longitudinally to see how their susceptibility interacts with their various environments, and how their ability to cope and self-regulate mediates or moderates the links between their susceptibility and their outcomes.

Some researchers have studied developmental psychopathology and resilience in children and families at the extreme ends of the spectrum of environmental problems, such as maltreatment (e.g., Cicchetti, 2016) and socio-economic advantages, such as affluence (e.g., Luthar & Becker, 2002). Although affluence is often thought to render privilege to developing youth, a number of risks may also predominate, such as the easy availability of drugs and alcohol, and the pressure to succeed and achieve (Ansary, McMahon & Luthar, 2016). By conducting research with youth and their families at the extreme ends of the environmental spectrum, it becomes possible to compare the effects of non-normative life experiences to normative ones and to identify those who might benefit from preventive interventions; furthermore, it becomes possible with such identified groups to conduct randomized control trials (RCTs) to see which preventive intervention strategies are most effective (Cicchetti, 2016).

Consistent with the goals and rationale of Wave 4 researchers, Dante Cicchetti states that:

> Determining the multiple levels at which change is engendered through RCT's will provide insight into the mechanisms of change, the extent to which neural plasticity may be promoted, and the interrelations between biological and psychological processes in the development of maladaptation, psychopathology, and resilience in maltreated children. (Cicchetti, 2016, p. 205)

The primary goal of preventive interventions is to alter the environment to promote adaptation; however, there is increasing evidence from the field of ***behaviour epigenetics*** that experiences with social and physical environments also have an effect on the ***epigenome*** (Cicchetti, 2016; Keating, 2016, 2017; Lester, Conradt & Marsit, 2016). In other words, the expression of our genetic make-up may also be directly affected by our ongoing experiences with the environment. The emergent field of behaviour epigenetics involves examining such explanations of human behaviours on the basis of the environmental impact (e.g., maltreatment, affluence and enrichment) and how that environment interacts with genetic molecular processes that allow genes to be expressed; although DNA itself is *not* transformed, how the DNA gets activated and whether or not the genetic information it contains gets *expressed* is affected by our interactions with the social and physical environments (Lester et al., 2016). The prefix "epi" in epigenetic and epigenome means "on", "upon", or "over" and refers to this new functional layer of genetic expression that forms based on the person's interaction with the environment; this functional layer contains genetic markers that result from the interaction with the environment and that can be repeatedly assessed by taking samples of cells from saliva, tissue or blood (Lester et al., 2016).

The influence of the Human Genome Project, which provided a comprehensive blueprint for human genetics, is widespread and growing (National Human Genome Research Institute, 2016a, 2016b). The importance of the field of epigenetics for the future study of psychopathology and resilience should thus not be underestimated as it holds great promise for enhancing understanding of psychopathology and resilient functioning through research on the genetic moderation of treatment efficacy (Belsky & van IJzendoorn, 2015; Cicchetti, 2016; also see the introduction to the special section on epigenetics in *Child Development* (Volume 87, Number 1) by Lester et al., 2016). That is, there are now several recently identified genetic patterns (e.g., involving the hormone cortisol, and the neurotransmitters dopamine and serotonin) that have been studied in conjunction with various environmental predictors (e.g., parenting, adversity) and developmental outcomes (e.g., prosocial or antisocial behaviours); consistent with a differential susceptibility perspective, the findings of these studies suggest that the same underlying genetic pattern can operate "for the better" leading to positive outcomes when the environment is positive, or can operate "for the worse" leading to negative outcomes when the environment is negative (Belsky & van IJzendoorn, 2015, p. 1). Belsky and van IJzendoorn (2015) suggest that variation in the efficacy of interventions may be moderated by the genetic make-up of the individual and that experimental intervention research can assist in improving our understanding of what will work with whom.

Importantly, Cicchetti (2016) notes that genetic (G) x environment (E) interactions that have permeated developmental research for decades should now be replaced with the inclusion of a developmental (D) perspective into the formula so that G x E becomes G x E x D; findings from the field of behaviour epigenetics will make it possible to see how earlier gene-environment interactions at one developmental period (e.g., infancy, early childhood) affect gene-environment interactions at later developmental periods (e.g., adolescence, adulthood).

As researchers continue to sort out the implications of genetics for adaptive and maladaptive development, other psychosocial preventive interventions to promote resilience with adolescents and their families have focused on the importance of improving individual well-being, family conflict resolution and effective family communication. Weersing et al. (2016) examined predictors and moderators of the effectiveness of a cognitive-behavioural prevention programme (CBP) in a sample of adolescents from families with a high risk of depression; the researchers found that CBP was effective for adolescents, but only if the parents themselves were not actively depressed at the time that the intervention began. Thus, parental depression status was a powerful moderator of the intervention effectiveness; characteristics of the adolescents (e.g., hopelessness, anxiety) were also important in the prediction of treatment outcomes. Weersing et al. (2016) suggest that preventive intervention programmes may have to be scheduled to optimize their effects at times when family members are well enough to benefit; family members should be clinically stable and the targets of treatment should be those that are potentially modifiable (e.g., reducing anxiety, improving hopefulness). They also review other research that shows that active parental depression makes it difficult to treat adolescent depression, and that treating parental depression has a positive effect on youth outcomes, although the reasons for these effects are not entirely clear (Weersing et al., 2016). However, it appears that the co-regulation of emotion, similar to what has been found between infants and their depressed caregivers, may be a possible mechanism at work here as well, albeit in an older sample of parents and children.

While emotional co-regulation among older family members has not been a dominant area of study in parent–adolescent communication literature, there are some studies with families that have examined similar relevant processes such as negative and positive emotion reciprocity between parents and their children (see also Chapters 10 and 11). In a study by Lindsey et al. (2002), marital conflict spilled over and was related to the quality of emotions expressed between mothers and their preadolescent sons; mothers who reciprocated their sons' negative emotions had sons who displayed more aggression and had less peer acceptance, and boys who reciprocated their mothers' negative emotions displayed more aggression. However, boys who reciprocated their mothers' positive emotions were better liked and accepted by their peers. The quality of the marital relationship and the quality of parent–child interaction are thus critically important in understanding what needs to be targeted in preventive interventions to promote resilience. In another separate longitudinal study of the effects of maladaptive marital conflict on children from 2 to 10 years of age, Brock and Kochanska (2016) found that severe, destructive parental arguments undermined attachment security in daughters and increased their risk for developing internalizing problems over the period of their childhood; emotional tension from unresolved interparental conflict was also linked to internalizing problems in both sons and daughters. Preventive interventions that focus on the marital relationship and conflict resolution between parents have been found to have long-term benefits for children (e.g., Cowan, Cowan & Barry, 2011). As addressed next, the Iowa Youth and Family Project (IYFP) provides a good example of how the construct of resilience has been applied to the study of marital and parent–child relationships (Conger & Conger, 2002).

In their review of the first decade of their longitudinal research on resilience in rural Iowa American families, Rand Conger and Katherine Conger (2002) describe how marital couples (G1: Generation 1) and their 7th-grade adolescent children (approximately 12 years old; G2: Generation 2) adapted over time to economic adversity after a decline in agriculture affected many regional businesses and farmers. They also studied resilience in the children as they transitioned from childhood to adolescence and then again as they transitioned from adolescence into emerging adulthood. Their results showed that children's responses to economic hardship were indirectly affected by the parents' responses to the economic adversity. In spite of economic pressures, resilience was evident in parents when they supported each other in their videotaped interactions, when they demonstrated effective problem-solving skills together, and had a sense of mastery and control over themselves. The youth showed resilience to family economic pressures when there was support from their parents, siblings and other adults outside of the family. During developmental transitional periods, the nurturance, support and involvement of parents played a significant role in youth resilience (Conger & Conger, 2002). Some couples in this Iowa sample, however, showed little or no distress despite the economic adversity.

In a follow-up longitudinal study of *couple resilience* within the Iowa sample, the G1 parents were assessed again later when their now G2 adult children were involved in romantic relationships; for both generations of couples, economic pressures predicted increases in hostility during couple interactions (e.g., negative affect, non-verbal behaviours, and facial expressions) while effective problem-solving skills (open discussion of problems with potential solutions) served as a protective factor (Masarik et al., 2016). Thus, across both G1 and G2 generations, couples who were more effective at problem solving did not experience an increase in hostility when under economic pressure, while those who were less effective did. Additional studies on this longitudinal data set addressed the role of social support as a protective buffer for emotional disorders in those G2 children traumatized by maltreatment (Feldman, Conger & Burzette, 2004) and the role of positive parenting in promoting resilience from one generation to the next (Schofield, Conger & Neppl, 2014).

The study by Schofield et al. (2014) demonstrated the importance of *intergenerational resilience* as assessed by positive parenting (parental warmth, prosocial responsive behaviours such as sympathy and respect, and non-defensive, open, positive assertiveness), and by two personal resources: *parental efficacy*, whereby parents believe that their investments in their children will lead to positive outcomes, and *active coping strategy use*, whereby parents report actively trying to solve problems – for instance, by addressing the cause or looking to others for help. These three potential sources of intergenerational resilience (positive parenting, the personal resource of parental efficacy, and the personal resource of active coping) were examined with respect to G1 parents interacting with their G2 children initially, and later on by G2 parents interacting with their G3 (Generation 3) children. There were several important key findings. First, as might be expected, positive parenting in G1 predicted positive parenting in G2, although the positive correlation was moderate. Second, G1 positive parenting interacted with G2 personal resources to predict parenting behaviour at G2. That is, when G1 positive parenting was relatively low and either of the two personal resources was high in G2, then positive parenting was protected in G2, and G2 parents still showed adaptive parenting. Third, when G1 positive parenting was relatively high and both personal resources were low in G2, G2 still showed positive parenting. Thus, these results show that there is more than one pathway to showing positive parenting behaviours.

Imagine yourself as a parent. You, as a parent, can have a history of being the recipient of positive parenting behaviours and thus model these behaviours with your own children; this modelling of positive parenting may be effective even if you are low in some personal resources (such as not having great confidence in your own effectiveness as a parent, and not having effective active coping strategies at your disposal). Because positive parenting is what you know and understand best from your own childhood, that is what you would use with your own children. Interestingly though, and this is most important for preventive interventions, even when adults in the Schofield et al. (2014) study had a history of being parented by parents who were low in positive parenting, if they were high in either or both of the personal resources (parental efficacy, active coping) they were still able to demonstrate positive parenting with their own G3 children. In other words, even if your parents were not good role models, you can use your own personal resources to be a good parent. This latter finding is important for two reasons. First, a person's history of being parented is not modifiable – but personal efficacy beliefs and active coping strategies are modifiable. Thus, individuals with a history of being parented by parents who were low in positive parenting would likely benefit the most from training and interventions to promote their parental efficacy and active coping strategy use. Second, once parents begin to use positive parenting with their children, this may have the effect of a positive developmental cascade for future generations given that the effects of positive parenting on the next generation in the Schofield et al. (2014) study were robust and protected parents even when the parent was relatively lower in personal resources.

Promoting resilience in families often involves finding ways to promote positive parenting, cooperative family interactions, and family happiness and well-being, as will be addressed in the following final section of this chapter and book. However, this is not to overlook the possible benefits of learning how to handle stress well as highlighted in the research of Shapero et al. (2015), in which early stress experiences acted as a buffer to later emotional problems and symptoms. Consistent with other literature that they review (e.g., Boyce & Ellis, 2005), Shapero et al. (2015) found evidence for a *steeling effect* in which childhood experiences of moderately severe stressful situations seemed to later buffer and protect adolescents from depressive symptoms when they encountered subsequent everyday proximal stressors. Thus, one source of resilience for many people is the fact that they have already overcome so many stresses, that they have become hardened or resistant to some extent to negative outside influences. Nonetheless, even though experiencing the negative emotions that go along with stressful life experiences can potentially give individuals some skills that are needed to cope in the future, pursuing a future of happiness is still something that individuals and families, at least in Western cultures, strive for (Gilbert, 2006), as discussed next.

## Promoting Resilience and Happiness in Families: Everyday Life Solutions

Positive emotions, such as interest and happiness, have been found to facilitate motivation as well as cognitive information processing, creative and flexible thinking, and decision-making processes (Isen, 1993). As noted in earlier sections of this chapter and throughout the past chapters of this book, researchers have more often focused on the regulation of negative emotions and coping with stresses as a means of facilitating adaptive development than they have on the regulation of positive emotions. As noted in Chapter 10 on emotion regulation, positive emotions may need to be up-regulated or down-regulated depending on personal preferences and the situation (e.g., Gross, 2008). Specifically promoting the occurrence of positive emotional experiences in families can potentially enhance their resilience and help them to develop emotional competence. Table 12.1 displays

**Table 12.1** Summary Chart of Carolyn Saarni's (1999) Eight Emotional Competence Skills

| Eight Emotional Competence Skills (Saarni, 1999) | Description of Goals for Family Members |
|---|---|
| 1: Emotion self-awareness and self-understanding | Having insight into understanding the causes and consequences of your own emotions. |
| 2: Awareness and understanding of others' emotions | Reflective insight into understanding the causes and consequences of emotions in other family members. |
| 3: Ability to use a vocabulary of emotion and expression | Using language to effectively facilitate emotion communication among family members. |
| 4: Capacity for empathic involvement | Having the will and desire to care deeply about others and to act in a moral, prosocial way according to your social values. |
| 5: Ability to differentiate inner subjective emotional experience from outer externally detectable emotional expressions | Understanding that there are complexities involved in coordinating one's inner life with outer expressions. |
| 6: Capacity for adaptive coping with aversive emotions and distressing circumstances | Demonstrating age-appropriate emotion regulation by inhibiting impulses and using adaptive coping strategies. |
| 7: Awareness of emotional communication within relationships | Being emotionally attuned to self and others during interactions by attending to emotional cues. Promoting positive emotion reciprocity during communication by showing forgiveness when wronged or expressing gratitude where appropriate, for example. |
| 8: Capacity for emotional self-efficacy | Believing that you have the ability and resources to act in accordance with your values. A cultural environment that is supportive, civil and respectful facilitates emotional self-efficacy. Emotional self-efficacy also involves resilience to face adversities even in non-supportive situations. |

eight emotional competence skills identified by Carolyn Saarni (1999) as potential targets for preventive interventions and for family emotion socialization; these have been addressed throughout the current book. Theories of emotional competence and the implementation of preventive interventions are increasingly focusing on maintaining and enhancing positive emotions rather than on just addressing negative emotion management (Tugade & Fredrickson, 2007).

Fredrickson's (1998, 2001) broaden and build theory of positive emotions, introduced in Chapter 10, proposes that experiencing positive emotions has immediate broadening effects on a person's attention and thought-action repertoire; furthermore, experiencing emotional states such as joy, contentment, interest and love over time results in the build-up of social, physical and intellectual resources that are related to happiness and well-being. For example, positive affect motivates and promotes prosocial acts of generosity, kindness, friendliness and helping behaviours, and may be reciprocated by the recipient with expressions of forgiveness for past slights and wrongs or with gratitude for that which the person received, thus promoting the relationship and encouraging further spiralling opportunities for positive reciprocity and openness in communication (e.g., Fredrickson & Cohn, 2008; Isen, 1993). Fredrickson and Cohn (2008) suggest that positive emotions lead to more open and flexible responses to other people; joy leads to creativity and a playful attitude, interest to an urge to explore and experience novelty, contentment to relaxing, savouring the moment and counting blessings, and love to a desire to share all of the above in warm, safe and close relationships. Thus, family members can become transformed and can become more creative, knowledgeable, healthy, socially integrated and resilient over time with repeated positive emotional experiences (Fredrickson & Cohn, 2008). Interestingly, some people who display resilience are proficient at *undoing* the harmful effects of negative emotions (e.g., physiological effects of stress on the cardiovascular system) by deliberately activating positive emotions such as happiness (Fredrickson & Cohn, 2008).

Ed Diener (2000, 2013) discusses happiness in terms of *subjective well-being (SWB)*, which can be defined as having many pleasant emotional experiences in contrast to unpleasant ones, experiencing many pleasures and few pains, engaging in subjectively enjoyable and interesting activities, and generally feeling satisfied with life. Some empirical evidence from data collected across the world suggests that SWB, which results in better health and longevity, is higher in married adults, those with relatively higher incomes up to a point (with many mediating and moderating factors), and those with religious or spiritual means of coping such as meditation; showing forgiveness, gratitude and concern for others has also been linked to SWB (e.g., Diener, 2013; Diener & Scollon, 2014).

The pursuit of happiness through enhancing pleasurable positive affect and reducing unpleasant negative affect has been called *hedonia*; in contrast, stemming from the writings of Aristotle, *eudaimonia* refers to having psychological well-being by living a full, meaningful and deeply satisfying life while fulfilling one's potential (Deci & Ryan, 2008; Robinson, 2004; Ryan, Huta & Deci, 2008; Waterman, 1993). As described further in History Feature Box 12, emotional deficits were initially the focus of targeted study and interventions, and have since transitioned over time to greater attention being given to the influence of strengths, positive adaptation and the effects of resilience as family members strive for well-being and eudaimonia.

**History Feature Box 12**

**Back Then and Now: From Emotional Deficits to Well-Being and Resilience**

Throughout recorded history, children and adults in the general population with any form of physical, mental, behavioural or emotional deficits were often viewed with disdain and subjected to abuse, neglect, abandonment or public ridicule (e.g., Donahue, Hersen & Ammerman, 1995; deMause, 1974). During the Middle Ages and even into contemporary times in some cultures, evil spirits or demons have been cited as influential causes in the development and maintenance of psychopathology; in Western history, it was not until after the periods of the Renaissance and Enlightenment from about 1300 to 1600 AD that some relatively reasonable views of treating children humanely and with affection began to emerge (Donahue et al., 1995). Although many educational, medical and legal reforms took place since then, it was not until the 20th century that classification of emotional problems and psychopathology was undertaken in a comprehensive manner by medical professionals (see History Feature Box 11). To help individuals to overcome or at least manage their maladaptive functioning and their negative emotions, it is important to identify the *causes* of symptoms of developmental psychopathology and emotional problems to target the goals to be addressed during treatments.

Psychopathology and *adaptational failures* are thought to occur when individuals deviate from expectations and are not meeting their age-appropriate developmental milestones (Mash & Wolfe, 2013; Rutter & Sroufe, 2000). While the emphasis on vulnerability to psychopathology and the associated risks involved has been an important focus of studies in recent decades (e.g., Ingram & Price, 2001), other researchers are now focusing on *positive psychology* in which the emphasis is placed on why it is good to feel good (Fredrickson, 2003), and why we should foster resilience. Mihaly Csikszentmihalyi and Martin Seligman were the catalysts and inspiration for the positive psychology approach (Csikszentmihalyi, 2009). At the subjective level, they emphasized "well-being, contentment, and satisfaction (in the past); hope and optimism (for the future); and flow and happiness (in the present)" (Seligman & Csikszentmihalyi, 2000, p. 5). Seligman and Csikszentmihalyi (2000, p. 5) emphasize positive traits such as "the capacity for love and vocation, courage, interpersonal skill, aesthetic sensibility, perseverance, forgiveness, originality, future mindedness, spirituality, high talent, and wisdom" and group characteristics, such as "civic virtues and the institutions that move individuals towards better citizenship: responsibility, nurturance, altruism, civility, moderation, tolerance, and work ethic". The goal of positive psychology has been to foster flourishing in individuals, in their families, and in the communities in which they live.

The contemporary research of Daniel McAdams at the Foley Center for the Study of Lives (www.sesp.northwestern.edu/foley) is a good example of how to understand individuals and their families through the stories they tell about overcoming emotional losses and suffering through eventual redemption. The development of the ***redemptive self*** is a common American narrative or life story found in historical records extending from the 17th-century Puritans to 19th-century African American slaves to contemporary politicians, entertainers and the general American public; an important part of the rags-to-riches American dream is having a life story in which a person grew up under adverse conditions but somehow managed to find redemption and resiliently overcome the adversity (McAdams, 2008a, 2008b). Although the life stories and narratives of Americans often emphasize striving to overcome suffering through finding redemption, such strivings are not necessarily reflected in Eastern cultures, Greek tragedies, nor in European existentialist views, where there are potential benefits, such as deepened interpersonal intimacy, that sometimes occur as the result of family members sharing pain and suffering (McAdams, 2008a, 2008b). Thus, life stories and resilience are not just about what is good and positive overcoming what is bad and negative. That is, even after redemption what is bad and negative is interwoven into the life stories of individuals and family members.

***Narrative identity*** is an individual's subjective life story created to imbue meaning to his or her life (Bauer, McAdams & Pals, 2008). The development of a narrative identity is a process situated in various contexts that is characterized by both *stability*, where the self-concept endures, and *changes* in the self-concept, where individuals can look to their memories and project into their future to reinvent themselves in a creative new way with the goal of redeeming themselves and doing things better the next time around (McLean, Pasupathi & Pals, 2007). The person may experience eudaimonic well-being associated with resilience when the life story emphasizes personal growth, transformation from deep pain and suffering to having enhanced insightful awareness, and redemption that is shaped by the person's cultural background (Bauer et al., 2008). Similarly, resilience at the family level may occur when family members generate narratives about difficult shared emotional events (e.g., a major loss, death, trauma, disaster) that are coherent and well-integrated life stories that show how emotional well-being was restored over time through readjustments, transformations and growth.

Individuals within families have multiple ***possible selves*** (Markus & Nurius, 1986; see Chapter 8) and family members serve as role models for each other regarding life possibilities. Each of us has multiple *past* possible selves that affect how we view ourselves now in the present, and we each have multiple *future* possible selves that we imagine ourselves to be based on our optimism and hope, or on fears of what we could become; although these possible selves are unique to each of us, others, such as our family members, can profoundly influence and constrain our possible selves in some deeply significant ways (Markus & Nurius, 1986). Family members can support each other in the development of their narrative identities and the various ways in which they see themselves. For example, incorporating an empathic sense of self into one's narrative identity during adolescence may be promoted both by having opportunities to show empathy towards others and by being on the receiving end of empathy during interactions with parents and other family members (e.g., Soucie, Lawford & Pratt, 2012).

Laura King and her colleagues have conducted studies that examine *lost possible selves*, in which the person's life story contains past dreams and goals that were never realized and for which there may be little realistic hope that they ever will be; lost possible selves are who we used to wish to be (King & Mitchell, 2015). Among the groups studied are divorced women (King & Raspin, 2004), gay men and lesbians (King & Smith, 2004), and parents of children with Down's Syndrome (King & Patterson, 2000); Loevinger's ego development (see Chapter 9) figures prominently in the work of King and her colleagues as a means of assessing how deeply and complexly a person has reflected on his or her life experiences. The research of King and her colleagues show that while people are motivated towards happiness in the here and now, happiness and eudaimonic well-being is not all there is; to have more than one chance at redemption and thus, to be able to bounce back in a resilient way, it is also important for individuals to demonstrate age-appropriate maturity, coherence and complexity in their life stories by interpreting and integrating their past lost possible selves into who they are currently and who they want to be in the future (e.g., King & Hicks, 2006; King & Mitchell, 2015).

As noted by Waterman (1993), the processes involved in eudaimonia include searching for the *daimon*, which refers to the "true self" in the Greek language, and attempting to realize one's full potential, sometimes called self-realization. Hedonistic pursuits tend to focus on materialistic goals or *outcomes*, are extrinsically motivated, and involve acquisitions such as wealth, power or pleasurable activities; eudaimonia, in contrast, involves intrinsic motivational goals (personal growth, living according to one's values, prosocial concerns for society) and is linked to the *process* of how to live well (Ryan et al., 2008). The two constructs are interrelated (e.g., the eudaimonic long-term process of living life well may result in attaining a pleasurable hedonic outcome though that was not the intended goal). However, the constructs are not identical because they have different goals and some routes to achieving short-term pleasures through hedonistic goals involve greed, exploiting others and compromising values (Ryan et al., 2008).

Even though family members may desire positive affect and hedonic/eudaimonic forms of well-being, family life is sometimes made quite unpleasant by the everyday reality of overt arguments and unresolved conflicts that may span from one generation to the next with potential links to maladaptive behaviours (e.g., Rothenberg, Hussong & Chassin, 2016). In families, it is possible for conflicts that are riddled with negative affect to escalate and become more overt as children transition into adolescence due to the continuing need for parents to regulate and guide their children at a time during which youth are struggling to gain more autonomy (Hakim-Larson & Hobart, 1987). What, then, will help families to maintain a sense of well-being and eudaimonia? The construct of mindfulness (see Chapter 10) is one that has been linked to both eudaimonia and resilience. Ryan et al. (2008) suggest that acting with a sense of mindful awareness is an important feature of eudaimonic living. According to Ryan et al. (2008), humans share a basic need for competence, relatedness and autonomy, which is facilitated by eudaimonic living; this is accomplished by achieving prosocial goals and demonstrating values for their own sake, thus leading to personal growth, physical and mental health, and the nurturing and strengthening of interpersonal relationships, as well as community ties. Furthermore, with eudaimonic living, individuals operate in a consensual manner with others, yet make deliberate autonomous decisions with mindful awareness of their actions (Ryan et al., 2008).

Mindfulness has been applied with success to parent training for the purpose of enhancing parent–adolescent communication and as a solution to promoting resilience and happiness during family interactions. As shown in Table 12.2, Duncan, Coatsworth and Greenberg (2009) have summarized the features of ***mindful parenting*** by reviewing research studies that have shown the benefits of mindfulness in family interactions. Instead of emotionally reacting in an automatic or impulsive way, individuals can operate in a mindful way by reflecting on the potential choices available in the moment, thus enabling them to make intentional choices with fewer regrets. For parents who take the time to reflect and be mindful, this means that hedonistic, self-centred goals (that which makes the parent feel good short term) is more likely to give way to eudaimonic parenting goals that are more child- and family-centred based on parental values and longer-term goals (Duncan et al., 2009).

Intervention research using mindfulness-based parenting approaches has been shown to be promising in strengthening resilience in families with both children and adolescents (e.g., Coatsworth et al., 2015; Lippold et al., 2015). One way that mindful parenting can promote resilience is by helping parents to calm and soothe themselves so that they are better able to reduce

**Table 12.2** Role of Mindful Parenting Practices in Parenting Interactions (Duncan, Coatsworth & Greenberg, 2009)

| Mindful parenting dimensions | Effective parenting behaviors promoted through this practice | Parenting behaviors decreased through this practice |
|---|---|---|
| Listening with full attention | • Correctly discern child's behavioral cues<br>• Accurately perceive child's verbal communication | • Reduced use and influence of congni-tive constructions and expectations |
| Nonjudgmental acceptance of self and child | • Healthy balance between child-oriented, parent-oriented, and relationship-oriented goals<br>• Sense of parenting self-efficacy<br>• Appreciation for child's traits | • Reduction in self-directed concerns<br>• Fewer unrealistic expecta-tions of child's attributes |
| Emotional awareness of self and child | • Responsiveness to child's needs and emotions<br>• Greater accuracy in responsibility attributions | • Less dismissing of child's emotions<br>• Less discipline that results from parent's strong neg-ative emotion (e.g., anger, disappointment, shame) |
| Self-regulation in the parenting relationship | • Emotion regulation in the parenting context<br>• Parenting in accordance with goals and values | • Less overreactive/ "automatic" discipline<br>• Less dependence on child's emotions |
| Compassion for self and child | • Positive affection in the parent–child relationship<br>• More forgiving view of own parenting efforts | • Less negative affect dis-played in the parent–child relationship<br>• Less self-blame when parenting goals are not achieved |

Source: *Clinical Child and Family Psychology Review*. A model of mindful parenting: Implications for parent–child relationships and prevention research. Volume 12(3). 2009. p. 259. L. Duncan, J. Coatsworth and M. Greenberg, Copyright © The Author(s) (2009). This article is published with open access at Springerlink.com. With permission of Springer.

their negative reactions to their children's expressions and behaviours; when parents are more mindful and less reactive, their children are less likely to view their parents as overcontrolling (Lippold et al., 2015). All in all, the use of mindfulness can help to enhance the balance of positive to negative affect in parent–adolescent communication and relationships; the positive emotional quality of the parent–adolescent relationship is related to more disclosure by adolescents to their parents and more parental solicitation of information to start conversations with their adolescent (Lippold et al., 2015).

## Summary of Chapter Key Points

The experience of adversity and losses is a common human experience that often results in challenges to mental health and overall emotional well-being. Historically, individuals suffering from these and other challenges to their mental and emotional well-being were viewed primarily from the perspective of having an illness or psychopathology in need of treatment or a cure. Currently, researchers and mental health professionals are targeting alternative ways to counteract adversity and losses over the lifespan, such as preventive interventions and ways to promote and facilitate resilience. Exciting contemporary research linking the fields of resilience science, prevention science, epigenetics and developmental psychopathology point to the various developmental pathways that can result from the interaction of genetic expression within various contexts over time. Resilience can be promoted in families by explicitly supporting parents and adult family relationships (e.g., between couples and from one generation to the next) in their management of negative emotions and in their provision of positive emotional experiences within the family context. Although promoting happiness appears to be a favoured Western emotional goal to promote resilience, more research is needed on what it means to be resilient in a variety of cultures. The construct of mindfulness holds promise for strengthening our understanding of resilience in both individuals and parent–child relationships. The emotional life of families may perhaps be understood best by how they may deepen the meaning of their emotional bonds with each other through the losses, suffering and pain that they have shared together as well as the joys, pleasures and happiness they have experienced together.

## Further Reading

Masten, A. S. (2014). *Ordinary magic: Resilience in development.* New York: Guilford Press.

Along with other early pioneers of resilience research, Ann S. Masten has made numerous contributions to the study of ways to promote adaptive functioning in families; her important research contributions are summarized at various points throughout her book. Masten summarizes much of the past literature on resilience in a concise and integrative manner over the course of the four waves of resilience science. Her title reflects the fact that resilience, as remarkable and magical as it may seem to be, is nonetheless common because basic ordinary protections, such as a loving family, physical health, or community supports (religious institutions, adequate schooling) may remain intact. In her book, Masten details changes in resilience science over the four waves, the meaning of the short list, and how resilience is manifest in neurobiology as well as in family functioning and in various cultures. Among her recommendations for increasing resilience is to increase the assets and resources of family members and to promote resilience by planning in advance for the possibility of severe adversity, traumas or disasters.

Saarni, C. (1999). *The development of emotional competence*. New York: The Guilford Press.

Carolyn Saarni's seminal and classic book on the topic of emotional competence is highly relevant to contemporary research and a pleasure to read. In addition to providing a review of the early studies conducted on the eight basic skills of emotional competence, Saarni provides the reader with interesting stories and case studies of children and families struggling with becoming more emotionally competent. Saarni covers a wide range of topics in a comprehensive manner including, where relevant, studies and interpretations of the development of emotional competence from non-Western cultures.

## Relevant Films

Hochberg, T. (2010). *Other rituals: Parents' stories of meaning making* [DVD]. Other rituals ©Todd Hochberg. All rights reserved. Available from www.toddhochberg.com

In this emotionally moving DVD, Todd Hochberg shares his photos, video footage and stories of families as they grieve over the loss of their beloved young children. Each parent interviewed describes uniquely meaningful rituals and activities used to cope with their losses. One family had multiple birthday celebrations during the short life of the child. Another family focused on the use of religious ceremonies to help during their triplets' transition to a new form of life. In another case, a father handcrafted the casket for his child's burial. Finally, another father had a tattoo put on his arm of his beloved child's favourite toy as a remembrance of the child. These rituals afforded family members opportunities to make healing connections among themselves and with their lost loved ones.

NOVA/WGBH (Producer). (2010). *This emotional life: In search of ourselves – and happiness* [DVD]. USA: Public Broadcasting Service (PBS). Available from www.pbs.org/video

*This emotional life: In search of ourselves – and happiness* is an excellent must-see six-hour Public Broadcasting Service series hosted by Daniel Gilbert on the science behind the real everyday emotional lives of people seeking happiness and well-being. Three two-hour DVDs cover the topics of relationships in *Family, Friends & Lovers*, the regulation of anger, sadness and fear in *Facing Our Fears*, and resilience and the pursuit of happiness in *Rethinking Happiness*. The stories told by the individuals interviewed involved their relationships, thus demonstrating how emotions are co-regulated through social interactions. Clearly delineated stories and topics within each DVD make it suitable for promoting discussions among viewers.

# References


ABC News-20/20 (1998). *The secret life of boys [DVD]*. New York: Films Media Group.

Abidin, R. R. (1990). Introduction to the special issue: The stresses of parenting. *Journal of Clinical Child Psychology, 19*(4), 298.

Abidin, R. R. (1992). The determinants of parenting behavior. *Journal of Clinical Child Psychology, 21*(4), 407–412. doi:10.1207/s15374424jccp2104_12

Achenbach, T. M. (2014). Developmental, quantitative, and multicultural assessment of psychopathology. In M. Lewis & K. D. Rudolph (Eds.), *Handbook of developmental psychopathology (3rd ed.)* (pp. 67–85). doi:10.1007/978-1-4614-9608-3_4

Adrian, M., Zeman, J. & Veits, G. (2011). Methodological implications of the affect revolution: A 35-year review of emotion regulation assessment in children. *Journal of Experimental Child Psychology*, 110(2),171–197. doi: 10.1016/j.jecp.2011.03.009

Ainsworth, M. D. S., Bell, S. M. V. & Stayton, D. J. (1973). Individual differences in strange situation behavior of one-year-olds. In L. J. Stone, H. T. Smith & L. B. Murphy (Eds.), *The competent infant: Research and commentary* (pp. 1150–1161). New York: Basic Books.

Ainsworth, M. D. S. & Wittig, B. (1969). Attachment and exploratory behavior of one-year olds in a Strange Situation. In B. Foss (Ed.), *Determinants of infant behavior* (Vol. 4, pp. 113–136). London: Methuen.

Ajrouch, K. J. (1999). Family and ethnic identity in an Arab-American community. In M. Suleiman (Ed.), *Arabs in America: Building a new future* (pp. 129–139). Philadelphia, PA: Temple University Press.

Ajrouch, K. J. (2000). Place, age, and culture: Community living and ethnic identity among Lebanese American adolescents. *Small Group Research, 31*, 447–469.

Akyil, Y., Prouty, A., Blanchard, A. & Lyness, K. (2014). Parents' experiences of intergenerational value transmission in Turkey's changing society: An interpretative phenomenological study. *Journal of Family Psychotherapy, 25*(1), 42–65. doi:10.1080/08975353.2014.881690

Aldao, A., Sheppes, G. & Gross, J. (2015). Emotion regulation flexibility. *Cognitive Therapy and Research, 39*(3), 263–278.

Al-Khatib, H. (2003). Language alternation among Arabic and English youth bilinguals: Reflecting or constructing social realities? *International Journal of Bilingual Education and Bilingualism, 6*, 409–422. doi:10.1080/13670050308667794

Al-Krenawi, A. & Lightman, E. S. (2000). Learning achievement, social adjustment, and family conflict among Bedouin-Arab children from polygamous and monogamous families. *The Journal of Social Psychology, 140*(3), 345–355. doi:10.1080/00224540009600475

Alzheimer's Association (2014). Retrieved from www.alz.org/dementia/types-of-dementia.asp

Amer, M. M. (2014). Arab American acculturation and ethnic identity across the lifespan: Sociodemographic correlates and psychological outcomes. In S. C. Nassar-McMillan, K. J. Ajrouch & J. Hakim-Larson (Eds.), *Biopsychosocial perspectives on Arab Americans: Culture, development, and health* (pp. 153–173). doi:10.1007/978-1-4614-8238-3_8

American Psychiatric Association (2013). *Diagnostic and Statistical Manual of Mental Disorders, 5th Edition.* Arlington, VA: American Psychiatric Association.

American Psychiatric Association (2016). *History of the DSM.* Retrieved from www.psychiatry.org/psychiatrists/practice/dsm/history-of-the-dsm

Ansar, N. S., McMahon, T. J. & Luthar, S. S. (2016). Trajectories of emotional–behavioral difficulty and academic competence: A 6-year, *person-centered*, prospective study of affluent suburban adolescents. *Development and Psychopathology.* Advance online publication. doi:10.1017/S0954579416000110

Arain, M., Haque, M., Johal, L., Mathur, P., Nel, W., Rais, A., Sandhu, R., Sharma, S. (2013). Maturation of the adolescent brain. *Neuropsychiatric Disease and Treatment, 9*, Article ID 449–461.

Arnander, P. & Skipwith, A. (2007). *The son of a duck is a floater.* London: Stacey International.

Arnold, M. B. (1960). *Emotion and personality: Vol. 1. Psychological aspects.* New York: Columbia University Press.

Are, F. & Shaffer, A. (2015). Family emotion expressiveness mediates the relations between maternal emotion regulation and child emotion regulation. *Child Psychiatry and Human Development.* Advance online publication. doi:10.1007/s10578-015-0605-4

Asian Americans and Pacific Islanders (2015). *Who are we?* Retrieved from www.socialsecurity.gov/aapi/who.htm

Asian American & Pacific Islander Initiative (AAPI) (2015). *Asian American and Pacific Islander – Primer.* Retrieved from www.epa.gov/aapi/primer.htm

Austin, E. J., Saklofske, D. H., Huang, S. H. S. & McKenney, D. (2004). Measurement of trait emotional intelligence: Testing and cross-validating a modified version of Schutte et al.'s (1998) measure, *Personality and Individual Differences, 36*, 555–562.

Baltes, P. B., Reese, H. W. & Lipsitt, L. P. (1980). Life-span developmental psychology. *Annual Review of Psychology, 31*(1), 65–110. doi:10.1146/annurev.ps.31.020180.000433

Bandura, A. (1977). Self-efficacy: Toward a unifying theory of behavioral change. *Psychological Review, 84*(2), 191–215. doi:10.1037/0033-295X.84.2.191

Bandura, A. (1982). Self-efficacy mechanism in human agency. *American Psychologist, 37*(2), 122–147. doi:10.1037/0003-066X.37.2.122

Bandura, A. (1989). Regulation of cognitive processes through perceived self-efficacy. *Developmental Psychology, 25*(5), 729–735. doi:10.1037/0012-1649.25.5.729

Barchard, K. A. & Hakstian, A. R. (2004). The nature and measurement of emotional intelligence abilities: Basic dimensions and their relationships with other cognitive ability and personality variables. *Educational and Psychological Measurement, 64*, 437–462.

Bariola, E., Gullone, E. & Hughes, E. K. (2011). Child and adolescent emotion regulation: The role of parental emotion regulation and expression. *Clinical Child and Family Psychology Review, 14*(2), 198–212. doi:10.1007/s10567-011-0092-5

Barkley, R. A. (2013). Distinguishing sluggish cognitive tempo from ADHD in children and adolescents: Executive functioning, impairment, and comorbidity. *Journal of Clinical Child and Adolescent Psychology, 42*(2), 161–173.

Barkley, R. A. (2015). *Attention-deficit hyperactivity disorder: A handbook for diagnosis and treatment (4th ed.)*. New York: Guilford Press.

Bar-On, R. (1997). *BarOn Emotional Quotient – Inventory (BarOn EQ-I)*. Available from Psychcorp, www.psychcorp.com.

Barrett, K. C. & Campos, J. J. (1987). Perspectives on emotional development II: A functionalist approach to emotions. In J. D. Osofsky (Ed.), *Handbook of infant development (2nd ed.)* (pp. 555–578). Oxford, England: Wiley.

Bartoletti, M. M. (2006). *Effectiveness of Mruk's self-esteem change program on psychological and physiological measures of well-being* (Order No. 3275687). Available from ProQuest Dissertations & Theses Global (304910277).

Bates, J. E., Goodnight & Fite (2008). Temperament and emotion. In M. Lewis, J. M. Haviland-Jones & L. Feldman Barrett (Eds.), *Handbook of emotions (3rd ed.)* (pp. 485–496). New York: Guilford.

Bauer, J. J. & McAdams, D. P. (2004). Growth goals, maturity, and well-being. *Developmental Psychology, 40*(1), 114–127. doi:10.1037/0012-1649.40.1.114

Bauer, J. J., McAdams, D. P. & Pals, J. L. (2008). Narrative identity and eudaimonic well-being. *Journal of Happiness Studies, 9*(1), 81–104. doi:10.1007/s10902-006-9021-6

Baumeister, R. F., Smart, L. & Boden, J. M. (1996). Relation of threatened egotism to violence and aggression: The dark side of high self-esteem. *Psychological Review, 103*(1), 5–33. doi: 10.1037/0033-295X.103.1.5

BBC News (2011). *Profile: Arab League*. Retrieved from http://news.bbc.co.uk/2/hi/middle_east/country_profiles/1550797.stm

Beauchaine, T. P. (2015). Future directions in emotion dysregulation and youth psychopathology. *Journal of Clinical Child and Adolescent Psychology, 44*(5), 875–896. doi:10.1080/15374416.2015.1038827

Beitin, B. K. & Aprahamian, M. (2014). Family values and traditions. In S. C. Nassar-McMillan, K. J. Ajrouch & J. Hakim-Larson (Eds.) (pp. 67–88). *Biopsychosocial perspectives on Arab Americans: Culture, development, and health*. New York: Springer.

Bellak, L. & Bellak, S. S. (1974). *Children's Apperception Test (C.A.T.)*. New York: C.P.S. Publishing.

Bellamy, S. & Hardy, C. (2015). Factors predicting depression across multiple domains in a national longitudinal sample of Canadian youth. *Journal of Abnormal Child Psychology, 43*(4), 633–643. doi:10.1007/s10802-014-9940-3

Belsky, J. & van IJzendoorn, M. H. (2015). What works for whom? Genetic moderation of intervention efficacy. *Development and Psychopathology, 27*(1), 1–6. doi:10.1017/S0954579414001254

Benjafield, J. G. (2010). *A history of psychology (3rd ed.)*. Don Mills, Ontario: Oxford University Press Canada.

Benjafield, J. G. (2012). *Psychology: A concise history*. Don Mills, Ontario: Oxford University Press Canada.

Bernat, D. H., Oakes, J. M., Pettingell, S. L. & Resnick, M. (2012). Risk and direct protective factors for youth violence. *American Journal of Preventive Medicine, 43*(2), S57–S66. doi:10.1016/j.amepre.2012.04.023

Biederman, J., Faraone, S. V., Milberger, S., Jetton, J. G., Chen, L., Mick, E., … Russell, R. L. (1996). Is childhood oppositional defiant disorder a precursor to adolescent conduct disorder? Findings from a four-year follow-up study of children with ADHD. *Journal of the American Academy of Child & Adolescent Psychiatry, 35*(9), 1193–1204. doi:10.1097/00004583-199609000-00017

Bierman, K. L., Coie, J., Dodge, K., Greenberg, M., Lochman, J., McMohan, R., … Conduct Problems Prevention Research Group. (2013). School outcomes of aggressive-disruptive children: Prediction from kindergarten risk factors and impact of the Fast Track prevention program. *Aggressive Behavior, 39*(2), 114–130. doi:10.1002/ab.21467

Blanchard-Fields, F. (2009). Flexible and adaptive socio-emotional problem solving in adult development and aging. *Restorative Neurology and Neuroscience, 27*(5), 539–550.

Blechman, E. A., Prinz, R. J. & Dumas, J. E. (1995). Coping, competence, and aggression prevention: I. Developmental model. *Applied & Preventive Psychology, 4*(4), 211–232. doi:10.1016/S0962-1849(05)80024-1

Block, J. & Block, J. H. (2006). Venturing a 30-year longitudinal study. *American Psychologist, 61*(4), 315–327. doi:10.1037/0003-066X.61.4.315

Block, J. & Block, J. H. (2010). "Block and Block Longitudinal Study, 1969–1999", Retrieved from http://hdl.handle.net/1902.1/NGQCIPIDUK, Harvard Dataverse, V1.

Bocknek, E. L., Brophy-Herb, H. E., Fitzgerald, H. E., Schiffman, R. F. & Vogel, C. (2014). Stability of biological father presence as a proxy for family stability: Cross-racial associations with the longitudinal development of emotion regulation in toddlerhood. *Infant Mental Health Journal, 35*(4), 309–321. doi:10.1002/imhj.21454

Bodenmann, G. (2005). Dyadic coping and its significance for marital functioning. In T. A. Revenson, K. Kayser & G. Bodenmann (Eds.), *Decade of behavior. Couples coping with stress: Emerging perspectives on dyadic coping* (pp. 33–49). Washington, D.C.: American Psychological Association. doi:10.1037/11031-002

Bodie, G., Vickery, A., Cannava, K. & Jones, S. (2015). The role of "active listening" in informal helping conversations: Impact on perceptions of listener helpfulness, sensitivity, and supportiveness and discloser emotional improvement. *Western Journal of Communication, 79*(2), 151–173.

Bonoti, F. & Misalidi, P. (2015). Social emotions in children's human figure drawings: Drawing shame, pride and jealousy. *Infant and Child Development*. Advance online publication. doi:10.1002/icd.1918

Borstelmann, L. J. (1983). Children before psychology: Ideas about children from antiquity to the late 1800s. In P. H. Mussen (Ed.), *Handbook of child psychology* (Vol. 1, pp. 1–40). New York: Wiley.

Boss, P. (2016). The context and process of theory development: The story of ambiguous loss. *Journal of Family Theory & Review, 8(3)*, 269–286. doi:10.1111/jftr.12152

Boswell, J. (1988). *The kindness of strangers: The abandonment of children in Western Europe from late antiquity to the Renaissance*. New York: Pantheon Books.

Bowlby, J. (1969). *Attachment and loss: Vol. 1, Attachment*. New York: Basic Books.

Boyatzis, R. E. & Sala, F. (2004). The Emotional Competence Inventory (ECI). In G. Geher (Ed.), *Measuring emotional intelligence: Common ground and controversy* (pp. 147–180). Hauppauge, NY: Nova Science.

Boyce, W. T. & Ellis, B. J. (2005). Biological sensitivity to context: I. An evolutionary–developmental theory of the origins and functions of stress reactivity. *Development and Psychopathology, 17*(2), 271–301. doi:10.1017/S0954579405050145

Boyer, W. (2013). Getting back to the woods: Familial perspectives on culture and preschoolers' acquisition of self-regulation and emotion regulation. *Early Childhood Education Journal, 41*(2), 153–159. doi:10.1007/s10643-012-0536-7

Brackett, M. A. & Mayer, J. D. (2003). Convergent, discriminant, and incremental validity of competing measures of emotional intelligence. *Personality and Social Psychology Bulletin, 29*, 1147–1158.

Brackett, M. A., Mayer, J. D. & Warner, R. M. (2004). Emotional intelligence and its relation to everyday behaviour. *Personality and Individual Differences, 36*, 1387–1402.

Brant, C. C. (1990). Native ethics and rules of behaviour. *The Canadian Journal of Psychiatry / La Revue canadienne de psychiatrie, 35*(6), 534–539.

Brent, S. S. (1984). *Psychological and social structures*. Hillsdale, NJ: Erlbaum.

Bretherton, I. (2003). Mary Ainsworth: Insightful observer and courageous theoretician. In G. A. Kimble & M. Wertheimer (Eds.), *Portraits of pioneers in psychology* (Vol. 5). Hillsdale, NJ: Erlbaum.

Bretherton, I. & Beeghly, M. (1982). Talking about internal states: The acquisition of an explicit theory of mind. *Developmental Psychology, 18*(6), 906–921. doi:10.1037/0012-1649.18.6.906

Bretherton, I., Fritz, J., Zahn-Waxler, C. & Ridgeway, D. (1986). Learning to talk about emotions: A functionalist perspective. *Child Development, 57*(3), 529–548. doi:10.2307/1130334

Bretherton, I. & Munholland, K. A. (2008). Internal working models in attachment relationships: Elaborating a central construct in attachment theory. In J. Cassidy & P. R. Shaver (Eds.), *Handbook of attachment: Theory, research, and clinical applications (2nd ed.)* (pp. 102–127). New York: Guilford Press.

Bridges, K. (1932). Emotional development in early infancy. *Child Development, 3*, 324–341.

Bridgett, D. J., Burt, N. M., Edwards, E. S. & Deater-Deckard, K. (2015). Intergenerational transmission of self-regulation: A multidisciplinary review and integrative conceptual framework. *Psychological Bulletin, 141*(3), 602–654. doi:10.1037/a0038662

Brock, R. L. & Kochanska, G. (2016). Interparental conflict, children's security with parents, and long-term risk of internalizing problems: A longitudinal study from ages 2 to 10. *Development and Psychopathology, 28*(1), 45–54. doi:10.1017/S0954579415000279

Brody, L. R. (2000). The socialization of gender differences in emotional expression: Display rules, infant temperament, and differentiation. In A. H. Fischer (Ed.), *Studies in emotion and social interaction. Second series. Gender and emotion: Social psychological perspectives* (pp. 24–47). New York: Cambridge University Press.

Brody, L. R. & Hall, J. A. (2008). Gender and emotion in context. In M. Lewis, J. M. Haviland-Jones & L. F. Barrett (Eds.), *Handbook of emotions (3rd ed.)* (pp. 395–408). New York: Guilford Press.

Bronfenbrenner, U. (1994). Ecological models of human development. In *International Encyclopedia of Education, Vol. 3 (2nd ed.)* (1643–1647). Oxford: Elsevier. Reprinted in: Gauvain, M. & Cole, M. (Eds.), Readings in the development of children, *(2nd ed.)* (1993, pp 37–43). New York: Freeman.

Broth, M. R., Goodman, S. H., Hall, C. & Raynor, L. C. (2004). Depressed and well mothers' emotion interpretation accuracy and the quality of mother-infant interaction. *Infancy, 6*(1), 37–55. doi: 10.1207/s15327078in0601_2

Buck, R. (1977). Nonverbal communication of affect in preschool children: Relationships with personality and skin conductance. *Journal of Personality and Social Psychology, 35*(4), 225–236. doi:10.1037/0022-3514.35.4.225

Bugental, D. B. (1992). Affective and cognitive processes within threat-oriented family systems. In I. E. Sigel, A. V. McGillicuddy-DeLisi & J. J. Goodnow (Eds.), *Parental belief systems: The psychological consequences for children (2nd ed.)* (pp. 219–248). Hillsdale, NJ: Erlbaum.

Burnett, S., Thompson, S., Bird, G. & Blakemore, S.-J. (2011). Pubertal development of the understanding of social emotions: Implications for education. *Learning and Individual Differences, 21*(6), 681–689. doi:10.1016/j.lindif.2010.05.007

Camras, L. A. (2011). Differentiation, dynamical integration and functional emotional development. *Emotion Review, 3*(2), 138–146. doi:10.1177/1754073910387944

Camras, L. A. & Fatani, S. S. (2008). The development of facial expressions: Current perspectives on infant emotions. In M. Lewis, J. M. Haviland-Jones & L. F. Barrett (Eds.), *Handbook of emotions (3rd ed.)* (pp. 291–303). New York: Guilford Press.

Cappa, K. A., Begle, A. M., Conger, J. C., Dumas, J. E. & Conger, A. J. (2011). Bidirectional relationships between parenting stress and child coping competence: Findings from the PACE study. *Journal of Child and Family Studies, 20*(3), 334–342. doi:10.1007/s10826-010-9397-0

Carey, W. B. & McDevitt, S.C. (1995). *Coping with children's temperament: A guide for professionals.* New York: Basic Books.

Carr, A. (1998). The inclusion of fathers in family therapy: A research based perspective. *Contemporary Family Therapy, 20*(3), 371–383. Retrieved from http://resolver.scholarsportal.info/resolve/08922764/v20i0003/371_tiofiftarbp

Carstensen, L. L., Gottman, J. M. & Levenson, R. W. (1995). Emotional behavior in long-term marriage. *Psychology and Aging, 10*(1), 140–149. doi:10.1037/0882-7974.10.1.140

Carstensen, L. L., Turan, B., Scheibe, S., Ram, N., Ersner-Hershfield, H., Samanez-Larkin, G. R., Brooks, K. P. & Nesselroade, J. R. (2011). Emotional experience improves with age: Evidence based on over 10 years of experience sampling. *Psychology and Aging, 26*(1), 21–33. doi:10.1037/a0021285

Carver, C. S. & Scheier, M. F. (1990). Origins and functions of positive and negative affect: A control-process view. *Psychological Review, 97*(1), 19–35. doi:10.1037/0033-295X.97.1.19

Cassidy, J. & Shaver, P. R. (Eds.) (2008). *Handbook of attachment: Theory, research, and clinical applications (2nd ed.).* New York: Guilford.

Causadias, J., Salvatore, J. & Sroufe, L. (2012). Early patterns of self-regulation as risk and promotive factors in development: A longitudinal study from childhood to adulthood in a high-risk sample. *International Journal of Behavioral Development, 36*(4), 293–302. doi:10.1177/0165025412444076

Chan, D. W. (2003). Dimensions of emotional intelligence and their relationships with social coping among gifted adolescents in Hong Kong. *Journal of Youth and Adolescence, 32*, 409–418.

Chaplin, T. M. & Aldao, A. (2013). Gender differences in emotion expression in children: A meta-analytic review. *Psychological Bulletin, 139*(4), 735–765. doi: 10.1037/a0030737

Chaplin, T. M., Cole, P. M. & Zahn-Waxler, C. (2005). Parental socialization of emotion expression: Gender differences and relations to child adjustment. *Emotion, 5*(1), 80–88. doi:10.1037/1528-3542.5.1.80

Chawla, N. & Wadsworth, S. M. (2012). The impact of an Operation Purple Camp Intervention on military children and adolescents' self-perception of social acceptance, athletic competence, and global self-worth. *The American Journal of Family, 40*, 267–278.

Chen, S. H., Zhou, Q., Main, A. & Lee, E. H. (2015). Chinese American immigrant parents' emotional expression in the family: Relations with parents' cultural orientations and children's emotion-related regulation. *Cultural Diversity and Ethnic Minority Psychology, 21*(4), 619–629. doi:10.1037/cdp0000013

Cheng, C. (2001). Assessing coping flexibility in real-life and laboratory settings: A multimethod approach. *Journal of Personality and Social Psychology, 80*(5), 814–833. doi:10.1037/0022-3514.80.5.814

Chess, S. & Thomas, A. (1977). Temperament and the parent-child interaction. *Pediatric Annals, 6*, 574–582.

Ciarrochi, J., Chan, A. Y. C. & Bajgar, J. (2001). Measuring emotional intelligence in adolescents. *Personality and Individual Differences, 31*, 1105–1119.

Cicchetti, D. (2014). Illustrative developmental psychopathology perspectives on precursors and path ways to personality disorder: Commentary on the special issue. *Journal of Personality Disorders, 28*(1), 172–179. doi:10.1521/pedi.2014.28.1.172

Cicchetti, D. (2016). Socioemotional, personality, and biological development: Illustrations from a multilevel developmental psychopathology perspective on child maltreatment. *Annual Review of Psychology, 67*, 187–211. doi:10.1146/annurev-psych-122414-033259

Cicchetti, D. & Banny, A. (2014). A developmental psychopathology perspective on child maltreatment. In M. Lewis & K. D. Rudolph (Eds.), *Handbook of developmental psychopathology (3rd ed.)* (pp. 723–741). New York: Guilford Press. doi: 10.1007/978-1-4614-9608-3_37

Cicchetti, D. & Natsuaki, M. N. (2014). Multilevel developmental perspectives toward understanding internalizing psychopathology: Current research and future directions. *Development and Psychopathology, 26*(4, Pt 2), 1189–1190. doi:10.1017/S0954579414000959

Cicchetti, D. & Rogosch, F. A. (1996). Equifinality and multifinality in developmental psychopathology. *Development and Psychopathology, 8*(4), 597–600. doi:10.1017/S0954579400007318

Cicchetti, D., Rogosch, F. A. & Toth, S. L. (2006). Fostering secure attachment in infants in maltreating families through preventive interventions. *Development and Psychopathology, 18*(3), 623–649. doi:10.1017/S0954579406060329

Clark, K. B. & Clark, M. P. (1947). Racial identification and preference in Negro children. Reprinted in T. M. Newcomb & E. L. Hartley (Eds.), *Readings in social psychology* (pp. 269–278). New York: Henry Holt and Company.

Clark, K. & Clark, M. (1950). Emotional factors in racial identification and preference in Negro children. *The Journal of Negro Education, 19*(3), 341–350. doi:10.2307/2966491

Coatsworth, J. D., Duncan, L. G., Nix, R. L., Greenberg, M. T., Gayles, J. G., Bamberger, K. T., … Demi, M. A. (2015). Integrating mindfulness with parent training: Effects of the mindfulness-enhanced strengthening families program. *Developmental Psychology, 51*(1), 26–35. doi:10.1037/a0038212

Cohn, J. F. & Tronick, E. Z. (1988). Mother-infant face-to-face interaction: Influence is bidirectional and unrelated to periodic cycles in either partner's behavior. *Developmental Psychology, 24*(3), 386–392. doi:10.1037/0012-1649.24.3.386

Cohn, L. D. & Westenberg, P. M. (2004). Intelligence and maturity: Meta-analytic evidence for the incremental and discriminant validity of Loevinger's measure of ego development. *Journal of Personality and Social Psychology, 86*(5), 760–772. doi:10.1037/0022-3514.86.5.760

Colarossi, L. G. & Eccles, J. S. (2000). A prospective study of adolescents' peer support: Gender differences and the influence of parental relationships. *Journal of Youth and Adolescence, 29*(6), 661–678. doi: 10.1023/A:1026403922442

Cole, D. A. (1990). Relation of social and academic competence to depressive symptoms in childhood. *Journal of Abnormal Psychology, 99*(4), 422–429. doi:10.1037/0021-843X.99.4.422

Cole, D. A. (1991). Preliminary support for a competency-based model of depression in children. *Journal of Abnormal Psychology, 100*(2), 181–190. doi:10.1037/0021-843X.100.2.181

Cole, P. M., Michel, M. K. & Teti, L.O'D. (1994). The development of emotion regulation and dysregulation: A clinical perspective. *Monographs of the Society for Research in Child Development, 59*(2–3), 73–100, 250–283. doi:10.2307/1166139

Cole, P. M. & Tan, P. Z. (2007). Emotion socialization from a cultural perspective. In J. E. Grusec & P. D. Hastings (Eds.), *Handbook of socialization: Theory and research* (pp. 516–542). New York: Guilford Press.

Cole, M. & Wertsch, J. V. (1996). Beyond the individual-social antinomy in discussions of Piaget and Vygotsky. *Human Development, 39*(5), 250–256. doi:10.1159/000278475

Coleman, P. K. (2003). Reactive attachment disorder in the context of the family: A review and call for further research. *Emotional and Behavioural Difficulties, 8*, 205–216.

Coleman, P. K. & Karraker, K. H. (1998). Self-efficacy and parenting quality: Findings and future applications. *Developmental Review, 18*(1), 47–85. doi:10.1006/drev.1997.0448

Compas, B. E., Jaser, S. S., Dunbar, J. P., Watson, K. H., Bettis, A. H., Gruhn, M. A. & Williams, E. K. (2014). Coping and emotion regulation from childhood to early adulthood: Points of convergence and divergence. *Australian Journal of Psychology, 66*(2), 71–81. doi: 10.1111/ajpy.12043

Condon, W. S. & Sander, L. W. (1974). Synchrony demonstrated between movements of the neonate and adult speech. *Child Development, 45(2)*, 456–462. doi:10.2307/1127968

Conger, R. D. & Conger, K. J. (2002). Resilience in Midwestern families: Selected findings from the first decade of a prospective, longitudinal study. *Journal of Marriage and the Family, 64*(2), 361–373.

Coopersmith, S. (1967a). *The antecedents of self-esteem*. San Francisco: W. H. Freeman & Co.

Coopersmith, S. (1967b/1975/2002). *Coopersmith Self-Esteem Inventory*. Retrieved from www.mindgarden.com/85-coopersmith-self-esteem-inventory#horizontalTab3

Cornelius, R. R. (1996). *The science of emotion: Research and tradition in the psychology of emotions*. Englewood Cliffs, NJ: Prentice-Hall.

Cornelius, R. R. (2006). Magda Arnold's Thomistic theory of emotion, the self-ideal, and the moral dimension of appraisal. *Cognition and Emotion, 20*(7), 976–1000. doi: 10.1080/02699930600616411

Cowan, C. P., Cowan, P. A. & Barry, J. (2011). Couples' groups for parents of preschoolers: Ten-year outcomes of a randomized trial. *Journal of Family Psychology, 25*(2), 240–250. doi:10.1037/a0023003

Crabtree, S. A. (2007). Culture, gender and the influence of social change amongst Emirati families in the United Arab Emirates. *Journal of Comparative Family Studies, 38*(4), 575–587.

Crawford, L. E. (2009). Conceptual metaphors of affect. *Emotion Review, 1*(2), 129–139. doi:10.1177/1754073908100438

Crocker, A. D. & Hakim-Larson, J. (1997). Predictors of pre-adolescent depression and suicidal ideation. *Canadian Journal of Behavioural Science/Revue canadienne des sciences du comportement, 29*(2), 76–82. doi: 10.1037/0008-400X.29.2.76

Crowe, M., Raval, V. V., Trivedi, S. S., Daga, S. S. & Raval, P. H. (2012). Processes of emotion communication and control: A comparison of India and the United States. *Social Psychology, 43*(4), 205–214. doi:10.1027/1864-9335/a000121

Crowley, R. J. & Mills, J.C. (1989). *Cartoon magic: How to help children discover their rainbows within.* New York: Magination Press.

Csikszentmihalyi, M. (2009). The promise of positive psychology. *Psihologijske Teme, 18*(2), 203–211.

Cuijpers, P., Weitz, E., Karyotaki, E., Garber, J. & Andersson, G. (2015). The effects of psychological treatment of maternal depression on children and parental functioning: A meta-analysis. *European Child & Adolescent Psychiatry, 24*(2), 237–245. doi:10.1007/s00787-014-0660-6

Culbertson, J. L. (1999). Focus chapter: Research methods with children. In P. C. Kendall, J. N. Butcher & G. N. Holmbeck (Eds.), *Handbook of research methods in clinical psychology (2nd ed.)* (pp. 619–633). Hoboken, NJ: John Wiley.

Cummings, E. M. & Miller-Graff, L. E. (2015). Emotional security theory: An emerging theoretical model for youths' psychological and physiological responses across multiple developmental contexts. *Current Directions in Psychological Science, 24*(3), 208–213. doi:10.1177/0963721414561510

Damasio, A. (2010). *Self comes to mind: Constructing the conscious brain.* New York: Vintage Books.

Darwin, C. (1872/2008). *The expression of the emotions in man and animals.* London: The Folio Society.

Darwin, C. (1909/1937). *The origin of species.* New York: P.F. Collier & Son, Corporation.

Davidson Films Inc., Films for the Humanities & Sciences & Films Media Group. (2007). *John Bowlby: Attachment theory across generations* (Giants of Psychology). New York, N.Y.: Films Media Group.

Davies, P. T. & Cummings, E. M. (1994). Marital conflict and child adjustment: An emotional security hypothesis. *Psychological Bulletin, 116*(3), 387–411. doi:10.1037/0033-2909.116.3.387

Davis-Sowers, R. (2012). "It just kind of like falls in your hands": Factors that influence Black aunts' decisions to parent their nieces and nephews. *Journal of Black Studies, 43(3)*, 231–250. doi:10.1177/0021934711415243

Davitz, J. R. (1969). *The language of emotions.* New York: Academic Press.

Deci, E. L. & Ryan, R. M. (2008). Hedonia, eudaimonia, and well-being: An introduction. *Journal of Happiness Studies, 9*(1), 1–11. doi:10.1007/s10902-006-9018-1

Delgado-Romero, E. A., Nevels, B. J., Capielo, C., Galvan, N. & Torres, V. (2013). Culturally alert counseling with Latino/Latina Americans. In G. McAuliffe & Associates (Ed.), *Culturally alert counseling: A comprehensive introduction (2nd ed.)* (pp. 293–314). Thousand Oaks: Sage.

DeMause, L. (1974). *The history of childhood.* New York: Psychohistory Press.

Demo, D. H., Small, S. A. & Savin-Williams, R. C. (1987). Family relations and the self-esteem of adolescents and their parents. *Journal of Marriage and the Family, 49*(4), 705–715. doi:10.2307/351965

Denham, S. A. (1998). *Emotional development in young children.* New York: Guilford.

Denham, S. A., Bassett, H. H. & Wyatt, T. (2007). The socialization of emotional competence. In J. E. Grusec P. D. Hastings (Ed.), (pp. 614–637). New York, US: Guilford.

Denissen, J. J. A., van Aken, M. A. G., Penke, L. & Wood, D. (2013). Self-regulation underlies temperament and personality: An integrative developmental framework. *Child Development Perspectives, 7*(4), 255–260.

Dennis, T. A., Cole, P. M., Wiggins, C. N., Cohen, L. H. & Zalewski, M. (2009). The functional organization of preschool-age children's emotion expressions and actions in challenging situations. *Emotion, 9*(4), 520–530. doi:10.1037/a0016514

DeRivera, J. (1984). Development and the full range of emotional experience. In C. Z. Malatesta & C. E. Izard (Eds.), *Emotion in adult development* (pp. 45–63). Beverly Hills, CA: Sage.

Derks, D., Fischer, A. H. & Bos, A. E. R. (2008). The role of emotion in computer-mediated communication: A review. *Computers in Human Behavior, 24*(3), 766–785. doi: 10.1016/j.chb.2007.04.004

Derryberry, D. & Rothbart, M. K. (1988). Arousal, affect, and attention as components of temperament. *Journal of Personality and Social Psychology, 55*(6), 958–966. doi: 10.1037/0022-3514.55.6.958

Derryberry, D. & Rothbart, M. (2001). Early temperament and emotional development. In A. F. Kalvaboer & A. Gramsbergen (Eds.), *Handbook of brain and behaviour in human development* (pp. 967–988). Great Britain: Kluwer Academic.

Desbordes, G., Gard, T., Hoge, E. A., Hölzel, B. K., Kerr, C., Lazar, S. W., Olendzki, A. & Vago, D. R. (2015). Moving beyond mindfulness: Defining equanimity as an outcome measure in meditation and contemplative research. *Mindfulness, 6*(2), 356–372. doi:10.1007/s12671-013-0269-8

Dingfelder, S. F. (2005). Closing the gap for Latino patients. *APA Monitor on Psychology, 36*(1), 58–61. Washington, D.C.: American Psychological Association.

Diamond, G. M., Shahar, B., Sabo, D. & Tsvieli, N. (2016). Attachment-based family therapy and emotion-focused therapy for unresolved anger: The role of productive emotional processing. *Psychotherapy, 53*(1), 34–44. doi:10.1037/pst000

Diaz-Aguado, M. J. & Martinez, R. (2015). Types of adolescent male dating violence against women, self-esteem, and justification of dominance and aggression. *Journal of Interpersonal Violence, 30*(15), 2636–2658. doi: 10.1177/0886260514553631

Diehl, M., Coyle, N. & Labouvie-Vief, G. (1996). Age and sex differences in strategies of coping and defense across the life span. *Psychology and Aging, 11*(1), 127–139. doi:10.1037/0882-7974.11.1.127

Diener, E. (2000). Subjective well-being: The science of happiness and a proposal for a national index. *American Psychologist, 55*(1), 34–43. doi:10.1037/0003-066X.55.1.34

Diener, E. (2013). The remarkable changes in the science of subjective well-being. *Perspectives on Psychological Science, 8*(6), 663–666. doi:10.1177/1745691613507583

Diener, E. & Scollon, C. N. (2014). The what, why, when, and how of teaching the science of subjective well-being. *Teaching of Psychology, 41*(2), 175–183. doi:10.1177/0098628314530346

DiGiuseppe, R. (1995). Developing the therapeutic alliance with angry clients. In H. Kassinove (Ed.), *Series in clinical and community psychology. Anger disorders: Definition, diagnosis, and treatment* (pp. 131–149). Philadelphia: Taylor & Francis.

Disney PIXAR (2015). *Inside Out.* Distributed by Buena Vista Home Entertainment, Inc.

Dix, T. (1991). The affective organization of parenting: Adaptive and maladaptative processes. *Psychological Bulletin, 110*(1), 3–25. doi:10.1037/0033-2909.110.1.3

Dix, T., Ruble, D. N., Grusec, J. E. & Nixon, S. (1986). Social cognition in parents: Inferential and affective reactions to children of three age levels. *Child Development, 57*(4), 879–894. doi:10.2307/1130365

Dodge, K. A. (1980). Social cognition and children's aggressive behavior. *Child Development, 51*(1), 162–170. doi:10.2307/1129603

Donahue, B., Hersen, M. & Ammerman, R. T. (1995). Historical overview. In M. Hersen & R.T. Ammeran (Eds.), *Advanced abnormal child psychology* (pp. 3–19). Hillsdale, NJ: Erlbaum.

Donaldson, S. K. & Westerman, M. A. (1986). Development of children's understanding of ambivalence and causal theories of emotions. *Developmental Psychology, 22*(5), 655–662. doi:10.1037/0012-1649.22.5.655

Dozier, M., Stovall-McClough, K. C. & Albus, K. E. (2008). Attachment and psychopathology in adulthood. In J. Cassidy & P. R. Shaver (Eds.), *Handbook of attachment: Theory, research, and clinical applications (2nd ed.)* (pp. 718–744). New York: Guilford Press.

Drewes, M. J. & Westenberg, M. (2001). The impact of modified instructions on ego-level scores: A psychometric hazard or indication of optimal ego level? *Journal of Personality Assessment, 76*(2), 229–249. doi:10.1207/S15327752JPA7602_07

Duggins, S. D., Kuperminc, G. P., Henrich, C. C., Smalls-Glover, C. & Perilla, J. L. (2016). Aggression among adolescent victims of school bullying: Protective roles of family and school connectedness. *Psychology of Violence, 6*(2), 205–212. doi:10.1037/a0039439

Dunbar, A. S., Perry, N. B., Cavanaugh, A. M. & Leerkes, E. M. (2015). African American parents' racial and emotion socialization profiles and young adults' emotional adaptation. *Cultural Diversity and Ethnic Minority Psychology, 21*(3), 409–419. doi: 10.1037/a0037546

Duncan, L., Coatsworth, J. & Greenberg, M. (2009). A model of mindful parenting: Implications for parent–child relationships and prevention research. *Clinical Child and Family Psychology Review, 12*(3), 255–270. doi:10.1007/s10567-009-0046-3

Dunn, J. (2007). Siblings and socialization. In J. E. Grusec & P. D. Hastings (Eds.), *Handbook of socialization: Theory and research* (pp. 309–327). New York: Guilford.

Dunsmore, J. C. (2015). Effects of person- and process-focused feedback on prosocial behavior in middle childhood. *Social Development, 24*(1), 57–75. doi:10.1111/sode.12082

Dunsmore, J. C., Booker, J. A., Ollendick, T. H. & Greene, R. W. (2016). Emotion socialization in the context of risk and psychopathology: Maternal emotion coaching predicts better treatment outcomes for emotionally labile children with oppositional defiant disorder. *Social Development, 25*(1), 8–26. doi:10.1111/sode.12109

Eamon, M. K. (2001). The effects of poverty on children's socioemotional development: An ecological systems analysis. *Social Work, 46*(3), 256–266. doi:10.1093/sw/46.3.256

Eccles, J. S. (1999). The development of children ages 6 to 14. *The Future of Children, 9*(2), 30–44. doi:10.2307/1602703

Eisenberg, N., Cumberland, A. & Spinrad, T. L. (1998a). Parental socialization of emotion. *Psychological Inquiry, 9*(4), 241–273. doi:10.1207/s15327965pli0904_1

Eisenberg, N., Spinrad, T. L. & Cumberland, A. (1998b). The socialization of emotion: Reply to commentaries. *Psychological Inquiry, 9*(4), 317–333. doi: 10.1207/s15327965pli0904_17

Ekman, P. (1989). *Why kids lie: How parents can encourage truthfulness.* New York: Penguin.

Ekman, P. (1994). How are emotions distinguished from moods, temperament, and other related affective constructs? Moods, emotions, and traits. In P. Ekman & R. J. Davidson (Eds.), *Series in affective science. The nature of emotion: Fundamental questions* (pp. 56–58). New York: Oxford University Press.

Ekman, P. & Friesen, W. V. (1975). *Unmasking the face.* Englewood Cliffs, NJ: Prentice-Hall.

Ekman, P. & Friesen, W. V. (1978). *Facial action coding system: A technique for the measurement of facial movement.* Palo Alto, CA: Consulting Psychologists Press.

Ekman, P. (2003/2007). *Emotions revealed: Recognizing faces and feelings to improve communication and emotional life.* New York: St. Martin's Press.

Ekmekci, H., Yavuz-Muren, H. M., Emmen, R. A. G., Mesman, J., IJzendoorn, M. H., Yagmurlu, B. & Malda, M. (2015). Professionals' and mothers' beliefs about maternal sensitivity across cultures: Toward effective interventions in multicultural societies. *Journal of Child and Family Studies, 24*(5), 1295–1306. doi:10.1007/s10826-014-9937-0

Elder, G., H., Jr., Modell, J. & Parke, R. D. (1993). *Children in time and place: Developmental and historical insights*. New York: Cambridge University Press.

Elder, G. H., Jr. & Hareven, T. K. (1993). Rising above life's disadvantage: From the Great Depression to war. In G. H. Elder, Jr., J. Modell & R. D. Parke (Eds.), *Cambridge studies in social and emotional development. Children in time and place: Developmental and historical insights* (pp. 47–72). New York: Cambridge University Press.

Ellis, B. J., Boyce, W. T., Belsky, J., Bakermans-Kranenburg, M. J. & Van IJzendoorn, M. H. (2011). Differential susceptibility to the environment: An evolutionary–neurodevelopmental theory. *Development and Psychopathology, 23*(1), 7–8. doi:10.1017/S0954579410000611

Emmen, R. A. G., Malda, M., Mesman, J., Ekmekci, H. & van IJzendoorn, M. H. (2012). Sensitive parenting as a cross-cultural ideal: Sensitivity beliefs of Dutch, Moroccan, and Turkish mothers in the Netherlands. *Attachment & Human Development, 14*(6), 601–619. doi:10.1080/14616734.2012.727258

Engel, S. (1995). *The stories children tell: Making sense of the narratives of childhood.* New York: W.H. Freeman & Co.

Erickson, B. M. (2005). Scandinavian families: Plain and simple. In M. McGoldrick, J. Giordano & N. Garcia-Preto (Eds.), *Ethnicity and family therapy (3rd ed.)* (pp. 641–653). New York: Guilford.

Erikson, E. H. (1963). *Childhood and society (2nd ed.).* New York: Norton.

Esposito, J. L. (Ed.) (2003). *The Oxford dictionary of Islam.* New York: Oxford University Press.

European Union (2013). Eurostat-European Commission. Statistics explained archive. Vol. 2 – Social statistics, December 2012. Retrieved from http://ec.europa.eu/eurostat/documents/4031688/5930084/KS-FM-13-002-EN.PDF/37dc8192-c5df-49b3-98a6-2b005beb75bf?version=1.0

Evans, D. E. & Rothbart, M. K. (2007). Developing a model for adult temperament. *Journal of Research in Personality, 41*(4), 868–888. doi:10.1016/j.jrp.2006.11.002

Evans, K. M. & George, R. (2013). African Americans. In G. J. McAuliffe (Ed.), *Culturally alert counseling: A comprehensive introduction (2nd ed.)* (pp. 146–230). Thousand Oaks, CA: Sage.

Evans, L. D., Kouros, C., Frankel, S. A., McCauley, E., Diamond, G. S., Schloredt, K. A. & Garber, J. (2015). Longitudinal relations between stress and depressive symptoms in youth: Coping as a mediator. *Journal of Abnormal Child Psychology, 43*(2), 355–368. doi:10.1007/s10802-014-9906-5

Evans, L. D., Kouros, C. D., Samanez-Larkin, S. & Garber, J. (2016). Concurrent and short-term prospective relations among neurocognitive functioning, coping, and depressive symptoms in youth. *Journal of Clinical Child & Adolescent Psychology, 45*(1), 6–20. doi:10.1080/15374416.2014.982282

Fabes, R. (2002). *Emotions and the family*. New York: Haworth Press.

Fabes, R. A., Valiente, C. & Leonard, S. A. (2003). Introduction: Part 1: General family/marriage processes. *Marriage & Family Review, 34*(1–2), 3–11. doi:10.1300/J002v34n01_01

Fainsilber, L. & Ortony, A. (1987). Metaphorical uses of language in the expression of emotions. *Metaphor & Symbolic Activity*, *2*(4), 239–250. doi:10.1207/s15327868ms0204_2

Fanning, P. & McKay, M. (Eds.). (2000). *Family guide to emotional wellness*. Oakland, CA: New Harbinger Publications.

Farb, N. A. S., Anderson, A. K., Irving, J. A. & Segal, Z. V. (2014). Mindfulness interventions and emotion regulation. In J. J. Gross (Ed.), *Handbook of emotion regulation (2nd ed.)* (pp. 548–567). New York: Guilford Press.

Farver, J. A. M., Xu, Y., Eppe, S., Fernandez, A. & Schwartz, D. (2005). Community violence, family conflict, and preschoolers' socioemotional functioning. *Developmental Psychology*, *41*(1), 160–170. doi:10.1037/0012-1649.41.1.160

Feather, N. T. (2004). Value correlates of ambivalent attitudes toward gender relations. *Personality and Social Psychology Bulletin*, *30*, 3–12.

Feldman, B. J., Conger, R. D. & Burzette, R. G. (2004). Traumatic events, psychiatric disorders, and pathways of risk and resilience during the transition to adulthood. *Research in Human Development*, *1*(4), 259–290. doi:10.1207/s15427617rhd0104_3

Feldman, R. (2007). On the origins of background emotions: From affect synchrony to symbolic expression. *Emotion*, *7*(3), 601–611. doi:10.1037/1528-3542.7.3.601

Feldman, R., Bamberger, E. & Kanat-Maymon, Y. (2013). Parent-specific reciprocity from infancy to adolescence shapes children's social competence and dialogical skills. *Attachment & Human Development*, *15*(4), 407–423. doi:10.1080/14616734.2013.782650

Field, T. (1982). Affective displays of high-risk infants during early interactions. In T. Field & A. Fogel (Eds.), *Emotion and early interaction* (pp. 101–125). Hillsdale, NJ: Erlbaum.

Field, T., Healy, B., Goldstein, S. & Guthertz, M. (1990). Behavior-state matching and synchrony in mother-infant interactions of nondepressed versus depressed dyads. *Developmental Psychology*, *26*, 7–14.

Fiese, B. H., Sameroff, A. J., Grotevant, H. D., Wamboldt, F. S., Dickstein, S., Fravel, D. L., … Schiller, M. (1999). The stories that families tell: Narrative coherence, narrative interaction, and relationship beliefs. *Monographs of the Society for Research in Child Development*, *64*(2), 1–162. doi: 10.1111/1540-5834.00017

Fiese, B. H., Sameroff, A. J., Grotevant, H. D., Wamboldt, F. S., Dickstein, S. & Fravel, D. L. (2001). Observing families through the stories that they tell: A multidimensional approach. In P. Kerig & K. M. Lindahl (Eds.), *Family observational coding systems: Resources for systemic research*. Mahwah, NJ: Erlbaum.

Fiese, B. H. & Wamboldt, F. S. (2003). Coherent accounts of coping with a chronic illness: Convergences and divergences in family measurement using a narrative analysis. *Family Process*, *42*, 439–451.

Fitton, V. A. (2012). Attachment theory: History, research, and practice. *Psychoanalytic Social Work*, *19*(1–2), 121–143. doi:10.1080/15228878.2012.666491

Fitzgerald, J. M. (1996). The distribution of self-narrative memories in younger and older adults: Elaborating the self-narrative hypothesis. *Aging, Neuropsychology, and Cognition*, *3*(3), 229–236. doi:10.1080/13825589608256626

Fitzgerald, J. M. (2010). Culture, gender, and the first memories of black and white American students. *Memory & Cognition, 38*(6), 785–796. doi:10.3758/MC.38.6.785siegal

Fivush, R. (2011). The development of autobiographical memory. *Annual Review of Psychology, 62*, 559–582. doi: 10.1146/annurev.psych.121208.131702

Fivush, R., Brotman, M. A., Buckner, J. P. & Goodman, S. H. (2000). Gender differences in parent–child emotion narratives. *Sex Roles, 42*(3–4), 233–253. doi: 10.1023/A:1007091207068

Fivush, R., Haden, C. A. & Reese, E. (2006). Elaborating on elaborations: Role of maternal reminiscing style in cognitive and socioemotional development. *Child Development, 77*(6), 1568–1588. doi:10.1111/j.1467-8624.2006.00960.x

Fivush, R. & Nelson, K. (2004). Culture and language in the emergence of autobiographical memory. *Psychological Science, 15*(9), 573–577. doi: 10.1111/j.0956-7976.2004.00722.x

Fivush, R. & Nelson, K. (2006). Parent-child reminiscing locates the self in the past. *British Journal of Developmental Psychology, 24*(1), 235–251. doi:10.1348/02615 1005X57747

Fogel, A. & Thelen, E. (1987). Development of early expressive and communicative action: Reinterpreting the evidence from a dynamic systems perspective. *Developmental Psychology, 23*(6), 747–761. doi:10.1037/0012-1649.23.6.747

Foley, S., Kovacs, Z., Rose, J., Lamb, R., Tolliday, F., Simons-Coghill, M., … Sarten, T. (2013). International collaboration on prevention of shaken baby syndrome an ongoing project/intervention. *Paediatrics and International Child Health, 33*(4), 233–238. doi:10.1179/2046905513Y.0000000093

Folkman, S., Lazarus, R. S., Dunkel-Schetter, C., DeLongis, A. & Gruen, R. J. (1986). Dynamics of a stressful encounter: Cognitive appraisal, coping, and encounter outcomes. *Journal of Personality and Social Psychology, 50*(5), 992–1003. doi:10.1037/0022-3514.50.5.992

Fonagy, P., Gergely, G. & Target, M. (2008). Psychoanalytic constructs and attachment theory and research. In J. Cassidy & P. R. Shaver (Eds.), *Handbook of attachment: Theory, research, and clinical applications (2nd ed.)* (pp. 783–810). New York: Guilford Press.

Fosco, G. & Grych, J. (2013). Capturing the family context of emotion regulation: A family systems model comparison approach. *Journal of Family Issues, 34*(4), 557–578. doi:10.1177/0192513X12445889

Fox, N. A. & Calkins, S. D. (2000). Multiple-measure approaches to the study of infant emotion. In M. Lewis & J. M. Haviland-Jones (Eds.), *Handbook of emotions (2nd ed.)* (pp. 203–219). New York: Guilford.

Fox, N. A., Snidman, N., Haas, S. A., Degnan, K. A. & Kagan, J. (2015). The relations between reactivity at 4 months and behavioral inhibition in the second year: Replication across three independent samples. *Infancy, 20(1)*, 98–114. doi:10.1111/infa.12063

Francis, K. J. & Wolfe, D. A. (2008). Cognitive and emotional differences between abusive and non-abusive fathers. *Child Abuse & Neglect, 32*(12), 1127–1137. doi:10.1016/j.chiabu.2008.05.007

Franklin, J. C., Jamieson, J. P., Glenn, C. R. & Nock, M. K. (2015). How developmental psychopathology theory and research can inform the Research Domain Criteria (RDoC) project. *Journal of Clinical Child and Adolescent Psychology, 44*(2), 280–290. doi:10.1080/15374416.2013.873981

Franks, D. D. & Gecas, V. (1992). Autonomy and conformity in Cooley's self-theory: The looking-glass self and beyond. *Symbolic Interaction, 15(1),* 49–68.

Fredrickson, B. L. (1998). What good are positive emotions? *Review of General Psychology, 2*(3), 300–319. doi:10.1037/1089-2680.2.3.300

Fredrickson, B. L. (2001). The role of positive emotions in positive psychology: The broaden-and-build theory of positive emotions. *American Psychologist, 56*(3), 218–226. doi:10.1037/0003-066X.56.3.218

Fredrickson, B. L. (2003). The value of positive emotions: The emerging science of positive psychology is coming to understand why it's good to feel good. *American Scientist, 91*(4), 330–335.

Fredrickson, B. L. & Cohn, M. A. (2008). Positive emotions. In M. Lewis, J. M. Haviland-Jones & L. F. Barrett (Eds.), *Handbook of emotions (3rd ed.)* (pp. 777–796). New York: Guilford Press.

Freud, S. (1910). The origin and development of psychoanalysis. *The American Journal of Psychology, 21*(2), 181–218. doi: 10.2307/1413001

Freud, S. (1914). *Psychopathology of everyday life.* Originally published 1901; translated by Brill AA. London: T. Fisher Unwin.

Frijda, N. H. (2008). The psychologists' point of view. In M. Lewis, J. M. Haviland-Jones & L. F. Barrett (Eds.), *Handbook of emotions (3rd ed.)* (pp. 68–87). New York: Guilford.

Frijda, N. H. & Mesquita, B. (1994). The social roles and functions of emotions. In S. Kitayama & H. R. Markus (Eds.), *Emotion and culture: Empirical studies of mutual influence* (pp. 51–87). Washington, D.C.: American Psychological Association.

Frost, D. M. (2013). The narrative construction of intimacy and affect in relationship stories: Implications for relationship quality, stability, and mental health. *Journal of Social and* Personal Relationships, 30(3), 247–269. doi:10.1177/0265407512454463

Gagne, J. R., Miller, M. M. & Goldsmith, H. H. (2013). Early—but modest—gender differences in focal aspects of childhood temperament. *Personality and Individual Differences, 55*(2),95–100. doi:10.1016/j.paid.2013.02.006

Gambrel, L. E., Faas, C., Kaestle, C. E. & *Savla*, J. (2016). Interpersonal neurobiology and couple relationship quality: A longitudinal model. *Contemporary Family Therapy: An International Journal.* Advance online publication. doi:10.1007/s10591-016-9381-y

Gao, M. & Han, Z. R. (2016). Family expressiveness mediates the relation between cumulative family risks and children's emotion regulation in a Chinese sample. *Journal of Child and Family Studies, 25*(5), 1570–1580. doi:10.1007/s10826-015-0335-z

Garber, J. (1984). Classification of childhood psychopathology: A developmental perspective. *Child Development, 55*(1), 30–48. doi:10.2307/1129833

Garber, J. & Cole, D. A. (2010). Intergenerational transmission of depression: A launch and grow model of change across adolescence. *Development and Psychopathology, 22*(4), 819–830.doi:10.1017/S0954579410000489

Gardner, R. A. (1992). *The psychotherapeutic techniques of Richard A. Gardner (Rev. ed.).* Creskill, NJ: Creative Therapeutics.

Garmezy, N. (1991). Resilience and vulnerability to adverse developmental outcomes associated with poverty. *American Behavioral Scientist, 34*(4), 416–430. doi:10.1177/0002764291034004003

Garner, P. W. (1995). Toddlers' emotion regulation behaviors: The roles of social context and family expressiveness. *The Journal of Genetic Psychology: Research and Theory on Human Development, 156*(4), 417–430. doi:10.1080/00221325.1995.9914834

Garrett, M. T., Garrett, J. T., Grayshield, L., Williams, C., Portman, T. A. A., Rivera, E. T., King, G., Ogletree, T., Parrish, M. & Kawulich, B. (2013). Culturally alert counseling with Native Americans. In G. J. McAuliffe (Ed.), *Culturally alert counseling: A comprehensive introduction (2nd ed.)* (pp. 185–230). Thousand Oaks, CA: Sage.

Garrod, A. C., Smulyan, L., Powers, S. I. & Kilkenny, R. (2012). *Adolescent portraits: Identity, relationships, and challenges, 7th ed.* Boston, MA: Pearson Education.

Gaskins, S. (2013). The puzzle of attachment: Unscrambling maturational and cultural contributions to the development of early emotional bonds. In N. Quinn & J. M. Mageo (Eds.), *Culture, mind, and society. Attachment reconsidered: Cultural perspectives on a Western theory* (pp. 33–64). doi:10.1057/9781137386724.0005

Gershoff, E. T., Grogan-Kaylor, A., Lansford, J. E., Chang, L., Zelli, A., Deater-Deckard, K., Dodge, K. A. & Dodge, K. A. (2010). Parent discipline practices in an International sample: Associations with child behaviors and moderation by perceived normativeness. *Child Development, 81*(2), 487–502. doi: 10.1111/j.1467-8624.2009.01409.x

Gilbert, D. (2006). *Stumbling on happiness.* New York: Alfred A. Knopf.

Giordano, J. & McGoldrick, M. (1996). European families: An overview. In M. McGoldrick, J. Giordano & J. K. Pearce (Eds.), *Ethnicity and family therapy (2nd ed.)* (pp. 427–441). New York: Guilford.

Gleser, G. C. & Ihilevich, D. (1969). An objective instrument for measuring defense mechanisms. *Journal of Consulting and Clinical Psychology, 33*(1), 51–60. doi:10.1037/h0027381

Glick, P. & Fiske, S. T. (2001). An ambivalent alliance: Hostile and benevolent sexism as complementary justifications for gender inequality. *American Psychologist, 56*, 109–118.

Goddard, C. (2014). Interjections and emotion (with special reference to "surprise" and "disgust"). *Emotion Review, 6(1)*, 53–63. doi: 10.1177/1754073913491843

Goldsmith, H. H., Buss, A. H., Plomin, R., Rothbart, M. K., Thomas, A., Chess, S., Hinde, R. & McCall, R. B. (1987). What is temperament? Four approaches. *Child Development*, 58(2),*505–529*. doi:10.2307/1130527

Goodwin, C. J. (2010). *Annotated readings in the history of modern psychology.* Hoboken, NJ: Wiley.

Goodwin, C. J. (2015). *A history of modern psychology (5th ed.).* Hoboken, NJ: Wiley.

Goodnow, J. J. & Collins, W. A. (1990). *Essays in developmental psychology series. Development according to parents: The nature, sources, and consequences of parents' ideas.* Hillsdale, NJ: Erlbaum.

Gosling, S. D., Vazire, S., Srivastava, S., John, O. P. (2004). Should we trust web-based studies? A comparative analysis of six preconceptions about internet questionnaires. *American Psychologist, 59*, 93–104.

Gottlieb, G. (1991). Experiential canalization of behavioral development: Theory. *Developmental Psychology, 27(1)*, 4–13. doi:10.1037/0012-1649.27.1.4

Gottlieb, G. & Lickliter, R. (2007). Probabilistic epigenesis. *Developmental Science, 10*(1), 1–11. doi:10.1111/j.1467-7687.2007.00556.x

Gottman, J. M. (1980). Consistency of nonverbal affect and affect reciprocity in marital interaction. *Journal of Consulting and Clinical Psychology, 48*(6), 711–717. doi: 10.1037/0022-006X.48.6.711

Gottman, J. (with J. DeClaire) (1997). *The heart of parenting: Raising an emotionally intelligent child.* New York: Simon & Schuster.

Gottman, J. M. (2011). *The science of trust: Emotional attunement for couples.* New York: Norton.

Gottman, J. M., Katz, L. F. & Hooven, C. (1996). Parental meta-emotion philosophy and the emotional life of families: Theoretical models and preliminary data. *Journal of Family Psychology, 10*, 243–268.

Gottman, J. M., Katz, L. F. & Hooven, C. (1997). *Meta-emotion: How families communicate emotionally.* NJ: Erlbaum.

Gottman, J. M. & Levenson, R. W. (2002). A two-factor model for predicting when a couple will divorce: Exploratory analyses using 14-year longitudinal data. *Family Process, 41(1)*, 83–96. doi:10.1111/j.1545-5300.2002.40102000083.x

Government of Canada, Aboriginal Affairs and Northern Development Canada (2014). *First Nations people in Canada.* Retrieved from www.aadnc-aandc.gc.ca/eng/1303134042666/1303134337338

Gralinski, J. H. & Kopp, C. B. (1993). Everyday rules for behavior: Mothers' requests to young children. *Developmental Psychology, 29*(3), 573–584. doi: 10.1037/0012-1649.29.3.573

Granic, I. (2005). Timing is everything: Developmental psychopathology from a dynamic systems perspective. *Developmental Review, 25*(3–4), 386–407. doi:10.1016/j.dr.2005.10.005

Greenberg, L. S. (1993). Emotion and change processes in psychotherapy. In M. Lewis & J. M. Haviland (Eds.), *Handbook of emotions* (pp. 499–508). New York: Guilford Press.

Greenberg, L. S. (2008). The clinical application of emotion in psychotherapy. In M. Lewis, J. M. Haviland-Jones & L. F. Barrett (Eds.), *Handbook of emotions (3rd ed.)* (pp. 88–101). New York: Guilford Press.

Greenberg, L. S. & Pascual-Leone, A. (2006). Emotion in psychotherapy: A practice-friendly research review. *Journal of Clinical Psychology, 62*(5), 611–630. doi:10.1002/jclp.20252

Greene, R. W. & Doyle, A. E. (1999). Toward a transactional conceptualization of oppositional defiant disorder: Implications for assessment and treatment. *Clinical Child and Family Psychology Review, 2*(3), 129–148. doi:10.1023/A:1021850921476

Greenspan, S. I. & Porges, S. W. (1984). Psychopathology in infancy and early childhood: Clinical perspectives on the organization of sensory and affective-thematic experience. *Child Development, 55*(1), 49–70. doi:10.2307/1129834

Greenstein, T. (2006). *Methods of family research (2nd ed.)*. Thousand Oaks, CA: Sage. doi: 10.4135/9781412990233

Griffith, V. (2005). *Dr. James Pennebaker: Writing to heal.* Office of Public Affairs, University of Texas at Austin. Retrieved from www.utexas.edu/features/2005/writing/

Griffiths, M. (2003). The therapeutic use of videogames in childhood and adolescence. *Clinical Child Psychology and Psychiatry, 8*, 547–554.

Griffiths, P. E. & Tabery, J. (2008). Behavioral genetics and development: Historical and conceptual causes of controversy. *New Ideas in Psychology, 26(3)*, 332–352. doi:10.1016/j.newideapsych.2007.07.016

Gross, J. J. (2008). Emotion regulation. In M. Lewis, J. M. Haviland-Jones & L. F. Barrett (Eds.), *Handbook of emotions (3rd ed.)* (pp. 497–512). New York: Guilford Press.

Gross, J. J. (2014). Emotion regulation: Conceptual and empirical foundations. In J. J. Gross (Ed.), *Handbook of emotion regulation (2nd ed.)* (pp. 3–20). New York: Guilford Press.

Gross, J. J. & Thompson, R. A. (2007). Emotion regulation: Conceptual foundations. In J. J. Gross (Ed.), *Handbook of emotion regulation* (pp. 3–24). New York: Guilford Press.

Grossman, A. W., Churchill, J. D., McKinney, B. C., Kodish, I. M., Otte, S. L. & Greenough, W. T. (2003). Experience effects on brain development: Possible contributions to psychopathology. *Journal of Child Psychology and Psychiatry, 44*(1), 33–63. doi:10.1111/1469-7610.t01-1-00102

Grühn, D., Lumley, M. A., Diehl, M. & Labouvie-Vief, G. (2013). Time-based indicators of emotional complexity: Interrelations and correlates. *Emotion, 13*(2), 226–237. doi: 10.1037/a0030363

Grusec, J. E. & Davidov, M. (2007). Socialization in the family: The roles of parents. In J. E. Grusec & P. D. Hastings (Eds.), *Handbook of socialization: Theory and research* (pp. 284–308). New York: Guilford.

Grusec, J. E. & Davidov, M. (2010). Integrating different perspectives on socialization theory and research: A domain-specific approach. *Child Development, 81*(3), 687–709. doi:10.1111/j.1467-8624.2010.01426.x

Grusec, J. E. & Davidov, M. (2015). Analyzing socialization from a domain-specific perspective. In J. E. Grusec & P. D. Hastings (Eds.), *Handbook of socialization: Theory and research (2nd ed.)* (pp. 158–181). New York: Guilford.

Grusec, J. E., Goodnow, J. J. & Kuczynski, L. (2000). New directions in analyses of parenting contributions to children's acquisition of values. *Child Development, 71*(1), 205–211. doi:10.1111/1467-8624.00135

Grusec, J. E., Hastings, P. & Mammone, N. (1994). Parenting cognitions and relationship schemas. In J. G. Smetana (Ed.), *New directions for child development, No. 66. Beliefs about parenting: Origins and developmental implications* (pp. 5–19). San Francisco: Jossey-Bass.

Grysman, A. & Hudson, J. A. (2013). Gender differences in autobiographical memory: Developmental and methodological considerations. *Developmental Review, 33*(3), 239–272. doi:10.1016/j.dr.2013.07.004

Gudykunst, W. B., Matsumoto, Y., Ting-Toomey, S. & Nishida, T. (1996). The influence of cultural individualism-collectivism, self construals, and individual values on communication styles across cultures. *Human Communication Research, 22*(4), 510–543. doi:10.1111/j.1468-2958.1996.tb00377.x

Guindon, M. H. (2002). Toward accountability in the use of the self-esteem construct. *Journal of Counseling & Development, 80*(2), 204–214.

Guindon, M. H. (Ed.). (2010). *Self-esteem across the lifespan: Issues and interventions.* New York: Routledge/Taylor & Francis Group.

Gump, B. B., Matthews, K. A. & Räikkönen, K. (1999). Modeling relationships among socioeconomic status, hostility, cardiovascular reactivity, and left ventricular mass in African American and White children. *Health Psychology, 18*(2), 140–150. doi:10.1037/0278-6133.18.2.140

Hakim-Larson, J. & Hobart, C. J. (1987). Maternal regulation and adolescent autonomy: Mother-daughter resolution of story conflicts. *Journal of Youth and Adolescence, 16*(2), 153–166. doi:10.1007/BF02138917

Hakim-Larson, J. & Nassar-McMillan, S. C. (2008). Middle Eastern Americans and counseling. In G. McAuliffe (Ed.), *Culturally alert counseling: A comprehensive introduction* (pp. 293–322). Thousand Oaks: Sage.

Hakim-Larson, J., Parker, A., Lee, C., Goodwin, J. & Voelker, S. (2006). Measuring parental meta-emotion: Psychometric properties of the Emotion-Related Parenting Styles Self-Test. *Early Education and Development, 17*(2), 229–251. doi:10.1207/s15566935eed1702_2

Hakim-Larson, J., Dunham, K., Vellet, S., Murdaca, L. & Levenbach, J. (1999). Parental affect and coping. *Canadian Journal of Behavioural Science/Revue canadienne des sciences du comportement,* 31(1),5–18. doi:10.1037/h0087069

Hakim-Larson, J. & Mruk, C. (1997). Enhancing self-esteem in a community mental health setting. *American Journal of Orthopsychiatry, 67*(4), 655–659. doi:10.1037/h0080264

Hakim-Larson, J., Nassar-McMillan, S. & Paterson, A. D. (2013). Culturally alert counseling with Middle Eastern Americans. In G. McAuliffe (Ed.), *Culturally alert counseling: A comprehensive introduction (2nd ed.)* (pp. 293–322). Thousand Oaks, CA: Sage.

Hakoyama, M. & MaloneBeach, E. E. (2013). Predictors of grandparent–grandchild closeness: An ecological perspective. *Journal of Intergenerational Relationships, 11*(1), 32–49. doi:10.1080/15350770.2013.753834

Halberstadt, A. G. (1986). Family socialization of emotional expression and nonverbal communication styles and skills. *Journal of Personality and Social Psychology, 51*(4), 827–836. doi:10.1037/0022-3514.51.4.827

Halberstadt, A. G., Cassidy, J., Stifter, C. A., Parke, R. D. & Fox, N. A. (1995). Self-expressiveness within the family context: Psychometric support for a new measure. *Psychological Assessment, 7*(1), 93–103. doi: 10.1037/1040-3590.7.1.93

Halberstadt, A. G., Denham, S. A. & Dunsmore, J. C. (2001). Affective social competence. *Social Development, 10*, 79–119.

Halberstadt, A. G., Dennis, P. A. & Hess, U. (2011). The influence of family expressiveness, individuals' own emotionality, and self-expressiveness on perceptions of others' facial expressions. *Journal of Nonverbal Behavior, 35*(1), 35–50. doi:10.1007/s10919-010-0099-5

Halberstadt, A. G., Dunsmore, J. C., Bryant, A., Jr., Parker, A. E., Beale, K. S. & Thompson, J. A. (2013). Development and validation of the Parents' Beliefs About Children's Emotions Questionnaire. *Psychological Assessment, 25*(4), 1195–1210. doi:10.1037/a0033695

Halberstadt, A. G. & Eaton, K. L. (2002). A meta-analysis of family expressiveness and children's emotion expressiveness and understanding. In R. A. Fabes (Ed.), *Emotions and the family* (pp. 35–62). Binghampton, NY: Haworth.

Hall, E. T. (1976). *Beyond culture*. New York: Doubleday.

Hall, J. A., Carter, J. D. & Horgan, J. G. (2000). Gender differences in nonverbal communication of emotion. In A. H. Fischer (Ed.), *Studies in emotion and social interaction. Second series. Gender and emotion: Social psychological perspectives* (pp. 97–117). New York: Cambridge University Press.

Hamner, T. & Turner, P. H. (1996). *Parenting in contemporary society (3rd ed.)*. Boston: Allyn & Bacon.

Hardy, K. V. & Laszloffy, T. A. (1995). The cultural genogram: Key to training culturally competent family therapists. *Journal of Marital and Family Therapy, 21*, 227–237.

Harkins, D. A. (1993). Parent goals and styles of storytelling. In J. Demick, K. Bursik & R. DiBiase (Eds.), *Parental development* (pp. 61–74). Hillsdale, NJ: Erlbaum.

Harkness, S. & Super, C. M. (Eds.) (1996). *Parents' cultural belief systems: Their origins, expressions, and consequences*. New York: Guilford.

Harrigan, M. M. (2010). Exploring the narrative process: An analysis of the adoption stories mothers tell their internationally adopted children. *Journal of Family Communication, 10*(1), 24–39. doi:10.1080/15267430903385875

Harris, P. L. (1989). *Children and emotion: The development of psychological understanding.* Cambridge, MA: Basil Blackwell.

Harter, S. (1985). *The self-perception profile for children.* Unpublished manual, University of Denver, Denver, CO.

Harter, S. (1988). *The self-perception profile for adolescents.* Unpublished manual, University of Denver, Denver, CO.

Harter, S. (2012). *The construction of the self: Developmental and sociocultural foundations (2nd. ed).* New York: Guilford Press.

Harter, S. & Buddin, B. J. (1987). Children's understanding of the simultaneity of two emotions: A five-stage developmental acquisition sequence. *Developmental Psychology, 23*(3), 388–399. doi: 10.1037/0012-1649.23.3.388

Harter, S., Bresnick, S., Bouchey, H. A. & Whitesell, N. R. (1997). The development of multiple role-related selves during adolescence. *Development and Psychopathology, 9*(4), 835–853. doi:10.1017/S0954579497001466

Harter, S., Low, S. M. & Whitesell, N. R. (2003). What have we learned from Columbine: The impact of the self-system on suicidal and violent ideation among adolescents. *Journal of School Violence, 2(3),* 3–26.

Harter, S., Marold, D. B. & Whitesell, N. R. (1992). Model of psychosocial risk factors leading to suicidal ideation in young adolescents. *Development and Psychopathology, 4*(1), 167–188. doi:10.1017/S0954579400005629

Harter, S., Waters, P. & Whitesell, N. R. (1998). Relational self-worth: Differences in perceived worth as a person across interpersonal contexts among adolescents. *Child Development, 69*(3), 756–766. doi:10.2307/1132202

Harter, S. & Whitesell, N. R. (1989). Developmental changes in children's understanding of single, multiple, and blended emotion concepts. In C. Saarni & P. L. Harris (Eds.), *Cambridge studies in social and emotional development. Children's understanding of emotion* (pp. 81–116). New York: Cambridge University Press.

Harwood, R. L. (1992). The influence of culturally derived values on Anglo and Puerto Rican mothers' perceptions of attachment behavior. *Child Development, 63*(4), 822–839. doi:10.2307/1131236

Hawley, D. R. (2000). Clinical implications of family resilience. *The American Journal of Family Therapy, 28*(2), 101–116. doi:10.1080/019261800261699

Hawley, D. R. & DeHaan, L. (1996). Toward a definition of family resilience: Integrating Life-Span and family perspectives. *Family Process, 35*(3), 283–298. doi:10.1111/j.1545-5300.1996.00283.x

Hess, U., Houde, S. & Fischer, A. (2014). Do we mimic what we see or what we know? In C. von Scheve & M. Salmela (Eds.), *Series in affective science. Collective emotions: Perspectives from psychology, philosophy, and sociology* (pp. 94–107). doi:10.1093/acprof:oso/9780199659180.003.0007

Hesse, E. & Main, M. (2000). Disorganized infant, child, and adult attachment: Collapse in behavioral and attentional strategies. *Journal of the American Psychoanalytic Association, 48*(4), 1097–1127. doi:10.1177/00030651000480041101

Heubeck, B. G., Butcher, P. R., Thorneywork, K. & Wood, J. (2016). Loving and angry? Happy and sad? Understanding and reporting of mixed emotions in mother–child relationships by 6- to 12-year-olds. *British Journal of Developmental Psychology, 34*(2), 245–260. doi: 10.1111/bjdp.12128

Hochberg, T. (2010). Other rituals: Parents' stories of meaning making [DVD]. Other rituals©Todd Hochberg. All rights reserved. Available from www.toddhochberg.com

Hoffman, M. L. (2008). Empathy and prosocial behavior. In M. Lewis, J. M. Haviland-Jones & L. F. Barrett (Eds.), *Handbook of emotions (3rd ed.)* (pp. 440–455). New York: Guilford Press.

Holodynski, M. (2013). The internalization theory of emotions: A cultural historical approach to the development of emotions. *Mind, Culture, and Activity, 20*(1), 4–38. doi:10.1080/10749039.2012.745571

Holodynski, M. & Friedlmeier, W. (2005). *Development of emotions and emotion regulation*. New York: Springer.

Holahan, C. K., Holahan, C. J., Velasquez, K. E. & North, R. J. (2008). Longitudinal change in happiness during aging: The predictive role of positive expectancies. *The International Journal of Aging & Human Development, 66*(3), 229–241. doi:10.2190/AG.66.3.d

Hooghe, A. & Neimeyer, R. A. (2013). Family resilience in the wake of loss: A meaning-oriented contribution. In D. S. Becvar (Ed.), *Handbook of family resilience* (pp. 269–284). New York: Springer. doi: 10.1007/978-1-4614-3917-2_16

Hopkins, K. D., Taylor, C. L., D'Antoine, H. & Zubrick, S. R. (2012). Predictors of resilient psychosocial functioning in Western Australian aboriginal young people exposed to high family-level risk. In M. Ungar (Ed.), *The social ecology of resilience: A handbook of theory and practice* (pp. 425–440). New York: Springer.

Hughes, D. & Johnson, D. (2001). Correlates in children's experiences of parents' racial socialization behaviors. *Journal of Marriage and Family, 63*(4), 981–995. doi:10.1111/j.1741-3737.2001.00981.x

Huth-Bocks, A. C., Muzik, M., Beeghly, M., Earls, L. & Stacks, A. M. (2014). Secure base scripts are associated with maternal parenting behavior across contexts and reflective functioning among trauma-exposed mothers. *Attachment & Human Development, 16*(6), 535–556. doi:10.1080/14616734.2014.967787

Hy, L. X. & Loevinger, J. (1996). *Measuring ego development (2nd ed.)*. Hillsdale, NJ: Erlbaum.

Ingram, R. E. & Price, J. M. (Eds.). (2001). *Vulnerability to psychopathology: Risk across the lifespan*. New York: Guilford Press.

International Labour Organization (2016). *About the International Programme on the Elimination of Chid Labour (IPEC)*. Retrieved from www.ilo.org/ipec/programme/lang--en/index.htm

Isen, A. M. (1993). Positive affect and decision making. In M. Lewis & J. M. Haviland (Eds.), *Handbook of emotions* (pp. 261–277). New York: Guilford Press.

Izard, C. E. (1993). Organizational and motivational functions of discrete emotions. In M. Lewis & J. M. Haviland (Eds.), *Handbook of emotions* (pp. 631–641). New York: The Guilford Press.

Izard, C. E. & Abe, J. A. (2004). Developmental changes in facial expressions of emotions in the Strange Situation during the second year of life. *Emotion, 4,* 251–265.

Izard, C. E. & Ackerman, B. P. (2000). Motivational, organizational, and regulatory functions of discrete emotions. In M. Lewis & J. M. Haviland-Jones (Eds.), *Handbook of emotions (2nd ed.)* (pp. 253–264). New York: Guilford.

Jaffee, S. R., Moffitt, T. E., Caspi, A. & Taylor, A. (2003). Life with (or without) father: The benefits of living with two biological parents depend on the father's antisocial behavior. *Child Development, 74*(1), 109–126. doi:10.1111/1467-8624.t01-1-00524

James, W. (1890/2013). *The principles of psychology.* Oxford, England: Dover Publications.

James, B. (1994). *Handbook for treatment of attachment-trauma problems in children.* New York: Lexington.

Jamil, H., Hakim-Larson, J., Farrag, M., Kafaji, T., Duqum, I. & Jamil, L. H. (2002). A retrospective study of Arab American mental health clients: Trauma and the Iraqi refugees. *American Journal of Orthopsychiatry, 72*(3), 355–361. doi:10.1037/0002-9432.72.3.355

Jarrett, C. (2012). *Mirror neurons: The most hyped concept in neuroscience?* Retrieved from www.psychologytoday.com/blog/brain-myths/201212/mirror-neurons-the-most-hyped-concept-in-neuroscience

Jarrett, C. (2013). A calm look at the most hyped concept in neuroscience – Mirror neurons. *Brain Watch.* Retrieved from www.wired.com/2013/12/a-calm-look-at-the-most-hyped-concept-in-neuroscience-mirror-neurons/

Jespersen, K., Kroger, J. & Martinussen, M. (2013). Identity status and ego development: A meta-analysis. *Identity: An International Journal of Theory and Research, 13*(3), 228–241. doi:10.1080/15283488.2013.799433

John, O. P. & Eng, J. (2014). Three approaches to individual differences in affect regulation: Conceptualizations, measures, and findings. In J. J. Gross (Ed.), *Handbook of emotion regulation (2nd ed.)* (pp. 321–345). New York: Guilford Press.

John, O. P. & Srivastava, S. (1999). The Big Five Trait taxonomy: History, measurement, and theoretical perspectives. In L. A. Pervin & O. P. John (Eds.), *Handbook of personality: Theory and research (2nd ed.)* (pp. 102–138). New York: Guilford.

Johnson, S. M. (2008). Emotionally focused couple therapy. In A. S. Gurman (Ed.), *Clinical handbook of couple therapy (4th ed.)* (pp. 107–137). New York: Guilford Press.

Johnson, S. & Capdevila, R. (2014). "That's just what's expected of you … so you do it": Mothers discussions around choice and the MMR vaccination. *Psychology & Health, 29*(8), 861–876. doi:10.1080/08870446.2014.892940

Johnson-Laird, P. N. & Oatley, K. (1989). The language of emotions: An analysis of a semantic field. *Cognition and Emotion, 3*(2), 81–123. doi: 10.1080/02699938908408075

Jones, T. L. & Prinz, R. J. (2005). Potential roles of parental self-efficacy in parent and child adjustment: A review. *Clinical Psychology Review, 25*(3), 341–363. doi:10.1016/j.cpr.2004.12.004

Jongsma, A. E., Peterson, L. M. & McInnis, W. P. (1996). *The child and adolescent psychotherapy treatment planner*. New York: Wiley.

Judge, T. A. & Bono, J. E. (2001). Relationship of core self-evaluations traits—self-esteem, generalized self-efficacy, locus of control, and emotional stability—with job satisfaction and job performance: A meta-analysis. *Journal of Applied Psychology, 86*(1), 80–92. doi:10.1037/0021-9010.86.1.80

Kabat-Zinn, J. (2015). Mindfulness. *Mindfulness, 6*(6), 1481–1483. doi:10.1007/s12671-015-0456-x

Kagan, J. (1994). *Galen's prophecy: Temperament in human nature*. New York: Basic.

Kaminski, J. W., Valle, L. A., Filene, J. H., Boyle, C. L. (2008). A meta-analytic review of components associated with parent training program effectiveness. *Journal of Abnormal Child Psychology, 36(4)*, 567–589. doi: 10.1007/s10802-007-9201-9

Karney, B. R. & Bradbury, T. N. (1995). The longitudinal course of marital quality and stability: A review of theory, methods, and research. *Psychological Bulletin, 118*(1), 3–34. doi:10.1037/0033-2909.118.1.3

Kaslow, F. W. (2013). Divorced fathers and their families: Legal, economic, and emotional dilemmas. New York: Springer. doi:10.1007/978-1-4614-5535-6

Katz, L. F., Maliken, A. C. & Stettler, N. M. (2012). Parental meta-emotion philosophy: A review of research and theoretical framework. *Child Development Perspectives, 6*(4), 417–422.

Katz, L., Stettler, N. & Gurtovenko, K. (2016). Traumatic stress symptoms in children exposed to intimate partner violence: The role of parent emotion socialization and children's emotion regulation abilities. *Social Development, 25*(1), 47–65. doi:10.1111/sode.12151

Katz, L. F. & Windecker-Nelson, B. (2006). Domestic violence, emotion coaching, and child adjustment. *Journal of Family Psychology, 20*(1), 56–67. doi:10.1037/0893-3200.20.1.56

Kaufman, J., Gelernter, J., Hudziak, J. J., Tyrka, A. R. & Coplan, J. D. (2015). The Research Domain Criteria (RDoC) project and studies of risk and resilience in maltreated children. *Journal of the American Academy of Child & Adolescent Psychiatry, 54*(8), 617–625. doi:10.1016/j.jaac.2015.06.001

Kaye, L. K., Malone, S. A. & Wall, H. J. (2017). Emojis: Insights, affordances, and possibilities for psychological science. *Trends in Cognitive Sciences, 21*(2), 66–68. doi:10.1016/j.tics.2016.10.007

Kazdin, A. E. (Ed.). (1998). *Methodological issues & strategies in clinical research (2nd ed.)*. Washington, D.C.: American Psychological Association.

Kazdin, A. E. & Weisz, J. R. (1998). Identifying and developing empirically supported child and adolescent treatments. *Journal of Consulting and Clinical Psychology, 66*(1), 19–36. doi:10.1037/0022-006X.66.1.19

Keating, D. P. (2016). Transformative role of epigenetics in child development research: Commentary on the special section. *Child Development, 87*(1), 135–142. doi:10.1111/cdev.12488

Keating, D. P. (2017). *Born anxious: The lifelong impact of early life adversity – and how to break the cycle.* New York: St. Martin's Press.

Kellas, J. K. (2005). Family ties: Communicating identity through jointly told family stories. *Communication Monographs, 72*(4), 365–389. doi: 10.1080/03637750500322453

Kellas, J. K. & Trees, A. R. (2006). Finding meaning in difficult family experiences: Sense-making and interaction processes during joint family storytelling. *Journal of Family Communication, 6*(1), 49–76. doi:10.1207/s15327698jfc0601_4

Keller, H. (2013). Attachment and culture. *Journal of Cross-Cultural Psychology, 44*(2), 175–194. doi:10.1177/0022022112472253

Keltner, D. & Ekman, P. (2000). Facial expression of emotion. In M. Lewis & J. M. Haviland-Jones (Eds.), *Handbook of emotions (2nd ed.)* (pp. 236–249). New York: The Guilford Press.

Keppel, B. (2002). Kenneth B. Clark in the patterns of American culture. *American Psychologist, 57(1)*, 29–37. doi: 10.1037/0003-066X.57.1.29

Kerig, P. K. (2001). Introduction and overview: Conceptual issues in family observtional research. In P. K Kerig & K. M Lindahl (Eds.), *Family observational coding systems* (pp. 1–22). Mahwah, NJ: Lawrence Erlbaum.

Kerig, P. K. & Lindahl, K. M. (Eds.) (2001). *Family observational coding systems: Resources for systemic research.* Mahwah, NJ: Erlbaum.

Keyes, E. F. (2000). Mental health status in refugees: An integrative review of current research. *Issues in Mental Health Nursing, 21*(4), 397–410. doi: 10.1080/016128400248013

Kilner, J. M. & Lemon, R. N. (2013). What we know currently about mirror neurons. *Current Biology, 23, R1057–R1062.* doi:dx.doi.org/10.1016/j.cub.2013.10.051

Kim, B. S. K. & Park, Y. S. (2013). East and Southeast Asian Americans. In G. McAuliffe (Ed.), *Culturally alert counseling: A comprehensive introduction (2nd ed.).* (pp. 188–219). Thousand Oaks, CA: Sage.

King, L. A. & Hicks, J. A. (2006). Narrating the self in the past and the future: Implications for maturity. *Research in Human Development, 3*(2–3), 121–138. 10.1207/s15427617rhd0302&3_4

King, L. A. & Mitchell, G. L. (2015). Lost possible selves and personality development. In K. E. Cherry (Ed.), *Traumatic stress and long-term recovery: Coping with disasters and other negative life events* (pp. 309–325). Cham, Switzerland: Springer International Publishing.

King, L. A. & Patterson, C. (2000). Reconstructing life goals after the birth of a child with Down Syndrome: Finding happiness and growing. *International Journal of Rehabilitation & Health*, *5*(1), 17–30. doi:10.1023/A:1012955018489

King, L. A. & Raspin, C. (2004). Lost and found possible selves, subjective well-being, and ego development in divorced women. *Journal of Personality*, *72*(3), 603–632. doi:10.1111/j.0022-3506.2004.00274.x

King, L. A. & Smith, N. G. (2004). Gay and straight possible selves: Goals, identity, subjective well-being, and personality development. *Journal of Personality*, *72*(5), 967–994. doi:10.1111/j.0022-3506.2004.00287.x

Kira, I. A., Amer, M. M. & Wrobel, N. H. (2014). Arab refugees: Trauma, resilience, and recovery. In S. C. Nassar-McMillan, K. J. Ajrouch & J. Hakim-Larson (Eds.), *Biopsychosocial perspectives on Arab Americans: Culture, development, and health* (pp. 175–195). doi:10.1007/978-1-4614-8238-3_9

Kirmayer, L., Simpson, C. & Cargo, M. (2003). Healing traditions: Culture, community and mental health promotion with Canadian Aboriginal peoples. *Australasian Psychiatry*, *11* Supplement, S15–S23.

Kitayama & H. R. Markus (Eds.) (1994). *Emotion and culture: Empirical studies of mutual influence*. Washington, D.C.: American Psychological Association.

Klimes-Dougan, B. & Garber, J. (2016). Regulatory control and depression in adolescents: Findings from neuroimaging and neuropsychological research. *Journal of Clinical Child and Adolescent Psychology*, *45*(1), 1–5. doi:10.1080/15374416.2015.1123637

Kochanska, G. (1997). Multiple pathways to conscience for children with different temperaments: From toddlerhood to age 5. *Developmental Psychology*, *33(2)*, 228–240. doi:10.1037/0012-1649.33.2.228

Kochanska, G., Brock, R. L., Chen, K.-H., Aksan, N. & Anderson, S. W. (2015). Paths from mother-child and father-child relationships to externalizing behavior problems in children differing in electrodermal reactivity: A longitudinal study from infancy to age 10. *Journal of Abnormal Child Psychology*, *43*(4), 721–734. doi:10.1007/s10802-014-9938-x

Kochanska, G., Friesenborg, A. F., Lange, L. A. & Martel, M. M. (2004). Parents' personality and infants' temperament as contributors to their emerging relationship. *Journal of Personality and Social Psychology*, *86*, 744–759. doi:10.1037/0022-3514.86.5.744

Kohlberg, L., Yaeger, J. & Hjertholm, E. (1968). Private speech: Four studies and a review of theories. *Child Development*, *39*(3), 691–736. doi:10.2307/1126979

Kopp, C. B. (1982). Antecedents of self-regulation: A developmental perspective. *Developmental Psychology*, *18*(2), 199–214. doi:10.1037/0012-1649.18.2.199

Kovecses, Z. (2000). *Metaphor and emotion: Language, culture, and body in human feeling. studies in emotion and social interaction second series*. Cambridge, MA: Cambridge University Press.

Kramer, L. (2014). Learning emotional understanding and emotion regulation through sibling interaction. *Early Education and Development*, *25*(2), 160–184. doi:10.1080/10409289.2014.838824

Kranstuber, H., Carr, K. & Hosek, A. M. (2012). "If you can dream it, you can achieve it." Parent memorable messages as indicators of college student success. *Communication Education, 61*(1), 44–66. doi:10.1080/03634523.2011.620617

Kraut, R., Olson, J., Banaji, M., Bruckman, A., Cohen, J. & Couper, M. (2003). *Psychological Research Online: Opportunities and challenges.* Retrieved from the website of the American Psychological Association, www.apa.org.

Kraut, R., Olson, J., Banaji, M., Bruckman, A., Cohen, J. & Couper, M. (2004). Psychological research online: Report of Board of Scientific Affairs' Advisory Group on the conduct of research on the internet. *American Psychologist, 59,* 105–117.

Kreutzer, J. S., Mills, A. & Marwitz, J. H. (2016). Ambiguous loss and emotional recovery after traumatic brain injury. *Journal of Family Theory & Review, 8*(3), 386–397. doi:10.1111/jftr.12150

Kuczynski, L. & Kochanska, G. (1995). Function and content of maternal demands: Developmental significance of early demands for competent action. *Child Development, 66(3),* 616–628. doi:10.2307/1131938

Labella, M. H., Narayan, A. J. & Masten, A. S. (2015). Emotional climate in families experiencing homelessness: Associations with child affect and socioemotional adjustment in school. *Social Development.* Advance online publication. doi:10.1111/sode.12154

Labouvie-Vief, G. (2015). *Integrating emotions and cognition throughout the lifespan.* Switzerland: Springer. doi: 10.1007/978-3-319-09822-7

Labouvie-Vief, G., DeVoe, M. & Bulka, D. (1989). Speaking about feelings: Conceptions of emotion across the life span. *Psychology and Aging, 4*(4), 425–437. doi:10.1037/0882-7974.4.4.425

Labouvie-Vief, G. & Medler, M. (2002). Affect optimization and affect complexity: Modes and styles of regulation in adulthood. *Psychology and Aging, 17*(4), 571–588. doi:10.1037/0882-7974.17.4.571

Labouvie-Vief, G. & Hakim-Larson, J. (1989). Developmental shifts in adult thought. In S. Hunter & M. Sundel (Eds.), *Sage sourcebooks for the human services series, Vol. 7. Midlife myths: Issues, findings, and practice implications* (pp. 69–96). Thousand Oaks, CA: Sage Publications.

Labouvie-Vief, G., Hakim-Larson, J., DeVoe, M. & Schoeberlein, S. (1989). Emotions and self-regulation: A life span view. *Human Development, 32*(5), 279–299. doi:10.1159/000276480

Labouvie-Vief, G., Hakim-Larson, J. & Hobart, C. J. (1987). Age, ego level, and the life-span development of coping and defense processes. *Psychology and Aging, 2*(3), 286–293. doi: 10.1037/0882-7974.2.3.286

Lagacé-Séguin, D. G. & Coplan, R. J. (2005). Maternal emotional styles and child social adjustment: Assessment, correlates, outcomes and goodness of fit in early childhood. *Social Development, 14*(4), 613–636. doi:10.1111/j.1467-9507.2005.00320.x

Laible, D. & Panfile, T. (2009). Mother-child reminiscing in the context of secure attachment relationships: Lessons in understanding and coping with negative emotions. In J. A. Quas & R. Fivush (Eds.), *Emotion and memory in development: Biological, cognitive, and social considerations* (pp. 166–195). New York: Oxford.

Lakoff, G. & Johnson, M. (1980). The metaphorical structure of the human conceptual system. *Cognitive Science, 4*(2), 195–208. doi:10.1207/s15516709cog0402_4

Lamb, M. E., Ketterlinus, R. D. & Fracasso, M. P. (1992). Parent-child relationships. In M. H. Bornstein & M. E. Lamb (Eds.), *Developmental psychology: An advanced textbook (3rd ed.)* (pp. 465–518). Hillsdale, NJ: Lawrence Erlbaum.

Landy, S. & Menna, R. (2006). *Early intervention with multi-risk families: An integrative approach.* Baltimore: Paul H Brookes Publishing.

Larsen, R. J., Diener, E. & Emmons, R. A. (1986). Affect intensity and reactions to daily life events. *Journal of Personality and Social Psychology, 51*(4), 803–814. doi:10.1037/0022-3514.51.4.803

Larsen, J. T., Berntson, G. G., Poehlmann, K. M., Ito, T. A. & Cacioppo, J. T. (2008). The psychophysiology of emotion. In M. Lewis, J. M. Haviland-Jones & L. F. Barrett (Eds.), *Handbook of emotions (3rd ed.)* (pp. 180–195). New York: Guilford Press.

Larson, M., Vaughn, M. G., Salas-Wright, C. P. & Delisi, M. (2015). Narcissism, low self-control, and violence among a nationally representative sample. *Criminal Justice and Behavior, 42*(6), 644–661. doi:10.1177/0093854814553097

Laskey, B. J. & Cartwright-Hatton, S. (2009). Parental discipline behaviours and beliefs about their child: Associations with child internalizing and mediation relationships. *Child: Care, Health and Development, 35*(5), 717–727. doi:10.1111/j.1365-2214.2009.00977.x

Lazarus, R. S. (1991). *Emotion and adaptation.* New York: Oxford University Press.

Lazarus, R. S. & Folkman, S. (1984). *Stress, appraisal, and coping.* New York: Springer.

LeDoux, J. (1996). *The emotional brain: The mysterious underpinnings of emotional life.* New York: Simon & Schuster.

LeDoux, J. (2002). *The synaptic self: How our brains become who we are.* New York: Viking.

LeDoux, J. E. & Phelps, E. A. (2008). Emotional networks in the brain. In M. Lewis, J. M. Haviland-Jones & L. F. Barrett (Eds.), *Handbook of emotions (3rd ed.)* (pp. 159–179). New York: Guilford Press.

Lee, E. (1996). Asian American families: An overview. In M. McGoldrick, J. Giordano & J. K. Pearce (Eds.). *Ethnicity and family therapy (2nd ed.)* (pp. 227–248). New York: Guilford.

Lelkes, O. (2010). *Eurostat-Methodologies and working papers. Social participation and social isolation.* Retrieved from http://ec.europa.eu/eurostat/documents/3888793/5847145/KS-RA-10-014-EN.PDF/e9a887c8-1b36-43cf-bb63-1bd62ac87ed8?version=1.0

Lerner, R. M. (1984). *On the nature of human plasticity.* Cambridge: Cambridge University Press. doi:10.1017/CBO9780511666988

Lerner, R. M. (2002). *Concepts and theories of human development (3rd ed.).* Mahwah, NJ: Erlbaum.

Lester, B. M., Conradt, E. & Marsit, C. (2016). Introduction to the special section on epigenetics. *Child Development, 87*(1), 29–37. doi:10.1111/cdev.12489

Leung, P. K. & Boehnien, J. (1996). Vietnamese families. In M. McGoldrick, J. Giordano & J. K. Pearce (Eds.). *Ethnicity and family therapy (2nd ed.)*. New York: Guilford.

Levant, R. F., Allen, P. A. & Lien, M.-C. (2014). Alexithymia in men: How and when do emotional processing deficiencies occur? *Psychology of Men & Masculinity, 15*(3), 324–334.

Levant, R. F. & Kopecky, G. (1995). *Masculinity reconstructed: Changing the rules of manhood.* New York: Dutton/Plume.

Levy, R. I. (1982). On the nature and functions of the emotions: An anthropological perspective. *Social Science Information/sur les sciences sociales, 21*(4–5), 511–528. doi:10.1177/053901882021004002

Levy, T. M. (Ed.). (2000). *Handbook of attachment interventions.* San Diego, CA: Academic Press.

Lewis, M. (1989). Cultural differences in children's knowledge of emotional scripts. In C. Saarni & P. L. Harris (Eds.), *Cambridge studies in social and emotional development. Children's understanding of emotion* (pp. 350–373). New York: Cambridge University Press.

Lewis, M. (2008a). The emergence of human emotions. In M. Lewis, J. M. Haviland-Jones & L. F. Barrett (Eds.), *Handbook of emotions (3rd ed.)* (pp. 304–319). New York: Guilford.

Lewis, M. (2008b). Self-conscious emotions: Embarrassment, pride, shame, and guilt. In M. Lewis, J. M. Haviland-Jones & L. F. Barrett (Eds.), *Handbook of emotions (3rd ed.)* (pp. 742–756). New York: Guilford.

Lewis, M. (2014). *The rise of consciousness and the development of emotional life.* New York: Guilford.

Lidstone, J., Meins, E. & Fernyhough, C. (2011). Individual differences in children's private speech: Consistency across tasks, timepoints, and contexts. *Cognitive Development, 26*(3), 203–213. doi:10.1016/j.cogdev.2011.02.002

Lilgendahl, J. P., Helson, R. & John, O. P. (2013). Does ego development increase during midlife? The effects of openness and accommodative processing of difficult events. *Journal of Personality, 81*(4), 403–416. doi:10.1111/jopy.12009

Lind, K., Toure, H., Brugel, D., Meyer, P., Laurent-Vannier, A. & Chevignard, M. (2016). Extended follow-up of neurological, cognitive, behavioral and academic outcomes after severe abusive head trauma. *Child Abuse & Neglect, 51*, 358–367. doi: 10.1016/j.chiabu.2015.08.001

Lindahl, K. M. (2001). Methodological issues in family observational research. In P. K. Kerig & K. M. Lindahl (Eds.), *Family observational coding systems* (pp.23–32). Mahwah, NJ: Erlbaum.

Lindquist, K. A. & Barrett, L. F. (2008). Emotional complexity. In M. Lewis, J. M. Haviland-Jones & L. F. Barrett (Eds.), *Handbook of emotions (3rd ed.)* (pp. 513–530). New York: Guilford Press.

Lindquist, K. A., MacCormack, J. K. & Shablack, H. (2015). The role of language in emotion: Predictions from psychological constructionism. *Frontiers in Psychology, 6*, Article ID 444.

Lindsay, D. L., Pajtek, S., Tarter, R. E., Long, E. C. & Clark, D. B. (2014). Amygdala activation and emotional processing in adolescents at risk for substance use disorders. *Journal of Child & Adolescent Substance Abuse, 23*(3), 200–204.

Lindsey, E. W., MacKinnon-Lewis, C., Campbell, J., Frabutt, J. M. & Lamb, M. E. (2002). Marital conflict and boys' peer relationships: The mediating role of mother-son emotional reciprocity. *Journal of Family Psychology, 16*, 466–477.

Lippold, M. A., Duncan, L. G., Coatsworth, J. D., Nix, R. L. & Greenberg, M. T. (2015). Understanding how mindful parenting may be linked to mother–adolescent communication. *Journal of Youth and Adolescence, 44*(9), 1663–1673. doi:10.1007/s10964-015-0325-x

Livas-Dlott, A., Fuller, B., Stein, G. L., Bridges, M., Mangual Figueroa, A. & Mireles, L. (2010). Commands, competence, and cariño: Maternal socialization practices in Mexican American families. *Developmental Psychology, 46(3)*, 566–578. doi:10.1037/a0018016

Loevinger, J. (1966). The meaning and measurement of ego development. *American Psychologist, 21*(3), 195–206. doi:10.1037/h0023376

Loevinger, J. (1994). Has psychology lost its conscience? *Journal of Personality Assessment, 62*(1), 2–8. doi:10.1207/s15327752jpa6201_1

Loevinger, J. & Wessler, R. (1970). *Measuring ego development 1: Construction and use of a sentence completion test.* San Francisco: Jossey-Bass.

Lord, S. E., Eccles, J. S. & McCarthy, K. A. (1994). Surviving the junior high school transition: Family processes and self-perceptions as protective and risk factors. *The Journal of Early Adolescence, 14*(2), 162–199. doi:10.1177/027243169401400205

Luangrath, A. W., Peck, J. & Barger, V. A. (2017). Textual paralanguage and its implications for marketing communications. *Journal of Consumer Psychology, 27*(1), 98–107. doi:10.1016/j.jcps.2016.05.002

Lucas, R. E. & Diener, E. (2008). Subjective well-being. In M. Lewis, J. M. Haviland-Jones & L. F. Barrett (Eds.), *Handbook of emotions (3rd ed.)* (pp. 471–484). New York: Guilford Press.

Luciana, M. (2016). Executive function in adolescence: A commentary on regulatory control and depression in adolescents: Findings from neuroimaging and neuropsychological research. *Journal of Clinical Child & Adolescent Psychology, 45*(1), 84–89. doi:10.1080/15374416.2015.1123638

Lucy, J. A. (1997). Linguistic relativity. *Annual Review of Anthropology, 26*, 291–312. doi: 10.1146/annurev.anthro.26.1.291

Lunkenheimer, E. S., Hollenstein, T., Wang, J. & Shields, A. M. (2012). Flexibility and attractors in context: Family emotion socialization patterns and children's emotion regulation in late childhood. *Nonlinear Dynamics, Psychology, and Life Sciences, 16*(3), 269–291.

Luthar, S. S. (1991). Vulnerability and resilience: A study of high-risk adolescents. *Child Development, 62*(3), 600–616. doi:10.2307/1131134

Luthar, S. S. (2015). Mothering mothers. *Research in Human Development, 12*(3–4), 295–303. doi:10.1080/15427609.2015.1068045

Luthar, S. S. & Becker, B. E. (2002). Privileged but pressured?: A study of affluent youth. *Child Development, 73*(5), 1593–1610. doi:10.1111/1467-8624.00492

Luthar, S. S., Cicchetti, D. & Becker, B. (2000). Research on resilience: Response to commentaries. *Child Development, 71*(3), 573–575. doi:10.1111/1467-8624.00168

Luthar, S. S. & Suchman, N. E. (2000). Relational psychotherapy mothers' group: A developmentally informed intervention for at-risk mothers. *Development and Psychopathology, 12*(2), 235–253. doi:10.1017/S0954579400002078

Maccoby, E. & Jacklin, C. N. (1974). *The psychology of sex differences*. Stanford, CA: Stanford University Press.

Mace, N. L. & Rabins, P. V. (2011). *The 36-hour day (5th ed.)*. Baltimore, MD: The Johns Hopkins University Press.

Macklem, G. L. (2008). *Practitioner's guide to emotion regulation in school-aged children*. New York: Springer.

Magai, C. (2008). Long-lived emotions: A life course perspective. In M. Lewis, J. M. Haviland-Jones & L. F. Barrett (Eds.), *Handbook of emotions (3rd ed.)* (pp. 376–392). New York: Guilford.

Main, M. & Solomon, J. (1986). Discovery of an insecure-disorganized/disoriented attachment pattern. In T. B. Brazelton & M. W. Yogman (Eds.), *Affective development in infancy* (pp. 95–124). Westport, CT: Ablex Publishing.

Malatesta, C. (1981). Affective development over the lifespan: Involution or growth? *Merrill-Palmer Quarterly of Behavior and Development, 27*(2), 145–173. Retrieved from www.jstor.org.ezproxy.uwindsor.ca/stable/23083757

Malatesta, C. Z. & Izard, C. E. (Eds.) (1984). *Emotion in adult development*. Beverly Hills, CA: Sage Publications.

Mansson, D. H. (2013). Affectionate communication and relational characteristics in the grandparent–grandchild relationship. *Communication Reports, 26*(2), 47–60. doi:10.1080/08934215.2013.798670

Marinosson, G. (1998). The ethnographic approach. *Educational and Child Psychology, 15*, 34–43.

Markus, H. R. & Kitayama, S. (1991). Culture and self: Implications for cognition, emotion, and motivation. *Psychological Review, 98*, 224–253.

Markus, H. & Nurius, P. (1986). Possible selves. *American Psychologist, 41*(9), 954–969. doi:10.1037/0003-066X.41.9.954

Martinez-Torteya, C., Dayton, C. J., Beeghly, M., Seng, J. S., McGinnis, E., Broderick, A., … Muzik, M. (2014). Maternal parenting predicts infant biobehavioral regulation among women with a history of childhood maltreatment. *Development and Psychopathology, 26*(2), 379–392. doi:10.1017/S0954579414000017

Masarik, A. S., Martin, M. J., Ferrer, E., Lorenz, F. O., Conger, K. J. & Conger, R. D. (2016). Couple resilience to economic pressure over time and across generations. *Journal of Marriage and Family, 78*(2), 326–345. doi:10.1111/jomf.12284

Mash, E. J. & Wolfe, D. A. (2013). *Abnormal child psychology (5th ed.)*. Belmont, CA: Wadsworth Cengage.

Masten, A. S. (2007). Resilience in developing systems: Progress and promise as the fourth wave rises. *Development and Psychopathology, 19*(3), 921–930. doi:10.1017/S0954579407000442

Masten, A. S. (2014). *Ordinary magic: Resilience in development*. New York: Guilford.

Masten, A. S. & Cicchetti, D. (2010). Developmental cascades. *Development and Psychopathology, 22*(3), 491–495. doi:10.1017/S0954579410000222

Masten, A. S. & Cicchetti, D. (2012). Risk and resilience in development and psychopathology: The legacy of Norman Garmezy. *Development and Psychopathology, 24*(2), 333–334. doi:10.1017/S0954579412000016

Masten, A. S. & Coatsworth, J. D. (1998). The development of competence in favorable and unfavorable environments: Lessons from research on successful children. *American Psychologist, 53*(2), 205–220. doi:10.1037/0003-066X.53.2.205

Masten, A. S., Desjardins, C. D., McCormick, C. M., Kuo, S. I-C. & Long, J. D. (2010). The significance of childhood competence and problems for adult success in work: A developmental cascade analysis. *Development and Psychopathology, 22*(3), 679–694. doi:10.1017/S0954579410000362

Masten, A. S., Hubbard, J. J., Gest, S. D., Tellegen, A., Garmezy, N. & Ramirez, M. (1999). Competence in the context of adversity: Pathways to resilience and maladaptation from childhood to late adolescence. *Development and Psychopathology, 11*(1), 143–169. doi:10.1017/S0954579499001996

Masten, A. S. & Narayan, A. J. (2012). Child development in the context of disaster, war, and terrorism: Pathways of risk and resilience. *Annual Review of Psychology, 63*, 227–257. doi:10.1146/annurev-psych-120710-100356

Masten, A. S. & Obradović, J. (2006). Competence and resilience in development. *Annals of the New York Academy of Sciences, 1094*(1), 13–27. doi: 10.1196/annals.1376.003

Masten, A. S. & Obradović, J. (2008). Disaster preparation and recovery: lessons from research on resilience in human development. *Ecology and Society, 13*(1), 9. [online] URL: www.ecologyandsociety.org/vol13/iss1/art9/

Masten, A. S. & Tellegen, A. (2012). Resilience in developmental psychopathology: Contributions of the Project Competence Longitudinal Study. *Development and Psychopathology, 24*(2), 345–361. doi:10.1017/S095457941200003X

Matsumoto, D. & Hwang, H. S. (2012). Culture and emotion: The integration of biological and cultural contributions. *Journal of Cross-Cultural Psychology, 43*(1), 91–118. doi: 10.1177/0022022111420147

Mayer, J. D., Salovey, P. & Caruso, D. R. (2005). The Mayer-Salovey-Caruso Emotional Intelligence Test Youth Version (MSCEIT-YV). Research version. Toronto, Canada: Multi Health Systems.

Mayer, J. D., Salovey, P., Caruso, D. R. & Sitarenios, G. (2003). Measuring emotional intelligence with the MSCEIT V2.0. *Emotion, 3*, 97–105.

McAdams, D. P. (2001). The psychology of life stories. *Review of General Psychology, 5*, 100–122.

McAdams, D. P. (2008a). Personal narratives and the life story. In O. P. John, R. W. Robins & L. A. Pervin (Eds.), *Handbook of personality: Theory and research (3rd ed.)* (pp. 242–262). New York: Guilford Press.

McAdams, D. P. (2008b). American identity: The redemptive self. *The General Psychologist, 43(1)*, 20–27.

McAdams, D. P., Bauer, J. J., Sakaeda, A. R., Anyidoho, N. A., Machado, M. A., Magrino-Failla, K., White, K. W. & Pals, J. L. (2006). Continuity and change in the life story: A longitudinal study of autobiographical memories in emerging adulthood. *Journal of Personality, 74*(5), 1371–1400. doi:10.1111/j.1467-6494.2006.00412.x

McAdams, D. P., Reynolds, J., Lewis, M., Patten, A. H. & Bowman, P. J. (2001). When bad things turn good and good things turn bad: Sequences of redemption and contamination in life narrative and their relation to psychosocial adaptation in midlife adults and in students. *Personality and Social Psychology Bulletin, 27*(4), 474–485. doi: 10.1177/0146167201274008

McAuliffe, G. (Ed.) (2008a). *Culturally alert counseling: A comprehensive introduction (2nd ed.)*. Thousand Oaks: Sage.

McAuliffe, G. (2008b). *Resource Guide. Key practices in culturally alert counselling: A demonstration of skills* (pp. 7–9). Retrieved from www.sagepub.com/upm-data/24164_Resoure_Guide_for_A_Demonstration_of_Skills.pdf

McCartney, K., Burchinal, M. R. & Bub, K. L. (2006). Best practices in quantitative methods for developmentalists. *Monographs of the Society for Research in Child Development, 71*(3), 1–145. doi:10.1111/j.1540-5834.2006.00401a.x

McClelland, D. C. (1985). *Human motivation.* Cambridge, UK: Cambridge University Press.

McClelland, D. C., Koestner, R. & Weinberger, J. (1989). How do self-attributed and implicit motives differ? *Psychological Review, 96*, 690–702.

McCord, B. L. & Raval, V. V. (2016). Asian Indian immigrant and White American maternal emotion socialization and child socio-emotional functioning. *Journal of Child and Family Studies, 25*(2), 464–474. doi:10.1007/s10826-015-0227-2

McGill, D. W. & Pearce, J. K. (1996). American families with English ancestors from the Colonial era: Anglo Americans. In M. McGoldrick, J. Giordano & J. K. Pearce (Eds.), *Ethnicity and family therapy (2nd ed.)* (pp. 451–466). New York: Guilford.

McGillicuddy-DeLisi, A. V. (1992). Parents' beliefs and children's personal-social development. In I. E. Sigel, A. V. McGillicuddy-DeLisi & J. J. Goodnow (Eds.), *Parental belief systems: The psychological consequences for children (2nd ed.)* (pp. 115–142). Hillsdale, NJ: Erlbaum.

McGoldrick, M. (1996). Irish families. In M. McGoldrick, J. Giordano & J. K. Pearce (Eds.), *Ethnicity and family therapy (2nd ed.)* (pp. 544–566). New York: Guilford.

McGoldrick, M., Giordano, J. & Pearce, J. K. (Eds.). (1996). *Ethnicity and family therapy (2nd ed.)*. New York: Guilford.

McLean, K. C., Pasupathi, M. & Pals, J. L. (2007). Selves creating stories creating selves: A process model of self-development. *Personality and Social Psychology Review, 11*(3), 262–278. doi:10.1177/1088868307301034

McShane, K. E. & Hastings, P. D. (2004). Culturally sensitive approaches to research on child development and family practices in first peoples communities. *First Peoples Child and Family Review, 1*(1), 33–48.

Meins, E. (2013). Sensitive attunement to infants' internal states: Operationalizing the construct of mind-mindedness. *Attachment & Human Development, 15*(5–6), 524–544. doi:10.1080/14616734.2013.830388

Meins, E., Fernyhough, C., Wainwright, R., Gupta, M. D., Fradley, E. & Tuckey, M. (2002). Maternal mind-mindedness and attachment security as predictors of theory of mind understanding. *Child Development, 73*(6), 1715–1726. doi:10.1111/1467-8624.00501

Meltzoff, A. N. & Moore, M. K. (1977). Imitation of facial and manual gestures by human neonates. *Science, 198*(4312), 75–78. doi:10.1126/science.198.4312.75

Merriam-Webster (1977). Webster's new collegiate dictionary: A Merriam-Webster. Springfield, MA: G. & C. Merriam Company.

Mesman, J. & Emmen, R. A. G. (2013). Mary Ainsworth's legacy: A systematic review of observational instruments measuring parental sensitivity. *Attachment & Human Development, 15*(5–6), 485–506. doi:10.1080/14616734.2013.820900

Mesman, J., Oster, H. & Camras, L. (2012). Parental sensitivity to infant distress: What do discrete negative emotions have to do with it? *Attachment & Human Development, 14*(4), 337–348. doi:10.1080/14616734.2012.691649

Mesquita, B., De Leersnyder, J. & Albert, D. (2014). The cultural regulation of emotions. In J. J. Gross (Ed.), *Handbook of emotion regulation (2nd ed.)* (pp. 284–301). New York: Guilford Press.

Miklósi, M., Szabó, M., Martos, T., Galambosi, E. & Forintos, D. P. (2013). Cognitive emotion regulation strategies moderate the effect of parenting self-efficacy beliefs on parents' anxiety following their child's surgery. *Journal of Pediatric Psychology, 38*(4), 462–471. doi:10.1093/jpepsy/jss174

Miklowitz, D. J. & Cicchetti, D. (2006). Editorial: Toward a life span developmental psychopathology perspective on bipolar disorder. *Development and Psychopathology, 18*(4), 935–938. doi:10.1017/S0954579406060469

Milardo, R. M. (2005). Generative uncle and nephew relationships. *Journal of Marriage and Family, 67(5)*, 1226–1236. doi:10.1111/j.1741-3737.2005.00212.x

Milardo, R. (2009). *The forgotten kin: Aunts and uncles.* New York: Cambridge University Press.

Miller, S. A. (2013). *Developmental research methods (4th ed.).* Thousand Oaks, CA: Sage.

Mills, J. C. & Crowley, R. J. (1986). *Therapeutic metaphors for children and the child within.* New York: Brunner/Mazel.

Mohammad Bin Rashid School of Government (2014). *Internet of everything.* Retrieved from www.mbrsg.ae/HOME/NEWS-AND-EVENTS/News/Internet_of_Everything.aspx

Moffitt, T. E. & Caspi, A. (2001). Childhood predictors differentiate life-course persistent and adolescence-limited antisocial pathways among males and females. *Development and Psychopathology, 13*(2), 355–375. doi:10.1017/S0954579401002097

Moreland, A. & Dumas, J. (2008). Evaluating child coping competence: Theory and measurement. *Journal of Child & Family Studies, 17*(3), 437–454. doi:10.1007/s10826-007-9165-y

Morgan, C. D. & Murray, H. (1935). A method for investigating fantasies: The Thematic Apperception Test. *Archives of Neurological Psychiatry, 34*, 289–306.

Morris, A. S., Silk, J. S., Steinberg, L., Myers, S. S. & Robinson, L. R. (2007). The role of the family context in the development of emotion regulation. *Social Development, 16*(2), 361–388. doi:10.1111/j.1467-9507.2007.00389.x

Morton, J. B. & Trehub, S. E. (2001). Children's understanding of emotion in speech. *Child Development, 72*(3), 834–843. doi:10.1111/1467-8624.00318

Morton, J. B., Trehub, S. E. & Zelazo, P. D. (2003). Sources of inflexibility in 6-year-olds' understanding of emotion in speech. *Child Development, 74*(6), 1857–1868. doi:10.1046/j.1467-8624.2003.00642.x

Mruk, C. J. (1995). *Self-esteem: Research, theory, and practice.* New York: Springer.

Mruk, C. J. (2006). *Self-esteem research, theory, and practice: Toward a positive psychology of self-esteem (3rd ed.).* New York: Springer.

Mruk, C. J. (2013). *Self-esteem and positive psychology: Research, theory, and practice (4th ed.).* New York: Springer.

Mullin, B. C. & Hinshaw, S. P. (2007). Emotion regulation and externalizing disorders in children and adolescents. In J. J. Gross (Ed.), *Handbook of emotion regulation* (pp. 523–541). New York: Guilford Press.

Munger, M. P. (2003). *The history of psychology: Fundamental questions.* New York: Oxford.

Murray, H. A. & Bellak, L. (1973). Thematic Apperception Test. Available from Psychcorp, www.psychcorp.com.

Murray, L., Pella, J. E., De Pascalis, L., Arteche, A., Pass, L., Percy, R., … Cooper, P. J. (2014). Socially anxious mothers' narratives to their children and their relation to child representations and adjustment. *Development and Psychopathology, 26*(4, Pt 2), 1531–1546. doi:10.1017/S0954579414001187

Nafisi, A. (2003). *Reading Lolita in Tehran: A memoir in books.* New York: Random House.

Nassar-McMillan, S. C., Ajrouch, K. J. & Hakim-Larson, J. (Eds.). (2014). *Biopsychosocial perspectives on Arab Americans: Culture, development, and health.* New York: Springer.

Nassar-McMillan, S. C. & Hakim-Larson, J. (2014). Clinical applications with individuals of Middle Eastern and Northern African descent. In D.W. Sue, M. E. Gallardo & H. A. Neville (Eds.), *Case Studies in Multicultural Counseling and Therapy* (pp. 61–75). Hoboken, NJ: Wiley.

National Human Genome Research Institute (2016a). *Epigenomics.* Retrieved from www.genome.gov/27532724

National Human Genome Research Institute (2016b). *The NHGRI Brochure.* Retrieved from www.genome.gov/27561939/new-nhgri-brochure-highlights-major-genomics-research-areas/

Nelson, K. (2014). A matter of meaning: Reflections on forty years of JCL. *Journal of Child Language, 40*(Supp 1), 93–104. doi:10.1017/S0305000914000154

Neugarten, B. L. (Ed.). (1968). *Middle age and aging: A reader in social psychology.* Chicago: University of Chicago Press.

Newmark, G. (2008). *How to raise emotionally healthy children: Meeting the five critical needs of children ... and parents too!* Tarzana, CA: NMI Publishers.

Nichols, M. P. & Schwartz, R. C. (1995). *Family therapy: Concepts and methods (3rd ed.).* Boston: Allyn and Bacon.

Niederkrotenthaler, T., Xu, L., Parks, S. E. & Sugerman, D. E. (2013). Descriptive factors of abusive head trauma in young children—United States, 2000–2009. *Child Abuse & Neglect, 37*(7), 446–455. doi:10.1016/j.chiabu.2013.02.002

NOVA/WGBH (Producer) (1986). *Life's first feelings [DVD].* Boston, MA: Public Broadcasting System.

NOVA/WGBH (Producer). (2010). *This emotional life: In search of ourselves—and happiness.* [DVD]. USA: Public Broadcasting Service (PBS). Available from www.pbs.org/video/

Nucci, L. (1994). Conceptions of personal issues: A domain distinct from moral or societal concepts. In B. Puka (Ed.), *Moral development: A compendium, Vol. 2. Fundamental research in moral development* (pp. 294–301). New York: Garland Publishing. (Reprinted from "Child Development," 1981, 52, pp. 114–121)

Nydell, M. K. (2006). *Understanding Arabs: A guide for modern times (4th ed.).* Boston, MA: Intercultural Press.

Oatley, K. & Jenkins, J. M. (1996). *Understanding emotions.* Cambridge, MA: Blackwell.

Oberman, L. M. & Ramachandran, V. S. (2008). Preliminary evidence for deficits in multisensory integration in autism spectrum disorders: The mirror neuron hypothesis. *Social Neuroscience, 3*, 348–355.

Obradović, J. (2016). Physiological responsivity and executive functioning: Implications for adaptation and resilience in early childhood. *Child Development Perspectives, 10*(1), 65–70. doi:10.1111/cdep.12164

Obradović, J., Burt, K. B. & Masten, A. S. (2010). Testing a dual cascade model linking competence and symptoms over 20 years from childhood to adulthood. *Journal of Clinical Child and Adolescent Psychology, 39*(1), 90–102. doi:10.1080/15374410903401120

O'Brien, E. J. & Epstein, S. (1988). *MSEI: The Multidimensional self-esteem inventory.* Lutz, Fl: Psychological Assessment Resources.

Okado, Y. & Bierman, K. L. (2015). Differential risk for late adolescent conduct problems and mood dysregulation among children with early externalizing behavior problems. *Journal of Abnormal Child Psychology, 43*(4), 735–747. doi:10.1007/s10802-014-9931-4

Ortony, A., Clore, G. L. & Foss, M. A. (1987). The referential structure of the affective lexicon. *Cognitive Science, 11*(3), 341–364. doi:10.1207/s15516709cog1103_4

Oster, H. (2005). The repertoire of infant facial expressions: An ontogenetic perspective. In J. Nadel & D. Muir (Eds.), *Emotional development: Recent research advances* (pp. 261–292). New York: Oxford University Press.

Osofsky, J. D. (Ed.). (1987). *Handbook of infant development (2nd ed.).* Oxford, England: Wiley.

Padilla-Walker, L. M. (2014). Parental socialization of prosocial behavior: A multidimensional approach. In L. M. Padilla-Walker & G. Carlo (Eds.), *Prosocial development: A multidimensional approach* (pp. 131–155). doi:10.1093/acprof:oso/9780199964772.003.0007

Paivio, S. C. (2013). Essential processes in emotion-focused therapy. *Psychotherapy, 50*(3), 341–345. doi:10.1037/a0032810

Paley, B., Cox, M. J. & Kanoy, K.W. (2001). The Young Family Interaction Coding System. In P. K. Kerig & K. M. Lindahl (Eds.), *Family observational coding systems* (pp. 273–288). Mahwah, NJ: Lawrence Erlbaum.

Papoušek, H. & Papoušek, M. (1989). Intuitive parenting: Aspects related to educational psychology. *European Journal of Psychology of Education, 4*(2), 201–210. doi:10.1007/BF03172602

Papoušek, M. (2007). Communication in early infancy: An arena of intersubjective learning. Infant Behavior & Development, 30(2), 258–266. doi:10.1016/j.infbeh.2007.02.003

Papoušek, M., Papoušek, H. & Symmes, D. (1991). The meanings of melodies in motherese in tone and stress languages. *Infant Behavior & Development, 14*(4), 415–440. doi:10.1016/0163-6383(91)90031-M

Pappa, I., Szekely, E., Mileva-Seitz, V. R., Luijk, M. P. C. M., Bakermans-Kranenburg, M. J., van IJzendoorn, M. H. & Tiemeier, H. (2015). Beyond the usual suspects: A multidimensional genetic exploration of infant attachment disorganization and security. *Attachment & Human Development, 17*(3), 288–301. doi:10.1080/14616734.2015.1037316

Parke, R. (2004). Development in the family. *Annual Review of Psychology, 55*, 365–399.

Parker, A. E., Halberstadt, A. G., Dunsmore, J. C., Townley, G., Bryant, A., Jr., Thompson, J. A. & Beale, K. S. (2012). "Emotions are a window into one's heart": A qualitative analysis of parental beliefs about children's emotions across three ethnic groups: Abstract. *Monographs of the Society for Research in Child Development, 77*(3), vii. doi:10.1111/j.1540-5834.2012.00676.x

Pasalich, D. S., Witkiewitz, K., McMahon, R. J., Pinderhughes, E. E. & Conduct Problems Prevention Research Group. (2016). Indirect effects of the fast track intervention on conduct disorder symptoms and callous-unemotional traits: Distinct pathways involving discipline and warmth. *Journal of Abnormal Child Psychology, 44*(3), 587–597. doi:10.1007/s10802-015-0059-y

Paterson, A. D., Babb, K. A., Camodeca, A., Goodwin, J., Hakim-Larson, J., Voelker, S. & Gragg, M. (2012). Emotion-Related Parenting Styles (ERPS): A short form for measuring parental meta-emotion philosophy. *Early Education and Development, 23*(4), 583–602. doi:10.1080/10409289.2011.569316

Patterson, G. R., Forgatch, M. S. & DeGarmo, D. S. (2010). Cascading effects following intervention. *Development and Psychopathology, 22*(4), 949–970. doi:10.1017/S0954579410000568

Patterson, G. R. & Stoolmiller, M. (1991). Replications of a dual failure model for boys' depressed mood. *Journal of Consulting and Clinical Psychology, 59*(4), 491–498. doi:10.1037/0022-006X.59.4.491

Pennebaker, J. W. & Seagal, J. D. (1999). Forming a story: The health benefits of narrative. *Journal of Clinical Psychology, 55*(10), 1243–1254. 10.1002/(SICI)1097-4679(199910)55:10<1243::AID-JCLP6>3.0.CO;2-N

Perez Rivera, M. B. & Dunsmore, J. C. (2011). Mothers' acculturation and beliefs about emotions, mother-child emotion discourse, and children's emotion understanding in Latino families. *Early Education and Development, 22*(2), 324–354. doi:10.1080/10409281003702000

Perry, W. G., Jr. (1970). *Forms of intellectual and ethical development in the college years*. Oxford, England: Holt, Rinehart & Winston.

Petrides, K. V., Frederickson, N. & Furnham, A. (2004). The role of trait emotional intelligence in academic performance and deviant behavior at school. *Personality and Individual Differences, 36*(2), 277–293. doi:10.1016/S0191-8869(03)00084-9

Petrides, K. V. & Furnham, A. (2003). Trait emotional intelligence: Behavioural validation in two studies of emotion recognition and reactivity to mood induction. *European Journal of Personality, 17*(1), 39–57. doi:10.1002/per.466

Petrides, K. V., Pita, R. & Kokkinaki, F. (2007). The location of trait emotional intelligence in personality factor space. *British Journal of Psychology, 98*(2), 273–289. doi:10.1348/000712606X120618

Petrides, K. V., Sangareau, Y., Furnham, A. & Frederickson, N. (2006). Trait emotional intelligence and children's peer relations at school. *Social Development, 15*(3), 537–547. doi:10.1111/j.1467-9507.2006.00355.x

Piaget, J. (1962). *Play, dreams, and imitation in childhood*. New York: Norton.

Pickren, W. & Rutherford, A. (2010). *A history of psychology in modern context*. Hoboken, NJ: Wiley.

Pine, D. S., Lissek, S., Klein, R. G., Mannuzza, S., Moulton, J. L. III, Guardino, M. & Woldehawariat, G. (2004). Face-memory and emotion: Associations with major depression in children and adolescents. *Journal of Child Psychology and Psychiatry, 45*(7), 1199–1208. doi: 10.1111/j.1469-7610.2004.00311.x

Pinker, S. (2008). Introduction (xix–xxii). In C. Darwin (1872/2008), *The expression of the emotions in man and animals*. London: The Folio Society.

Plutchik, R. (2000). *Emotions in the practice of psychotherapy: Clinical implications of affect theories*. Washington, D.C.: American Psychological Association.

Pollack, W. S. (2006). The "war" for boys: Hearing "real boys'" voices, healing their pain. *Professional Psychology: Research and Practice, 37*(2), 190–195. doi:10.1037/0735-7028.37.2.190

Pollak, S. D. & Tolley-Schell, S. A. (2003). Selective attention to facial emotion in physically abused children. *Journal of Abnormal Psychology, 112*(3), 323–338. doi:10.1037/0021-843X.112.3.323

Ponzetti, J. J. (2011). The forgotten kin: Aunts and uncles by Robert Milardo. Aunting: Cultural practices that sustain family and community life by Laura Ellingson and Patricia Sotirin. *Journal of Intergenerational Relationships, 9*(2), 213–220. doi:10.1080/15350770.2011.567920

Posada, G., Gao, Y., Wu, F., Posada, R., Tascon, M., Schöelmerich, A., … Schoelmerich, A. (1995). The secure-base phenomenon across cultures: Children's behavior, mother's preferences, and experts' concepts. *Monographs of the Society for Research in Child Development, 60*(2–3), 27–48. doi:10.2307/1166169

Povinelli, D. J., Landau, K. R. & Perilloux, H. K. (1996). Self-recognition in young children using delayed versus live feedback: Evidence of a developmental asynchrony. *Child Development, 67*(4), 1540–1554. doi:10.2307/1131717

Pratt, M. W., Norris, J. E., Arnold, M. L. & Filyer, R. (1999). Generativity and moral development as predictors of value-socialization narratives for young persons across the adult life span: From lessons learned to stories shared. *Psychology and Aging, 14*(3), 414–426. doi:10.1037/0882-7974.14.3.414

Pratt, M. W., Norris, J. E., van de Hoef, S. & Arnold, M. L. (2001). Stories of hope: Parental optimism in narratives about adolescent children. *Journal of Social and Personal Relationships,18*(5), 603–623. doi:10.1177/0265407501185003

Quas, J. A. & Fivush, R. (Eds.). (2009). *Emotion and memory in development: Biological, cognitive, and social considerations.* New York: Oxford.

Quinn, N. & Mageo, J. M. (Eds.) (2013). *Attachment reconsidered: Cultural perspectives on a Western theory.* New York, NY: Palgrave Macmillan.

Ramachandran, V. S. & Hirstein, W. (1997). Three laws of qualia: What neurology tells us about the biological functions of consciousness. *Journal of Consciousness Studies, 4*(5–6), 429–457.

Ramsden, S. R. & Hubbard, J. A. (2002). Family expressiveness and parental emotion coaching: Their role in children's emotion regulation and aggression. *Journal of Abnormal Child Psychology, 30*(6), 657–667. doi:10.1023/A:1020819915881

Raval, V. V., Raval, P. H. & Deo, N. (2014). Mothers' socialization goals, mothers' emotion socialization behaviors, child emotion regulation, and child socioemotional functioning in urban India. *The Journal of Early Adolescence, 34*(2), 229–250. doi:10.1177/0272431613485821

Reck, C., Hunt, A., Fuchs, T., Weiss, R., Noon, A., Moehler, E., Downing, G., Tronick, E. Z. & Mundt, C. (2004). Interactive regulation of affect in postpartum depressed mothers and their infants: An overview. *Psychopathology, 37*, 272–280. doi: 10.1159/000081983

Reese, E., Bird, A. & Tripp, G. (2007). Children's self-esteem and moral self: Links to parent-child conversations. *Social Development, 16*(3), 460–478. doi:10.1111/j.1467-9507.2007.00393.x

Reese, E. & Newcombe, R. (2007). Training mothers in elaborative reminiscing enhances children's autobiographical memory and narrative. *Child Development, 78*(4), 1153–1170. doi:10.1111/j.1467-8624.2007.01058.x

Rentzsch, K., Wenzler, M. P. & Schütz, A. (2016). The structure of multidimensional self-esteem across age and gender. *Personality and Individual Differences, 88*, 139–147. doi: 10.1016/j.paid.2015.09.012

Resnick, M. D., Bearman, P. S., Blum, R. W., Bauman, K. E., Harris, K. M., Jones, J., Tabor, J., Beuhring, T., Sieving, R. E., Shew, M., Ireland, M., Bearinger, L. H. & Udry J. R. (1997). Protecting adolescents from harm. Findings from the National Longitudinal Study on Adolescent Health. *Journal of the American Medical Association, 278*(10), 823–832.

Richardson, J. B., Jr. (2009). Men do matter: Ethnographic insights on the socially supportive role of the African American uncle in the lives of inner-city African American male youth. *Journal of Family Issues, 30*(8), 1041–1069. doi:10.1177/0192513X08330930

Richmond, L. J. & Guindon, M. H. (2013). Culturally alert counseling with European Americans. In G. McAuliffe (Ed.), *Culturally alert counseling: A comprehensive introduction* (pp. 231–262). Thousand Oaks, CA: Sage.

Ridgeway, D., Waters, E. & Kuczaj, S. A. (1985). Acquisition of emotion-descriptive language: Receptive and productive vocabulary norms for ages 18 months to 6 years. *Developmental Psychology, 21*(5), 901–908. doi:10.1037/0012-1649.21.5.901

Riordan, M. A. & Kreuz, R. J. (2010). Cues in computer-mediated communication: A corpus analysis. *Computers in Human Behavior, 26*(6), 1806–1817. doi:10.1016/j.chb.2010.07.008

Rivers, S. E., Brackett, M. A., Reyes, M. R., Mayer, J. D., Caruso, D. R. & Salovey, P. (2012). Measuring emotional intelligence in early adolescence with the MSCEIT-YV: Psychometric properties and relationship with academic performance and psychosocial functioning. *Journal of Psychoeducational Assessment, 30*(4), 344–366. doi:10.1177/0734282912449443

Rizzolatti, G. & Craighero, L. (2004). The mirror-neuron system. *Annual Review of Neuroscience, 27*, 169–192. doi:10.1146/annurev.neuro.27.070203.144230

Roberts, B. W. & DelVecchio, W. F. (2000). The rank-order consistency of personality traits from childhood to old age: A quantitative review of longitudinal studies. *Psychological Bulletin, 126*(1), 3–25. doi:10.1037/0033-2909.126.1.3

Roberts, G. E. & McArthur, D. S. (1989). *Roberts Apperception Test for Children.* Available from Western Psychological Services, www.wpspublish.com.

Robertson, J. & Robertson, J. (1989). *Separation and the very young.* Oxford, England: Free Association Books.

Robin, A. L. (1998). Training families with ADHD adolescents. In R. A. Barkley (Ed.), *Attention-deficit hyperactivity disorder: A handbook for diagnosis and treatment (2nd ed.)* (pp. 413–457). New York: Guilford Press.

Robin, A. L. & Foster, S. L. (1989). *Negotiating parent-adolescent conflict: A behavioral-family systems approach.* New York: Guilford Press.

Robinson, D. N. (2004). *The great ideas of philosophy (2nd ed.).* Lectures 1–30. Chantilly, VA: The Great Courses.

Rockwood, C. (Ed.) (2007). *Chambers biographical dictionary (8th ed.).* Edinburgh: Chambers Harrap Publishers Ltd.

Rogoff, B. (2003). *The cultural nature of human development.* New York: Oxford.

Roisman, G. I., Newman, D. A., Fraley, R. C., Haltigan, J. D., Groh, A. M. & Haydon, K. C. (2012). Distinguishing differential susceptibility from diathesis–stress: Recommendations for evaluating interaction effects. *Development and Psychopathology, 24*(2), 389–409. doi:10.1017/S0954579412000065

Rosenberg, M. (1965). *Society and the adolescent self-image.* Princeton, NJ: Princeton University Press.

Ross, S. & Jennings, K.D. (1995). Development and psychopathology. In M. Hersen & R.T. Ammerman (Eds.), *Advanced abnormal child psychology* (pp. 49–57). Hillsdale, NJ: Erlbaum.

Rothbart, M. K. (2006). *Mary Rothbart's Temperament Questionnaires.* Retrieved from www.bowdoin.edu/~sputnam/rothbart-temperamentquestionnaires/instrument-descriptions/

Rothbart, M. K. (2007). Temperament, development, and personality. *Current Directions in Psychological Science, 16*(4), 207–212. doi:10.1111/j.1467-8721.2007.00505.x

Rothbart, M. K. & Bates, J. E. (1998). Temperament. In W. Damon (Series Ed.) & N. Eisenberg (Vol. Ed.), *Handbook of child psychology: Vol. 3 Social, emotional, and personality development (5th ed.)* (pp. 105–176). New York: Wiley.

Rothbart, M. K., Chew, K. H. & Garstein, M. A. (2001). Assessment of temperament in early development. In L. T. Singer & P. S. Zeskind (Eds.), *Biobehavioral assessment of the infant* (pp. 109–208). New York: Guilford.

Rothbart, M. K. & Putnam, S. P. (2002). Temperament and socialization. In L. Pulkinnen & A. Caspi (Eds.), *Paths to successful development: Personality in the life course* (pp. 19–45). Cambridge, UK: Cambridge University Press.

Rothbaum, F., Weisz, J., Pott, M., Miyake, K. & Morelli, G. (2000). Attachment and culture: Security in the United States and Japan. *American Psychologist, 55*(10), 1093–1104. doi:10.1037/0003-066X.55.10.1093

Rothenberg, W. A., Hussong, A. M. & Chassin, L. (2016). Intergenerational continuity in high-conflict family environments. *Development and Psychopathology, 28*(1), 293–308. doi:10.1017/S0954579415000450

Russell, B. (2004). *History of Western philosophy.* London: The Folio Society.

Russell, J. A. (1991). Culture and the categorization of emotions. *Psychological Bulletin, 110*(3), 426–450. doi:10.1037/0033-2909.110.3.426

Russell, S. T., Crockett, L. J., Shen, Y.-L. & Lee, S.-A. (2008). Cross-ethnic invariance of self-esteem and depression measures for Chinese, Filipino, and European American adolescents. *Journal of Youth and Adolescence, 37*(1), 50–61. doi:10.1007/s10964-007-9231-1

Rutter, M. (1999). Resilience concepts and findings: Implications for family therapy. *Journal of Family Therapy, 21*(2), 119–144. doi:10.1111/1467-6427.00108

Rutter, M. (2013). Developmental psychopathology: A paradigm shift or just a relabeling? *Development and Psychopathology, 25*(4, Pt 2), 1201–1213. doi:10.1017/S0954579413000564

Rutter, M. & Sroufe, L. A. (2000). Developmental psychopathology: Concepts and challenges. *Development and Psychopathology, 12*(3), 265–296. doi:10.1017/S0954579400003023

Ryan, R. M., Huta, V. & Deci, E. L. (2008). Living well: A self-determination theory perspective on eudaimonia. *Journal of Happiness Studies, 9*(1), 139–170. doi:10.1007/s10902-006-9023-4

Saarni, C. (1984). An observational study of children's attempts to monitor their expressive behavior. *Child Development, 55*(4), 1504–1513. doi:10.2307/1130020

Saarni, C. (1998). Issues of cultural meaningfulness in emotional development. *Developmental Psychology, 34*, 647–652.

Saarni, C. (1999). *The development of emotional competence*. New York, NY: Guilford.

Saarni, C. (2000). The social context of emotional development. In M. Lewis & J. M. Haviland-Jones (Eds.), *Handbook of emotions (2nd ed.)* (pp. 306–322), New York, NY: Guilford.

Sabatelli, R. M., Buck, R. & Dreyer, A. (1982). Nonverbal communication accuracy in married couples: Relationship with marital complaints. *Journal of Personality and Social Psychology, 43*(5), 1088–1097. doi:10.1037/0022-3514.43.5.1088

Salovey, P. & Mayer, J. D. (1990). Emotional intelligence. *Imagination, Cognition and Personality, 9*(3), 185–211. doi: 10.2190/DUGG-P24E-52WK-6CDG

Salovey, P., Mayer, J. D. & Caruso, D. (2002). The positive psychology of emotional intelligence. In C. R. Snyder & S. J. Lopez (Eds.), *Handbook of positive psychology* (pp. 159–171). New York: Oxford University Press.

Salmon, K., Dadds, M. R., Allen, J. & Hawes, D. J. (2009). Can emotional language skills be taught during parent training for conduct problem children? *Child Psychiatry and Human Development, 40*(4), 485–498. doi: 10.1007/s10578-009-0139-8

Saltzman, W., Pynoos, R., Lester, P., Layne, C. & Beardslee, W. (2013). Enhancing family resilience through family narrative co-construction. *Clinical Child and Family Psychology Review, 16*(3), 294–310. doi:10.1007/s10567-013-0142-2

Samhan, H. H. (2014). Intra-ethnic diversity and religion. In S. C. Nassar-McMillan, K. J. Ajrouch & J. Hakim-Larson (Eds.) (pp. 45–65). *Biopsychosocial perspectives on Arab Americans: Culture, development, and health*. New York: Springer.

Schachter, S. & Singer, J. (1962). Cognitive, social, and physiological determinants of emotional state. *Psychological Review, 69*(5), 379–399. doi:10.1037/h0046234

Scherer, K. R. (2005). What are emotions? And how can they be measured? *Social Science Information, 44(4)*, 693–727.

Scherer, K. R., Banse, R. & Wallbott, H. G. (2001). Emotion inferences from vocal expression correlate across languages and cultures. *Journal of Cross-Cultural Psychology, 32*(1), 76–92. doi: 10.1177/0022022101032001009

Schmitt, D. P. & Allik, J. (2005). Simultaneous administration of the Rosenberg Self-Esteem Scale in 53 Nations: Exploring the universal and culture-specific features of global self-esteem. *Journal of Personality and Social Psychology, 89*(4), 623–642. doi:10.1037/0022-3514.89.4.623

Schnall, S. (2005). The pragmatics of emotion language. *Psychological Inquiry, 16*(1), 28–31.

Schofield, T. J., Conger, R. D. & Neppl, T. K. (2014). Positive parenting, beliefs about parental efficacy, and active coping: Three sources of intergenerational resilience. *Journal of Family Psychology, 28*(6), 973–978. doi:10.1037/fam0000024

Schutte, N. S. & Malouff, J. M. (1999). *Measuring emotional intelligence and related constructs*. New York: The Edwin Mellen Press.

Schutte, N. S., Malouff, J. M., Hall, L. E., Haggerty, D. J., Cooper, J. T., Golden, C. J. & Dornheim, L. (1998). Development and validation of a measure of emotional intelligence. *Personality and Individual Differences, 25*, 167–177.

Schutz, L. E. (2007). Models of exceptional adaptation in recovery after traumatic brain injury: A case series. *The Journal of Head Trauma Rehabilitation, 22(1)*, 48–55. doi: 10.1097/00001199-200701000-00006

Scott, S. A., Scammell, J. L., Metler, S., Williams, K. & Hakim-Larson, J. (July, 2014). Mothers' elaboration prompting and narrative exploration in children with autism spectrum disorder or another developmental disability. Poster presented at 9th International Conference on Child and Adolescent Psychopathology, London, UK.

Seedall, R. B. & Wampler, K. S. (2016). Couple emotional experience: Effects of attachment anxiety in low and high structure couple interactions. *Journal of Family Therapy*. Advance online publication. doi:10.1111/1467-6427.12113

Seldes, G. (1985). *The great thoughts*. New York: Ballantine.

Seligman, M. E. P. & Csikszentmihalyi, M. (2000). Positive psychology: An introduction. *American Psychologist, 55*(1), 5–14. doi:10.1037/0003-066X.55.1.5

Selman, R. (1980). *Growth of interpersonal understanding: Developmental and clinical analyses*. New York: Academic Press.

Selman, R. L. (1981). The development of interpersonal competence: The role of understanding in conduct. *Developmental Review, 1*(4), 401–422. doi:10.1016/0273-2297(81)90034-4

Shai, D. & Belsky, J. (2011a). When words just won't do: Introducing parental embodied mentalizing. *Child Development Perspectives, 5*(3), 173–180. doi:10.1111/j.1750-8606.2011.00181.x

Shai, D. & Belsky, J. (2011b). Parental embodied mentalizing: Let's be explicit about what we mean by implicit. *Child Development Perspectives, 5*(3), 187–188. doi:10.1111/j.1750-8606.2011.00195.x

Shantz, C. U. (1975). *The development of social cognition*. Chicago: University of Chicago Press.

Shantz, C. (1987). Conflicts between children. *Child Development, 58*(2), 283–305. doi:10.2307/1130507

Shapero, B., Hamilton, J., Stange, J., Liu, R., Abramson, L. & Alloy, L. (2015). Moderate childhood stress buffers against depressive response to proximal stressors: A multi-wave prospective study of early adolescents. *Journal of Abnormal Child Psychology, 43*(8), 1403–1413. doi:10.1007/s10802-015-0021-z

Sharpe, W. & Isidore of Seville (1964). Isidore of Seville: The Medical Writings. An English Translation with an Introduction and Commentary. *Transactions of the American Philosophical Society, 54*(2), 1–75. Retrieved from www.jstor.org/stable/1005938

Shaver, P. R. & Mikulincer, M. (2014). Adult attachment and emotion regulation. In J. J. Gross (Ed.), *Handbook of emotion regulation (2nd ed.)* (pp. 237–250). New York: Guilford Press.

Shaver, P., Schwartz, J., Kirson, D. & O'Connor, C. (1987). Emotion knowledge: Further exploration of a prototype approach. *Journal of Personality and Social Psychology, 52*(6), 1061–1086. doi:10.1037/0022-3514.52.6.1061

Shen, A. C.-T. (2009). Self-esteem of young adults experiencing interparental violence and child physical maltreatment: Parental and peer relationships as mediators. *Journal of Interpersonal Violence, 24*(5), 770–794. doi: 10.1177/0886260508317188

Shennum, W. A. & Bugental, D. B. (1982). The development of control over affective expression in nonverbal behavior. In R. S. Feldman (Ed.), *Development of nonverbal behavior in children* (pp. 101–121). New York: Springer-Verlag.

Shewark, E. A. & Blandon, A. Y. (2015). Mothers' and fathers' emotion socialization and children's emotion regulation: A within-family model. *Social Development, 24*(2), 266–284. doi:10.1111/sode.12095

Shields, A. & Cicchetti, D. (1998). Reactive aggression among maltreated children: The contributions of attention and emotion dysregulation. *Journal of Clinical Child Psychology, 27*(4), 381–395. doi:10.1207/s15374424jccp2704_2

Shields, A., Ryan, R. M. & Cicchetti, D. (2001). Narrative representations of caregivers and emotion dysregulation as predictors of maltreated children's rejection by peers. *Developmental Psychology, 37*(3), 321–337. doi:10.1037/0012-1649.37.3.321

Shiner, R. L., Buss, K. A., McClowry, S. G., Putnam, S. P., Saudino, K. J. & Zentner, M. (2012). What is temperament now? Assessing progress in temperament research on the twenty-fifth anniversary of Goldsmith et al. (1987). *Child Development Perspectives, 6*(4), 436–444.

Shirk, S., Burwell, R. & Harter, S. (2003). Strategies to modify low self-esteem in adolescents. In M. A. Reinecke, F. M. Dattilio & A. Freeman (Eds.), *Cognitive therapy with children and adolescents: A casebook for clinical practice (2nd ed.)* (pp. 189–213). New York: Guilford Press.

Shobris, J. G. (1994). The dualism of psychology. *Genetic, Social, and General Psychology Monographs, 120*(4), 373–392.

Shortt, J. W., Katz, L. F., Allen, N. B., Leve, C., Davis, B. & Sheeber, L. B. (2016). Emotion socialization in the context of risk and psychopathology: Mother and father socialization of anger and sadness in adolescents with depressive disorder. *Social Development, 25*(1), 27–46. doi:10.1111/sode.12138

Shure, M. B. & Spivack, G. (1982). Interpersonal problem-solving in young children: A cognitive approach to prevention. *American Journal of Community Psychology, 10*(3), 341–356. doi:10.1007/BF00896500

Shweder, R. A. (1993). The cultural psychology of the emotions. In M. Lewis & J. M. Haviland (Eds.), *Handbook of emotions* (pp. 417–431). New York: Guilford.

Shweder, R. A., Haidt, J., Horton, R. & Joseph, C. (2008). The cultural psychology of the emotions: Ancient and renewed. In M. Lewis, J. M. Haviland-Jones & L. F. Barrett (Eds.), *Handbook of emotions (3rd ed.)* (pp. 409–427). New York: Guilford.

Siegel, D. J. (1999). *The developing mind: How relationships and the brain interact to shape who we are*. New York: Guilford.

Siegel, D. J. (2001). Toward an interpersonal neurobiology of the developing mind: Attachment relationships, "mindsight," and neural integration. *Infant Mental Health Journal, 22*(1–2), 67–94. 10.1002/1097-0355(200101/04)22:1<67::AID-IMHJ3>3.0.CO;2-G

Siegel, D. J. (2006). An interpersonal neurobiology approach to psychotherapy: Awareness, mirror neurons, and neural plasticity in the development of well-being. *Psychiatric Annals, 36*(4), 248–256.

Siegling, A. B., Vesely, A. K., Petrides, K. V. & Saklofske, D. H. (2015). Incremental validity of the Trait Emotional Intelligence Questionnaire–Short Form (TEIQue–SF). *Journal of Personality Assessment, 97*(5), 525–535. doi:10.1080/00223891.2015.1013219

Sigel, I. E. & McGillicuddy-De Lisi, A. V. (2002). Parent beliefs are cognitions: The dynamic belief systems model. In M. H. Bornstein (Ed.), *Handbook of parenting: Vol. 3. Being and becoming a parent (2nd ed.)* (pp. 485–508). Mahwah, NJ: Erlbaum.

Sigel, I. E., McGillicuddy-DeLisi, A. V. & Goodnow, J. J. (Eds.) (1992) *Parental belief systems: The psychological consequences for children (2nd ed.)*. Hillsdale, NJ: Erlbaum.

Skinner, M. K. (2015). Environmental epigenetics and unified theory of the molecular aspects of evolution: A neo-Lamarckian concept that facilitates neo-Darwinian evolution. *Genome Biology and Evolution, 7*(5), 1296–1302.

Skovholt, K., Grønning, A. & Kankaanranta, A. (2014). The communicative functions of emoticons in workplace e-mails: :-). *Journal of Computer-Mediated Communication, 19*(4), 780–797. doi:10.1111/jcc4.12063

Small, S. A. (1988). Parental self-esteem and its relationship to childrearing practices, parent-adolescent interaction, and adolescent behavior. *Journal of Marriage and the Family, 50*(4), 1063–1072. doi:10.2307/352115

Smetana, J. G. (Ed.). (1994). *New directions for child development, No. 66. Beliefs about parenting: Origins and developmental implications*. San Francisco: Jossey-Bass.

Smith, J. P., Glass, D. J. & Fireman, G. (2015). The understanding and experience of mixed emotions in 3–5-year-old children. *The Journal of Genetic Psychology: Research and Theory on Human Development, 176*(2), 65–81. doi:10.1080/00221325.2014.1002750

Solomon, R. C. (1993). The philosophy of emotions. In M. Lewis & J. M. Haviland (Eds.), *Handbook of emotions* (pp. 3–15). New York: Guilford.

Solomon, R. C. (2000). The philosophy of emotions. In M. Lewis & J. M. Haviland-Jones (Eds.), *Handbook of emotions (2nd ed.).* New York: Guilford Press.

Solomon, R. C. (2002). Back to basics: On the very idea of "basic emotions." *Journal for the Theory of Social Behaviour, 32*(2), 115–144. doi:10.1111/1468-5914.00180

Solomon, R. C. (2008). The philosophy of emotions. In M. Lewis, J. M. Haviland-Jones & L. F. Barrett (Eds.), *Handbook of emotions (3rd ed.)* (pp. 3–16). New York: Guilford.

Solomon, J. & George, C. (Eds.). (1999). *Attachment disorganization.* New York: Guilford.

Solomon, J. & George, C. (Eds.). (2011). *Disorganized attachment and caregiving.* New York: Guilford.

Soltis, K., Davidson, T. M., Moreland, A., Felton, J. & Dumas, J. E. (2015). Associations among parental stress, child competence, and school-readiness: Findings from the PACE study. *Journal of Child and Family Studies, 24*(3), 649–657. doi:10.1007/s10826-013-9875-2

Somerville, L. H. & Casey, B. J. (2010). Developmental neurobiology of cognitive control and motivational systems. *Current Opinion in Neurobiology, 20*(2), 236–241. doi:10.1016/j.conb.2010.01.006

Sorce, J. F., Emde, R. N., Campos, J. J. & Klinnert, M. D. (1985). Maternal emotional signaling: Its effect on the visual cliff behavior of 1-year-olds. *Developmental Psychology, 21*(1), 195–200. doi:10.1037/0012-1649.21.1.195

Soucie, K. M., Lawford, H. & Pratt, M. W. (2012). Personal stories of empathy in adolescence and emerging adulthood. *Merrill-Palmer Quarterly, 58*(2), 141–158. doi:10.1353/mpq.2012.0010

Srivastava, S., John, O. P., Gosling, S. D. & Potter, J. (2003). Development of personality in early and middle adulthood: Set like plaster or persistent change? *Journal of Personality and Social Psychology, 84*, 1041–1053.

Sroufe, L. (1996). *Emotional development: The organization of emotional life in the early years.* New York. NY: Cambridge University Press.

Statistics Canada (2008). Retrieved from www12.statcan.gc.ca/census-recensement/2006/rt-td/ap-pa-eng.cfm

Staub, E. (1989). Individual and societal (group) values in a motivational perspective and their role in benevolence and harmdoing. In N. Eisenberg, J. Reykowski & E. Staub (Eds.), *Social and moral values: Individual and societal perspectives* (pp. 45–61). Hillsdale, NJ: Erlbaum.

Stavrianopoulos, K., Faller, G. & Furrow, J. L. (2014). Emotionally focused family therapy: Facilitating change within a family system. *Journal of Couple & Relationship Therapy, 13*(1), 25–43. doi:10.1080/15332691.2014.865976

Steele, H. & Steele, M. (2014). Attachment disorders: Theory, research, and treatment considerations. In M. Lewis & K. D. Rudolph (Eds.), *Handbook of developmental psychopathology (3rd ed.)* (pp. 357–370). doi: 10.1007/978-1-4614-9608-3_18

Stein, T., Carey, W. B. & Snyder, D. M. (2004). Is this a behavior problem or normal temperament? (Challenging cases: behaviors that concern parents). *Pediatrics, 114 (5), p.SS1400(7).*

Stein, N. L. & Levine, L. J. (1990). Making sense out of emotion: The representation and use of goal-structured knowledge. In N. L. Stein, B. Leventhal & T. Trabasso (Eds.), *Psychological and biological approaches to emotion* (pp. 45–73). Hillsdale, NJ: Erlbaum.

Steinberg, E. A. & Drabick, D. A. G. (2015). A developmental psychopathology perspective on ADHD and comorbid conditions: The role of emotion regulation. *Child Psychiatry and Human Development, 46*(6), 951–966. doi:10.1007/s10578-015-0534-2

Stern, D. N. (1999). Vitality contours: The temporal contour of feelings as a basic unit for constructing the infant's social experience. In P. Rochat (Ed.), *Early social cognition: Understanding others in the first months of life* (pp. 67–80). Mahwah, NJ: Erlbaum.

Sterns, P. E. (Ed.) (2008). *Oxford encyclopedia of the modern world: Slave trade*. Oxford University Press. Retrieved online from www.oxfordreference.com

Stewart, S. L. (2009). One Indigenous academic's evolution: A personal narrative of Native health research and competing ways of knowing. *First Peoples Child & Family Review*, 4(1), 57–65.

Stiles, J. & Jernigan, T. L. (2010). The basics of brain development. *Neuropsychology Review, 20*(4), 327–348. doi:10.1007/s11065-010-9148-4

Stipek, D. (1992). The child at school. In M. H. Bornstein & M. E. Lamb (Eds.), *Developmental psychology: An advanced textbook (3rd ed.)* (pp. 579–625). Hillsdale, NJ: Erlbaum.

Strang, N. M., Hanson, J. L. & Pollak, S. D. (2012). Physiological measures of emotion from a developmental perspective: State of the science: The importance of biological methods in linking social experience with social and emotional development. *Monographs of the Society for Research in Child Development, 77*(2), 61–66. doi:10.1111/j.1540-5834.2011.00662.x

Stronach, E. P., Toth, S. L., Rogosch, F. & Cicchetti, D. (2013). Preventive interventions and sustained attachment security in maltreated children. *Development and Psychopathology, 25*(4), 919–930. doi:10.1017/S0954579413000278

Sue, S., Kuraski, K. S. & Srinivasan, S. (1999). Ethnicity, gender, and cross-cultural issues in clinical research. In P. C. Kendall, J. N. Butcher & G. N. Holmbeck (Eds.), *Handbook of research methods in clinical psychology (2nd ed.)* (pp. 54–71). New York: Wiley.

Suveg, C., Payne, M., Thomassin, K. & Jacob, M. L. (2010). Electronic diaries: A feasible method of assessing emotional experiences in youth? *Journal of Psychopathology and Behavioral Assessment, 32*(1), 57–67. doi:10.1007/s10862-009-9162-0

Suveg, C., Sood, E., Barmish, A., Tiwari, S., Hudson, J. L. & Kendall, P. C. (2008). "I'd rather not talk about it": Emotion parenting in families of children with an anxiety disorder. *Journal of Family Psychology, 22*(6), 875–884. doi:10.1037/a0012861

Swick, K. J. & Williams, R. D. (2006). An analysis of Bronfenbrenner's bioecological perspective for early childhood educators: Implications for working with families experiencing stress. *Early Childhood Education Journal, 33*, 371–378. doi: 10.1007/s10643-006-0078-y

Tafarodi, R., Shaughnessy, S., Yamaguchi, S. & Murakoshi, A. (2011). The reporting of self-esteem in Japan and Canada. *Journal of Cross-Cultural Psychology, 42*(1), 155–164.

Tafarodi, R. W. & Swann, W. B., Jr. (1996). Individualism-collectivism and global self-esteem: Evidence for a cultural trade-off. *Journal of Cross-Cultural Psychology, 27*(6), 651–672. doi: 10.1177/0022022196276001

Tan, E. S. (1996). *Film and the structure of narrative film: Film as an emotion machine.* Mahwah, NJ: Lawrence Erlbaum.

Tau, G. Z. & Peterson, B. S. (2010). Normal development of brain circuits. *Neuropsychopharmacology, 35*(1), 147–168. doi:10.1038/npp.2009.115

Talavage, T. M., Nauman, E. A., Breedlove, E. L., Yoruk, U., Dye, A. E., Morigaki, K. E., Feuer, H. & Leverenz, L. J. (2014). Functionally-detected cognitive impairment in high school football players without clinically-diagnosed concussion. *Journal of Neurotrauma, 31*(4), 327–338. doi:10.1089/neu.2010.1512

Taylor, G. J., Bagby, R. M. & Luminet, O. (2000). Assessment of alexithymia: Self-report and observer-rated measures. In R. Bar-On & J. D. A. Parker (Eds.), *The handbook of emotional intelligence: Theory, development, assessment, and application at home, school, and in the workplace* (pp. 301–319). San Francisco: Jossey-Bass.

Teglasi, H. & Rothman, L. (2001). Stories: A classroom-based program to reduce aggressive behavior. *Journal of School Psychology, 39*, 71–94.

Thelen, E. & Smith, L. B. (1994). *MIT Press/Bradford book series in cognitive psychology. A dynamic systems approach to the development of cognition and action.* Cambridge, MA: The MIT Press.

Thelen, E. & Smith, L. B. (2006). Dynamic systems theories. In R. M. Lerner & W. Damon (Eds.), *Handbook of child psychology* (*6th ed.*): *Vol. 1, Theoretical models of human development* (pp. 258–312). Hoboken, NJ: John Wiley.

Thomas, A., Chess, S. Birch, H. G., Hertzig, M. E. & Korn, H. J. (1963). *Behavioral individuality in early childhood.* New York: New York University Press.

Thompson, R. A. (1994). Emotion regulation: A theme in search of definition. *Monographs of the Society for Research in Child Development, 59*(2–3), 25–52, 250–283. doi:10.2307/1166137

Thompson, R. A. (2009). Relationships, stress, and memory. In J. A. Quas & R. Fivush (Eds.), *Emotion and memory in development: Biological, cognitive, and social considerations* (pp. 355–373). New York: Oxford.

Thompson, R. A. (2014). Socialization of emotion and emotion regulation in the family. In J. J. Gross (Ed.), *Handbook of emotion regulation (2nd ed.)* (pp. 173–186). New York: Guilford Press.

Thorson, A. R., Rittenour, C. E., Kellas, J. K. & Trees, A. R. (2013). Quality interactions and family storytelling. *Communication Reports, 26*(2), 88–100. doi:10.1080/08934215.2013.797482

Teigen, K. H. (1994). Yerkes-Dodson: A law for all seasons. *Theory & Psychology, 4*(4), 525–547. doi:10.1177/0959354394044004

Tomkins, S. S. (1962). Amplification, attenuation and affects. In S. S. Tomkins, *Affect, imagery, consciousness, Vol. 1. The positive affects* (pp. 88–107). doi:/10.1037/14351-003

Tomkins, S. S. (1978). Script theory: Differential magnification of affects. In H. Howe & A. Dienstbier (Eds.), *Nebraska Symposium on Motivation* (Vol. 26, pp. 201–236). Lincoln: University of Nebraska Press.

Tomkins, S. S. (1981). The quest for primary motives: Biography and autobiography of an idea. *Journal of Personality and Social Psychology, 41*(2), 306–329. doi:10.1037/0022-3514.41.2.306

Tomkins, S. S. & McCarter, R. (1964). What and where are the primary affects? Some evidence for a theory. *Perceptual and Motor Skills, 18*(1), 119–158. doi:10.2466/pms.1964.18.1.119

Tops, M., Van Peer, J. M., Korf, J., Wijers, A. A. & Tucker, D. M. (2007). Anxiety, cortisol, and attachment predict plasma oxytocin. *Psychophysiology, 44*, 444–449.

Toth, S. L., Gravener-Davis, J. A., Guild, D. J. & Cicchetti, D. (2013). Relational interventions for child maltreatment: Past, present, and future perspectives. *Development and Psychopathology, 25*(4, Pt 2), 1601–1617. doi:10.1017/S0954579413000795

Tracy, J. L., Cheng, J. T., Robins, R. W. & Trzesniewski, K. H. (2009). Authentic and hubristic pride: The affective core of self-esteem and narcissism. *Self and Identity, 8*(2–3), 196–213. doi:10.1080/15298860802505053

Tracy, J. L., Robins, R. W. & Lagattuta, K. H. (2005). Can children recognize pride? *Emotion, 5*(3), 251–257. doi: 10.1037/1528-3542.5.3.251

Triandis, H. C. (1994). Major cultural syndromes and emotion. In S. Kitayama & H. R. Markus (Eds.), *Emotion and culture: Empirical studies of mutual influence* (pp. 285–306). Washington, D.C.: American Psychological Association.

Trimble, J. E. & Dickson, R. (2005). *Ethnic gloss*. In C. B. Fisher & R. M. Lerner (Eds.), *Encyclopedia of applied developmental science* (pp. 412–415) Volume I. Thousand Oaks: Sage.

Tronick, E. (2007). *The neurobehavioral and social-emotional development of infants and children*. New York, NY: Norton.

Tronick, E. & Beeghly, M. (2011). Infants' meaning-making and the development of mental health problems. *American Psychologist, 66*(2), 107–119. doi:10.1037/a0021631

Tsai, J. L. (2007). Ideal affect: Cultural causes and behavioral consequences. *Perspectives on Psychological Science, 2*(3), 242–259. doi:10.1111/j.1745-6916.2007.00043.x

Tsai, J. L., Knutson, B. & Fung, H. H. (2006). Cultural variation in affect valuation. *Journal of Personality and Social Psychology, 90*(2), 288–307. doi:10.1037/0022-3514.90.2.288

Tsai, J. L., Louie, J. Y., Chen, E. E. & Uchida, Y. (2007). Learning what feelings to desire: Socialization of ideal affect through children's storybooks. *Personality and Social Psychology Bulletin, 33*(1), 17–30. doi:10.1177/0146167206292749

Tugade, M. M. & Fredrickson, B. L. (2007). Regulation of positive emotions: Emotion regulation strategies that promote resilience. *Journal of Happiness Studies, 8*(3), 311–333. doi:10.1007/s10902-006-9015-4

Twenge, J. M. & Campbell, W. K. (2002). Self-esteem and socioeconomic status: A meta-analytic review. *Personality and Social Psychology Review, 6*(1), 59–71. doi:10.1207/S15327957PSPR0601_3

Twenge, J. M. & Campbell, W. K. (2008). Increases in positive self-views among high school students: Birth-cohort changes in anticipated performance, self-satisfaction, self-liking, and self-competence. *Psychological Science, 19*(11), 1082–1086. doi:10.1111/j.1467-9280.2008.02204.x

Twenge, J. & Crocker, J. (2002). Race and self-esteem: Meta-analyses comparing Whites, Blacks, Hispanics, Asians, and American Indians and comment on Gray-Little and Hafdahl (2000). *Psychological Bulletin, 128*(3), 371–408.

UCSF Memory and Aging Center (2016). Retrieved from http://memory.ucsf.edu/

Umaña-Taylor (2013). Ethnic identity development among Latino adolescents … Who, what, when, where??? *Society for Research on Adolescence*. Retrieved from www.s-r-a.org/print/581

Umaña-Taylor, A. J. & Guimond, A. B. (2010). A longitudinal examination of parenting behaviors and perceived discrimination predicting Latino adolescents' ethnic identity. *Developmental Psychology, 46*(3), 636–650. doi:10.1037/a0019376

UNICEF (2015). *Child labour*. Retrieved from www.unicef.org/protection/57929_child_labour.html

United Nations High Commissioner for Refugees (2016). *Figures at a glance*. Retrieved from www.unhcr.org/en-us/figures-at-a-glance.html

United Nations Statistics Division (October 31, 2013). *UNdata: A world of information*. Retrieved from http://unstats.un.org/unsd/methods/m49/m49regin.htm#europe

U.S. Census Bureau (2011). *The Hispanic population: 2010*. Retrieved from www.census.gov/prod/cen2010/briefs/c2010br-04.pdf

U.S. Department of the Interior, Indian Affairs (2015). *Who we are*. Retrieved from http://bia.gov/WhoWeAre/

Valsiner, J. (Ed.). (2005). *Heinz Werner and developmental science*. New York, NY: Kluwer Academic/Plenum Publishers. doi:10.1007/b108487

Van Bergen, P. V., Salmon, K., Dadds, M. R. & Allen, J. (2009). The effects of mother training in emotion-rich, elaborative reminiscing on children's shared recall and emotion knowledge. *Journal of Cognition and Development, 10*(3), 162–187. doi:10.1080/15248370903155825

van der Pol, L. D., Groeneveld, M. G., van Berkel, S. R., Endendijk, J. J., Hallers-Haalboom, E. T., Bakermans-Kranenburg, M. J. & Mesman, J. (2015). Fathers' and mothers' emotion talk with their girls and boys from toddlerhood to preschool age. *Emotion, 15*(6), 854–864. doi:10.1037/emo0000085

van IJzendoorn, M. H. & Bakermans-Kranenburg, M. J. (2012). A sniff of trust: Meta-analysis of the effects of intranasal oxytocin administration on face recognition, trust to in-group, and trust to out-group. *Psychoneuroendocrinology, 37*(3), 438–443. doi:10.1016/j.psyneuen.2011.07.008

van IJzendoorn, M. H. & Sagi-Schwartz, A. (2008). Cross-cultural patterns of attachment: Universal and contextual dimensions. In J. Cassidy & P. R. Shaver (Eds.), *Handbook of attachment: Theory, research, and clinical applications (2nd ed.)*, pp. 880– 905. New York: Guilford.

van IJzendoorn, M. H., Schuengel, C. & Bakermans-Kranenburg, M. J. (1999). Disorganized attachment in early childhood: Meta-analysis of precursors, concomitants, and sequelae. *Development and Psychopathology*, 11, 225–249.

Varga, S. & Krueger, J. (2013). Background emotions, proximity and distributed emotion regulation. *Review of Philosophy and Psychology*, *4*(2), 271–292. doi:10.1007/s13164-013-0134-7

Vaughn, B. E., Kopp, C. B. & Krakow, J. B. (1984). The emergence and consolidation of self-control from eighteen to thirty months of age: Normative trends and individual differences. *Child Development*, *55*(3), 990–1004. doi:10.2307/1130151

Vidal, L., Ares, G. & Jaeger, S. R. (2016). Use of emoticon and emoji in tweets for food-related emotional expression. *Food Quality and Preference*, *49*, 119–128. doi:10.1016/j.foodqual.2015.12.002

Vinik, J., Johnston, M., Grusec, J. E. & Farrell, R. (2013). Understanding the learning of values using a domains-of-socialization framework. *Journal of Moral Education*, *42*(4), 475–493. doi:10.1080/03057240.2013.817329

Volling, B. L., McElwain, N. L. & Miller, A. L. (2002). Emotion regulation in context: The jealousy complex between young siblings and its relations with child and family characteristics. *Child Development*, *73*(2), 581–600. doi:10.1111/1467-8624.00425

von Soest, T., Wichstrøm, L. & Kvalem, I. L. (2016). The development of global and domain-specific self-esteem from age 13 to 31. *Journal of Personality and Social Psychology*, *110*(4), 592–608. doi:10.1037/pspp0000060

Vogel, D. L., Wester, S. R., Heesacker, M. & Madon, S. (2003). Confirming gender stereotypes: A social role perspective. *Sex Roles*, *48*(11–12), 519–528. doi: 10.1023/A:1023575212526

Vygotsky, L. S. (1962). *Thought and language*. Cambridge, MA: MIT Press.

Waddington, C. H. (1957). *The strategy of the genes*. London: George Allen & Unwin.

Waggoner, J. E. (2010). Temperature-based metonymies for emotions in children and adults. *Psychological Reports*, *106*(1), 233–245. doi:10.2466/PR0.106.1.233-245

Waggoner, J. E. & Palermo, D. S. (1989). Betty is a bouncing bubble: Children's comprehension of emotion-descriptive metaphors. *Developmental Psychology*, *25*(1), 152–163. doi: 10.1037/0012-1649.25.1.152

Walker-Andrews, A. S. (2008). Intermodal emotional processes in infancy. In M. Lewis, J. M. Haviland-Jones & L. F. Barrett (Eds.), *Handbook of emotions (3rd ed.)* (pp. 364–375). New York: Guilford Press.

Walsh, F. (1996). The concept of family resilience: Crisis and challenge. *Family Process*, *35*(3), 261–281. doi:10.1111/j.1545-5300.1996.00261.x

Waterman, A. S. (1993). Two conceptions of happiness: Contrasts of personal expressiveness (eudaimonia) and hedonic enjoyment. *Journal of Personality and Social Psychology*, *64*(4), 678–691. doi:10.1037/0022-3514.64.4.678

Waters, E. & Deane, K. E. (1985). Defining and assessing individual differences in attachment relationships: Q-methodology and the organization of behavior in infancy and early childhood. *Monographs of the Society for Research in Child Development, 50*(1–2), 41–65. doi:10.2307/3333826

Waters, H. S. & Waters, E. (2006). The attachment working models concept: Among other things, we build script-like representations of secure base experiences. *Attachment & Human Development, 8*(3), 185–197. doi:10.1080/14616730600856016

Waters, H. S. & Rodrigues-Doolabh, L. (2001, April). Are attachment scripts the building blocks of attachment representations? Paper presented at the meeting of the Society for Research in Child Development. Retrieved from www.psychology.sunysb.edu/attachment/srcd2001/srcd2001.htm

Waters, T. E. A., Bosmans, G., Vandevivere, E., Dujardin, A. & Waters, H. S. (2015). Secure base representations in middle childhood across two Western cultures: Associations with parental attachment representations and maternal reports of behavior problems. *Developmental Psychology, 51*(8), 1013–1025. doi:10.1037/a0039375

Waters, T. E. A. & Fivush, R. (2015). Relations between narrative coherence, identity, and psychological well-being in emerging adulthood. *Journal of Personality, 83*(4), 441–451. doi:10.1111/jopy.12120

Weersing, V. R., Shamseddeen, W., Garber, J., Hollon, S. D., Clarke, G. N., Beardslee, W. R., … Brent, D. A. (2016). Prevention of depression in at-risk adolescents: Predictors and moderators of acute effects. *Journal of the American Academy of Child & Adolescent Psychiatry, 55*(3), 219–226. doi:10.1016/j.jaac.2015.12.015

Werner, H. (1957). *Comparative psychology of mental development (rev. ed.)*. Oxford, England: International Universities Press.

Westenberg, P. M., Drewes, M. J., Goedhart, A. W., Siebelink, B. M. & Treffers, P. D. A. (2004). A developmental analysis of self-reported fears in late childhood through mid-adolescence: Social-evaluative fears on the rise? *Journal of Child Psychology and Psychiatry, 45*(3), 481–495. doi:10.1111/j.1469-7610.2004.00239.x

Westenberg, P. M., Siebelink, B. M., Warmenhoven, N. J. C. & Treffers, P. D. A. (1999). Separation anxiety and overanxious disorders: Relations to age and level of psychosocial maturity. *Journal of the American Academy of Child & Adolescent Psychiatry, 38*(8), 1000–1007. doi:10.1097/00004583-199908000-00016

Westenberg, P. M. & Gjerde, P. F. (1999). Ego development during the transition from adolescence to young adulthood: A 9-year longitudinal study. *Journal of Research in Personality, 33*(2), 233–252. doi:10.1006/jrpe.1999.2248

White, G. M. (1993). Emotions inside out: The anthropology of affect. In M. Lewis & J. M. Haviland (Eds.), *Handbook of emotions* (pp. 29–39). New York: Guilford Press.

White, G. M. (2000). Representing emotional meaning: Category, metaphor, schema, discourse. In M. Lewis and J. M. Haviland-Jones (Eds.), *Handbook of Emotions (2nd ed.)* (pp. 30–44). New York: Guilford Press.

Whiting, D. L., Deane, F. P., Simpson, G. K., McLeod, H. J. & Ciarrochi, J. (2017). Cognitive and psychological flexibility after a traumatic brain injury and the implications for treatment in acceptance-based therapies: A conceptual review. *Neuropsychological Rehabilitation, 27*(2), 263–299. doi:10.1080/09602011.2015.1062115

Wicker, B., Keysers, C., Plailly, J., Royet, J., Gallese, V. & Rizzolatti, G. (2003). Both of us disgusted in my insula. *Neuron, 40*(3), 655–664. doi:doi:10.1016/S0896-6273(03)00679-2

Widen, S. C. & Russell, J. A. (2008). Young children's understanding of others' emotions. In M. Lewis, J. M. Haviland-Jones & L. F. Barrett (Eds.), *Handbook of Emotions (3rd ed.)* (pp. 348–363). New York: Guilford Press.

Wierzbicka, A. (1992). The semantics of interjection. *Journal of Pragmatics, 18*(2–3), 159–192. doi:10.1016/0378-2166(92)90050-L

Wilson, B. J., Berg, J. L., Zurawski, M. E. & King, K. A. (2013). Autism and externalizing behaviors: Buffering effects of parental emotion coaching. *Research in Autism Spectrum Disorders, 7*(6), 767–776. doi:10.1016/j.rasd.2013.02.005

Winsler, A. (2003). Introduction to special issue: Vygotskian perspectives in early childhood education. *Early Education and Development, 14*(3), 253–269.

Wols, A., Scholte, R. H. J. & Qualter, P. (2015). Prospective associations between loneliness and emotional intelligence. *Journal of Adolescence, 39*, 40–48. doi:10.1016/j.adolescence.2014.12.007

Wörmann, V., Holodynski, M., Kärtner, J. & Keller, H. (2012). A cross-cultural comparison of the development of the social smile: A longitudinal study of maternal and infant imitation in 6- and 12-week-old infants. *Infant Behavior & Development, 35*(3), 335–347. doi:10.1016/j.infbeh.2012.03.002

Yoon, E., Langrehr, K. & Ong, L. Z. (2011). Content analysis of acculturation research in counseling and counseling psychology: A 22-year review. *Journal of Counseling Psychology, 58*, 83–96. doi:10.1037/a0021128

Yoshikawa, H. (1994). Prevention as cumulative protection: Effects of early family support and education on chronic delinquency and its risks. *Psychological Bulletin, 115*(1), 28–54.doi: 10.1037/0033-2909.115.1.28

Yoshimoto, D. K. (2005). Marital meta-emotion: Emotion coaching and dyadic interaction. *Dissertation Abstracts International: Section B: The Sciences and Engineering, 66*(6-B), 3448. (UMI No. AAI0808307)

Yow, W. Q. & Markman, E. M. (2011). Bilingualism and children's use of paralinguistic cues to interpret emotion in speech. *Bilingualism: Language and Cognition, 14*(4), 562–569. doi: 10.1017/S1366728910000404

Zajonc, R. B. (1984). On the primacy of affect. *American Psychologist, 39*(2), 117–123. doi: 10.1037/0003-066X.39.2.117

Zeev, W. (2015). Effects of childhood experience of violence between parents and/or parent-to-child violence on young Israeli adults' global self-esteem. *Violence and Victims, 30(4)*, 699–713. doi.org/10.1891/0886-6708.VV-D-13-00126

Zeman, J., Dallaire, D. & Borowski, S. (2016). Socialization in the context of risk and psychopathology: Maternal emotion socialization in children of incarcerated mothers. *Social Development, 25*(1), 66–81. doi:10.1111/sode.12117

Zeman, J., Klimes-Dougan, B., Cassano, M. & Adrian, M. (2007). Measurement issues in emotion research with children and adolescents. *Clinical Psychology: Science and Practice, 14*(4), 377–401. doi:10.1111/j.1468-2850.2007.00098.x

Zentner, M. & Bates, J. E. (2008). Child temperament: An integrative review of concepts, research programs, and measures. *European Journal of Developmental Science*, 2*(1–2)*, 7–37.

Zurbriggen, E. L. & Sturman, T. S. (2002). Linking motives and emotions: A test of McClelland's hypotheses. *Personality and Social Psychology Bulletin, 28*, 521–535.

# Glossary

**affect mirroring** The socialization process by which parents interpret their children's emotional states and reflect them back to them in a manner that demonstrates how to regulate affect (Holodynski, Friedlmeier).

**affect optimization** Optimizing well-being through the use and experience of emotions as exemplified in the work of M. Powell Lawton with older adults (Labouvie-Vief, Medler; Magai).

**affect reciprocity** In dyadic communication, how one member of a dyad reciprocates the valence of emotion demonstrated by the other (e.g., reciprocating positive affect with positive affect, negative with negative, positive with negative, or negative with positive).

**affect valuation theory** A theory that proposes that ideal affect or how you would ideally like to feel in certain situations varies from one culture to another (Tsai).

**affective schemas** Mental representations of relatively stable modes of reacting emotionally that are influenced by the processes of assimilation and accommodation (Piaget).

**affective social competence** The ability to effectively manage affect, communicate an awareness and acceptance of affect in self and others, and to be responsive to others' affective communications (Halberstadt, Denham, Dunsmore).

**alexithymia** A maladaptive condition in which individuals have difficulty describing their own feelings and states of emotional arousal (Taylor, Bagby, Luminet).

**authentic self-esteem** Feeling good about the self in a way that shows a balance between humility and vanity, and that involves making realistic attributions about the self based on specific situations, tasks, and one's own behaviours (Mruk; Lewis).

**autobiographical memories** Memories of the self that situate a person across time and space and that give emotional meaning to the person's life stories and identities (Fivush, Nelson; Fitzgerald; McAdams).

**background emotions** Observable shifts over time in indicators of emotion in the face, body language, muscle tone and gestures (Damasio; Feldman).

**behaviour epigenetics** A field of study that examines social and physical environmental effects on the epigenome (i.e., modifiable functional layer of genes that affects genetic expression). The focus is on examining changes in the epigenome at various points in time and as passed on across generations (Cicchetti; Keating; Lester, Conradt, Marsit).

**behavioural inhibition** A temperamental quality characterized by low reactivity to the environment and inhibited behaviours when confronted with novel stimulation (Kagan).

**brain plasticity** The idea that structural and functional aspects of the brain change in a flexible manner over the course of development and in reaction to the environment.

**broaden and build theory** A theory that maintains that positive emotions help to build a strong foundation of trust in the environment and thus lead to the creative consideration of broader possibilities and the promotion of well-being or happiness (Frederickson).

**callous-unemotional traits** A deficit in the ability to experience and demonstrate prosocial emotions, remorse, guilt and empathy (DSM-5).

**canalization** The constraining or narrowing of options or pathways as development proceeds (Waddington).

**coercive parenting** A parenting style in which a repetitive negative cycle of emotional interaction and coercion develops between the parent and child (Patterson, Forgatch, DeGarmo).

**cognitive appraisal** Thought processes that involve how people evaluate, interpret and give meaning to their emotional experiences (Arnold; Lazarus).

**cohort effects** Group differences that are due to commonalities of a generation rather than to age.

**collectivistic** A term that describes cultures in which emphasis is placed more on the group needs and value maintenance than on the individual's needs and rights (Triandis).

**conceptual metaphor** Using a more concrete emotion concept, such as "boiling with anger" to stand for an abstract one, such as "anger" (Kovecses; Lakoff, Johnson).

**conceptual metonymy** Using part of an emotion concept (drop in temperature with fear) such as having "cold feet", to stand for another part or the whole emotion concept such as "fear" (Kovecses; Lakoff, Johnson).

**coping flexibility** The ability to flexibly switch from using one coping strategy to another, an ability that is especially important when the controllability of a situation changes (Cheng).

**core relational themes** The fundamental theme underlying each emotion that reveals how cognition is linked to motivation. Evident during encounters between a person and an environment that can result in harm or benefits to the person (Lazarus).

**cultural genogram** A family tree examining two or more generations with an emphasis on the various ethnic backgrounds and cultural values that may coincide or be in conflict with each other (Hardy, Laszloffy).

**cumulative protections** Protective factors (including preventive interventions) that can accumulate over time and thus pile up and add to resilience (Yoshikawa).

**decoding (judgement) accuracy** Accurately interpreting the intended emotional feeling conveyed by someone else.

**defensive self-esteem** Feeling good about the self due to an exaggerated, unrealistic and excessive sense of either self-worth or competence, or both (Mruk).

**depression composite** A composite of variables that assess self-worth, affect and feelings of hopelessness that together predict suicidal ideation (Harter, Marold, Whitesell).

**developmental psychopathology** An approach to research and clinical work that considers continuities and discontinuities in development over the lifespan, and adaptive and maladaptive functioning with relatively more emphasis on prevention and resilience than diagnosis and treatment (Rutter, Sroufe).

**differential susceptibility** A model of biological susceptibility to the influence of the environment in which a person may be more susceptible both to risks in adverse environments and to enhanced development in enriched environments (Boyce, Ellis).

**differentiation and dynamical integration (DDI)** A perspective that integrates theories of emotional expressions with a dynamic systems point of view. Physiological, cognitive and social aspects of development along with conscious self-awareness become integrated and organized and result in specific emotions such as anger, sadness, fear or happiness (Camras).

**difficult temperament** A relatively stable pattern of temperament characterized by overactivity, unpredictability, negative moods and emotional expressions, and difficulties in social situations (Chess, Thomas).

**display rules** Implicit or explicit rules learned within social and cultural settings that specify how, when, where and with whom emotions can be expressed (Ekman, Friesen).

**dual failure** A model in which children with conduct disorder show deficits both academically and socially (Patterson, Stoolmiller).

**dyadic coping** Joint efforts made by dyad partners to cope with stress to address their common goals (Bodenmann).

**dyadic reciprocity** Collaboration between family members of a dyad as they interact harmoniously to accomplish the goals of a joint activity (Feldman, Bamberger, Kanat-Maymon).

**dyadic stress** Stressful life experiences that affect both members of dyads in the family at about the same time and place (Bodenmann).

**dynamic systems** A construct derived from mathematics and physics that has been applied to psychology. Various components of a single system may develop or change independently of each other but may coalesce and stabilize at a given point in time as they are attracted to a particular attractor state (Thelen, Smith).

**easy-going temperament** A relatively stable pattern of temperament characterized by alertness, attentiveness and primarily positive affect in social situations (Chess, Thomas).

**effortful control** A temperamental quality that involves the ability to inhibit and regulate behaviours (Rothbart, Putnam; Evans).

**elaborative reminiscing style** Involves the parent adding new details and relevant new information while guiding a child's interpretations as the child remembers past emotional events (Fivush, Nelson; Laible, Panfile).

**emotion acceptance, awareness and coaching** The three underlying component processes that are important for parental meta-emotion philosophy and socialization of emotion in children (Gottman).

**emotion scripts** Scripts for the causes and consequences of specific emotions linked to common events and routines within a given culture (Saarni; White; Widen, Russell).

**emotional attunement** Attempts by partners in a couple to pay attention to and understand each other's emotions and to make sincere attempts to repair each other's hurt feelings in an empathic manner (Gottman).

**emotional biases** A bias towards particular emotional experiences and expressions in personality over time that are nonetheless subject to possible change (Magai).

**emotional competence** The age-appropriate ability to demonstrate knowledge and understanding of emotions in self and others through non-verbal and verbal communication and emotional expression and regulation. Demonstrated when emotions are experienced that are consistent with individuals' own values and that of their culture (Saarni).

**emotional self-efficacy** Feeling that you have the capacity, skills and resources needed to achieve a desired emotional outcome (Saarni).

**emotionally focused family therapy (EFFT)** Application of emotion-focused therapy to family members with the goal of transforming maladaptive attachment-related emotions to adaptive emotions that benefit the family relationships (Johnson).

**emotion-focused therapy (EFT)** A type of therapy in which the processing of emotions is targeted by facilitating awareness during emotion arousal, emotion regulation, reflection on emotions, and transformation of their meaning (Greenberg).

**emotion-related socialization behaviours (ERSBs)** Emotion-relevant parenting practices meant to teach children about their own and others' emotions and how, when and where to display or control emotions according to the situation or culture (Eisenberg, Cumberland, Spinrad).

**epigenome** Functional layer of genetic information that contains genetic markers that result from interactions with the environment (Lester, Conradt, Marsit).

**ethnic gloss** Use of a broad and overgeneralized categorical label when discussing culture that implies that all people within a broad geographical area hold the same views (e.g., Asia); to avoid ethnic gloss, it is helpful to specify regions or countries wherever possible (Trimble, Dickson).

**ethnic identity affirmation** The degree to which individuals have positive or affirming feelings about their own ethnic identities (Umaña-Taylor).

**ethnographic approach** A research approach that makes use of recording observations and data that is collected in natural settings among the people of a given culture.

**executive functions** A set of cognitive skills that include inhibitory control, working memory and cognitive flexibility that assist individuals in regulating attention, behaviour and emotions (Obradović).

**expression accuracy** Conveying the intended emotional feeling accurately for others to interpret through non-verbal channels.

**externalizing disorder** Disorders in which the primary features are behavioural misconduct and angry disruptions that disturb others.

**facial feedback** Hypothesis that emotional feelings arise from arousal feedback originating in skin changes (e.g., flushed, goosebumps) and muscle movements (Tomkins, McCarter).

**facial mimicry** Mimicry of another person's facial expression, such as when an adult opens his or her mouth in surprise and an infant mimics the expression (Meltzoff, Moore).

**five domains of socialization** Five domains in which parents make attempts to socialize their children according to their goals. The domains are protection, reciprocity, control, guided learning and group participation.

**four horsemen of the apocalypse** Four behaviours that are part of a communication pattern that occurs when partners are on a pathway that predicts a break-up or divorce. These are defensiveness, criticism, stonewalling and contempt (Gottman).

**functional neurocircuitry** Connections or circuits between brain regions that serve particular functions.

**heterochronic** The idea that the various components of a system may develop in an uneven manner with some components developing earlier than others.

**individualistic** A term that describes cultures in which emphasis is placed more on the individual's needs and rights than on group needs and value maintenance (Triandis).

**interactional synchrony** Correspondence in the movements of infants to the speech sounds they hear in the social environment (Condon, Sander).

**inter-informant agreement** A form of reliability in which the degree of agreement is assessed among various informants (e.g., mother, father and teacher) as they rate the same behaviours (e.g., a child's aggression).

**internalization theory** Developmental theory that emotional expressions are signs for actions and serve a regulatory function; in infancy, the signs are co-constructed and co-regulated with caregivers, but become increasingly internalized with increases in reflection and self-regulation in later development (Holodynski, Friedlmeier).

**internalizing disorder** Disorders in which the primary features involve emotional dysfunction, such as anxiety and depression.

**intuitive parenting** Parenting behaviours that have evolved to allow parents to intuitively respond to their infants' emotional and cognitive needs as the infants are learning (H. Papoušek, M. Papoušek).

**jealousy complex** Complexity of possible primary emotions, such as anger, fear or sadness, that may underlie jealous feelings in a triad such as a parent with two siblings (Volling, McElwain, Miller).

**launch and grow model** A model of adolescent depression that proposes that maternal depression launches risk factors for children that eventually lead to adolescent depression (Garber, Cole).

**linguistic relativity** The idea originating from Edward Sapir and Benjamin Whorf that perceptions and experiences, including those involving emotions, depend upon or are relative to the linguistic terms available to describe the perceptions and experiences (Lucy; Russell).

**looking-glass self** The idea originating from Charles Horton Cooley that others affect how we view ourselves and their appraisals of us are reflected back to us (Franks, Gecas).

**measurement equivalence** Measuring the same or equivalent underlying constructs with different groups of people who vary by age, gender or culture.

**mentalization** The ability to reflect on the internal mental states of self and others that develops during interactions with important others (Fonagy, Gergely, Target).

**meta-analyses** Compiling the results from a number of studies measuring the same construct by taking the average of the strength of the relations among the variables that are common among the studies.

**mindful parenting** The ability of parents to attentively engage in the process of mindful self- and other-awareness while parenting by reflecting on their parenting choices in the moment and by making intentional decisions with less possibility of later regrets (Duncan, Coatsworth, Greenberg).

**mindfulness** Attending to and being aware of one's own experiences whether they arise from internal experiences or external stimulation, and doing so in the present moment in a non-judgemental manner (Kabat-Zinn).

**mind-mindedness** The tendency in parents to treat their young children as thinking and feeling beings with minds of their own (Meins).

**mirror neurons** Neurons that are activated through direct experience and by observing or imitating another person (Rizzolatti, Craighero).

**mixed methods** A research approach that integrates both qualitative and quantitative data.

**narrative coherence** A codable feature of oral or written narratives that assesses how complete and comprehensible the narrative is and how internally consistent the details are (Fiese; Waters, Fivush).

**narrative identity** The life story created by a person to give his or life meaning (Bauer, McAdams, Pals).

**negative emotionality** A temperamental quality that involves aspects of fear, anger and sadness (Rothbart, Putnam; Evans).

**ontogenetic** Developmental changes that occur within individuals over the lifespan.

**orienting sensitivity** A temperamental quality that involves sensitivity to attending to stimulation within the self or the environment (Rothbart, Putnam; Evans).

**orthogenetic principle** Principle that development proceeds over time from being less to more complex, differentiated and hierarchically organized (Werner).

**paralinguistic features** Features of language that convey meanings, including emotional meanings such as sound patterns, rhythms of speech, voice intonations and interjections. Such paralanguage may also be text-based and include the use of emoji and emoticons.

**parental beliefs** Mental representations that parents have about any aspect of their functioning as a parent (Sigel, McGillicuddy-DeLisi).

**parental embodied mentalization (PEM)** Parents' ability to consider the infant as a mentalistic partner while they are interacting non-verbally through facial expressions, bodily movements and making bodily contact (Shai, Belsky).

**parental meta-emotion philosophy (PMEP)** How parents think and feel about their own emotions and those of their children (Gottman, Katz, Hooven).

**parental prearming** Parental attempts to prepare their children for how to handle possible future emotionally laden situations (Padilla-Walker).

**parental self-efficacy beliefs** Parents' perception of their own capability of performing the role of being a parent (Coleman, Karraker).

**perceived physical appearance** How individuals perceive and evaluate their physical appearance which then influences their sense of self-worth or worthiness of being liked or loved (Harter).

**phylogenetic** Changes that occur within species over historical time.

**possible selves** Possibilities for the kind of selves individuals aspire to be in the future, or the kind of selves they used to wish to be in the past (Markus, Nurius).

**pragmatics** Features of communication patterns that convey the underlying social intentions and emotional meaning of a form of interaction, such as using polite, respectful terminology and greetings.

**primary emotions** Biologically based emotional reactions that are adaptive, or learned emotional reactions that are maladaptive that form the underlying foundation for the processing of emotions. Construct used in emotion-focused therapy (Greenberg).

**probabilistic epigenesis** A developmental systems theory that emphasizes that higher forms or levels of complexity that emerge from earlier ones cannot be predictably determined from earlier ones, and are thus probabilistic in nature (Gottlieb).

**process model of emotion regulation** Five categories of ways to regulate emotion: selecting a situation relevant to goals, modifying the situation to regulate emotions in self or others, directing attention in the moment to regulate emotions, changing thoughts to reappraise the situation and thus alter emotion, and finally modulating or altering emotional responses directly by attempts to enhance or suppress emotions (Gross).

**qualia** The unique conscious quality of how human sensory and perceptual experiences feel to the person having the experience (Ramachandran, Hirstein).

**racial socialization** Efforts by older family members with younger ones to instil racial pride and enhance awareness and caution about how to counteract racial prejudice and discrimination (Evans, George).

**randomized control trial (RCT) interventions** Interventions in which participants are randomly assigned to a manualized intervention or to a comparison group as a control; therapists who conduct the treatments are supervised and checks are made to ensure therapists follow the manual (Cicchetti).

**reaction range** Term originating from Theodosius Dobzhansky and Irving Gottesman that was used in the past to refer to the limits on phenotype set by a person's genotype (Griffiths, Tabery).

**redemptive self** A common part of life narratives in which individuals first experience adversity that contaminates their life stories, but then manage to resiliently overcome it leading to redemption (McAdams).

**reference values** Goals, standards and norms incorporated by individuals as they self-regulate and that eventually supersede their temperamental characteristics (Denissen et al.).

**regulatory capacity** A temperamental quality in infants similar to effortful control in children in which infants are able to stay focused and show pleasure in low-intensity activities (Shiner et al.).

**relational intervention** An intervention approach that emphasizes empathically assisting mothers to understand the reasons for how they react to their infants, and then helping them to modify their interactions with the goal of improving their emotional relationship (Stronach, Toth, Rogosch, Cicchetti).

**scaffolding** Provision of appropriate resources, support and assistance when engaging in the process of socialization (Vygotsky).

**secondary emotions** Defensive emotional reactions that occur when primary emotional reactions are hindered or blocked. Construct used in emotion-focused therapy (Greenberg).

**secure base scripts** A research paradigm in which a series of words is used to prompt participants to tell attachment-relevant stories (H. S. Waters, Rodrigues-Doolabh; H. S. Waters, E. Waters).

**self-esteem moments** Important events or turning points during a person's life that have the potential to significantly influence a person's sense of self-worth or competence in either a positive or negative direction (Mruk).

**self-organizing tendencies** A term used in dynamic systems models that refers to the tendency for systems to be attracted to the goal of self-organizing and stabilizing in a preferred configuration given the current conditions (Thelen, Smith).

**sequential designs** A combination of cross-sectional, longitudinal and time-lag research designs meant to optimize the advantages and minimize the disadvantages of each (Lerner).

**slow-to-warm-up temperament** A relatively stable pattern of shy temperament characterized by a cautious reluctance to engage in activities or to interact with others (Chess, Thomas).

**social or affective referencing** Using the emotional reactions of others as a reference for how to feel and respond emotionally (Sorce, Emde, Campos, Klinnert).

**state of action readiness** A consequence of emotion that prepares the organism to get ready to act, such as by approaching or avoiding (Frijda).

**still-face paradigm** A research paradigm in which mothers hold a neutral facial expression and ignore their infants' bids for attention and responsiveness; this pattern often occurs in mothers who are depressed (Field; Tronick).

**surgency** A temperamental quality that involves positive emotions and a tendency to be social and outgoing (Rothbart, Putnam; Evans).

**theory of mind** Belief system concerning the internal mental and emotional states of self and others (Bretherton, Beeghly).

**three primary ethics** Ethical values that are emphasized to varying degrees in different cultures. These are ethics of autonomy, community and divinity (Shweder).

**vitality contours** Patterns of affective arousal in infants, such as accelerating, fading or explosive bursts, that indicate how infants are experiencing and perceiving their environments (Stern).

**zone of proximal development** A zone of learning and comprehension that is just beyond a student's current level. Effective teachers/parents provide challenging material within this zone and assist their students/children via scaffolding (Vygotsky).

# Author Index

## C

D



E

## L

M

## Y



## Z

# Subject Index